MW01046506

THE GREAT BLACK JOCKEYS

BLACK

EDWARD HOTALING

THE
GREAT
JOCKEYS

THE LIVES AND TIMES
OF THE MEN WHO
DOMINATED AMERICA'S
FIRST NATIONAL SPORT

FORUM

An Imprint of Prima Publishing

A Marthe, Greg, et Luc

Cover: Shelby "Pike" Barnes on Proctor Knott beats Tony Hamilton on Salvator in 1888 at the inaugural Futurity Stakes. The race was worth $40,900, the richest annual event yet in American sports. Third was Galen, ridden by his trainer, Turner.

Cover spine and flap: Wallace Hicks and Jimmy Lee.

Preceding page: Jimmy Winkfield on Alan-a-Dale. Courtesy of Kentucky Derby Museum.

A portion of the preface appeared as an essay in the *Los Angeles Times*. The author's chapter nine account of black jockeys in the Belmont Stakes appeared in a slightly different form as an article in the *New York Times*.

FORUM is an imprint of Prima Publishing, 3875 Atherton Road, Rocklin, California, 95765.

PRIMA PUBLISHING and colophon are registered trademarks of Prima Communications, Inc.

Library of Congress Cataloging-in-Publication Data on File

ISBN 0-7615-1437-6

99 00 01 02 AA 10 9 8 7 6 5 4 3 2 1
Printed in the United States of America

How to Order
Single copies may be ordered from Prima Publishing, P.O. Box 1260BK, Rocklin, CA 95677; telephone (916) 632-4400. Quantity discounts are also available. On your letterhead, include information concerning the intended use of the books and the number of books you wish to purchase.

Visit us online at *www.primapublishing.com*

CONTENTS

A PREFACE: JIMMY THE GREEK FOR LUNCH

I SUPPOSE THIS BOOK was born on the day I interviewed Jimmy the Greek and somehow managed to cause one of the biggest media frenzies of recent times. In the end, it was all about nothing, really—a matter of no importance, silly even. It does seem that, more and more, we know too much about things that don't matter and not enough about things that do. The other day, though, I got to thinking that a review of my moment with the Greek might unravel the riddle—why Americans could obsess on the size of football and basketball players, for example, yet know nothing about their great black jockeys.

Here's what happened. On a freezing January morning, I took a television crew down to the Mall in Washington to report on a ceremony for Martin Luther King's Birthday. It was here that he had revealed his dream to thousands of marchers in front of the Lincoln Memorial, but I expected the ceremony would resonate for me for a more personal reason: I had played a tiny role in the dissemination of his last speeches, after falling under his spell from afar. I was living in Paris when King exploded on the scene. From that distance, none of the other civil rights figures came into focus, but King, a beacon of human rights, beamed across the sea and quickly became an American icon. When he came to Paris, I was a little startled to see an icon disguised as an unimposing man of medium height in a plain brown suit, but a few years later, when I moved to New York, I found myself enthralled with him again. It was in the last year of his truncated life but in the dawn of "all-news radio."

The New York CBS station suddenly found itself no longer confined to four-minute newscasts but facing gaping holes of air time, and we were free to plug the holes with almost anything we wanted. Overly aggressive as always, I produced long reports on King's latest appearances, packed with his passionate exhortations of the day or night before. For the first time at something close to its real power, King's voice began bouncing about the bedrooms and BMWs of America's opinion makers on their way into midtown, or so I immodestly imagined. Accustomed to fifteen-second sound bites, they now woke to three- to eight-minute human-rights alarms.

But on that cold King's Birthday in 1988, when they played "I have a dream" over the loudspeakers, it moved exactly nobody. The only people at the ceremony were National Park Service employees and a few District of Columbia officials. I decided to rescue the story—which was rare in television, where few stories were worth rescuing, but I did not want to let King go so quietly. Maybe our crew could discern whether the civil rights issue had expired at last, as that ceremony implied, by doing a little MOS on Connecticut Avenue, a videotaped "man-on-the-street" sampling of a few people's opinions. If people thought the movement was dead, it was.

So these three old guys out for a stroll stopped by, and before I could ask them my question, they asked me theirs. What was I doing?

I told them.

With the mysterious radar of the elderly, they said, "You ought to talk to Jimmy the Greek. He's there in Duke's, eating lunch."

Why not stick a famous face in my MOS? I could hardly have found a better candidate than Jimmy "the Greek" Snyder, *né* Demetrios Synodinos in Steubenville, Ohio. The country's most colorful professional gambler, he had marketed himself as a network TV oddsmaker on football games and had become the only interesting presence in millions of living rooms on autumn Sunday afternoons. Everybody knew him. Asked about the odds on a possible American-Soviet summit, Secretary of State George Schultz said, "If you were in a statistical frame of mind, and if Jimmy the

Greek was here, maybe the possibility would be something between 2 and 4 [out of 10]." The Greek's success rested not on odds-
making but on an asset seen only once or twice a decade on TV, a
personality. Even though he did not fit the lifeless corporate mold,
he was paid an estimated $500,000 to $750,000 a year, which
would translate to many times that today, for his undeniable appeal
as a familiar grouch. Snyder was in town for Sunday's championship playoff game between Washington and Minnesota.

So our crew marched into Duke Ziebert's fancy glass house of
a deli, celebrated for its big pickles but not as big as the one Jimmy
was about to land in. Duke led us to the Greek's table, and I shoved
the microphone in the puss that was a map of the Aegean islands,
and said we were doing a piece for Martin Luther King Day on
civil rights, and asked, "Is there anything you still think we need to
do, or do you think we don't need to worry about civil rights anymore?" Of course, Snyder had no idea he was talking to something
of an attack journalist who couldn't let go of King.

The Greek: "Yeah, pretty soon they're going to have to equalize it for the blacks, for the Greeks, the Jews, and for everybody. I
mean, let's make it equal for everybody. You know."

He obviously had something to say. As it turned out, it was
about "them."

EH: "Is it equal? What about sports?"

The Greek: "They've got everything. If they take over coaching like everybody wants them to, there's not going to be anything
left for the white people. I mean, all the players are black. I mean
the only thing that the whites control is the coaching jobs. Now
I'm not being derogatory about it, but that's all that's left for them.
The black talent is beautiful. It's great. It's out there. The only
thing left for the whites is a couple of coaching jobs."

EH: "Yeah, but do we need to get more black coaches?"

The Greek: "Oh, it's all right with me. I'm sure that they'll
take over that pretty soon, too."

He had praised the black talent, but it was still "us" and
"them," as it was for most Americans. Thinking I should quit while
ahead, I lucked into an excuse sitting at a nearby table. It was

David Brinkley, the equally celebrated commentator and recent fellow denizen of NBC's halls. Thinking David, I pulled away from Jimmy, but he was not to be upstaged. He barked at the crew and gestured toward me.

The Greek: "Let me ask *him* a question."

EH: "Ask . . . ask!"

As Jerry Nachman wrote in the *New York Post*, "Slowly, as in the cheap novels, they turned. The newsman. The camera. The lens. The light. The videotape deck. The microphone." Jerry's own cheap novel continued: "All the equipment stood poised, the electronic firing squad it often is, inches from the Greek's lined face."

The Greek: "I don't want this on . . . I'm just . . ."

Snyder was "apparently trying to hedge the career bet he was about to make," Nachman noted. "The camera stayed where it was—in his face."

The Greek: "There isn't much left for the white guys anymore."

EH: "Well, uh, actually there is."

The Greek: "Where?"

EH: "Well, they can make big progress in basketball, for example, or in football . . ."

The Greek: "There's ten people, there's ten players on a basketball court. If you find two whites, you're lucky; either four out of five, or nine out of ten, are black. Now that's because they practice, and they play and practice and play. They're not lazy like the white athlete is."

This was clearly a dangerous discussion.

EH: "Yeah, but you know, another thing is, the predominantly white schools don't emphasize sports."

The Greek: "That's not the reason."

We were like two guys in a bar, though there was no obvious sign that Jimmy had been drinking.

The Greek: "The black is the better athlete to begin with. Because he's been bred to be that way, because of his high thighs and big thighs that goes up into his back, and they can jump higher and run faster because of their bigger thighs, you see. The white man has to overcome that. But they don't try hard enough to overcome it."

He was getting much too real for today's corporate "newsrooms," but like Snyder himself, I did not happen to be a corporate team player, and I let him wander into weirder territory.

The Greek: "In football and baseball and any game that you have to run a lot, I mean your thighs come into prominence, very much so, because that's what gauges your speed and your jump. In situations such as that, in basketball, your thighs' the things that make you jump high."

He became insistent.

The Greek: "I'm telling you that the black is the better athlete, and he practices to be the better athlete, and he is bred to be the better athlete, because this goes back all the way to the Civil War when during the slave trading the big, the owner, the slave owner, would breed his big black to his big woman, so that he could have a big black kid, you see. I mean that's where it all started."

That's where it all ended for Jimmy the Greek. In less than lunch one of the country's best-known sports commentators had not only complained that black athletes had taken over sports—although he blamed it on the lazy whites—but said they were "bred" for it. The bomb exploded that freezing Friday evening. Our station, the NBC outlet in Washington, led its evening newscast with excerpts from the interview and then made them available to the networks. In a bit more than an hour, tens of millions of Americans had listened to snatches of it, and on Saturday the Greek's philosophy was splashed over the papers from ocean to ocean.

I was ten years old when I had my first journalistic thrill. I walked into Carl Izzo's barbershop on Railroad Place in Saratoga Springs one August day and spotted, on a chair, the gigantic headline on the world's greatest newspaper, the tabloid *New York Daily News:*

BABE RUTH DIES

That stunning headline announcing the death of an American hero gave me an incredible rush. That sounds obscene, but I guess I was a journalist. Little did I dream, however, that one day a story of my own would be blasted to the known universe from the cover of the

Daily News. The paper had gotten a little fancy, so there was a line of smaller type on top:

Jimmy 'the Greek' Snyder
BLITZES BLACKS

That was nothing. On Saturday came a second explosion—the canning of the Greek by CBS—and an even rarer journalistic moment. The reaction to that got not only the *Daily News* front cover, as befits the apocalypse of the morning—

GREEK FIRED

—but the back, too—

GREEK TRAGEDY

Having hired him to speak his mind as a typical American, CBS had dumped him for speaking his mind as a typical American. But as the news was screamed to the millions again, I began wondering. Why was this bigger than the story I chased alone in Iran in my early twenties, a revolution in the making? Or the *real* Greek coup? Or the Six-Day War? If this was what big news was, why had I sailed to Cyprus with a Turkish fishing captain in his pajamas searching through the night for Famagusta? Where the shelled hotel really had collapsed like the proverbial deck of cards, one floor slab catching a fleeing heel, so that the corpse of the man to whom the heel belonged flew out from the deck, a gargoyle. Why had I rushed to the green line in Nicosia, where I stepped into a shower and heard the loudest sound of my life, a Turkish jet sending a missile through a wall four feet from my body?

In my years of living stupidly, Jimmy could not have prompted such living arrangements as ours during the war in Beirut. Where our Moslem neighbors shot up a Christian friend's apartment without inquiring whether I might be cowering inside. Where crossing a square with a four-year-old on one's shoulders seemed

best until one realized that it made Greg a better target for the
sniper. Where fierce Marthe commandeered a taxi from Palestin-
ian guerrillas to get back with milk for Greg and Luc. Where, after
our own house was shot up, Greg's lips turned blue as he realized it
was real (two-year-old Luc thought everything was wonderful).
Where kidnappers came, sending us flying *en famille* from one exploding neighborhood to another. And the last stupid mailbox in
the bombed St. Georges Hotel, recent headquarters of the escaped
correspondents, bore the name of this last stupid journalist on his
last stupid story—which was nothing next to Jimmy the Greek.

This was obvious with the next big explosion, the "third day"
coverage, as the story was picked up by the magazines—*Time*,
Newsweek, *People*, and the rest—and the columnists, editorial writers,
and cartoonists across the country. Not that I was complaining. I
might not have fathomed the news judgment involved, but I was living the dream of that ten-year-old in Carl Izzo's. It was my story now
on the barbershop chairs. I had stepped out of the corporate news-
room and found myself in a telephone booth, tearing off my clothes
and emerging as the former journalist Superman, a force for dumb.

The fourth newsquake was a never-ending series of after-
shocks. The story would not die. In March, when I interviewed the
filmmaker Steven Spielberg, he volunteered that my story was "the
coup of the year," though even he seemed a little startled at the
coverage. "Surprising impact," Spielberg told me. Three years
later, it reached a high in absurdity when the Associated Press ran
its "Today in History" column, naming world-shaking events that
happened on that day. For January 16, it listed:

"Ivan the Terrible was crowned Czar of Russia.

"General Dwight D. Eisenhower took command of the Allied
Invasion Force in London.

"Two manned Soviet 'Soyuz' spaceships become the first vehicles to dock in space and transfer personnel.

"Shah Mohammed Reza Pahlevi departed Iran for Egypt.

"Jimmy 'the Greek' Snyder was fired . . ."

Snyder finally responded in kind, filing court complaints in
New York that sought twenty million dollars from CBS, my station,

and me, among a few others. I was ecstatic, as this was the closest I would get to twenty million dollars for some time. Unfortunately for Jimmy, however, nothing came of it.

Now I would not say that my story did no good at all. As *USA Today* reported, it reignited the debate over the lack of a black head coach in professional football. It reminded people of King's legacy. Writing about the interview and the firing of the Greek, the *New York Times* national columnist Tom Wicker declared, "It couldn't have happened at a more appropriate time than the eve of the Martin Luther King birthday observances." Noting my query about whether the movement was dead, whether anything more needed to be done, William Raspberry wrote in the *Washington Post:* "An awful lot remains to be changed—in the behavior of those who run our enterprises and in the attitudes of the rest of us."

But the harm done may have outweighed all that. This moment on television ruined Snyder's career. Whether or not it affected his frail health and contributed to his death of heart failure eight years later, at age seventy-six, it did mar his last years. It did not matter that he merely had regurgitated a myth millions of others bought, especially after the purple 1957 novel *Mandingo*, about a fictional slave-rearing plantation. It did not matter that it had been repeated prominently by others in times that were less politically correct. The black track star Lee Evans, the 1968 Olympic gold medalist, had once told *Sports Illustrated*, "On the plantations, a strong black man was mated with a strong black woman. [Blacks] were simply bred for physical qualities."

It did not matter that in the vast documentation of slavery there is no evidence of widespread forced mating for physical characteristics. It would not even have been possible. The myth assumes that such breeding could have been accomplished in the two centuries of American slavery and would have remained effective a century afterward, whereas all we know of evolution shows it would take thousands of years. But it is easy to see why Evans, for example, would have bought it: he was surrounded by big athletes. The same reason applies to millions of white Americans who get their only extended look at African Americans in football and basketball games on television—who rarely venture into black neighborhoods, or even black and white neighborhoods. But those who hold to the myth are by no means only rural or older Americans, or white or black sports professionals, such as Snyder and Evans. Many are younger, suburban, and well educated, but they still live in worlds that are mostly white and work in offices where there are few blacks.

Behind the *Mandingo* myth is another: the ancient myth of white racial superiority, which on this issue states: they're big and we're smart. This is not about superiority at all, of course, but about fear. The statement really means: if they are like us, then what is so special about us? And the answer is disturbing to the insecure: nothing. Indeed, the differences between the races are not only superficial but infinitesimal—"just tiny," as the Harvard University paleontologist Stephen Jay Gould has noted, "when compared to the variation within races."

But Snyder's was not the only career to be marred by a moment on TV. This frenzy was simply the biggest in a continuing eruption of pseudo-scandals, dopey remarks magnified out of all proportion by us pseudo-journalists. In recent years CBS sports analyst Billy Packer blew up a storm when he casually referred to basketball star Allen Iverson, then a Georgetown University guard, as "a tough monkey." In 1997 golfer Fuzzy Zoeller was raked over the media coals for a lame joke about Masters champion Tiger Woods wanting to celebrate with fried chicken, watermelon, and collard greens.

And it was not just a few who were hurt. In some cases one man's goof was converted into a vast platform for racist propaganda. In the Jimmy the Greek instance, millions of people, black and white, had to endure having the breeding myth flung in their faces as the media, like pious pornographers, sold it while pretending to condemn it. There were only a few serious attempts to dispel the myth, notably in the *New York Times* by Tom Wicker and by Professor Richard S. Randall of New York University on the op-ed page and in *Time* by Jack E. White.

Everything is wrong with the little sound bites of "news"— especially these blown-up moments of political incorrectness—that substitute for public education and knowledge in America today. They provide no context. They bury whatever else is said, such as Snyder's provocative opinion that African American athletes have a better work ethic. And his apology. "I didn't mean for my remarks to come out the way they did," he commented right after his remarks were broadcast. "I was trying to emphasize how much harder so many blacks work at becoming better athletes than white athletes. And they work harder because they're hungrier. That many blacks run faster and jump higher than whites is a fact. Using the term 'bred' was wrong on my part, and I apologize for that, as I do for suggesting coaching was the only domain left for whites. Blacks could do well in that area, too, if given the opportunity."

In another comment, he said, "I offer full apologies to all those I may have offended, and this is from my heart. At seventy years old, I can't say much more than that right now." His remarks may have left some questions unanswered, but they were hardly the words of a racist. And he was convincing when he said he was "dumbfounded" by the uproar.

Those TV moments would dissolve if they were subjected to the slightest inquiry, and they have dissolved on several occasions, only too late. In the midst of his own storm, Billy Packer denied that his "tough monkey" remark was racial and said he meant it to be "endearing," had used it about whites, and never looked at anyone in terms of black or white. Iverson and Georgetown's black coach, John Thompson, agreed, saying Packer was not at all racist, so it was much ado about nothing. As for Zoeller and his limp joke about watermelons and greens, black golfers Jim Dent and Walter Morgan said they weren't offended by such foolishness.

All this correctness was warmed-over puritanism. Salem survived. One columnist even carried the torch of the zealots further by commenting that Woods himself should apologize for some sexual remarks about his fellow African Americans. Everybody, apparently, must wear a scarlet letter for every moronic remark.

And yet these politically prosecutable moments usually turn out to have been pure chance. Bill Ringle, of the Gannett News Service, quoted Snyder himself as saying, "Do you know the odds against me being in that restaurant, at that time, on that day, answering those questions?" To which Ringle added, "And that's without the odds against WRC-TV's having dispatched a 'Martin Luther King freak' to cover an event that disappointed him. Or of the reporter deciding to rescue the story. Or of the reporter's having run into 'those three old guys.'" On the basis of such quirks in the world of television a man's career is destroyed and a racist myth promoted.

But the real problem is not that many people harbor racial biases and occasionally let them slip out, but that they are afraid to discuss them, and therefore television is afraid to discuss them. They don't want their views to be exposed, and neither does television, so they cover them up with politically correct rhetoric, which glosses over the issue. This is the main reason why people won't discuss racism in depth and why mainstream television won't touch it, either. Deep down, they also fear that open discussion would lead to tolerance of others' rights and progress, which could be a threat to their own.

Had the corporations not wiped out so many good journalists in recent years, their news operations might have done what they should have, which was to bring Snyder and the others back on, to air their concerns. I offered this opinion to reporters after the interview and soon had company, which produced yet another cover story, in the *New York Post*:

Cosby cools racial furor
"Don't Hang Jimmy the Greek"

Television comedian Bill Cosby said Snyder shouldn't be fired. "These hangings going on don't make us better human beings. On the eve of celebrating Martin Luther King Day, we should be more forgiving." Snyder was forgiven by the Reverend Jesse Jackson. And Professor Randall of NYU wrote in the *Times*, "CBS's moral outrage would have more credibility if instead of firing Mr. Snyder, it had required him, and invited others, to participate in public discussions about why black athletes have come to dominate American sports, what this means, and why discriminatory barriers still exist." It would have produced tremendous viewership, too, so the decision not to do it perhaps proved that in television fear is stronger than greed.

Ten years later this obvious solution to America's racial discomfort, open discussion, still hasn't happened. Far from being able to discuss their problems, white and black Americans don't even know how to talk to each other. I discovered this when I had the pleasure of being black at odd moments—from the day after the interview through the following year and beyond. How did I change races? When the story broke, a wire service and several newspapers across the country assumed I was black, although most of the papers probably just picked it up from the wire service. Six days after the interview, the *Los Angeles Times* reported: "For the record: it has been erroneously reported that Ed Hotaling, the TV reporter who did the infamous interview with Snyder last Friday, is black. He is white."

By then, though, the error had traveled the country, and I got to be a black star, almost, launched by an editorial in the *Philadelphia Inquirer*, which put me in some pretty fancy company. Noting that the Greek had said those silly things to a black television reporter, it pointed out that the network's white brass was "far more outraged than Mssrs. Cosby or Jackson or, for that matter, Ed Hotaling, who conducted the interview."

Some odd things happened when white people found out I was different—that is to say, black. They started talking funny. After the interview, when those calls started coming in from around the country, a white editor on a leading newspaper kept complimenting me. His lavish words were echoed by a white reporter for another big paper. They both said that I had been "verrry calm, verrry level-headed, verrry professional throughout the whooole thing."

What, I wondered as I listened to all this on the phone, was going on? Why were they talking as if I were twelve years old? Did they think I was interning with "Children's Express"?

That was before I knew I was black. "Oh, we get that all the time," one black TV anchor explained. So whites often do talk differently to blacks. If you're white, you know that, but have you felt it?

Whites rushed to praise the black me. An Arizona caller said it was wonderful that, in spite of what Snyder had said, I had been so tolerant, defending his right to free speech. When I said I was white, the caller lost interest.

But why did people assume that a black reporter's reaction would be predictable? In fact, a number of blacks told me they thought the Greek should have been fired; a number disagreed. Yet many whites took it for granted that black reaction would be uniformly hostile and unforgiving. Black exceptions brought white sighs of relief, cross-country bouquets, and in the case of Cosby and Jackson, banner headlines in New York. Occasionally, my new racial role was uncomfortable. A writer for a monthly magazine phoned long after the interview and wondered, apologetically, if I were black. I hated to stonewall a fellow reporter, but now it seemed irrelevant. I told him I didn't care to say. He apologized again. It felt right, but rotten.

Why had that wire service and some newspapers assumed in the first place that the interviewer was black? The answer was simple. I was working on a Martin Luther King Day story, asking people about the decline of civil rights as an issue. These days, I learned, if you are interested in civil rights, you must be black. Thus, when a paper in upstate New York got the United Press International text of the interview, which began with the question, "Do you think there's anything we still need to do, or do you think we don't need to worry about civil rights anymore?" an editor inserted "blacks" in parentheses after "we." Who else, indeed, would ask that question? Sadly, almost nobody, it seems.

Not only do many Americans today see civil rights as a minority issue; they also remember King as a special-interest advocate. Three decades after his death, many recall him exclusively as a black leader, the way many concluded that only a black would be chasing a civil rights story. Shortly after my interview with Snyder, at a Washington dinner of veteran journalists, all white, I remarked that I was surprised so many people still viewed King strictly as a black hero. Hundreds of thousands of whites had supported him. Europeans had given him the Nobel Prize.

They looked at each other, a little startled. It was clear I was the one out of step.

"But that's what he was," some brilliant somebody said, as the others nodded in agreement, "a black leader."

It was good to feel black again. I have often wondered, though, whether those who fired the Greek thought that he had been all the more insensitive because they believed he said those things to a black reporter, whether that error might have been a factor in his dismissal and in the size of the scandal. It was yet another example of the unpredictable odds, the missing pieces, the lack of any discussion that might add context, that make these TV "scandals" so silly.

It was while researching my last book, *They're Off! Horse Racing at Saratoga*, that I discovered the great black jockeys (the reader will learn about an early Jimmy the Greek who declared in the 1860s that these equestrian athletes were so good it was obvious they were "bred" that way). If Snyder, or for that matter his bosses, had been aware of the black jockeys, they would have known that African Americans were hardly taking over sports in the late twentieth century. Quite the contrary, they had been in on the birth of American sports, dominating racing in the South, where the sport was concentrated, from the eighteenth century on. From the beginning, they rode side by side with a smaller number of great white riders, but in the face of slavery and then terrorism and racism, the black jockeys needed something else to stay on top, so this is a tale of courage.

I think almost all Americans will be delighted to discover the adventure of these long-lost athletes, a story that does matter. I hope you will, and that you'll share it with some kids you know.

Edward Hotaling
Washington, D.C.
December 1998

INTRODUCTION

Wow! Who's he?"
That's how many react when they see a picture of one of the great black jockeys.

"When did he ride?"

"How come I've never heard of him?"

Most people are oblivious to the fact that, two centuries before Jackie Robinson, blacks competed alongside whites in America's first national pastime. They are unaware of it because the black jockeys were not only ridden out of their profession but written out of history. Yet there they were, present at the birth of mainstream American sports—outperforming the superb equestrian George Washington and the would-be jockey Thomas Jefferson and thrilling hundreds of thousands from New York to New Orleans in the years before the Civil War, as their talent and courage overcame even slavery. There they were when freedom arrived, capturing the first Kentucky Derby and many of America's other major races. And here they are again, in the first history of the black jockeys. It's a lively, documented saga, illuminated by rare vintage photographs that testify to the triumphs of these exceptional Americans.

This is not black history. It is not white history. It is American history, never told before. It takes both a long and close view, introducing individual champions, nearly all of them forgotten since their days of glory, and a riveting historical cast—of poor and rich, whites and blacks, women and men, adults and children.

The story opens in Colonial days, when a young athlete named Austin Curtis rode and trained racehorses for one of the founding fathers of North Carolina—until the Revolution came, and the most murderous of the British officers and his troops rode into town. Presented here for the first time, this adventure ended with freedom not only for America but for Curtis personally.

Simon was another great jockey, renowned across half a continent, from Charleston to Middle Tennessee and down the Natchez Trace to the Mississippi. White historians, and black historians, too, have often treated those early African Americans simply as victims of slavery, mere "economic units" in what was, indeed, a vast criminal conspiracy to keep the plantations running. But Simon proved that they were hardly mere victims, or units, or even just laborers. They were men and women of faith and courage and

This jockey outfit may be the oldest athletic uniform in America. It was made by plantation workers in Waccamaw, South Carolina, for Colonel William Alston in the early 1800s. The silk jacket has red and green satin stripes; the pants are buckskin. Courtesy of Charleston Museum.

resistance, and not only that: they were often professionals, helping to manage the lumber industry of North Carolina, saving the rice economy of South Carolina with specialized talents the English desperately lacked, and running fabled horse farms, from the North Carolina–Virginia border to Louisiana.

In other words, although one would hardly know it from reading American histories, these people were not slaves in their own minds but merely under the rules of the cowardly terrorist system holding them—unarmed, of course, except for their minds and their talents. Simon, for example, made slavery a minor detail of his life, becoming the forerunner of the modern "showboating" super-athlete. Witty, hilariously sarcastic, vastly entertaining, Simon brazenly took on the most famous man of his day, the general and future president Andrew Jackson, not once but again and again.

And then there was the brilliant Charles Stewart. "Charley" made so much money even while a slave that at one time he had to have an agent handle it. Go figure. And despite rules against slaves crossing state lines, Stewart traveled the land from his native Virginia (scholars who limit their understanding to the supposed "rules" of slavery will have a lot of trouble figuring out Stewart). In New York, on Long Island, he witnessed the first modern sports spectacular, a horse race that brought out probably the biggest American crowd at any event yet, including wars. Once his racing days were over, he became a manager of thoroughbred operations, with employees of his own, not only in his native Virginia but in the Kentucky bluegrass and on the bayous of Louisiana—all while still hopelessly trapped in the state-sponsored crime of slavery.

"Hold him, Jesse!" shouted the president of the United States, Andrew Jackson. Jesse couldn't have weighed much more than a hundred pounds, but he was at the controls of a one-thousand-pound thoroughbred stallion. Jesse was a slave at the White House—and a professional athlete, a rider for the president's racing stable. If all of this sounds new and more than a little strange, it's not surprising: nobody at 1600 Pennsylvania Avenue today (the author inquired) knew the story, either. But at one time, in fact, the White House became a major sports operation, with a lot of slave help. The early 1800s also saw the fantastic career of the slave Cornelius, usually aboard Boston, one of the greatest racers of all time. Like Simon, Cornelius anticipated the modern superstar athlete, not as a showboater, which he definitely was not, but with his grueling professional schedule, especially around New York and the Northeast, where he became the first black jockey to win the repeated plaudits of the national press. Incredibly, the story of Cornelius is matched by that of Cato, who won his freedom in the midst of two Kentucky races that would be reported across the country and remembered in awe.

The Civil War did not ground the black jockeys. Seven months after the rebels began the game by shelling Fort Sumter off Charleston, the slave Abe was still riding in the Old South. Two years later, after the "Glory" regiment of black troops assaulted Fort Wagner in that same embattled harbor, a one-eyed fugitive slave named Sewell was capturing the opener at the country's greatest sports center yet, the Saratoga Race Course. The following year, as the Yankees blew up the rebel works at Petersburg and black troops charged into the breach, many of them to be murdered as they tried to surrender, the escapee Abe was basking in applause, from Missouri to New Jersey to New York. With the war's end, the black jockeys impressed the eagle-eyed publisher Horace Greeley at the biggest sporting festival the country had ever seen, one that foreshadowed the next century's Super Bowl and World Series. As for baseball, the second all-American pastime had yet to get organized on a national scale.

It bears repeating that Jackie Robinson did not "integrate" American professional sports. Almost as surprising as the long-buried accomplishments of the black jockeys is the story of how they competed right alongside white jockeys, sharpening the old saw that everything is equal on the turf and under it. This rare equality went on for more than two centuries before it was decided that American sports had to be "segregated." Until then, as the reader will see, the only race that mattered was the one around the track, the only colors that counted were the ones on their backs, if only for those minutes on horses. In fact, the competition frequently was reduced to two contestants, one white, one black. Few of the many black-white rivalries were more fascinating than the one between Abe Hawkins and Gilbert Watson Patrick, an Irish boy from Poughkeepsie known as "Gilpatrick." Their battle stretched all the way from antebellum days to beyond the Civil War, entertaining hundreds of thousands of slavery-weary, war-weary spectators.

The star of the century arrived in the late 1800s with the handsome Ike Murphy, who was a thoroughly modern athlete. One of the more cerebral performers of his day, a fabulous judge of pace, and a beacon of integrity, Ike had to fight the twin battles of the bulge and the bottle. He lost the former and was accused of losing the latter, so perhaps what was most modern about him was the way his life ended. The fans saw the end coming in the season of his most ballyhooed race. Murphy, sitting straight up in the conventional English manner, rode against the white "Snapper" Garrison, hunched over in the American crouch, producing the first photo finish and an early media frenzy. The frenzy turned paroxysmal a few weeks later when, to the shock of millions, Isaac Murphy, perhaps the greatest American athlete of his day, fell out of the saddle into a heap on the ground.

The Gay Nineties opened with the black jockeys at the top of their game and ready to share not only in the applause but in the profits of America's most popular sport. Shelby "Pike" Barnes, James "Soup" Perkins, and Willie Simms took turns as the year's top jockey, making them the leading athletes in the country's leading sport. Simms even took his act abroad, becoming one of the earliest Americans to ride in England. He taught the English the "American seat"—the crouch that at first shocked them and then overtook them––but he learned little in return, except that Americans hardly had a monopoly on racism.

But by the end of that supposedly gay decade, the black jockeys were on their way out, on a tide of social change and racism. The breakup of old horse farms in the South and border states, the hopelessness of sharecropping, and a reign of racist terror combined to cause a mass migration of African Americans to cities in the North. At the same time, Northern whites were horrified when they realized that freedom for African Americans was not simply a theory, and they were coming up to get it.

Jimmy Winkfield was the last of the great black jockeys. His response to being targeted in a Chicago "race war," in an attack that broke his horse's ribs and could have killed him, was simply to keep riding. In fact, he became the first rider since Ike Murphy to win back-to-back Kentucky Derbies. And after those head-turning successes, his response to being dumped by a powerful stable owner was, to his enormous credit, to blame it on himself. "I got too smart for my pants," he later said. But it drove him into exile and a dreamlike career across the Atlantic. Unable to become the American national riding champion, he became the Russian national champion and was soon enjoying a valet, a suite at the National Hotel in Moscow, and caviar for breakfast.

By the early 1900s, the great black jockeys had gone from winning the Kentucky Derby to not being able to get a mount in that Louisville classic (the exception of Henry King, tenth on Planet in 1921, merely proved the rule)—or almost anywhere else. For all intents and purposes, they had vanished from the American racetrack. The final chapter deals at the length with the reasons why: racism, the threat of violence, big money, a new way of life in the big Northern cities, and even Dixie diets and the Jimmy the Greek "theory." But what has been saddest about it, perhaps, is the fact that the sport that gave the black jockeys their days of glory has failed to bring them back in any significant numbers. And thanks to the elitism that has characterized what is a very expensive sport to stage, its chroniclers have tended to focus on the stable owners, leaving out the black jockeys, save for an occasional mention. So these first professional athletes not only disappeared from the American scene but vanished from the history books, burying what really is an exemplary epic, the story of their accomplishments, their courage, and their heroism. Here it is.

Match race at Tucker's Path, Brunswick County, Virginia. Austin Curtis (with whip in air) rides Trick'em, whose saddle cloth is marked WJ for owner Willie Jones. Modern painting by Sam Savitt. Courtesy of Helen K. Groves/American Quarter Horse Museum.

.I.

THE BIRTH *of* AMERICAN SPORTS

AUSTIN CURTIS AND

THE FOUNDING FATHERS

1607–1809

THEY WERE THE new people, the Americans, thousands of them streaming along the dusty roads toward the strange set of parallel lines on the grassy southern Virginia plain above the bright and furious Roanoke River. It would be judged the biggest crowd of Americans ever gathered before the Revolution or for nearly fifty years afterward. They came down from Petersburg, seventy miles north, across the cornfields and tobacco plantations, and they came up from the river port of Halifax, North Carolina, twenty miles south. They traveled by carriage, cart, horseback, and foot across the western Piedmont of both states. They arrived from the east, from the Virginia tidewater, from Norfolk, and from North Carolina's coastal plains—all converging at the two rigid paths. It was as if they were preparing for some unique American ritual, perhaps a joyous religious celebration if their smiles were any indication.

From the looks of them, it would have been hard to say what an American was. Apparently it could have been anybody. Thousands of English Americans gathered at the paths, whole families of them. They were farm wives, great planters, loose children, indentured servants, skilled and unskilled laborers from places like the tobacco and hemp warehouses in Halifax, and clerks from the stores and counting houses of Petersburg, the tobacco capital. Accounts by witnesses at other such events indicated that thousands of African Americans came as well, whole families of them, plantation workers and servants, craftsmen and sawyers, warehouse workers, professionals who produced naval supplies—turpentine, pitch, rosin—from North Carolina's towering longleaf pines and who made barrel staves, countless thousands of barrel staves, to be exported to the world.

Native American families ferried across the raging Roanoke to the gathering, doubtless by the hundreds, since probably two thousand lived in Halifax County. However, they did not live openly as Indians, displaying their customs, because the hated Tuscarora War settlement, half a century earlier, had required them to leave their Carolina home. Many had stayed nonetheless, hoping to pass for white, or for colored, or for anybody but expelled Indians. To the paths the Dutch and German Americans must have come from New York and Pennsylvania. The inevitable Yankee peddlers, who liked a crowd, came as well, although nobody did a better business than the tavern keeper hard by the paths. Among the mixed-up thousands were many Scots and Scots-Irish, the ones with the burrs on their tongues, who had been pouring into the area over the past few decades. A few had trekked deeper into Virginia and the Carolinas, even into Tennessee, where the opportunities had to be unlimited. But many of them had stopped here, at the beginning of the Piedmont, which stretched west to the Appalachians, where one day they, too, might be headed, though none thought about it today. Today just about everybody was at the race paths in Brunswick County, Virginia, providing a loud, unruly, inappropriate (especially inappropriate), and joyful (especially joyful) preview of a new people.[1]

It was America's biggest sporting event yet. The excitement on the Roanoke had been building for three months, ever since

Colonel Henry Delony, a planter from Mecklenburg County, Virginia, west of the paths, met Willie (he pronounced it Wiley) Jones, a Halifax County landowner and politician. It was about 1773—the exact year remains uncertain. The colonel had challenged Jones to a "quarter race," an American invention if there ever was one.

In the decades after the English settled Jamestown in 1607, the Eastern Seaboard was too wooded to lay out racecourses a mile or more long, like the ones back in England—so the Americans simply thought up a new sport. They hacked a pair of adjacent paths through the pines anywhere from ten to twenty-four feet wide but always a quarter of a mile long, so that performances in different races could be compared. Not just once but up to twenty times a day the Americans would fling a pair of horses down these rigid paths at full gallop, jockeys jostling each other and whips smacking as they passed two walls of roaring spectators. They called the new sport "quarter racing." Of course, they had to take breaks between races, and between their foolish and dangerous wagers on the horses, so invariably the paths were laid out next to a tavern. Sideshows, especially cockfights and wrestling— the latter highlighted by eye-gouging and both, it was hoped, as bloody as possible—rounded out the amusements.

Lieutenant Thomas Anburey, a British prisoner in Virginia during the Revolution, wrote of going "to see a diversion peculiar to this country, termed quarter racing, which is a match between two horses to run a quarter of a mile. . . . This diversion is a great favorite with the middling and lower classes, and they have a breed of horses which perform it with astonishing velocity."[2]

By the day of the Brunswick County contest, quarter racing had been America's biggest sport for almost a century, its first form of mass entertainment. But nowhere was it bigger than on the Virginia–North Carolina border, the "Race Horse Region," as it would soon be dubbed, which encompassed six counties on the Roanoke that had a total population of about seventy thousand. Four of the counties were in North Carolina: Northampton, Granville, Bute (later renamed Warren), and Halifax. Two were in southside Virginia: Mecklenburg and Brunswick. The Race Horse Region's black population, which was about twenty thousand, supplied most of the jockeys. Indeed, because racing was centered in the South, most of the thousands of athletes involved for two centuries, from the mid-1600s to the Civil War, were slaves. But they were also professionals, and they were openly recognized as such, for this was their highly specialized job. As will be seen, some would be paid in various ways, including cash.

Of course, there were many white riders as well, especially the "gentleman jockeys" who raced their own horses. Many were brilliant reinsmen, among them Thomas Jefferson, although Jefferson declared George Washington the best horseman of his age, even in that day of American cavaliers. No record has been located of either of them riding in a formal race, but Jefferson himself remembered wondering as a boy: ". . . which of these kinds of reputation should I prefer? That of a horse jockey? A foxhunter? An orator? Or the honest advocate of my country's rights?"[3] Many gentlemen did choose horse jockey—it was a hobby that often became a calling—but as the stakes rose, they increasingly dismounted in favor of the professionals, black or white. The black riders prevailed in the South, where there was far more racing, while the whites dominated in the North. A relatively few white professionals worked in the South as well.[4]

Almost as remarkable as the success of the slave jockeys was the fact that they competed alongside whites as athletic equals. As early as 1677, a white named Thomas Cocke rode for one Richard Ligon against "a boy of Chamberlaine" in the Richmond, Virginia, area for three hundred pounds of tobacco. In racing, "boy" simply meant, and still means, "jockey," white or black, but Thomas Chamberlaine's jockey was almost certainly black because white riders were usually identified by name in the court records, which was where this contest wound up. It is not clear who got the three hundred pounds of tobacco at stake because the case was settled out of court. More often, both riders in those one-on-one quarter races were black—and on this day in Brunswick County, one of them was America's first truly great professional athlete.[5]

THE JOCKEY was Austin Curtis—a slave, except in his own mind. Curtis was helping Willie Jones turn his Roanoke stable into the winningest, most profitable racing power in the American Colonies. As a modern quarter-racing authority, poring over ancient records, would put it, "Willie Jones was the fortunate owner of Austin Curtis, the best quarter horse jockey, trainer, and groom in the country." As that statement indicates, those first American jockeys did much more than ride. They were often grooms as well, responsible for the feeding, stabling, and exercising of one or more horses. As was the case with Curtis, they sometimes rose to the exalted level of trainer, supervising the conditioning of the horses, directing other jockeys, devising racing strategies, assisting in the purchase of horses—in other words, co-managing the business with the stable owner. Up to and beyond the Civil War, countless African American trainers managed, or helped manage, racing stables, which were the country's earliest major sports organizations. As one early authority noted, "training in the South was for the most part in colored hands." A few of the white stable owners were themselves great trainers, however, and a number of them hired white professional trainers.[6]

Their relationship may have been imbalanced—to put it mildly—but Willie Jones, in his early thirties, and Austin Curtis, in his early teens, were the first famous manager-athlete combination in America. However, when Colonel Delony bumped into Jones that day in about 1773, he reminded him that their sport was fast going out of style. The pioneers were taking quarter racing deeper into the woods (Kentucky would get its first quarter-mile strip in 1780) as proper oval courses opened outside one American town after another. So the colonel suggested that they make this final fling for a stake so big that neither of them would ever forget it. For anybody but Jones and Curtis, that might have been intimidating, since

the Race Horse Region was prime gambling as well as prime tobacco country.[7]

The planters sometimes raced their horses for a fortune's
worth of the Colonies' leading export—indeed, for entire crops of
tobacco. On one occasion, the stake was eighty thousand pounds
of the weed; on another, a hundred thousand pounds. By comparison, a poor tobacco farmer's whole crop might total four thousand.
But Delony and Jones outdid them all. Their two black jockeys
would ride for an astounding one hundred hogsheads, which were
huge, seaworthy containers, or the equivalent of about 147,000
pounds of top-quality leaf, officially inspected at Petersburg. Such
prizes were distributed as "tobacco notes," payable, in cases of
huge quantities such as this, upon sale abroad.

In a bit of wonderful luck, a few of the high-stakes capers of
Jones and Curtis have been preserved in letters by Jones's great-
nephew, Allen Jones Davie. From these we learn that when Jones
showed up in Brunswick County that morning, Curtis had a scary
message for him. They had just been had.[8]

Austin Curtis was getting ready to ride Paoli, a gelding of "uncommon beauty" but "apparently light for a quarter horse, his
muscles finely developed but not very heavy." He was a fine horse,
but their rival, Colonel Delony, had pulled one of the oldest scams
in sports: he had entered a borrowed nag, in this case an undefeated champion known as the Big Filly, "much heavier in all her
parts; evidently possessing great strength"—which would be a considerable advantage since each horse was required to carry 160
pounds. Curtis and the other jockey, a Delony slave named Ned,
probably each weighed under 100 pounds, so extra weight would
have been added to make 160: clearly, the going would be a lot easier for the Big Filly. Furious, Jones accused the horse's owner,
Colonel Jeptha Atherton, of breaking his earlier word that he
wouldn't loan the filly to Delony. But it was too late: Curtis and
Ned were at the poles on either side of the starting line, two black
athletes at the center of the biggest showdown in eighteenth-
century American sports. All thoughts of hemp and tobacco prices,

of the next day's work, of the long trip back home, of the revolutionary stirrings up north, of cockfights and eye-gouging, were put
aside as thousands of Americans stretched both sides of the quarter
mile, several deep.[9]

"The fame of the horses, the high reputation of the gentlemen
who made the race, the great wager," wrote Jones's great-nephew,
"all united to collect a large crowd. They lined the paths as a solid
wall the whole distance." He said it rivaled "in popularity and interest" the great 1823 match on Long Island between American Eclipse
and Henry, although that would be hard to imagine, as that latter
contest drew up to sixty thousand witnesses. While this throng,
which was riveted on Curtis and Ned, quite possibly included some
of the great Virginians of the day, it was no mere aristocratic *diver-
tissement*. It was an American crowd, almost democratic, if only for
the day. As John Bernard, a visiting English actor, said, describing
some minor races in Virginia, both sides of the quarter mile were
"generally lined by a motley multitude of negroes, Dutchmen, Yankee pedlers, and backwoodsmen, among whom, with long whips in
their hands to clear the ground, moved the proprietors and bettors."
The latter would cry out, "Two cows and calves to one!" or "Three
to one!" or "Four hogsheads of tobacco to one!" Anne Ritson, an
Englishwoman married to a Norfolk merchant, began a little poem
with "A race is a Virginian's pleasure" and ended it as follows:

> From ev'ry quarter they can come,
> With gentle, simple, rich and poor,
> The race-ground soon is cover'd o'er;
> Males, females, all, both black and white
> Together at this sport unite.[10]

Finally, as Davie wrote, "all eyes were toward the start as the
riders mounted." Curtis and Ned were in a profession that put a
premium on intelligence, bravery, and—especially at the start—independence. Quarter races were sometimes launched with the
crack of an official's pistol, the blare of a trumpet, the tap of a

drum, or a shout of "Go!" But the best of the riders did not start that way. Instead, they used a method called "turn and lock." Curtis and Ned were to turn their mounts in a tight circle and then take off if and when—and only if and when—the horses were "locked," or aligned with each other, not necessarily perfectly but with one of them at least up to the other's rear quarters. "Ready?" one would shout. If the second jockey answered, "Go!" they were off. But if the second rider did not like the way they were positioned and shouted "No!" they repeated the turn and tried again. This method put all of the responsibility on the jockey for a bad start, but it also gave him a chance to get off faster than his rival.[11]

Ned was a lot more experienced than Curtis, who couldn't have been much more than fourteen. The older man had studied both animals and knew he could count on the filly being relaxed, the gelding growing nervous. So he stalled, refusing to start out of the first turn, and again out of the second. As Paoli's nerves began to tell, Curtis realized that he could not cut Ned the slightest slack—the contest was too close. He had to come up with something, anything, to get the race off. According to Davie, who knew Curtis well in later years, the jockey told Jones after the race: "We made two turns and could not start. I saw old Ned did not mean to start fair. The Big Filly was cool as a cucumber. Paoli beginning to fret. You know, sir, we had nothing to spare; so I drew one foot, to induce Ned to think I was off my guard."

Would young Curtis have said "induce"? Possibly. Spoken language has certainly gone downhill since then. In any event, Curtis took a foot out of the stirrup, and the ruse worked. The unhitched foot caught Ned's eye, prompting him to start the race as they came out of their third circling and burst past the starting poles, whips snapping. "Paoli was in fine motion," Curtis said. "Ned locked me at the poles. Away we came." Davie said they took off "with the velocity of lightning." But Curtis had pulled a dangerous stunt with that dangling foot. He needed all the control he could get as the animal flew through the human corridor—which would have screamed in approval, as the English actor John Bernard said, "if the horses had happened to jostle and one of the riders been thrown off with a broken leg." This time, however, the crowd was not screaming at all. Maybe it was the size of the prize. Davie wrote, "All was silence; not a man drew his breath; nothing was heard but the clattering of the horses. They passed with the noise and speed of a tempest."

The jockeying for position, with the riders crossing paths, whipping each other, kneeing, and elbowing, was one of the great sights of the sport for bloodthirsty Americans. The wild ride of the quarter race inspired the so-called "American seat": the rider, in short stirrups, crouched over the horse's neck, both for better control and to free up the horse's action. By contrast, the traditional "English seat" was bolt upright, usually with long stirrups. John Randolph, a white gentleman jockey who made his home on the Roanoke and who was later a Virginia senator, became one of the first, but by no means the last, American jockeys to be compared with a monkey when he assumed the quarter-race crouch. Travelers' descriptions and paintings show that Native American horsemen out on the plains also used the natural crouch. British visitors, however, were shocked not only by the crouch but by how quickly the American races were over.

"It is the most ridiculous amusement imaginable," said Lieutenant Anburey, that British prisoner of war during the Revolution. "For if you happen to be looking another way, the race is terminated before you can turn your head." It did not take thirty seconds to fly the quarter mile, but to the crowd it felt much longer, for it was fierce, focused, unforgettable. Anybody who wonders today how such quick sprints could have drawn thousands from far beyond the Race Horse Region might also ask how the Kentucky Derby, which lasts all of two minutes, outdraws any couple of hours of football, baseball, or basketball. Nobody forgets the unmatched, fist-clenching, jaw-dropping intensity of those couple of minutes in Louisville.[12]

As Curtis and Ned charged madly past the huge walls of people, Jones watched from the finish line, doubtless distracted by the thought of what 147,000 pounds of Petersburg-inspected tobacco might bring in England. When Austin's loose foot whizzed by, however, he must have panicked. Maybe he saw all that golden weed go up in smoke prematurely. "The crowd was still silent; so close had been the contest," Davie said. "All felt the decision was yet doubtful. The judges met, compared notes, and finally determined Paoli had won by 23 inches." In other words, by a head: the clever young Curtis had outwitted and outraced the elder Ned. As it turned out, no other horse, no other jockey, ever beat the Big Filly. The celebration was wild. John Bernard described similar scenes thus: "The event was always proclaimed by a tornado of applause from the winner's party," the Negroes, he said, "in particular halloing, jumping, and clapping their hands in a frenzy of delight." His English phlegm was apparently startled into remission by the discovery of people who knew how to have a good time. Jones rode over to ask his teenaged jockey how it chanced that his foot hung loose. Allen Davie quoted Curtis as explaining, with maybe a bit of a grin if not a broad smile, "No chance at all, sir. Both horses did their utmost, and the loss of the stirrup has won the race."

WHAT WAS Curtis's share? As a slave, was he paid anything? There is no record of it, but the experiences of later slave jockeys suggest that he may well have gotten something, in cash or perks. Certainly their sport, their profession, set those athletes free for a few moments. Other slaves, not only jockeys, sometimes did get cash payments for specific jobs, and still more found an escape in their work. As Marvin L. Michael Kay and Lorin Lee Cary put it in *Slavery in North Carolina 1748–1775*, the slaves' work "framed their world, providing both pain and, ironically, a means by which they could mold a sense of self-worth." Though barely acknowledged by most historians, not only the labor but also the expertise of the African Americans was critical to the survival of the Southern colonies. In many cases it was labor that the whites were incapable of doing. In North Carolina, as Kay and Cary point out, it included work as supervisors, artisans—some of them actually making the plows that others drove—house-builders, boatmen, teamsters, spinners, and weavers. They helped develop the lumber industry—making staves, hoops, and ends for barrels for the West India trade. At a sawmill operated by African Americans near Wilmington, they turned out three thousand planks a day and could double that. Perhaps applying experience from iron production in Africa, they handled the main jobs at an ironworks called Chatham Furnace. In North Carolina's Lower Cape Fear, as in South Carolina, they successfully imported their own rice-growing methods from Africa.[13]

For the black jockeys and trainers, the work meant an opportunity to seek their personal best, a moment of triumph. But there was also another side for those less fortunate than Austin Curtis, those who had perhaps grown too big to ride, or for one reason or another were out of a job. A man advertised as a runaway in the *South Carolina Gazette* in 1754 sounded very much like a jockey in uniform:

ON SUNDAY THE 7th INSTANT (JULY) ran away from the Subscriber in *Charles Town*, a very hairy, short, thick, chubby negro fellow, named Marro, between 30 and 40 years old, Angola born, formerly the property of *Jonah Collins*, deceased, and lately belonging to *John Bulzigar* of *Orangeburgh*. He had on, when he went away, a checqued shirt . . . breeches with strings in the knees, an old hat cut in the form of a jockey cap and an old home-spun blue and white waistcoat; was lately bou't at vendue [bought at sale]; and it's imagined that if he is not harboured in or about *Charles Town*, he is gone towards *Orangeburgh* or *Santee*. Whoever takes him up in any part of the province above 10 miles from *Charles Town* shall have FIFTEEN POUNDS reward; and in the said town or within 10 miles thereof TEN POUNDS.[14]

Perhaps he could still ride and somehow still find work. Even as black jockeys stayed on the job, many faced the constant threat of punishment. John Bernard, the touring British actor, also noted that if blacks on the winning side cheered too much at a disaster for the opponents, "the defeated owner, or some friend for him, always dealt out retribution with his whip, for the purpose, as he termed it, of maintaining order." Allen Jones Davie told of a white trainer who gave a groom free rein in directing a jockey, but when the horse lost "is said to have punished his groom severely." He did not say what the punishment was, but "severe" could be terrible in that society. A beating sent its message beyond the crack of the whip. So did nailing a person's ears to a post and/or hacking them off, a not uncommon punishment for North Carolina slaves convicted of relatively minor crimes. Kay and Cary said some of the slaveowners offered "greater rewards for the return of their runaway slave's head than for the slave alive." The authors noted that a hundred slaves were executed in North Carolina for various crimes in a twenty-four-year period, from 1748 to 1772. They reported that the mode of death is known for fifty-six of them, starting with an unusual use of the gibbet (a post with an extended arm from which the body of someone already executed is hung as a warning): "One was chained alive in a gibbet to die slowly and horribly. Six were burned, two were castrated and then hanged, five were hanged and decapitated with their heads displayed on poles, one was hanged and burned, twenty-four were hanged, three died or were killed in jail, one committed suicide in jail, two died as a result of castration, seven slaves, most having been outlawed, were shot or beaten to death when captured, and five outlawed runaways drowned themselves to avoid capture and sadistic treatment."[15]

FOR THE captive African Americans, the pressures were often unbearable. But to resist them and to find an escape through work, religion, traditions from home, or love, was in and of itself a heroic act. Whatever pressures he may have known, Austin Curtis overcame them and in a real sense defeated slavery, dominating a sport that provided endless challenges and entertainment. Those early American quarter races were always "matches," as contests between only two horses were called. They were simply a case of one man matching his speedster against another's. But the Willie Jones–Austin Curtis stable at Halifax was so strong that few would take them on or bet against them, which meant that Jones and Curtis kept having to dream up scams, not only to lure an opponent but to build up the odds. "For a quarter racer as famous and successful as Willie Jones," as one authority put it, "the problem was not how to win, but how to get his bets down at favorable odds."[16]

Consider what happened around 1770. A stable owner named Sharrard had convinced the 6,500-odd residents—about 5,200 whites and 1,300 blacks—in backwoods Dobbs County, North Carolina, south of the Race Horse Region, that his blue-gray quarter horse, Blue Boar, was plain unbeatable. When he heard of a Scot named Henry coming in, setting up a general store, and rolling his *r*'s forever about his fast little saddle pony, he probably thought nothing of it. Everything was changing in North Carolina, general stores were popping up all over, Highland Scots and Scots-Irish were rushing in, and what would this one know about Blue Boar? So the magnificent Sharrard rode in on his champion to welcome young Henry to America—and make him an offer. He'd load the Boar with 160 pounds against the pony, who would have no weight requirement at all, zero: "160 pounds to a feather," as they put it. Deal.[17]

With everybody and his brother screaming for a piece of the Boar, the side bets quickly outgrew the cash prize of a hundred British pounds. Dobbs County residents bet more than their money on the Blue Boar nag. They bet horses and oxen. They even bet some of their slaves. Seeing and raising their bets, naïve Henry gambled the entire contents of his store and had it packed up—all the easier, the Sharrard crowd figured, for them to haul it away. At last, the race day came, and the county got the shock of its life: the Scot's little mammal somehow sailed home in front, defeating the legendary Blue Boar.

As the Piedmont dust settled, the Dobbs folks started to figure out that they'd been taken. But by that time Henry and his backers had already piled their winnings onto wagons—there's no indication of how many slaves were actually turned over—and were hurrying back north whence they came. Which turned out to be, of all places, Halifax Town. Henry's angels were none other than Willie Jones and company, who had arranged for the general store to be set up in the first place but who didn't appear until the night before the contest, bringing the empty wagons they'd be needing. As historian Mackay-Smith noted, Jones himself had bred Blue Boar, so he "knew exactly what he was racing against." Most important, the Scot's saddle horse, which stood just 13 hands, 3¾ inches tall (a hand is four inches, so this animal was a mere 4 feet, 7¾ inches tall) and weighed only 890 pounds, turned out to be one of Jones's undefeated chargers. With a perfect name: Trick'em.

The identity of Trick'em's rider is lost. It was not Jones's top jockey, since his name would have given the game away, though Austin Curtis was about to ride again. We do know something about the athlete who embarrassed Dobbs County, however, because Allen Davie, Jones's great-nephew, mentions him, though not by name, in one of his letters: "Of all those who attended that race from Halifax, none are now living, but the rider, now an old man; he was a slave of Gen. A. Jones, and was so small as to weigh about 50 lbs., at the time." General Allen Jones was Willie's brother and the letter-writer's grandfather, so we know where that old jockey spent his life—nine miles from Halifax, on the other side of the Roanoke River—and one day we might be able to trace more of his story, too. Strange to say, his feathery weight was no record. Eleven- and twelve-year-old riders were not uncommon. A diarist of the day was amazed to hear of one who weighed only forty-seven pounds and commented, "Strange that so little substance in a human Creature can have strength & skill sufficient to manage a Horse in a Match of Importance."[18]

Like Trick'em's rider, most jockeys went unidentified in contemporary newspapers and records. When it came to naming contestants, the order of priority was: owner, as in "Mr. Jones's gray mare"; then horse, if it had a name. The horse definitely would get a name if it was extremely good, its performances being carefully exaggerated in records or advertisements for its sale or breeding services. As for the jockeys, black or white, most accounts made no reference to them whatsoever, almost as if the horses ran bareback. Naturally, those advertising a horse for sale were not about to dilute his accomplishments by citing human help. On the extremely rare occasions when they did refer to a rider, the white jockeys might be identified by name, the black jockeys almost never. Of course, the fact that most of the latter were slaves didn't help their chances for recognition, or as the racing historian John Hervey succinctly put it: "In the South, being slave lads, they were ignored." Which makes the saga of Austin Curtis, preserved by Allen Jones Davie, all the more remarkable.

Curtis was back in the saddle and Jones was up to his old tricks on a May Thursday in the 1770s. Again they faced Colonel Jeptha Atherton, whose Big Filly had lost to Austin's loose foot. Again the setting was Brunswick County, at a formal racing strip called Tucker's Paths, just north of the border. Again it was big versus little. Atherton's hefty Mud Colt would lug 165 pounds against 130 for any opponent under 14 hands, 8 inches (5 feet, 4 inches). Smelling the prize of five hundred British pounds, as well as possible side action, Jones proved wily indeed. He appeared with a horse three-quarters of an inch too tall, then made a show of telling Curtis to trim the hooves. Still too tall. Angry for all to see, Jones had his jockey-groom trim some more, until the hooves started bleeding and the Atherton forces heaped more money on their Mud Colt. Plainly desperate, Jones inquired of Curtis if the little animal pulling their baggage cart "was not a horse of tolerable speed." The latter allowed as how he was better than one with no feet, so the poor cart beast was saddled and approved by the judges, and yet more money was piled on the Mud Colt.[19]

Again the race start was "turn and lock." Because each pilot knew he could win the race (Curtis had his reasons), they actually locked out of the first turn—and the Roanoke crowd must have been dumbfounded to see the cart puller metamorphose into a thing of beauty, "a horse of great power and fine action," said Davie. In the fabled hands of Austin Curtis, he clobbered the Mud Colt by no less than twenty-seven feet. He had metamorphosed, all right, into Trick'em. "You will observe," wrote Jones's great-nephew, "that it was intended from the beginning to run Trick'em, and the first horse was measured, his hoofs pared, only to induce betting."

It would not have been safe for Curtis, as a slave, to participate in Jones's scams. Black jockeys were hardly in a position to cheat. Quite the contrary. In 1769, only a few years previously, a race in Charleston, South Carolina, was declared suspect in part precisely because the riders were not black. First it was disclosed that the white jockey-groom Robert Gay had taken a bribe to lose a race and had even fingered the briber as a minor judge, one of His Majesty's justices of the peace for Berkeley County. The *South Carolina Gazette* reported, "After receiving the usual and proper punishment of the horse-whip, his worship was carried into a room by the gentlemen of the turf to protect him from the mob, who would otherwise have torn him to pieces." His worship confessed to trying to bribe Gay in an earlier event, prompting the *Gazette* to add, in an unusual compliment to the black jockeys: "In short there is great reason to suspect that *the Race has not been to the swift* since white grooms have rode our horses."[20]

CURTIS WAS far more than a jockey. He became Willie Jones's trainer, and therefore one of the most important trainers in the country. The job did not cease with the beginnings of the American Revolution in 1775; it just became more difficult, and in a sense more important, because Curtis's unwritten job description was to lead Jones's thoroughbred operation through whatever troubles lay ahead. Something of a Trick'em himself, Jones stunned everybody with his own metamorphosis on the eve of the Revolution, switching from playboy Tory and British sympathizer to radical, populist Whig. He became president of the North

Carolina Committee of Safety, which made him unofficial governor, one of the state's founding fathers.

But he was not ready to give up his lucrative racing activities. In October of 1778, as the rebels debated whether the British army might make a move into South Carolina, Willie Jones was dispatching Curtis north into Virginia to prepare for a horse race. Like many other leaders of America's enormously popular sport, Jones managed to avoid rules and regulations about what slaves could and could not do, including crossing state lines. A Williamsburg letter-writer told a friend that Austin's job was to repair a worn-out thoroughbred named Sterne for an important race. "Mr. Willie Jones sent his man Austin to keep Sterne, who was with him about a month before the day [of the race, October 27], who mended him greatly, but the rains was much against us." The correspondent did not say how the race turned out, but the fact that Jones dispatched Curtis on his own into Virginia, and that the trainer mended the horse "greatly," reveals the jockey-trainer's value as an employee.[21]

The British army did invade South Carolina in early 1780. There the goals of the murderous British cavalry raider Lieutenant-Colonel Banastre Tarleton included plundering the colony's many valuable thoroughbreds, most of them in the hands of African American grooms and trainers. Throughout the war a slave trainer named Tommy managed colonist David Ravenel's extensive breeding establishment, which included a legendary racer named Lucy. It was a dangerous job, especially when the British troops camped right on Ravenel's plantation after the Battle of Eutaw Springs. British raiders stole thirteen thoroughbred mares, five fillies, and three colts from John Huger's plantation near Charleston, but another slave manager named Mingo hid most of the stock and other valuables from the British. After the war, Huger freed Mingo and his wife for their loyalty, and the couple stayed on as employees.

In the autumn of 1780 Tarleton, in need of more horses for his troops, repeatedly tried to horsenap the imported English racer and sire Flimnap from another plantation near Charleston, the seat of an American officer, Major Isaac Harleston. The famous Flimnap was easy to spot—he was a long, strong bay (reddish brown in color) with a black mane, black legs, and black tail—but each time Tarleton's troops came looking, the African American grooms hid Flimnap in the swamps along Goose Creek. One morning, a British party captured a groom and offered him a large reward to reveal the steed's hiding place. The groom flat-out refused. Told it would cost him his life, he still kept silent and was promptly strung up on a tree in front of the manor house and left to die. After the British left, the servants ran out of the house, cut down the groom, and revived him. Then a groom slipped Flimnap into North Carolina—again a slave crossing state lines—where the champion racer was turned over to Austin Curtis for safekeeping.[22]

The following spring the war came to Curtis's neighborhood. As the British army of Lord Cornwallis moved north on its fateful advance toward Yorktown, Virginia, Tarleton's light force led the way into hostile Halifax. They charged and defeated some detached American units and then withdrew to a ravine a half mile from town to await Cornwallis, who was nearly fifty miles southeast of Tarleton. As he collected and secured a number of boats on the Roanoke below Halifax, Tarleton would write that he was "greatly assisted by some refugees and Negroes." Willie Jones's whereabouts just then would remain a mystery, not only to the British but to history; however, as a newly commissioned lieutenant colonel, whose militia unit had been watching Cornwallis, Jones was likely not far off.[23]

No record has been found of Austin Curtis's whereabouts either, but there is evidence that his job—protecting Jones's valuable thoroughbreds—had assumed military significance. Tarleton said his losses in taking Halifax "amounted only to three men wounded and a few horses killed and wounded," but his need for horses was greater than that indicated. He sent back to Cornwallis for help from some of the lord's mounted guards, "as it was rather hazardous for a corps of light dragoons, without carbines, and sixty infantry, to remain on the same ground many days and nights, near fifty miles from the army, in a populous and hostile country." His request was rejected. He was told "that the light company of the guards could not proceed for want of horses."

So Curtis's safeguarding of Joncs's very serviceable horses may indeed have denied the British a useful asset. They could have assisted Cornwallis in his advance, or helped Tarleton defend his position, allowing him more time for his assigned mission to collect intelligence on the state of the British forces to the north on the James River in Virginia. To contribute to the thick volume of "might-have-beens" in military history, Tarleton might have even learned enough to convince Cornwallis to turn back. Later, with the wonderful advantage of hindsight, Tarleton claimed that at the time he "deemed it probable that Lord Cornwallis would forego the expedition of James River and return . . . to the frontier of South Carolina," thus avoiding his world-shaking defeat at Yorktown in 1781.

Military speculation aside, one can only imagine Tarleton's reaction had he known that the recent great object of his desire, the famous English import Flimnap, was again within his grasp. As it was, Cornwallis, short of horses, arrived at Halifax himself and set up headquarters at "Jones' house," most likely Willie's—ironically the most celebrated horse haven in the area. The apparent ignorance of Cornwallis and Tarleton in regard to the locally famous Jones-Curtis stables did not speak well for the talents of the lord's advance man. At Halifax, Cornwallis prepared for his advance into Virginia by ordering Tarleton and his cavalry to reconnoiter the Roanoke countryside. They had not gone four miles when "his lordship, attended by six dragoons of his guard," furiously overtook them. It turned out Cornwallis had learned that two of Tarleton's troops had committed rape and robbery the night before. Determined to calm the population, and to show his army's discipline, Cornwallis instructed Tarleton to dismount his entire cavalry, "for the inspection of the inhabitants," as Tarleton put it, "and to facilitate the discovery of the villains who had committed atrocious outrages the preceding evening."

It was an extraordinary scene: British soldiers brought down from their high horses by their own commander and humiliated in front of the American townspeople. "A sergeant and one dragoon were pointed out, and accused of rape and robbery. They were conducted to Halifax, where they were condemned to death by martial law." From wherever he was, Austin Curtis was close to history. In a letter dated "Jones' plantation, May 15th 1781, five P.M.," on the eve of his fatal trip toward Virginia, Cornwallis sent an urgent message to Tarleton. "I would have you proceed tomorrow to the Nottoway and remain near Simcoe's infantry. [Benedict] Arnold is ordered to meet me on the Nottoway. [Anthony] Wayne's having joined Lafayette makes me rather uneasy for Arnold until we join. If you should hear of any movement of the enemy in force to disturb Arnold's march, you will give him every assistance in your power."[24]

When he reached Virginia, Cornwallis left no doubt as to the danger that Willie Jones, Austin Curtis, and their racing stable had just escaped. On the James River, Cornwallis established his headquarters in a country seat of another founding father, the outgoing governor, Thomas Jefferson, who was not there. Tarleton's advance troops had just chased him out of Monticello, Jefferson leaping on his horse and taking off through the woods toward Carter's Mountain. When Cornwallis got to Elkhill, Jefferson's plantation on the James, he practiced a policy of "total extermination," as Jefferson would put it. He destroyed all the crops, burned the barns, used the livestock ("as was to be expected") to feed his army, "and carried off all the horses capable of service: of those too young for service he cut the throats."

> He carried off also about 30 slaves. Had this been to give them freedom he would have done right, but it was to consign them to inevitable death from the small pox and putrid fever then raging in his camp. This I knew afterwards to have been the fate of 27 of them. I had never had any news of the remaining three . . .

From an estimate I made at that time I supposed the state of Virginia lost under Ld. Cornwallis's hands that year about 30,000 slaves, and that of these about 27,000 died of the small pox and camp fever, and the rest were partly sent to the West Indies and exchanged for rum, sugar, coffee and fruits, and partly sent to New York, from whence they went at the peace either to Nova Scotia, or to England. From this last place I believe they have lately been sent to Africa. History will never relate the horrors committed by the British army in the *Southern* states of America.[25]

AFTER THE Revolution, Curtis worked in the reflected glow of Willie Jones, who was both the hero of Halifax—North Carolina's social, commercial, and political capital—and the possessor of vast wealth accumulated through inheritance, land deals, racing, and gambling, with not a little help, of course, from Curtis himself. Jones's home, which he named the Groves, rose above Quankey Creek ("quankey" being a Native American term for red-tinted) on the edge of town. Sitting in a mossy-floored park of white oaks and sycamores, the house was surrounded by shrubbery, crepe myrtle, and mock oranges, but what made it remarkable was the celebrated window—reputedly America's first bow window, an expensive semicircular production. It gave him a view across the backyard toward his private "race ground," where he could watch the great former jockey Austin Curtis exercising his thoroughbreds.[26]

At the same time Curtis had his own household to care for. The records are silent on most of his personal life, such as the source of his family name, Curtis, or exactly where he lived. But his will would mention his wife, Nancy, and nine children, five boys and four girls. His namesake, Austin, probably the eldest, apparently had arrived in that dizzying year of 1776. According to the first federal census, in 1790, Jones had a very large number of slaves, 120, and he had one more whenever Austin and Nancy Curtis had a child—until one momentous day in 1791. On December 5, Jones took pen in hand and created a document that until now has lain buried in the North Carolina State Archives. "The petition of Willie Jones" to "the Honorable General Assembly of North Carolina" humbly stated "that a mulattoe slave of his, named Austin Curtis, by his attachment to his Country during the War, by his Fidelity to his Master, the said Willie Jones, and by his Honesty and good Behavior on all Occasions, has demonstrated that he deserves to be free.—

"The said Willie Jones therefore prays the General Assembly pass a Law to liberate the said Austin Curtis."

The petition was made into an Assembly bill, which stated "that the said Austin Curtis shall be, and he is hereby declared to be, free, by and under the Name of Austin Curtis Jones. And the said Austin Curtis, under the Name of Austin Curtis Jones, shall, from henceforward, be subject to, and enjoy the protection of the Laws, and the Benefits of the Constitution of the State of North Carolina, in the same manner as if he had been born a free man.— Any Law to the contrary notwithstanding."[27]

The bill was passed by both houses, after having been referred in the state Senate to the new "Committee appointed to draw a Bill for the emancipation of Slaves." Curtis's was one in a spate of individual emancipations for loyal slaves in the midst of the heady atmosphere of Revolutionary victory. It is unfortunate that Jones did not provide specifics on Curtis's "attachment to his Country during the War." His newly discovered petition, however, does tell us that Curtis was a mulatto, and the bill itself gave him the name Jones. He would sometimes use that name, but years later his family would revert to the name Curtis.

As a result of his emancipation, Austin Curtis Jones, who already had begun training thoroughbreds for the celebrated Willie Jones, moved into his own. He became an important transitional figure in the history of sports as he shifted easily into the future of horse racing: from quarter racing to training thoroughbreds for full-scale races, with as many as twenty or more entrants, on full-size ovals.

Horse racing was America's first modern sport, its first national pastime. Racing on full-size tracks actually began extremely early in this country, just one year after the 1664 Dutch surrender of New Amsterdam. The English celebrated it by building a two-mile oval at Hempstead Plains in Nassau County on Long Island and baptizing it New Market, after the well-loved English racing center. It was some six decades before other ovals began to appear, but by the 1770s the big racecourses were a feature of many towns, from New York City to Charleston. Manhattan had three. Philadelphia boasted a famous two-mile course, except that it was short of two miles.

"Timothy Matlack, J. Lukens, Palmer, and myself measured the new race track very exact," the Philadelphia German Jacob Hiltzheimer told his diary on September 4, 1767, "and find it lacks 144 yards of being two miles." This was also one of the earliest American uses of the term "racetrack" instead of the more common "racecourse" (other early uses of "track" suggest it may have started in Philadelphia). Out on Long Island, they were still trying to be as English as possible, and this included a widespread concern with proper uniforms, which reflected the early professionalism of the sport. On a visit to Hempstead Plains, Hiltzheimer noted, doubtless with German approval, "The rider of Regulus losing his cap, his second heat was given to Steady." Announcements for races at Annapolis and Upper Marlboro, Maryland, specified, "Each Jockey to appear with a neat waistcoat and half-boots." While the gentleman jockeys could get themselves up in the best-looking buckskin that the plantation tailor could turn out, and black jockeys were often left with the most minimal threads, the frequent written dress codes for the athletes did not discriminate, and they helped equalize the competition.[28]

The Pennsylvania Dutchman did not say whether the capless jockey was white or black, but most of the jockeys on the new northern courses were white, among them Irishman John Leary, who won the New York Subscription Plate on Smoaker in 1753. Leary has been called America's first professional jockey, but we now see that this ignores the countless earlier black professionals. While Leary may have been good, to judge from the wispy records, he was still not good enough to erase the claim made here for Austin Curtis as America's first truly great professional athlete.

As with the quarter-racing paths, far more of the big ovals were built in the South. The white gentleman jockeys were still prominent there. British actor John Bernard noted that he saw horses of all ages at the Williamsburg Races one day in 1799, and he added, "The riders were chiefly their owners." But hundreds of slave athletes were required to provide most of the riding talent as countless courses sprang up all over the South. Irish traveler Isaac Weld observed of the races at Petersburg, Virginia, in the late 1790s: "The horses are commonly rode by negro boys, some of whom are really good jockies." One modern Virginia study said that "in advertisements for runaway servants, Negroes are several times mentioned as skillful and experienced jockeys."[29]

Again their names were rarely recorded, so questions abound in the search for the individuals who did so much to create our first major sport. Consider, for example, George Washington's encounters with the black jockeys. The only rider mentioned in his writings is not a professional thoroughbred jockey but one Robert Sandford, to whom he paid 12 shillings "for pacing my horse" in a race at Accotink, a few miles south of Mount Vernon, on September 29, 1768. We do not know who Sandford was, except that he had a wife named Kerrenhappuck and kept the Eagle Tavern at Newgate. The horse was most likely a foxhunter and saddle horse. Other questions remain.[30]

Who was in the saddle on Thursday, May 28, and Friday, May 29, 1761, for two three-mile races at Alexandria in Virginia? Among the managers and judges of the events was Washington himself, who was then twenty-nine years old, back from the French and Indian War, and farming at nearby Mount Vernon. Could Washington have blamed a black rider for the four-pound bet he lost at the Williamsburg Races in 1759? Which of the professionals were up when he helped finance the Williamsburg

TO BE RUN FOR,
On *Thurſday the* 28*th Day of* May, *on the uſual Race Ground at* ALEXANDRIA,

A PURSE of FIFTY POUNDS, Three Times round the Ground (being near three Miles) the beſt in Three Heats, by any Horſe, Mare, or Gelding, 14 Hands to carry 10 Stone, below that Meaſure, Weight for Inches.

And, on the Day following, will be Run for, on the ſame Ground and Diſtance, A PURSE of TWENTY-FIVE POUNDS, by Four Year old Colts, 14 Hands to carry 9 Stone, below that Meaſure, Weight for Inches

The Horſes to be Entered on the Monday before the Race with the Managers, Mr. *George Waſhington*, Mr. *John Carlyle*, and Mr. *Charles Digges:* Each Horſe to pay Fifty Shillings Entrance on the Firſt Day, and Twenty-five Shillings the Second Day; and thoſe who do not enter their Horſes on the Monday aforeſaid, to pay double Entrance.

Three Horſes to Start or no Race.

All Differences that may ariſe, will be decided by the Managers.

An advertisement in the Virginia Gazette *in May 1761 announces two races put on by 29-year-old George Washington and friends at Alexandria, Virginia. Courtesy of author.*

Jockey Club purses through the 1760s? Which riders entertained him at Annapolis, Maryland, on several occasions in the early 1770s, or at Fredericksburg in Virginia?

Who was aboard during the Alexandria season when two of the entries were "a fine young horse called the *Roan Colt,*" the property of Thomas Jefferson, and Magnolio, owned by Washington, who was just back from the Revolutionary War, farming again at Mount Vernon, and soon to be president? A number of historians have made this Alexandria race meeting more wonderful than it was, reporting that the Jefferson and Washington chargers competed against each other, with Jefferson winning. They based their accounts on a misreading of a memoir by Thomas Peter, who married a daughter of Washington's stepson, John Custis. Peter saw Washington serve as a judge on the day that Magnolio lost. He thought that Jefferson's colt came home a winner but in a different event and on a different day.

Who was Altamont, unknown to researchers at Mount Vernon today but said to have been a former slave of Washington's and the constant navigator of a champion named Grey Medley? Foaled in 1791, this colt ran at Tappahannock in Virginia before he was taken west. It was an Irish-born surgeon, Dr. Redmond Dillon Barry, who brought to Tennessee both Grey Medley, perhaps its first important sire, and something still more important, the delicious Irish blade celebrated ever since as bluegrass.

The primary places of employment for the black riders were the countless ovals that had sprung up all over Virginia, Maryland, and the Carolinas. These courses were built and run by the local "jockey clubs," which were the first organizations of owners in American sports, forerunners to the modern "leagues." They were not clubs of professional jockeys, as the name might suggest, but racing associations founded by "gentleman jockeys" and others for the purpose of operating their own courses. From the beginning, the founders often declared the clubs were established "for the improvement of the breed," a notion snickered at ever since, but as Curtis could have explained, the breed would not survive without racing. The year 1730 brought the first English "blood," or "bred," horse to the Colonies. This arrival of the stallion Bulle Rock in Virginia was the beginning of increased selectivity by Colonial breeders. In 1791, publication of the *English General Stud Book*, listing the lineage of thoroughbreds, created a still more selective breed in America. So when the North Carolina planter Marmaduke Johnson decided to get into racing in the 1790s, he was a lot fussier than he might have been before.

Johnson commissioned the newly freed trainer and businessman Austin Curtis to buy him a filly "that after racing would make a good brood mare," a producer of champions. Curtis responded by making racing history again. Whereas quarter horses were bred for bursts of speed, thoroughbreds had to have "bottom," the endurance to go incredible distances—up to five "heats," or rounds, of as many as four miles each, or a total of twenty miles with only a half-hour rest between heats. This would be unthinkable today, when thoroughbreds rarely compete as far as two miles. Locally legendary for his courtesy, Curtis doubtless displayed his unshakable good manners when he consulted a breeder in Greensville County, Virginia. From him, for fifty Virginia pounds, he purchased a small gray, "handsome and finely formed," sired by the imported Medley and a half-sister to Grey Medley. Known far and wide as the Medley Mare, Curtis's purchase scored many victories—the number is not known—and lost only once, on a technicality. Far more important, said the racing historian John Hervey, "she proved the value of Curtis' judgment by becoming the premier matron of her time," the mother of "the greatest chain of race mares of which we have knowledge." Their names were Reality, Bonnets o' Blue, and Fashion. Or as another authority put it, she was "a veritable 'blue hen,'" foaling a seemingly endless line of champions, many of them fillies.[31]

By the mid-1790s, Willie Jones's racecourse at Halifax had turned into a major public venue for thoroughbred racing, and the renown of its leading trainer reached far beyond the Race Horse Region—and beyond his time. In 1832, Judge William Williams, secretary of the Nashville Jockey Club, would compare Curtis with two white horse breeders of that earlier era, Harry Hunter and Turner Bynum, the latter having bred the Big Filly, who was beaten by a dangling foot. Along with Hunter and Bynum, the judge wrote, with the usual bow to the racism of the day, "flourished Austin Curtis, a man of color indeed but one of judgment, skill and courteous manners. He knew how 'to get the length into them,' or to bring out their game. Under his auspices the fame of Collector grew, and the powers of Snap Dragon were developed." Collector and Snap Dragon were two great runners of the day.

The Jones-Curtis stable was also where the imported Flimnap, who had been rescued by his black groom during the Revolution, sired both Betsy Baker, a great racing filly, and Young Flimnap, whose blood survives in many modern pedigrees.[32]

Willie Jones died at the age of sixty, in 1801. By then Curtis had been a free man for ten years, but his emancipation had not meant emancipation for his children born under slavery. His son William, for example, was still a slave, and now he was transferred to another owner. Jones's will declared, "I give Austin C. Jones's son Billey to my son Willie but Austin is to have the use of him until my son Willie comes of age." Willie William Jones would become twenty-one four years after his father's death. Never married, he was quite close to Curtis, which perhaps was what made it possible for Curtis to acquire his own son later on. We know that Curtis did just that because his own testament notes that he gave his own son William his freedom.[33]

Austin Curtis's assets expanded considerably after the death of his former "master" and racing partner. Jones bequeathed him two hundred dollars and the use of a nearby house and plantation, with permission to clear fifty acres for cultivation until Jones's five-year-old son Robert Allen came of age, at which time the property would transfer to Robert, but only if he chose to live on it. Two years later, Curtis acquired 165 more acres along Quankey Creek for six hundred dollars, and five years after that, in 1808, another 145 acres for three hundred dollars. He also purchased an unknown amount of land from his letter-writing friend Allen Jones Davie.[34]

Once, when Davie had to vouch for the Medley Mare's pedigree, he said he could do so in part because "the blood was so stated by Austin Curtis (who purchased the mare for Mr. Johnson;) and who, though a man of color, was one on whom all who knew him relied." Although he tacked on that racial qualification ("though a man of color"), typical for whites of that time, Davie added proudly, "Austin was a *freed* man of my family." There was no qualification at all in an unusual item in the Raleigh, North Carolina, *Minerva*, on January 5, 1809. It was unusual because there were not many people, certainly not many black people, whose deaths made the newspaper in the state capital. This notice, with no cause of death given, followed briefer obituaries for a Wilmington merchant and a member of the North Carolina Assembly.[35]

DIED,

On the 10th ult., at Halifax (n.c.) AUSTIN JONES, a colored man, aged about 50 years—well known for many years past, as keeper of race horses; in the management of which useful animals, he particularly excelled. —His character was unblemished; his disposition mild and obliging—his deportment uniformly correct and complaisant—he possessed the esteem of *many*— the respect and confidence of all who knew him.

Andrew Jackson, as seen here in an early engraving,
conquered virtually every adversary he faced, but not the great jockey
Simon aboard Haynie's Maria. Courtesy of author.

.2.

RACING *on the*
FRONTIER

SIMON AND GENERAL ANDREW JACKSON

1780–1817

S IMON WAS FOUR and a half feet tall. "He was a hunch-back with very short body and remarkably long arms and legs" ran a rare first-hand description of him by a Tennessee congressman who had seen him ride. It was couched in the white attitudes of the day. "His color and hair were African, but his features were not. He had a long head and face, a high and delicate nose, a narrow but prominent forehead and a mouth indicative of humor and firmness. It was rumored that Simon was a prince in his native country."[1]

The congressman went on: "He was a native African and was brought with his parents when quite young to South Carolina, before the prohibition of the slave trade took effect." That was in 1808. According to Simon's death notice, he was born in 1780 or 1781. He probably arrived in America by 1790, or perhaps well before, when he was "quite young." The family likely would have been "quarantined" with other slaves at Sullivans Island in Charleston Harbor before being taken into the city. We can only guess at the horrors that awaited them, for the documentary record then leaps ahead to when Simon was well into a career as a jockey. It may seem incongruous to say that a slave could have a highly successful professional career, yet it was an achievement that Austin Curtis and countless other black Americans managed before Simon. By the end of the eighteenth century, the racehorse jockey's was considered a legitimate profession, and the skills of the best were much sought after, whether black or white.

It's very likely that for many their careers had their origins, or inspiration, in Africa. Perhaps, like the English "gentleman jockeys," Simon and other black riders acquired a love of horses back home, or from the stories told by their elders of their equestrian tradition in Africa. After all, many of the Africans arrived with valuable talents. Some brought rice-growing skills to South Carolina, skills that the English desperately lacked and that literally saved the colony. One slave advertisement shouted, "250 fine healthy NE-GROES just arrived from the Windward & Rice Coast," while another announced "a choice cargo of windward and gold coast negroes, who have been accustomed to the planting of rice." In West Africa's Gambia River valley, horsemen tended large herds of cattle, a job that became an African specialty on a smaller scale in South Carolina. Some of that colony's Africans were even dispatched on horseback into the American wilderness to trade with Indians. One, who learned the Indians' language, led a twenty-two-horse pack train through the woods to Savannah, Georgia. The white shipper was subsidized by the authorities "in Consideration of his said Negro's extraordinary Service and being Linguist."[2]

Horses were everywhere in early South Carolina. "Horses, the best Kind in the World," raved an English promoter in a London magazine in 1732, "are so plentiful that you seldom see anybody travel on foot, except Negroes, and they oftner on horseback." South Carolina developed a love of horses every bit as intense as Virginia's; indeed, it built formal racecourses well before the Old Dominion, with African American jockeys participating from the start. When Charleston formed a jockey club in 1734 (before any other American town; for that matter, before any English town), an advertisement for the club's first recorded race made it clear that black jockeys were already in action. It did so indirectly, declaring that this one-mile contest was for four horses, each "to carry ten stone weight and white men to ride." Specifying whites this time meant that blacks also competed.[3]

In that rare atmosphere of the Southern racecourses, slave jockeys competed on equal athletic terms alongside white riders, a story untold until now. In the previous chapter, we read about the anonymous Angolan-born jockey who ran away in his uniform shortly after he was sold at auction in 1754. A decade later, the owner of a horse named Moro declined a challenge by the owner of Centinel because "Centinel would have an experienced white rider and Moro be obliged to carry a white lad or Negro not so skilled in that profession." A week after that, the owner of a third horse, Veve, challenged both of them and revealed that his jockey would not be hard to miss. "If this challenge is accepted, his rider will be a new negro clad in white, with a plume of swan's feathers in his cap." All jockeys, including slave jockeys, were considered to be professionals, even if their individual talents were not equal—as Veve's owner conceded that his rider, like Moro's, was "not very skilful in that profession." Very early then, the African American athlete discovered that sports could be, not a way out, except under the luckiest of circumstances, but a way up.

South Carolina was far ahead of other colonies in developing the traditions of America's first national sport. The carefully considered attire of Veve's rider, with his feathered cap and white uniform, with breeches almost certainly in the buckskin that many Charleston jockeys wore, suggests this. There were the prizes, too. They were minor in value compared with the vast sums that were wagered, but they carried considerable prestige. That earliest recorded South Carolina race in 1734, for white men only, was for "a handsome saddle and bridle," a modest prize, though one beyond the reach of most South Carolinians. Two years later, there was a race at Charleston's Bowling Green for a "silver-hilted small sword." In 1743, South Carolina was inventing the modern sports trophy, offering "a handsome and fashionable silver punch bowl" in two races and "a handsome silver pint mug" in another, not to mention a saddle, bridle, and furniture in a fourth event.

By now, both South Carolina's and Virginia's racecourses were also helping to develop human foot races, creating America's earliest formal "track and field" events, and quite imaginative ones at that. One Carolina racing program, on an October Thursday in 1743, featured a mile foot race "by six people . . . no jostling allow'd" for "a very good handsome French embroider'd waistcoat." Curiously, the notice did not specify men, or whites. On Saturday "will be given, gratis, a very good silver lac'd hat, to be run for by four men or more." The runners were "to make the best way they can 200 yards, each man to be in a sack, all but his head; the person that comes in first shall have the hat."

Another major innovation in the development of American sports was South Carolina's use of "stop watches," as they were already called, for workouts and races. In a 1764 report on several races, the *Gazette* noted that "the stop watch was not run for, for want of horses." Instead, the watch would be offered in a future race, "by which time gentlemen may get their horses in order and have the chance to win the best watch for that purpose ever in the province." Thus, the performances of American athletes, black and white, were already being carefully calibrated. It was an early proof of America's passion for exact timing in sports, for the most precise statistics, a passion that England, for example, has never shared. Moreover, that 1764 report, an account of several races over several South Carolina tracks, made its own contribution to American sports history. It was the earliest extensive sports report in American journalism.

Thus, when Simon began riding in South Carolina, probably by his midteens, or in the mid-1790s, he was starting at the top of the sport, which immediately provided him with an unbeatable professional education and doubtless contributed to the supreme confidence, and often arrogance, for which he would become legendary. Though a slave, he was participating in an interracial sport at the highest level. He could watch if not yet ride some of the greatest horses of the day and pick up pointers from some of the best jockeys, black and white. He was coached and counseled by leading trainers, even by powerful Carolina planters, who, like other stable owners of that day, did much of their own training and strategizing. Racing did not get any better than in the horse-crazy state where Simon started out in the 1790s.

After the Revolution, puritan and anti-English sentiment combined to drive America's one organized sport out of the North. Horse racing was even banned in New York State, its previous northern stronghold, in 1802, on the admittedly accurate grounds that it was mostly gambling. The South, on the other hand, absolutely loved everything about it that the puritans hated—the gambling, the sport, the throwbacks to England's chivalric traditions. And Simon's South Carolina loved it most of all. Opened in the first president's first term, and named for him, Charleston's Washington Course was not only the new country's first major sports facility but for many years its finest. Like the earlier quarter races, it drew the mixed-up, almost democratic crowds that only sports could attract, a lesson lost on politicians then and on historians ever since. Women, for example, loved it.

"Charleston, South Carolina, is, we believe, the only place where ladies habitually grace the course with their likeness," declared one gallant.[4]

That was not quite true. Women all over the South loved the sport. As quarter racing—with its backwoods sideshows of cockfighting, gouging contests, and bare-knuckle boxing—gave way to "course racing" in or near the cities, many jockey clubs found women turning out in force. Granted, Charleston's women were special. Its boosters went on forever about the belles who grew like Spanish moss at the Washington Course. They went on so much that British visitor Margaret Hunter Hall felt a need to report after the Jockey Club Ball, "I never in my life saw so many ugly women gathered together." More than a century and a half after that gratuitous insult, a Charleston historian and gentleman was still fuming,

declaring Mrs. Hall "rude and ignorant." She certainly had not followed the rules.[5]

In Simon's day, said a secretary of the Jockey Club, "everything
combined . . . to render race-week in Charleston emphatically the
carnival of the state, when it was *unpopular,* if not *impossible* to be
out of spirits and not to mingle with the gay throng." The excitement was shared by everyone, he said, "from the Governor and the
ladies in the Grand Stand to the negroes who sat unmolested on
the fence tops." Perhaps a day on the fence tops was a temporary
escape from the molesters, but at times that era's great crime was
carried out on the spot. "It is no uncommon thing there," noted
Isaac Weld, the Irishman who toured the South in the 1790s, "to
see gangs of negroes staked at a horse race"—in other words, offered as the betting stakes. At the same time Simon and the other
black athletes had fashioned their escape from the worst of it.[6]

WE KNOW that Simon began his career in South Carolina, riding
with the best of them, because of an incident that took place half a
continent away. In 1808, Green Berry Williams, a prominent white
trainer in Tennessee, went south to tour the swamps of the Chicka-
saws and Cherokees, trying to make an American dollar by matching his speedy gelding Omar against any and all takers. Entering
the fall races at Natchez on the Mississippi River, he wrote to a
friend, Colonel George Elliott, back in Tennessee with an idea for
a killing. Williams advised Elliott, who had a large stable at Gallatin, to head down the five-hundred-mile Natchez Trace with fifteen to twenty of his horses, which they would put up as the stakes
in bets on Omar. Williams also told Elliott to bring a certain
jockey to ride Omar. A match race was quickly scheduled, and in
his mind Williams may have already spent his winnings. But when
the horses took to the course, the rival trainer was startled to see a
familiar four-and-a-half-foot hunchback materialize from the mists
of the lower Mississippi. "Alarmed" was the word used.[7]

"Simon's appearance on the field," recalled a friend of Williams, "alarmed the trainer of the other horse who had known him

in South Carolina." So intimidating was the mere sight of the former South Carolina jockey that the other trainer, also "suspecting
that Omar was a bite," a ruse (specifically, that the horse was a lot
better than Williams had let on), paid a forfeit fee and pulled out
of the match.

By 1808, when Simon was about twenty-seven, he was no
longer living in South Carolina. We do not know whether he ever
saw his parents again, or how much of his American boyhood he
had spent with them. Nor do we know when he left, although he
was said to have ridden, among other famous thoroughbreds, Dr.
Barry's Polly Medley, who won Tennessee's first notable horse race
at Gallatin in 1804. We do know that Simon remained a slave. Perhaps his owners, like so many other Carolinians—Andrew Jackson
among them—had joined the long queue of pioneers crossing the
Appalachians, bringing Simon into North Carolina's western lands,
now the state of Tennessee. There, probably as the result of a death,
Simon had become the slave of two as yet unidentified minors.

He was also known by a nickname, Monkey Simon. It was a
popular sobriquet for whites as well as blacks throughout that century and well into the next, especially for athletes, such as the white
professional baseball player Pete "Monkey" Hotaling. Still, neither
of Simon's two regular employers, stable owner Elliott and trainer
Williams, used the nickname when they later shared their memories of the great jockey. Nor did Judge Thomas Barry, secretary of
the Gallatin Jockey Club, in his own reminiscence. They held him
in awe, and in the recollections they left, they called him Simon.[8]

For all his advantages, Austin Curtis as a jockey had been
chained to Willie Jones. Simon, however, operated somewhat independently, indeed extremely so when compared with most slaves.
Yet he was ultimately under the control of the children's guardian,
Robert C. Foster, a Nashville lawyer. Sociologically inclined historians, if any had ever heard of Simon, might sum up his situation as
follows: It was common for some owners to hire out a few of their
slaves. It was done frequently by heirs or legal guardians like Foster.
Skilled slaves might also be loaned out. Simon's experiences offered

insights into the lives of slaves who won a degree of independence through their skills, which often exceeded those of white workers.

Novelist Toni Morrison said it better in her novel *Beloved:* "Men and women were moved around like checkers. Anybody Baby Suggs knew, let alone loved, who hadn't run off or been hanged, got rented out, loaned out, bought up, brought back, stored up, mortgaged, won, stolen or seized."[9]

Most times Foster hired out Simon to Colonel George Elliott. There is no record of where or how the jockey lived when he was not riding, but when he was, he often must have shared quarters with the other stable help at Elliott's farm, Wall Spring. This was where the Red River Road crossed Station Camp Creek a few miles northwest of Gallatin in Sumner County, Tennessee. Here Simon would have circled the splendid private racecourse across the street from the house. He would have enhanced his reputation as Wall Spring became a horsemen's mecca, where "every meal was prepared for 'company.'" He would have witnessed the neighbor Dr. Barry's introduction of Irish bluegrass, which was making middle Tennessee a new power in American racing.

Elliott may have been a good man to work for, known as he was as a thoroughbred breeder of "tact, sound judgment and fine capacity of detail," one of the best and wealthiest horsemen in all of Tennessee. As the races neared, this Sumner County militia colonel would canter down the road to a place about a mile before the ferry crossed the sea-green Cumberland River at Nashville. There workers gathered to be hired out at auction, and there, Elliott said, "I have often hired Simon, who, on account of his deformity and dissipated habits, usually cost me from twelve to fifteen dollars per annum."[10]

Foster, the lawyer-guardian, collected that twelve to fifteen dollars for the children. He must have been quite a bungler, for he might have done much better. Certainly Simon's deformity never reduced his earning power. As for his "dissipated habits," they have not been identified, but the possibilities are tantalizing. Simon knew how to have a good time. He strummed a wicked banjo, for instance, spitting out vicious ditties about all the wonderful folk of Sumner and Nashville's Davidson Counties. Perhaps they were habits that reflected his vast lack of respect for the system. Whatever they were, he must have had enough control over them to perform at his lonely level, earning perks, tips, side money, and fame while returning to the colonel thousands of dollars on his Gallatin Road investment of twelve to fifteen dollars.

On occasion Simon must have felt like a checker on a checkerboard. Elliott, who got him from Foster, who got him from the minors, sometimes gave him to somebody else. It was then that Simon, three times removed from the children and that much freer, often displayed the passion that kept him on top. There was the time Elliott entered the Nashville Jockey Club stakes but for some reason hired out Simon to a prominent Nashville physician, Dr. Robert Sappington, a rival for the same purse. Maybe Elliott did this to get a reluctant Sappington into the game. The doc's nag, Oscar, was a forbidding presence, with a lion's oversized shoulders and chest and a gigantic windpipe. Don't let this monster use himself up, Sappington warned Simon, worried less about the jockey's skills, maybe, than his loyalty.[11]

At the tap of the drum, Oscar flew away, soaring fifty yards in front, which "served to increase the doubts of Simon's fidelity." The doctor darted across the infield screaming at his rented rider to rein Oscar in. But Simon was already doing exactly that, and this was one slave who shouted back.

"You d—d fool, don't you see his mouth is wide open!" Simon yelled as he pulled so hard on the bit that it left Oscar's jaw gaping. He went on to earn the doctor a thousand dollars in two four-mile heats.

It hardly mattered whether Simon was riding for his usual boss or for a cretin. As Tennessee congressman Balie Peyton put it, "Simon always rode to win, if possible; if he had a weakness, it was in being too eager for success in a close contest." One day he tried even harder because he was loaned out a little too casually. Again Elliott was letting his contract rider try to beat one of his own horses, Paddy Carry. Again it may have been to get the other owner, a Colonel Stepp, into the race. Seeing Simon was irritated at being loaned out, Stepp goaded him, saying Elliott obviously didn't think he needed his jockey. Then he slipped Simon one hundred dollars.[12]

"Somewhat offended at the idea of being lent out," Peyton wrote, "and by no means indifferent to the money, Simon resolved to win the race if possible, and nodding his head said, 'I'll show 'em.'"

Simon used every tactic he could get away with, including threats. Drawing the inside rail, he steered his mare at Paddy as they went into each turn, forcing him to the outside and keeping the shorter inside route for the weaker mare. Out of the turns Paddy had to work to get back in it and chase the mare down on the straightaways. Or, as Peyton put it, "Simon, by his consummate skill and by intimidating the other rider, managed to run him far out on the turns while he rested his mare for a brush on the stretches."

At the last turn, Simon found his mare worn out. Again Paddy, "a game 4-miler," caught up with her. Again Simon "boldly swung out so far as to leave Paddy in the fence corner." Still it wasn't over, as the other rider dragged Paddy back into it. "The boy came up and attempted to pass on the inside, but Simon headed him off and growled at him all the way down the quarter stretch, beating him out by a neck." As Peyton concluded, "Simon could come within a hair's breadth of foul riding and yet escape the penalty."

Elliott was not impressed. Normally a serene man, he spun out of control. He had lost another thousand dollars and whined to Simon that he'd made Paddy run forty feet farther on every turn and rode "foul all the way down the quarter stretch."

"Well, Col. Elliott," said Simon, "I've won many a race that way for you, and it is the first time I ever heard you object."

BUT SIMON would not have become famous had it not been for another Tennessean out of South Carolina. Simon was about to square off with Andrew Jackson himself in one of the most colorful rivalries in American sports. The seventh president was also the father of the Tennessee turf, a founder of both the Nashville and nearby Clover Bottom courses. Although he once put a white rider, Billy Phillips, on his great stallion Truxton, Jackson usually resorted to black jockeys, possibly drawing a few from the slaves at his 640-acre homestead, the Hermitage, northeast of Nashville. As he climbed from lawyer and merchant to representative and senator to judge and general, his slave holdings rose—from fifteen in 1794 to ninety-five when he became president in 1829 to as many as two hundred at one point.[13]

Once again questions about the black jockeys remain. Who rode for the future president on his private course at the Hermitage? The staff there today has no idea. Who besides Billy Phillips steered the great Truxton as he amassed, Jackson boasted, more than twenty thousand dollars in prizes? Who was supposed to mount Truxton before the owner of the other horse, Ploughboy, withdrew from the race but failed to pay the forfeit fee? This led to a duel in which Jackson, hit first, aimed directly at Charles Dickinson's groin and did not miss, fatally wounding the man. In another incident, around 1806, who was the boy that the future president and his partner accepted in partial payment for goods at their store on the hill overlooking the Clover Bottom course? The boy was then loaned as part of a stakes in a horse race, switched from one owner to another, sold down the river, literally, and then sent back again, finally dying of an untreated sore on his leg.[14]

Once Jackson tried to get a new jockey from Wade Hampton, the great power of the Charleston turf and holder of an incredible three thousand slaves. On a May day in 1810, Brigadier General Hampton was on his way from Nashville to South Carolina with his Light Dragoons when Jackson sent him a query. Could he buy either of two slaves traveling with him (Hampton's rank allowed him four servants) to work as a jockey? Wade Hampton spoke to one of his officers and then wrote to Jackson. "I suggested my wish of sending back to you one of the Boys," he said. But the officer had advised against it. "They are family Negroes, & his impression was, the sale I had made & the *distance*, would create great affliction amongst their relations, were Either of the Boys left." Tearing the boy from his family was not the clinching reason, however. Hampton continued: "And when I found that neither of them could ride at less than 100 ls [lbs.] I gave over the idea."[15]

Jackson benefited handsomely not only from his black jockeys but from his black trainer, Dunwoody. Everybody at the Hermitage called him "Dun." Having bought him in 1806, Jackson relied heavily on him for three decades to care for his racing and breeding stock. According to the editors of Jackson's papers, Dunwoody "became de facto chief of the stables and a trainer widely admired by horse breeders in Middle Tennessee." When a prominent stable owner was supervising affairs at the Hermitage during Jackson's absence, Dun made it clear who was the authority: "What would you suppose," the stable owner wrote the general, "I am here a-keeping race Horses with old Dun & find I know as little of the matter as If I had never seen a horse."[16]

In 1811, with Dun and his slave jockeys at his command, Andrew Jackson stood ready to knock off another rival horse. Maria was her name. Her father was the imported Diomed, who had captured the first English Derby at Epsom, sired sixty-five offspring over there, and then crossed the Atlantic to sire some fifty more, among them saddle horses for Thomas Jefferson and John Marshall. Maria, Diomed's last and best daughter, was sold for a hundred dollars to Captain Jesse Haynie of Sumner County. They gave her the plainest of names, Haynie's Maria, but she was a lot better than her unimaginative name implied. The captain watched as she filled out: deep in the shoulders, huge ribs, lengthy body. Mercurial personality. "In training," Haynie would tell a friend, "she was very vicious, in exercise lazy, but in a race she ran free and always kindly." She would need a brilliant rider: Simon. Maybe the captain or her trainer, Green Berry Williams, got him in a deal with Colonel Elliott.

But neither Captain Haynie nor Simon could know their feud with Andrew Jackson would last four years, helping to shift the sport westward and create a new "race horse region" in middle Tennessee, with Kentucky right behind. Maybe the feud said something about the frontier spirit. Or about Jackson, who would not let it die even as he answered his country's several calls to battle. Or about Simon, who like the general could stand only one outcome—winning—and who survived even as the obscenity of slavery soiled the frontier and filled the Tennessee newspapers not with Simon's adventures but with slave-sale ads. What follows are Andrew Jackson's confrontations with Haynie's Maria and Simon, documented first by a friend of Haynie's, Judge Thomas Barry, the son of Dr. Barry, the bluegrass importer. Judge Barry got the details from Haynie himself and relayed them to the *American Turf Register* under his pen name, Grosvenor, in 1835. Later Balie Peyton, Jackson's friend, added details. A third commentator, the anonymous racing writer in the respected sporting journal *Spirit of the Times*, said that Simon was aboard Maria in all of the confrontations.[17]

IN THE fall of 1811, to spoil Maria's debut at age three, Major General Jackson trotted out Decatur, a Truxton colt named for Stephen Decatur, who had distinguished himself during the 1801–1805 naval battles at Tripoli. Who would besmirch such names? Simon would, and Jackson knew it. If Maria was a mystery to him, Simon wasn't. This may have been the day the six-foot, one-inch militia general issued an order to the four-foot, six-inch jockey.

"Now, Simon, when my horse comes up and is about to pass you, don't spit your tobacco juice in his eyes, and in the eyes of his rider, as you sometimes do."

"Well, *Gineral*," said Simon, dripping sarcasm, "I've rode a good deal agin your horses, but (with an oath) none were ever near enough to catch my spit." As a later nineteenth-century commentator would point out, Simon was famous for his wit—"cutting, withering, almost blighting. . . . He rarely failed to shiver a lance, in repartee, with even the most eminent that he chanced to come in contact with, and he met the most distinguished men of the times." He got away with it because of his tremendous talent, his handicap, and his size. "His position and natural deformity gave him the broadest liberties with all, white and black."

On that particular day, there was no way Jackson's colt could have caught Simon's spit. Decatur didn't even finish. He and four others were so far behind in the first two-mile heat that they were "distanced"—meaning they were ruled out of the race. To qualify for the second heat, they would have had to have been within a required distance of Maria and Simon as they flew across the finish line. Maria took the second heat from the remaining contender, leaving Jackson more than mortified.[18]

He of the titanic drive was outraged. "This defeat aroused the ire and combative spirit of Gen. Jackson almost as much as did his [later] defeat by Mr. [John Quincy] Adams for the presidency," his friend Peyton would write, "and he swore 'by the eternal' he would beat her if a horse could be found in the United States able to do it."

But before he found one, one of his former riders, Billy Phillips, was in the saddle and traversing the countryside with an urgent announcement: the House had voted for the War of 1812. In his 860 miles from Washington to Nashville, Billy sped through North Carolina's own town of Lexington, "his horse's tail and his own long hair streaming in the wind," crying: "Here's the stuff! WAR WITH ENGLAND!! WAR!"[19]

War was what the hermit craved. Try as he did, though, he couldn't get President James Madison to rush him to Canada with twenty-five hundred militiamen, so he distracted himself with his other great passion.

By OCTOBER of 1812, Jackson had bought a share of Maria's next rival, Dungannon. A highlight of Nashville's season, this match was presided over by Jackson's wife, the queen, Rachel Jackson herself. On such occasions, the Jacksons would appear with her niece Rachel Hays, "the greatest belle in the country." Of course, there was a rival belle, seventeen-year-old Polly Hall, whom the general had partnered around the dance floor. Nashville belles were different. They did not arrive in carriages like the pampered ladies and gentlemen of eastern racing centers, but on horseback. On the other hand, they sometimes had to go home "riding double," or triple, if their horses' owners had bet them out from under them. The parson might be on hand, too. Once a neighborhood preacher happened to be at the racecourse looking for a stray cow, or so he apparently claimed, and got swept up by a crowd cheering Polly Medley, perhaps with Simon aboard. He climbed on a fence, waved his hat, and screamed: "Look at Polly Medley! Look at Polly Medley! Look! She leaves (with an oath) a blue streak behind her!"[20]

The reader may again insert the oath of his or her choice since Balie Peyton was too discreet to spell it out. The parson was arraigned before his church, tried, and suspended.

Before this second contest began, there were, of course, many side wagers, and not all of them for cash. As Simon and Jackson could have verified, "betting your shirt" had a literal origin. When Truxton beat Greyhound a few years before, Jackson described himself as "eased in finances and replenished in my wardrobe." The clothes women bet were not shirts but gloves, sometimes boxes of them, which they needed in those days of unpardonable dust. While Rachel Jackson gathered the Davidson County ladies to watch her husband's horse emerge victorious, the Sumner County backers of Haynie's Maria "bet their last glove on her."

After the dust kicked up by six thoroughbreds running four miles—twice—had settled, Sumner County was better gauntleted. Maria had done in Dungannon worse than Decatur, not to mention the rest of the competition. There was more trouble at the Hermitage. "After this second defeat," wrote Peyton, "Gen. Jackson became terribly in earnest, and before he gave up the effort to beat Maria he ransacked Virginia, South Carolina, Georgia and Kentucky. He was almost as clamorous for a horse as was Richard in the battle of Bosworth Field." The next horse for his kingdom came from William R. Johnson of Virginia, whose father, Marmaduke Johnson, had been launched into the horse-racing business with his purchase of the Medley Mare. From the son (about whom we will find out much more in the next chapter), Jackson bought the four-mile champion Pacolet for three thousand dollars.

It was the least one horse trader could do for another: after all, the six-year-old had cost Johnson $179.

Jackson also got his war orders and took two divisions to Natchez to join the fight. It was a fruitless mission, ending with a painful march back, but his troops said he was like the toughest wood they could think of, and they gave him a nickname to go with it.

In the autumn of 1813, "Old Hickory" at last had the horse to beat Haynie's Maria and her wisecracking jockey. The dappled gray that William Johnson sent him stood 15½ hands, 2 inches taller than the 5-foot Maria. Pacolet would meet her in his specialty: four-mile heats. Jackson paid the hefty thousand-dollar entrance fee—and lost again to Maria.

How did the general take it? "At first Jackson became a very madman," said the anonymous racing writer who had known the trainer Green Berry Williams and some of the other principals. "He sent forth torrents of threats, swore bitter oaths, and declared that he would conquer Haynie's Maria. . . . He spent his money like water to obtain success, for he had never known defeat and could not brook it. . . . Some may think this was a small affair. Not so with General Jackson. He regarded nothing as a small affair. . . . Whatever of talent, energy, and will he possessed (few men possessed more than he of either) he concentrated with his utmost power upon the object, and fought unceasingly, and with a morbid impetuosity."[21]

Now a Virginia group claimed that some geldings back home could beat Maria. This inspired Haynie to declare that he would match her for four thousand dollars against any nag "in the world"—an embryonic form of the boast that if a certain contest was American, it was a global championship, such as the "World Series," even if nobody else cared about it. It started with the local jockey clubs, who ran their races for members but opened them "to the world." Haynie got an even farther-reaching response from a momentarily cowed Andrew Jackson: "Make the race $50,000, she can beat anything in God's whole creation."[22]

Nobody answered the challenge, but Jackson's frustration oiled Simon's mouth, and Simon could race it like a horse, with accompaniment. "Simon was an inimitable banjo player," Peyton reported, "and he improvised his songs, making humorous hits at everybody. Even Gen. Jackson did not escape him. Indeed no man was his superior in repartee." And that from a former congressman known for his eloquence. We don't have any recordings of a Simon song, but we do have a report of one of Simon's humorous routines—an early version of the "He was so ugly . . ." bit that has been handed down all the way from the likes of Simon to vaudeville comedians to Red Foxx and television sitcoms.

Peyton wrote that after the general's Pacolet had been beaten by Maria, "and when no friend dared to take a liberty with him," Simon met Jackson in a crowd and said, "Gineral, you were always ugly, but now you're a show. I could make a fortune by showing you as you now look, if I had you in a cage where you could not hurt the people who came to look at you." You can still hear them roaring at Simon's riff all the way back in Tennessee. Of all the characters peopling the Jackson biographies, the jockey, protected by his talent and his handicap, is one of the very few who ever talked back to him.

Of course, Old Hickory's other distractions continued. In October of 1813 he was off again in another war, the bloody expedition against the Creek (Muskogee) Indians and the start of his long campaign to remove the Indians of the Southeast.

WHILE IN Mobile in 1814, having defeated the Creeks and now preparing to attack Spanish Florida, Jackson wrote to James Jackson (no relation), who was handling his racing affairs that he should saddle up Pacolet again—to defeat Maria once and for all. The general was suspicious about their previous encounter. In the *Nashville Whig*, he and his friends claimed Pacolet had hurt a foreleg while crossing a bridge on the course, leaving him "crippled" and "disabled." The complaint sounds very whiny, but he challenged Maria and Simon to a rematch. When the time for the showdown came, however, Pacolet was still lame, forcing the conqueror of the Creeks to pay a forfeit and retreat again.[23]

"These repeated failures only made the General more inflexible," said his friend Peyton. So he got another horse. "He sent to South Carolina and bought Tam O'Shanter." It is difficult to imagine Jackson's state of mind: how a man with so many more important concerns would still be so single-mindedly consumed by his imperial drive to win everything, even a simple horse race. But Simon would have understood, and he probably found it very funny, too—since he was winning.

IN THAT autumn of 1814, Maria beat Tam O'Shanter for the Nashville Jockey Club purse. Later in the century, the *Spirit of the Times* sporting weekly summed up the qualities that kept Simon in front. "He was not only able to hold a steady rein and maintain a graceful easy seat, but no emergency ever came upon him so suddenly, so unexpectedly, as to cause him to lose his presence of mind or disturb his equanimity. No danger, no peril was too great for his courage to encounter, and he moved with steady nerve in the face of the most appalling and threatening conflicts. His integrity was as pure as his courage was firm." The flowery author added, " 'To conquer' was the motto emblazoned by nature upon his mind and heart."[24]

FOUR DEFEATS—of Decatur, Dungannon, Pacolet, and Tam O'Shanter—and a forfeit. How desperate was Andrew Jackson now? Verry, as he often spelled it, in the brogue of his Scots-Irish parents. From his Mobile headquarters, Jackson "sent to Kentucky and induced Mr. DeWett to come to the Hermitage with his mare . . . with a view of matching her against Maria." DeWett's mare was "reputed to be the swiftest mile nag in the United States." So Jackson went in with DeWett to match his mare against Haynie's for a thousand dollars.

To shorten the agony of the reader, on the eve of Jackson's departure from Mobile for yet another battle—this time against the

British—Maria beat the Kentucky mare at Clover Bottom. To shorten the agony of the British, the frenetic Andrew Jackson did win the Battle of New Orleans—and was soon back in Nashville for his next contest with Maria.

IT WAS 1815, four years into the grudge, and the Hero of New Orleans had DeWett bring back his mare. The match was very Jacksonian, almost neurotically forcing the enemy at every step: the fifteen-hundred-dollar purse was divided into three, with five hundred dollars each for the leader after a quarter mile, six hundred yards, and a half mile. Maria led all the way.

A WEEK later, Jackson again wagered a thousand dollars, this time hoping that Colonel Ed Ward's Western Light could beat Maria. He lost.[25]

STILL IN 1815, Jackson fielded DeWett's mare for a third time in what would turn out to be his ninth, and last, confrontation with Haynie's Maria and Simon. The event: two-mile heats. The place: McNairy's Bottom, near Sulphur Springs.

Recounting this one, Haynie's friend Judge Thomas Barry lavished praise on Simon. He was "fully equal to [Virginia stable owner John] Tayloe's Dick, or any other rider *that ever straddled a horse.*" Trainer Green Berry Williams ordered Simon to cover the first mile in about two minutes, keep that pace for another five hundred yards, and then uncork Maria and "distance" DeWett's pet, putting her out of the race. Distancing her in a two-mile heat meant beating her by 120 yards or more. The ultimate professional, Simon "obeyed his instructions strictly"—to put it mildly. He did the first mile in exactly two minutes. He kept the pace for another five hundred yards. Then, with DeWett's mare at Maria's hips, he amazed the crowd. "When Simon touched her with the spur such a *rush* was never seen, she made from there home *a gap* of one hundred and eighty-four yards, and run the last mile in 1m.48s [1 minute, 48 seconds]. All those who

witnessed this race say they never saw such a burst of speed, before or since."[26]

It was their final defeat of General Andrew Jackson. As an odd
footnote, Balie Peyton reported a much different final contest
against Jackson, although Peyton was a child at the time and did
not see it, and despite the fact that he said he based his own account on the original Barry-Haynie version. The biggest difference was that Peyton did not have Simon riding Maria, even
though this was the one race in which Judge Barry took pains to
single out Simon's great riding. Perhaps Peyton, one of Tennessee's great raconteurs, was simply determined to weave his own
tale, which was a good one.

As Peyton tells it, a Colonel Lynch of Virginia brought in "his
famous colored rider, Dick," to ride for General Jackson and Mr.
DeWett. Dick, "who professed to be a conjurer," frightened
Maria's rider, who was identified only as "also colored." In fact,
Dick warned him that if he attempted to pass him early in the race,
he would retaliate with magic. "He would lift him out of his saddle
or throw down his mare by a mere motion of his whip, which the
boy fully believed." That supposedly got Maria off to a slow start
and nearly cost her the race. It is amusing to consider how the brilliant Simon would have handled this out-of-state conjurer.[27]

What was indubitably, mortifyingly clear, however, was that
Maria and Simon had outgeneraled the general, and this finally
drove him out of the sport. Doubtless in a rage, irascible Old
Hickory suddenly emptied the Hermitage stalls, selling all his
thoroughbreds except Truxton. One of his biographers, Marquis
James, concluded, diplomatically, "The defeat of Western Light
and the DeWett mare by Jesse Haynie's Maria in 1815 had convinced General Jackson that the itinerant nature of official duties
made it impossible to attend properly to the minutiae of his racers'
training." Another Jackson admirer would write, "Upon the turf he
never met a conqueror, except in Berry Williams, Monkey Simon,
and Hanie's [sic] Maria, and it took the combined three to accomplish what so many fought for." Old Hickory would get back to his

thoroughbreds and his black jockeys at a later date, when he only had to be president.[28]

SIMON AND MARIA rode again, although not as an automatic team. Famous as he was, the slave jockey still had to go to Gallatin Road near the ferry to get himself hired out each year, though Colonel George Elliott continued to be his most regular employer. One day Robert Foster, the guardian of the children who had "inherited" Tennessee's greatest jockey, nearly ruined Simon's chances. The politician, who had no use for a jockey, actually started bidding against Elliott, trying to run up the price for Simon's services. Perhaps Foster had finally realized what a bargain Colonel Elliott had been getting for so long, since he usually paid only twelve to fifteen dollars a year. Foster kept outbidding the Colonel till the price had risen to thirty dollars, "the then price of a good field hand."[29]

"Simon watched the bidding with deepest interest," Elliott recalled, "as he was most anxious to remain in the stable and enjoy the fame and emoluments of riding Haynie's Maria and other distinguished winners."

But then Elliott suddenly stopped bidding. He figured he would stick Foster with the winning bid and try to hire Simon on the side. The jockey was steaming. With his overbidding, Foster was acting as if Simon were being sold, not just hired out, and it was jeopardizing the jockey's chances of working for Elliott. He turned on the guardian—"and said in his peculiarly sarcastic manner, with his head laid back, and one eye closed: 'Colonel Foster, by G-d, I am not a-selling, but a-*hirin'* for only one year!'"

"You impudent scoundrel," the politician exploded, shaking his cane, "do you know who you are talking to?" Foster had, after all, recently run for governor of Tennessee.

"I think I do," Simon said, unflustered. Then he reminded Foster, "with the most aggravating coolness," of the terrible drubbing he'd gotten at the polls. "If I am not mistaken, you are the same gentleman who made a small 'speriment for Governor once."

As the crowd burst into laughter, Elliott got Simon's services at the next bid.[30]

The mare had a few more races in her. She bested the undefeated Robin Grey in one-mile heats at Lexington, Kentucky, and then she and Simon were at Cage's Race Paths near Gallatin. Race Paths? Quarter races and other straight sprints were still popular in Tennessee. In a half-mile contest on this straightaway, in 1816, the Maria-Simon combo again faced Andrew Jackson, but only by proxy. They gave a tremendous head start, sixty feet, to a filly sired by Truxton and still beat her by two feet.

"This was the first race I ever saw, and I was greatly impressed with the beautiful riding of Monkey Simon," recalled Balie Peyton. The future congressman was only twelve years old at the time but doubtless already a superior judge of horsemanship, and soon to become one of the best gentleman jockeys of that era.

Running out of victims, Elliott took Haynie's champion to Waynesboro, Georgia, and challenged "the world." Nobody came out. At last, in 1817, Captain Jesse Haynie sold his Maria to a Pollard Brown for a thousand dollars. She had never lost even a heat in the hands of Simon, but when Brown raced his new purchase at Charleston, it did not mean a return to South Carolina for her old jockey. Simon would never ride her again. Aboard Maria for the four-mile heats was the most famous white jockey of the day, Samuel Purdy of New York. He was three or four pounds overweight. Maria lost by a few feet.

SIMON'S OTHER famous mounts ranged from Polly Medley, who was racing as early as 1804, to Walk-in-Water, who raced for nearly twenty years—until 1832. To compare and judge the performances of jockeys and their mounts across centuries, you have to take into account how much longer the races were back then. For example, Maria's record as outlined by Judge Barry was eleven wins and one loss, with Purdy aboard for the defeat. That was over a total distance of more than forty miles (the distance was not given for one race). The great twentieth-century champion

Man O'War racked up twenty victories and one loss—but over a total of only twenty and five-eighths miles. Man O'War's victories covered nineteen and seven-eighths miles; Maria's, with Simon up, more than thirty-two. "Haynie's Maria was a most extraordinary race nag at all distances, probably not inferior to any that has appeared in America since her day," Peyton wrote in 1873. The next century's John Hervey called her "one of the greatest of all American-bred race mares."

Simon's own record on the many champions of his day would benefit from similar statistical multiples when compared with modern jockeys' performances. Haynie's friend, Judge Barry, said in 1835 that Simon was the equal of any "that ever straddled a horse." Colonel Elliott was quoted as saying that Simon was "the coolest, bravest, wisest rider" he ever saw mount a horse. Green Berry Williams, who had trained Maria for Simon's victories and Purdy's defeat, never forgot him. Before his death in 1872, he would often reflect, "If I only had such a boy now, I would win many races that I lose." Congressman Peyton summed up the four-and-a-half-foot, physically handicapped slave by saying, "Simon was a distinguished character and made a conspicuous figure on the turf of Tennessee for many years."

But it was Old Hickory who would pay Maria and by extension Simon their greatest tribute. When Jackson was living in the White House—and operating a full-scale racing stable in Washington, as will be seen in chapter four—there was one small ghost who must have haunted his thoughts, charging through his nightmares on the back of a dark chestnut mare. Even as the bony, white-haired president waged his lifelong wars—now against "nullification" of federal laws by states, now against the Bank of the United States, now against Congress—Judge Barry, old Jesse Haynie's friend down in Tennessee, wouldn't let him forget it. As he wrote in the *Turf Register*, the bible of the sport, which the president almost certainly read: "Gen. Jackson has conquered all his own and his country's enemies—except Maria." Peyton would make the same point many years later: "Although Gen. Jackson conquered the Indians, defeated Packenham [at the Battle of New Orleans], beat Adams and Clay [for the presidency], crushed the monster bank under the heel of his military boot, he could not beat Maria in the hands of Uncle Berry." And the *Spirit of the Times*, the sporting weekly, would note that in a life "crowned with the rarest and most brilliant achievements," Jackson had to face "the history of his overthrow by Hanie's [sic] Maria, Uncle Berry, and Monkey Simon." At last, in weary retirement at the Hermitage, the general himself was said to have been asked by an old friend: "Was there anything that you ever undertook heartily and failed to accomplish?"[31]

"Nothing that I remember," came the reply, "except Haynie's Maria. I could not beat her."[32]

Andrew Jackson just wasn't fast enough to catch Simon's spit. Old sportsmen in the Valley of the Cumberland, according to the *Spirit*, would go on for years telling of Simon's "victorious career (he had few defeats)," but that journal also noted that the rest of Tennessee, the general public, quickly forgot him. What happened to him? The records are sparse, to put it mildly, but a newspaper report that was unearthed during the research for this book reveals that he died in the cholera epidemic that swept the middle basin of Tennessee in 1833, as Andrew Jackson's second presidential term was getting underway. In June of that year, the Tennessee newspaper noted that there had been sixty-two burials in a sixteen-day period. Simon's name was among those listed in the death toll for three days in Nashville. Interestingly, the list did not identify him as a slave, suggesting that, even if he had not been formally emancipated, he perhaps no longer lived as a slave—perhaps his technical status as a slave had become irrelevant, and he had simply become a town character, long since on his own. All of which, of course, is pure speculation. The notice does, however, give his age, the only record of it yet located. It also reveals that he had become known by his nickname, although it was not used in the reminiscences of his close acquaintances—Elliott, Williams, Barry, and Haynie.

Equally interesting was the fact that in the midst of the terrible epidemic, like death itself, the death notices did not discriminate, awarding equally brief mention to whites and blacks, infants and elderly, convicts and a state senator. A scourge that had American pioneers putting people in boxes as fast they could, as they had to, would not produce the sort of generous obituary that the black jockey and trainer Austin Curtis had earned. Yet in its own way, Simon's death notice was perhaps a tiny vignette of his life and times. The death toll for the three days appeared in the *Knoxville Republican*, which picked up its report from Nashville's *National Banner:*

DEATHS IN NASHVILLE BY CHOLERA

Saturday, June 8: Elizabeth Stevenson, aged 3 years; Hazer Dyer, aged 3; Robert Porter, Sen., aged 68.

Sunday, June 9: Infant slave of Mrs. Porter, aged 3. At the Penitentiary in this vicinity: Jackson Thomas, aged 20, free man of color.

Monday, June 10: A child, 9 months old, name not known; Isham Perdue, aged 54; Simon, negro man, commonly called Monkey Simon, aged 52; infant slave of Wm. E. Anderson, Esq.; negro woman at Captain Young's; Maria Frances James, aged 8 months. In the neighborhood: two convicts, Yates and Baldwin, from the Penitentiary; Peter, slave of Dyer Pearl, aged 65.[33]

Simon was probably buried in the City Cemetery of Nashville, but there is no marker. The records for the year 1833 have been lost.

A young Charles Stewart holds Johnson's Medley. The jockey-trainer was painted by Edward Troye. Courtesy of Kathleen Jeffords.

·3·

AN AMERICAN LIFE

CHARLES STEWART AND NAPOLEON

1808–1884

CHARLES STEWART WAS born in Virginia in about 1808. Seventy-six years later, when he was living in rural Louisiana, he told his story. Like many other Americans in 1884, he could neither read nor write, but one day a neighbor, Annie Porter, said to him, "Uncle Charles, I want you to come in this evening and tell me all you can remember that ever happened to you, from the very beginning, and let me see if I can not write it down so that people can read it." His memoir, introduced by Porter, was to appear that October in *Harper's New Monthly Magazine.*[1]

Of course, Stewart was excited about the project. "He went off to his own house, which is quite nearby," Porter said, "and for the rest of the day refused to speak or be spoken to, on the plea that he was 'studyin.' In the evening, at what he calls early candlelight, he appeared, arrayed in his Sunday clothes, and it being a warm night in June, the feeling of self-respect must have been genuine indeed which compelled him to put on a plush waistcoat, reaching nearly to his knees, heavy white velveteen trousers ending in a pair of shooting gaiters, the whole surmounted by a long black frock coat, a spotted silk cravat of vast size, and a small jockey's cap."[2]

A sketch of Stewart in this outfit would accompany his memoir. But what Porter and her readers did not know was that these were not, as we shall see, his Sunday clothes. And they represented more than mere self-respect, for the title that *Harper's* gave the memoir, "My Life as a Slave," hardly summarized the story. Charles Stewart had ridden to a career beyond his dreams as a top jockey for William R. Johnson, America's leading stable owner before the Civil War. Later, as a trainer with a managerial talent equal to that of Austin Curtis, this slave made so much money that he had to have an agent to handle it. This particular line of work also required dressing up if the trainer was to appear in a painting of a thoroughbred. When, half a century earlier, he had held a champion for a portrait, he had projected a casual elegance and a handsome grace in a black vest and open white shirt. Other black

Old Charles Stewart donned the formal wear of a trainer for this portrait for Harper's New Monthly Magazine *in 1884. Courtesy of author.*

trainers in antebellum portraits wore frock coats and top hats. They come across as racist images today, but the trainers were not going to be painted in work clothes. English pictures often showed white trainers in similar business attire.

So Stewart appeared in his frock coat, waistcoat, and silk cravat over the course of several evenings as he dictated his memoir and posed for the sketch, adding his jockey's cap, no doubt for accuracy. Porter said she took down his story "almost verbatim," altering nothing "except to make the details as consecutive and the dialect as intelligible as possible." Typical of the day, her attempts at "dialect"—spelling words the way she thought Stewart said them, such as "allers" for "always" and "clo's" for "clothes"—were usually unfortunate, not merely condescending but indecipherable. Discarding most but not all of them brings back his wonderful humor.

The way Charles Stewart remembered it, brimming with pride, if you searched the whole town of Pocahontas, Virginia, from end to end, "you couldn't have lit down on no bigger little yeller rascal than me when I first begin to take good notice of myself." His father—"that is, I hear folks say that was my daddy, and he allowed so hisself"—was the senior Charles Stewart. "He was free and so was all his folks." The memory of his father came on strong and brought a chuckle. "He lived in a good, large house and was a sea-faring man, a mighty light mulatto; he looked like one of these here Mexican somebodies."[3]

Pocahontas itself was easy enough to find. It was an island smack in the middle of the Appomattox River, right across from Petersburg. But anybody searching for little Charles might not have lit down on him at all, since his boyhood was split up between households. He might have been rascaling around the big house where his father lived with his wife and other children. Or he might have been at his father's sister's house, "where mammy stayed when she wasn't out home at ol' Marster Enoch Vaughan's, what she belonged to." Or he might have been two miles away, at Vaughan's place, on the north side of the river, up on Colonial Heights. "I took a spell of staying out there sometimes. Mammy's name was Sally."

Stewart couldn't decide which he had liked better. To be at his mother's and hear "the white gentlemen" rehearsing their war stories—some of them almost certainly about Lafayette training his cannon on Cornwallis as he came in from Austin Curtis's neighborhood and headed down the James River only thirty-five years before. Or "to set in the chimney-corner in my daddy's house and hear him a-tellin' and narratin' all about them whalin' voyages he went on, where the fishes has got calves and gives milk same as cows." His father, he said, "was mighty good to me, and I can recollect now how it was share-and-share alike with his other children, and how his sister, Aunt Mary Stevens, was always giving me cake and clothes and candy."

But one day a simple thing happened, and everybody's lives changed. Enoch Vaughan died. After that Sally lived in the Petersburg area; her son did not say where or how. Vaughan's daughter, Lizzie, "inherited" Charles, but happily, he was left at his father's. In fact, it was the chance of a lifetime for the senior Stewart. Just as Curtis and others had done, and as other free African Americans would continue to do in the pre–Civil War South, he would try to buy his son out of slavery—if he could. "They just left me at my daddy's, and he tried to buy me, but they wouldn't sell me, nor hear about it."

When Charles was eleven or twelve, and Lizzie Vaughan had become Lizzie Vaughan Pace, her husband ran out of money— "something I never could understand, 'cause I always heared he never had none nohow." One day, perhaps not surprisingly, when Charles's father was away, "they just up and sold me on my tracks to Colonel William R. Johnson." With that, Sally's son was placed on a little-known path, but one traveled by Curtis and Simon and a number of others—a career under slavery. Like Curtis working for Willie Jones and Simon in South Carolina, Charles was starting at the top, for as he pointed out, William Johnson was known as "the Napoleon of the Turf."

WILLIAM WAS the son of Marmaduke Johnson, who had begun his racing career in North Carolina when he hired Austin Curtis to purchase the Medley Mare for him. And it was William Johnson who later tried to save Andrew Jackson's face by sending him Pacolet, who wound up as just another victim for Simon and Haynie's Maria. In the days when the real Napoleon reigned over Europe, William Ransom Johnson dominated the American turf, entering, organizing, and winning events from Maryland to North Carolina, thanks in large measure to slave grooms, slave jockeys, and slave trainers. In just two seasons, 1807 and 1808, he entered sixty-three races and won all but two. Johnson's racing stable was far and away America's leading sports organization before the Civil War, and it helped turn the country's first major sport into an industry. Johnson trained not only his but others' thoroughbreds at his stables on the Petersburg racecourse, which like a number of other stables was called Newmarket, after the English mecca. He also had stables and a private course at his legendary estate, Oaklands, eighteen miles from Petersburg, where a sign over the entrance bore the old saying: "There is nothing so good for the inside of a man as the outside of a horse." It was about 1820 when the young Charles Stewart showed up on Napoleon's doorstep.[4]

As Charles himself told it: "The Colonel just dashed his eyes over me—I was monstrous lean and peart for twelve year old—and says to some of the quality that was a-settin' alongside: 'Here's a lightweight for my Newmarket stables and Arthur Taylor's handling. Do you know a horse when you see one, boy?'

"'Yes, sir,' I says: 'I knows a horse from a mule just as far I can see 'em both walk.'

"They all laughs at that, and the next thing they gives me some new clothes all fixed up, and I was sent down to the great big training stables my new marster owned at Newmarket."

Like Curtis and Simon before him, Charles immediately discovered the advantages of starting at the top of the race world, such as having sterling teachers. The trainer Arthur Taylor was born in England, and he would soon be considered the best antebellum trainer in the country—the standard by which others were judged. Green Berry Williams, for example, was dubbed "the

Arthur Taylor of the West." Like many others, Taylor had been a jockey. "A sly-looking little man," as one Johnson guest described him, he was never without an old beaver or rabbit or some other crushed hat, and his usual communication was a chuckle. Being around horses will do that to a person. Taylor had a white assistant, and at that moment, he had sixteen grooms for eight thorough-breds. Joining them, Charles learned quickly that working at a racing stable is an unforgettable experience, and it quietly threatened to become a life—of oneness with nature and communion with horses, of incurable wonder.[5]

The very first job he had was rubbing down Reality, the Medley Mare's gray daughter, to erase her tension after running. If Johnson's stable was the equivalent of the next century's New York Yankees, Reality was Babe Ruth. She is believed to have racked up more than twenty-five victories—an impressive total in those days of racing several miles at a stretch—and Johnson often cited her as the best nag he ever raced. But her new groom had his own worlds to conquer, and the lightweight was soon in the saddle, moving up to exercise boy and loving it.

"How I did love them horses! It appeared like they loved me, too, and when they turned their rainbow necks, all slick and shining . . . searching for me to come and give 'em their gallops—whew-e-e! How we did spin along that old Newmarket course, right after sunrise in the cool summer mornings!"

When he was about thirteen and weighed seventy pounds, he moved up again, from exercise boy to jockey. He rode his first race, "a mile and a repeat," on a nag named John Stanley, and from the lofty perch of a horse the child began to command Johnson's attention. Napoleon was always around, with his flowing, prematurely white mane and eyes "that just snapped fire at you." He was "what you call a plain gentleman, and didn't believe his coat and pants was the making of him. He treated his servants like they was the prime cut."

But for the weeks beginning on the second Tuesday in May and in October, Johnson did wear his good coat and pants. Inert in summer, the whole South swayed to the rhythm of Race Week in spring and fall, when boarding houses boiled over, taverns filled to the brim, families took in what relatives they could stand, shops raked in more money than during the whole rest of the year, and you couldn't see the other side of the street for the dust and the jumble of coaches-and-fours. Stewart's own memories often sound like nostalgia for slavery days, but maybe that was partly for Annie Porter's ears. In any case, his reminiscences also sound like the words of servants and journalists today, gawking at the rich and famous.[6]

"Them was the grandest times that ever lived. King of Heaven! It was a sight to see my ol' marster, and others like him, a-struttin' up and down with their shirts all frilled and ruffled down the front. Why, then you could build a ballroom as long as from here to the stable and fill it with folks, an every one of 'em the real stuff. But nowadays what's it like? Name o' Heaven! Blue trash, red trash, green trash, speckled trash—there's plenty of every qualification, but nary one that washes in lye soap and dries on the grass without fadin'."

Off to the races the slaveholders clopped, in their phaetons and Philadelphia gigs, the wives and daughters—former reigning "belles" and their successors—all set to bet their supplies of gloves. Their beaux, some on beautiful blooded steeds, stopped to flirt at one carriage after another, and when they got to the races, they didn't just sit and watch. As the young men did in England, Virginian spectators often raced around the outside of the course themselves to get a better view of the thundering herd driven by Stewart and the other professionals, their stables' colors glistening in the sun. Johnson's "blue and blue"—sky blue jacket, sky blue cap—was equivalent to a Super Bowl uniform. As he thought of those incredible days, Stewart called on the vernacular again. "Lord! How proud this nigger was when they called me, 'Johnson's Charles,' and I used to come a-clippin' down the track in a two-mile heat!"

"Johnson's Charles" meant a lot more than Johnson's slave. It meant the leading stable in the country and an athlete good enough to ride for it. It must have felt something like freedom when he heard the roar of the crowd, or rubbed down a champion everybody was talking about, or walked her through the neighborhood, as Charles often did in the cool of the Newmarket evenings. He clearly was no slave in his own eyes: he had risen above the system, which was more than the slave-holding William R. Johnson and the "real stuff" had done. And he had risen far above what most white boys of thirteen could hope for in America as well.

Nor did he fall victim to the bane of most jockeys. He had no trouble at all making the weights—keeping his weight at or under the maximum limit allowed for a race, which was usually very low for contests involving colts or fillies. He was not only small but almost malarial looking. "I was one of these here fever-an'-ague little fellers what ain't got no flesh to take off nohow." Small was in demand, of course, so his horizons widened. He was sent to ride in Johnson's old North Carolina stamping grounds—the first real trip he ever made. "I went all alone and when I got up on the stage at Petersburg in my new suit of store clothes, with ten dollars in my pocket and more to come, I was 'high come up,' I tell you. The stage was a high flyer, and I was sorry enough when she stopped at Warrenton." There, sitting around with the other "quality" in the middle of the old Race Horse Region, was "ol' Marmaduke Johnson, the daddy of 'em all."

Because slaves were widely prohibited from crossing state lines, many American historians and scholars may be shocked to learn of Stewart's travel into North Carolina all by himself, although probably with a *laissez-passer* from Napoleon. But, again, their talent and their sport conferred special privileges on the great black jockeys, providing them with an escape from the travel ban, among many other advantages. Interstate travel was not in the least unusual for them. Simon traveled from Tennessee to Natchez with Elliott, who was not his owner, and into Kentucky with Haynie's Maria. Charles Stewart and, as we shall see, many future black jockeys traveled between racecourses all over the country while they were still slaves. They enjoyed more than certain rights. Caught in a system from which there was no final escape, many exchanged friendship with their professional colleagues in the sport, white as well as black, superiors as well as inferiors, often including their slave masters. It summons a well-polished chestnut among racing people: "All men are equal on the turf and under it." Of course, they are not, and it was not affection that led to the special treatment and limited independence. It was talent and the almost equally rare ability, among whites or blacks, to assume responsibility, to do their personal best and maintain their own professional standards.[7]

Stewart's performances in North Carolina, or maybe his absence from Newmarket for six months, made an impression on Napoleon, who kept him at hand when he returned. "I stayed pretty quiet at home, close to marstar, training in the stables under Arthur Taylor and going back and forth 'twixt the stables and Oaklands, or Petersburg, or maybe Richmond." In other words, Stewart went wherever Johnson went, and he moved up again, to journeyman jockey.

"My, what a crowd and noise and screeching and hallooing there was that day."

During the last week of May 1823, fifteen-year-old Charles Stewart went to New York and got to witness the greatest American sporting event since Austin Curtis beat the jockey Old Ned in a quarter race on the Roanoke River fifty years earlier. This one was even more spectacular, one of the first of the North versus South matches, pitting New York's champion, American Eclipse, against Virginia's Henry, trained by Johnson's stable. It was a preview of modern American sports, with a truly national crowd, up to forty thousand Northerners and twenty thousand Southerners. To report the results, the New York *Evening Post* was ready to roll with America's first sports "extra." For those who were in a bigger hurry, Niblo's Garden Tavern had a white pennant to raise for an Eclipse victory, a black one for a Southern win. The scene at the course was also a hint of things to come. "Booths erecting, Flags flying, Pigs roasting, Fiddlers tuning, and all dust & confusion," said New York's *National Advocate*. "N.B.: Six Pick Pockets were yesterday lodged in Bridewell, being on their way to the Race Course to train in their profession." As for New York's state ban on racing, it had already been lifted for Queens County on Long Island, permitting the opening of the Union Course two years earlier.[8]

As it turned out, Charles was not the only African American rider who made it north. The black jockeys were already part of the scene at the New York course. Surveying all the heavy betting—totaling up to a hundred thousand dollars by one estimate—the *Advocate* said Henry was heavily backed by the Carolina and Virginia racing fraternity—"the knowing ones of the Peedee, the Santee, the Waccamaw, and the Roanoke who are all on the ground with their little *negers* and appear to be up to a thing or two." The italics suggest that the slur was still mostly a Southern habit; indeed, the same New York correspondent, joking about the race and picking American Eclipse, commented, "Nothing from the slave-holding states beats us liberty and equality boys." The coverage was full of references to the North-South rivalry in the presidential campaign, in which Secretary of State John Quincy Adams of Massachusetts would defeat Virginia-born Georgia senator William Crawford (and Andrew Jackson). Historians who have ignored sports all these years might note one of the *Advocate*'s more serious comments in that May of 1823: "These contests of North against South lay the foundation of Sectional jealousies and create a spirit of rivalry when there should be union."[9]

The Northern and Southern champions would run a possible total of twelve miles—if they ran all of a best-of-three contest of four-mile heats. As the first race got underway, the white boy William Crafts got into trouble on American Eclipse and lost. Afterward, with the huge crowd in a frenzy, a spectator stepped forth and dramatically tore open his coat to reveal his jockey's outfit—and his availability. It was the well-known Samuel Purdy, the white New Yorker who had lost Maria's race in South Carolina, and he was now substituted for Crafts on American Eclipse. Purdy won the second heat, and then Henry got a change of jockey, too. Johnson's inexperienced white boy, John Walden, had started the race, but he did poorly and was replaced by none other than Arthur Taylor for the third and fatal heat. Taylor protested that he was not in shape and had not ridden for some time, but to no avail. Thus, all four riders were white.

The hard-fought twelve miles ended with a stunning victory for Samuel Purdy. Indeed, a witness, John Randolph—"Randolph of Roanoke"—would rise in the House of Representatives a few days later and intone: "The renown of the performance of that day will go down in the history of civilized society, and transmit the name of Samuel Purdy as the most skillful of jockeys to the latest posterity." A fine kudo, but then Randolph was one of the losing Henry's backers, and it was in his interest to make Purdy look

The great white jockey Samuel Purdy on American Eclipse, winning the big North-South race at Union Course on Long Island in 1823, as portrayed on a souvenir scarf. Courtesy of National Museum of Racing and Hall of Fame.

good. Also, these days, posterity might be far more impressed if it could assume that the slaveholding Randolph, or for that matter any other member of Congress then, would have had the courage to transmit the name of a black jockey, had the occasion called for it. Indeed, many Tennessee authorities would have argued that, when it came to "the most skillful of jockeys," Simon had a far more impressive record than Purdy.

It is difficult to say, at this remove, whether Charles Stewart rather than Taylor should have been tapped by Henry's backers, who were calling the shots (Napoleon was out sick, missing the most celebrated race any of his chargers ever entered). But it was the beginning of a noticeable trend whenever the stakes rose, with a corresponding increase in prestige and publicity: namely, the selection of white jockeys, especially in future editions of the North-South races. But Charles Stewart did ride at that New York meeting, boarding Young Sir Archy and losing by about a head— just eighteen inches. "But I made my three hundred dollars and the finest suit of clothes you ever see. I tell you, I walked around like a ol' gobbler with a red flannel tail tied on to his hind leg when we got back home again."[10]

BACK HOME in Virginia, Stewart rode stakes events through the 1820s, keeping down to eighty pounds. He and John Walden became the stable's best two lightweights, and Johnson had taken to calling him Charley. Toward the end of the decade, Stewart racked up another achievement, becoming a trainer. As he recalled it, Napoleon announced to him one day, "Charley, my boy, I has laid out for you to have a stable of your own . . . I 'specs you to take everything into your own care and send home some of them lazy scoundrels that is hidin' out there, too thick to shake a stick at and just waitin' for me to go and scrattle 'em home." As he told of reaching this first rung of management, he remembered his mother. "I tell you I felt so fine that my own mother wouldn't have knowed me for her son. I had plenty of money and nobody to say

nothing to me. I just had to train and exercise my horses and send
'em up when they was wanted." When he recalled these proud moments of accomplishment, he always mentioned the feeling of independence they brought. It sounded like a sort of secret freedom.

Stewart's stable was a mile from Johnson's Newmarket operation. He was in charge of eleven black grooms and, as he put it,
"two white trash they called 'helpers.'" It must have been similar
to setups all across Virginia, where thoroughbreds were raised in
log stables on hard corn and thin highland grass, usually under
African American grooms. The bigger stables sometimes advertised for more grooms, who could be slaves or free, and if the latter, black or white. William Johnson and Colonel J. M. Selden, for
example, each advertised for grooms who would serve long ap-
prenticeships, Selden calling on planters to send him "a few likely
boys (from ten to thirteen or fourteen years old)" who would be
"bound for seven years to the business."[11]

As for the trainers, most of them were African Americans, too.
As the country's only major sport—and its first national pastime—
exploded during the 1820s and 1830s, trainers were in demand.
Selden's ad for grooms said that those hired would not be limited
to the work of grooms but would be "thoroughly instructed in the
art of training horses for the turf." This, he pointed out, was a
most profitable trade, "few others adding as much to the value of a
slave, or to the productive capacity of a free labouring man." Of
course, it was more difficult for a slave to reach the rank of head
trainer for a major stable, as Arthur Taylor did, or to thrive as an
independent operator like Green Berry Williams, but a number of
black trainers did just that. Selden's ad bragged that he had the
services of "William Alexander, a very judicious and worthy
man, reared in the stables of Col. W. R. Johnson, and a first-rate
trainer." Alexander, a black man, would instruct the grooms, black
or white. We can only speculate, but Charles Stewart must have
known Alexander, since he was raised as a groom in William Johnson's stables.[12]

At small stables, one person might be groom, jockey, and trainer, but not under Johnson. Leaving riding behind, Stewart became a full-time trainer under Arthur Taylor. He managed not only good nags—such as Tariff, who was later known as Bolivar and was Andrew Jackson's pride—but the best horses of the day. There was Bonnets o' Blue, "that I raised myself," who was third in the line of fabulous race mares that started with the Medley Mare and Reality. In 1831, Bonnets o' Blue was sent to Charleston to run against the horse Clara Fisher. The race was for five thousand dollars, but as usual the wagering on the side was much higher—a throwback, in fact, to the days when Austin Curtis rode for one hundred hogsheads of tobacco. The biggest bet of this day, if not the decade, was born when Johnson took one look at Clara Fisher. "If he just only walked by a horse to look at it, he could tell you just how far that horse could run," Stewart said. As the race got underway, Johnson focused on Clara Fisher and saw "a sign in one of her forelegs that she would lay down in running a mile and three-quarters." He cornered his friend John Crowell, President Jackson's crony, and told him to hurry back and bet every dollar he had on Bonnets o' Blue. Crowell did more than that: he staked three plantations on Johnson's mare and won.

WHILE SLAVEHOLDERS were gaily wagering chunks of their slave economy on slave-trained thoroughbreds, many also lived in justified fear that the slaves might rebel. And they did rebel in Charles Stewart's day, in thousands of escapes, in isolated attacks on whites, in major plots to overthrow the system. As Bonnets o' Blue was winning at Charleston in 1831, Nat Turner, a slave preacher, was organizing a revolt in Southampton County, Virginia, some miles south of Stewart's stable at Newmarket. Turner's famous rebellion that August killed about sixty whites, including his master; afterward, at least seventeen blacks, including Turner, were hanged and twelve transported out of the state. The revolt terrified whites in the South, who brought about still more monstrous "laws," if they can be called that, oppressing slaves and free African Americans. Today it remains a little-known fact that the threat of rebellion, even by slaves who were unarmed, was so real that ironclad slave jails were needed in Southern cities. Many of them were heavily fortified, and they held thousands who had tried to escape or who had been torn from their families and were being quartered there before being "sold" again.[13]

But the story Charles Stewart told to Annie Porter in 1884 breathed no hint of rebellion. Like almost everybody else, he was trying to survive, by his wits and talents, of which, it still seemed, he had as much as William R. Johnson. He moved up again, becoming a "stallion man," one of the managers of Johnson's sires, whose stud services were sold at high prices to owners of thoroughbred mares. Because there were no railroads to bring mares from far distances to Newmarket, Napoleon expanded his empire and went to them. Forming partnerships with other stable owners, he sent them stallions to be bred to the local mares from miles around. In 1832, again blithely ignoring any restrictions on slave travel, the powerful Johnson had "Charley" take the gray stallion Medley all the way to Carlton, the estate of the merchant heir John Charles Craig, near Germantown, Pennsylvania. There, as it turned out, the stallion man would be assured a place in history.

Craig commissioned a Swiss-born, London-trained painter, Edward Troye, to record the glories of Carlton, which for the moment included Medley, Reality's first foal and namesake of his great-grandsire. Troye portrayed the beautiful gray being held by Charles Stewart, the stunning image mentioned above. The portrait received a national audience that year when it appeared in the *American Turf Register,* and it would reappear in books for the next century and more. The twenty-four-year-old Troye must have liked Stewart, who was about the same age, for the handsome trainer almost steals the picture, exuding a certain class and somehow looking taller than he was, which was about five feet, four inches. That year at Carlton, Troye painted another trainer, who was posed with Craig's mare Trifle and was dressed formally in top hat, frock coat, and waistcoat. This was likely William Alexander, whom Craig had retained from Colonel Selden to prep the mare for the Baltimore Jockey Club purse (which she won).[14]

THE NEXT year, in 1833, Stewart decided to get married. What he—and especially his bride—had to go through was another of slavery's horrors. He said he asked a Colonel Buford if he could visit his farm near the Rock Spring meetinghouse, where Buford kept a number of South Carolina women before sending them to his plantations. There he met Betsey Dandridge, who was a Buford slave, although it is not clear whether or not she was one of the South Carolina women, since her father lived nearby. As Stewart told it, he got Dandridge's permission to ask her father if they could be engaged, and then he got the father's permission to seek the slaveowner's permission. This process was "normal" under the crime of slavery. What was less so, however, was that Charles intended to buy his wife, or so he claimed. Here he tests credulity. He may very well have been just showing off, flexing his former muscles, to Annie Porter.

Free African Americans could and often did buy their loved ones, and others, out of slavery, but Stewart was a slave. Yet he was also one of the most prominent horsemen around, basking in the reflected prestige and, to a tiny degree, power of one of the most celebrated men in Virginia. And slavery was, after all, a "peculiar institution," a vast corruption that masked all sorts of chaotic exceptions. Still pushing his story, Stewart said he figured Colonel Buford would start out by telling him: "Wa'al, Stewart, you can have Betsey a year or so first to see if she will suit you, and then we can talk about the price."

Then he learned that Buford had just sold the Rock Spring farm, and all its slaves, to Major Isham Puckett, another stable owner. So off Stewart went, looking for Puckett and finding him up in Richmond, in front of the court house. Despite the fact that Stewart had to seek out Puckett to get his permission to marry Betsy Dandridge, this would appear to have been an extraordinary confrontation: slaveholder versus slave, albeit not just any slave.

Stewart told Annie that he introduced himself "as bein' 'Colonel Johnson's Charles.'" There surely must have been something in the way he said it—his manner and inflection presenting himself not merely as Johnson's Charles but as *bein'* Johnson's Charles, which really was something to be. It seemed to impress Puckett. "He was just as affable as a settin' hen. I seed two or three gentlemen I knowed well a-standing by, but I didn't ask nobody to speak for me: I up and speaks for myself, and just as soon as I had sensed him with what I was saying, he laughs and says, "'Why, Charley, you can have her just as she stands for three hundred and fifty dollars.'

"I tell you I was pleased. Before a mule could kick, I jumped round to Mr. Jefferson Balls's office—he was Major Puckett's brother-in-law, and besides that he was the money agent for Colonel Johnson, and that's how come he was my agent, too. I drawed out three hundred and fifty dollars, for I had made a heap that last year, more than I could spend in clothes and tobacco, more especially, too, by reason that the Colonel always give 'em both to me; so as soon as I had drawed the money out I just hands it back again to Mr. Balls for Major Puckett, and says, 'This here sum is for the acquisition of Miss Betsey Dandridge and all the children we can raise; is that so, Mr. Balls, sir?'

"And he answers, 'yes,' and give me the papers to have and to hold her as long as she behaves herself."

The idea that an agent handled Stewart's money was not so far-fetched. The tradition of direct money payments to a small number of slaves for specific tasks had been established in the previous century; even the jockey Simon's "emoluments," as his employer called them, had sometimes included cash. Stewart's professional trust-worthiness, unusual independence, and increased responsibilities would have required an expense account of some kind, part of which could fairly be considered income and all of which could easily be controlled, since Stewart's agent was also Johnson's. As to his "purchase" of Betsey Dandridge, it might have been simply another case of the turf elite ignoring the rules, humoring Charles by letting him have Betsey while greasing Puckett's palm for his approval. Or it could have been considered a discreet payment from Johnson to his fellow turfman Puckett.

Stewart took his wife to his house next to his training stable, where the congratulatory gifts (including more cash) were piling up, also no surprise for such a celebrity. "I hauled some three cart-loads of wedding presents. Such furniture and fixins was as fine as they *could* be. Lord! When I look back to them days and think about all the money, and dogs and chickens and ducks and geese and pigs I had, and whole chests full of fine clothes, and more china than we could eat out of in a year, and the Colonel ready to hand me out a hundred dollars every time I asked for it, and think no more about them than about spitting out a chaw of tobacco!"

Betsey Stewart filled the house with the joy of cooking. "She cooked as good biscuits, hoe-cake, bacon fry, hominy mush, and coffee as any gal I seed; then, moreover, she could iron and wash my shirts, and keep things a-going right smart." But if the kitchen smelled of heaven, after a few years the marriage was going to hell. True to his male chauvinist form, Charles blamed Betsey, in whom he found one serious fault. She was a liar, he told Annie, unloading another one of his old horse chips: "A woman ought to tell some of the truth once a day, if it's only to limber up her tongue." To "cure" her, he moved earth and heaven, literally, applying some of the cruelty he must have learned from the other slaveholders.

"I tried 'suasion and finery, birch rods split fine, and a light hickory stick about as thick as my littlest finger, and I tried making her kin and my kin that had religion pray for her at the big camp-meeting."

What did he think Betsey was lying about? Was it about her boys, with a year between them? Were they his? From his telling, from Porter's telling of his telling, it is not entirely clear. After four years of marriage, "I just made up my mind to 'vorce her as quick as ever I could." Not only divorce her but sell her. "Certainly I couldn't be out of pocket for no such a hussy as she was." He asked himself whether it would be worthwhile to keep the boys. "No, she must have come of a bad breed, and a colt is most apt to take after the dam anyhow."

Again Stewart tests his far-off listeners' (if not Annie's) faith, as he flexes his memories and claims that, in the moral chaos of Petersburg, he again set about committing the same crime that had made him victim. He crossed town to see a horse trader named Jones, who had the best-looking nag Stewart had seen in a year, and for sale at "just the very price I paid for Betsey." So (he asked Annie to believe), he went back to Puckett, told him he could have Betsey back at the same price, and, with unfathomable cruelty, added that "'lowing for the wear and tear of the four year I had done kept her, I would throw the boys into the bargain." Had he really felt that way? Or was the old man just bragging that he could be as vicious and cruel as any white man? Or was he trying to comfort Annie, a white, by showing that he had participated in the crime, too, so maybe it was everybody's fault? The latter explanation doubtless would have comforted her editors at *Harper's*, which shared the racism of most of the Northern press.

THAT FALL he left Virginia forever, but not the empire of Napoleon. Colonel Johnson decided to send Stewart to Kentucky with Medley, to establish a breeding business there. It was an important job, the management of valuable thoroughbreds and their large stud fees in what was becoming America's new Race Horse Region. Stewart's own career, shifting westward, was paralleling the growth and development of America's first major sport. Perhaps Johnson's grand plan for Charley had also contributed to his "divorce." Perhaps Johnson, or Stewart, had not wanted Betsey and the boys to go—or she had not wanted to go. In any event, being single made it easier.

It was 1837. There were no rail lines through the Allegheny Mountains, so Medley had to travel the old-fashioned way. Stewart could go on horseback; the horse could not. Getting up there in years at thirteen, Medley walked all the way to Kentucky—six hundred miles by their probable route, southwest to the Cumberland Gap into Tennessee, and then northwest into Kentucky. What a sight they were, the spectacular gray and her escort, materializing out of a forest road in the middle of some frontier town, drawing a bunch of backwoods gawkers, many of whom had never seen such a statuesque animal before and never would again.

Stewart's destination was the farm of a new Johnson breeding partner, John S. Hurt, at Paris, northeast of Lexington. Later Johnson sent him other stallions, including the celebrated Monsieur Tonson, sired by Andrew Jackson's Pacolet. Rather than waiting for the local mares to visit, Stewart took the stallions around the countryside "en accordance wid marster's orders." And how did he read those orders, which Johnson sent regularly? Like many other rural Americans, Stewart could neither read nor write, although he knew his alphabet. In fact, back home in Virginia it had been illegal for the past several years even to teach African Americans to read and write. The Virginia legislators thought it would be a threat. Judging by all that Stewart accomplished in Kentucky without the benefit of literacy, those legislators were right to worry.

As he had with Craig in Pennsylvania, Colonel Johnson sent his written orders to Hurt, who read them to Stewart, who reported back through Hurt. It seems a risky way to have managed the financial affairs of some of the most expensive thoroughbred stallions in the country, but it worked. Annie Porter said other sources confirmed that Stewart "discharged his duties excellently, keeping long accounts in his head and handling the large sums of money which were constantly passing through his hands with scrupulous accuracy and care." As for the old jockey himself, he entertained Annie with his own view of things. "The squire or the judge was always somewhere about to read marster's letters to me. I never had no book learnin' myself, 'cause I never was willing, for I knowed my brain was too smart for to stand it. When anybody has got as much sense in the head as I had, they must take great care not to be fooling around trying to stuff more in, or the first thing they'll bust it open."

In Paris, Stewart found that distance lent not only enchantment—"I stayed there a long time and was just as happy as a king"—but a lot more. Even freedom: "I was just as free and independent as any gentleman in the land. I had my helpers and jockeys, grooms and stablemen under me, nobody was over me." From this comment, it would appear that he also functioned as a trainer in Paris. In any event, his work took him across the length of Kentucky at a time when Dr. Redmond Barry's blue Irish blade, that slender, calcium-rich annual, was turning the state into the world's premier breeding center. As Stewart could have verified, bluegrass really does turn blue during its late-May blooming, although it is rarely seen in its blue glory today because of mowing and cropping by livestock.

Traversing the state according to the demand for his stallions, Stewart established a second base at Bowling Green, 175 miles to the southwest, in an open prairie surrounded by forests. He took the gorgeous Monsieur Tonson, with his long, tapering, arched neck and majestic, muscular presence, to the state fair. Even Kentuckians were impressed when they beheld this stallion, "with me standing alongside, and we took the prizes of three fifty-dollar tankards." He got as close as he could to the Kentucky quality. Senator Henry Clay, the Great Compromiser, "was always around, and might peart and perlite the old man was, too."

Of course, despite the impression he liked to give, Stewart was hardly "as free and independent as any gentleman in the land." The sons of two of the most famous gentlemen of the day tried to buy him. Henry Clay Jr. offered Johnson thirty-five hundred dollars for him, "but the Colonel, he told him money couldn't buy me." Wade Hampton II got the same answer. "I had a heap of people after me, I tell you." But he felt too secure to encourage them. "I was too well off for that, and I heared folks say as how 'betwixt a two-edge sword you falls to the ground.'"

IN 1840, he found another reason "for staying just how I was and where I was." That was the same year Queen Victoria married Prince Albert "and made such a talkin' an' palaverin'." Stewart's new reason for staying in Kentucky was Mary Jane Mallory, "the likeliest looking and fairest behaving light-colored mulatto gal I ever seed in my life." She was a slave of a Mr. Robertson, and here again surfaced the mixed-up subterfuges inspired by slavery, especially in what was then still considered the West. Robertson agreed that Mallory could marry, but he wanted to hire her out at the same time.

"Mr. Robertson told me to marry her and welcome." But under the arrangement, Robertson was to receive a monthly fee from her earnings as a seamstress. The marriage now made, Stewart once again found domestic bliss in "a little house I had fixed up near the stables." If Betsey Stewart had been amazing in her Virginia kitchen, Mary Jane Stewart was a Kentucky wonder with a needle. "She clear-starched and sewed and 'broidered and worked the hand-loom and made more pretty things than I could count." It's clear she could have made a living at it because it was she, not Stewart, who paid Robertson. "She paid her marster, en course, regular, so much a month for her hire, but, lord, she never touched her earnings for that." Stewart added, drawing from the ego that made him a giant in his sport but not much of a husband, "I had plenty of money to hire as many wives as I wanted but this one was the onlyest one I ever did want."

He could still picture his old Kentucky home. "I can see that little house now, with the big white bed, all clean and sweet and hung with ruffled curtains, in one corner the cupboard full of flowered china . . . and the bright wood fire, piled up with hickory and ash logs, blazin' on the hearth, and Mary Jane settin' in front by the candle with her fine white sewin' and her pink calico dress."

They had a son and named him John after Mary Jane's father and her brother, who was skilled as a locksmith. Maybe for the first time ever, Stewart, about age thirty-three, began adjusting to family life, with Mary Jane and John looming large. Soon, he figured, Colonel Johnson would ask him to bring Medley and Monsieur Tonson back to Virginia, and he could see his mother again. As he considered the success he had created for himself, slavery or no slavery, he realized he had done it for her, too, and he wanted to share it with her. "I would fetch Mary Jane and Johnny along with me and show 'em to my folks in Petersburg, 'cause my mammy she was living there, and so was my brothers and sisters and a heap of kin, and I wanted 'em to see my wife and boy."

Before leaving, Stewart had determined to buy Mary Jane out of slavery, but when their son was about six months old, she developed a terrible cough and wouldn't eat. It seemed as though all of a sudden she became sickly and terribly lean. "I was badly scared, and I sent for the doctor," Stewart said. The doctor said "give that woman some port wine and plenty of food and keep her happy," so he took her to the nearby springs. His wealthy clients sent wine for her, "and the doctor gives her quinine and bark," but it was all to no avail. She died within two years of their marriage.

"I never grieved so over anybody in all the world. She was just as fond of me as I was of her."

Stewart's world fell apart. Suddenly he no longer liked Kentucky and didn't want to go back to Virginia either. He had someone write Johnson that he just wanted to go off to some new place. Johnson was stunned. He wrote back, reluctantly agreeing. But he made it clear that he would not part with him cheap, that Charley should pick his new "owner" himself, not vice versa, and that he was shocked it was happening at all. "Marster, he writ back that if I could find *a owner to suit me, that would pay his price for me*, I could go, though he had never expected to part with me *by sale*."

TALENT, IT SEEMS, attracts power, but doesn't always know it. Charles Stewart knew it, got it down pat when he was eleven or twelve years old, and kept attracting power for the rest of his life. Just as he was standing at this crossroads, he attracted the attention of Alexander Porter, a U.S. senator from Louisiana and the first president of the New Orleans Jockey Club, who was visiting Henry Clay. The patriarch of the Louisiana Porters (his descendants included Annie Porter herself), he was also a former Louisiana Supreme Court judge. "They *said* he was a great judge of the South and could make laws like a book, and I *knows* he was a great judge of a horse, so when he come to Bowling Green him and me got acquainted," said modest Charles Stewart.

Judge Porter—the senator was known in those parts by that more distinguished title—was looking for a head trainer for his stables on the Bayou Teche, "and would I like to go with him if he would buy me." Porter's sugar plantation on the Teche was in Franklin, Louisiana, a hundred miles southwest of New Orleans. Stewart negotiated for a week or two with the judge, "and the more I thinks about staying in Kentucky without Mary Jane, the more I says to myself that I can't on no account do it." They finally agreed Stewart would try working at the judge's stables for six months, after which time he could go back home if he didn't like it. If he did like it, the judge would pay Colonel Johnson thiry-five hundred dollars for him. As Stewart said some four decades later, "I bet there ain't many folks with that amount of money North or South."

But what about the baby? After his mother died, Johnny was left with his grandmother at Dr. Robertson's. "Mary Robertson, she had just took such a liking to the little feller that she had him around the house half the time." But now Stewart had to tell them he'd be leaving for good. He and Mrs. Mallory, the baby in her arms, went up to the house, and they met Mary Robertson and her husband sitting there on the colonnaded piazza. Stewart told them about his new prospects, how he would be moving yet again—leaving Kentucky to become a head trainer in Louisiana.

"The old gentleman stretched over and picked Johnny up and stood him on the little stool by him, and says, 'Well, Stewart, I see what you want is this little man, and you shall have him for $150 and not a penny more.' I tell you I *was* pleased, sho enough, and I paid the money, and got the receipt, and we toted Johnny into Bowling Green that very day."

As Austin Curtis and others had done, and as his own father had been unable to do, Charles Stewart bought his own son, but with an important difference: the father was still a slave. How many others, talented at locksmithing or other trades, had done the same under the chaotic "peculiar institution," regardless of what "laws" said about slaves owning "property"? Stewart told Annie he had never tried to buy Johnny before because that would have meant leaving him with his grandmother, where he wouldn't be safe if he didn't legally belong to the Robertsons. "Some folks is so curious," as he ominously put it, that he didn't know what would happen to a boy who "belonged to his own daddy"—a daddy whose job took him away so often.

But still, now that he'd bought Johnny's freedom, he couldn't take his son with him. The trip was more than eight hundred miles, and there was no one to take care of him when they arrived. In addition, he was traveling with Judge Porter; they couldn't be delayed with baby business. He decided to leave Johnny with Mary Jane's sister; then, he promised, he would send for him just as soon as he got settled in Louisiana. More than four decades later, the father spoke a single, terrible sentence: "And the end of the matter was I left him; and I ain't never seed that child since."

THE STALLION man hit the road with the judge, moving west again with America and its unifying, expanding sport. What route did they take? It must have depended on the judge's business. They might have taken stages 140 miles to Paducah, then steamboats down the Ohio and Mississippi. More likely, they rode a stage sixty-six miles to Nashville. The immigrant judge had first settled there on his arrival from Ireland, had perhaps seen Simon ride, and had stayed in Nashville until his mentor, Andrew Jackson, advised him to go west. His wife, the former Evalina Baker, was buried in the Tennessee capital, as the judge himself would be. From there, he and Stewart would have picked up the Natchez Trace to the Mississippi. As for Stewart, once again single and leaving family behind, and once again changing "owners," he found it exhausting. It went on forever—"goin' in steamboats and stages, stages and steamboats, for weeks and days till we come to New Orleans." Once there, he acted like a typical American tourist.

"If you asked anybody a question they answered you in French, and you might screech till you was deaf before they would let on that they knowed what you was talking about. I stood that kind of nonsense first-rate from white folks: if they couldn't talk no Christian language, I just felt sorry for 'em." Here he lapsed into the vernacular, and his imagination. "But when it come to a great big fool nigger a-doin' me that way, I just hits him a lick in his ol' black jaws that shut 'em up for that day."

Johnson's home near the Appomattox was called Oaklands. Porter's home in the town of Franklin, on the Bayou Teche, was Oaklawn Manor. There were Oaklands and Ashlands, Ash Groves and Oak Lawns, Twin Oaks and Twelve Oaks, all over the South, where a tree was something you lived by, but the wet, other-worldly landscape of St. Mary Parish, with its fields of cane and lakes and bayous and live oaks, frightened Stewart at first. He did not say so, but perhaps it also had to do with the fact that he was suddenly in the middle of a tropical sugar plantation, rather than surrounded by horse farms, as he had been in Virginia and Kentucky. Its three thousand watery acres stretched nearly a mile through the live oaks and jungle along both sides of the bayou's Irish Bend. This vast farm was run on the backs of slaves who could not draw comfort from sugarcane as Stewart had from thoroughbreds. Still, for them, the plantation of this relatively liberal Whig politician was superior to many in the Deep South, the lesser of the horrors, its "Negro quarters" made up of a two-story hospital, a church, and streets of small frame houses, rather than cabins. With its large sugar mill, it was operated like the successful small industry it was. Of the 320 slaves, nearly all worked in the fields. Some 20 were employed in the three-story Greek Revival manor house.[15]

Stewart began to feel more at home as he walked around the racecourse and stables. Once again, his situation was special. Porter had invested $3,500 in him at a time when the other slaves at Oaklawn were valued on the southern Louisiana labor market at an average of $280 each. Stewart, of course, was not an average slave, and he was now personally in charge of the biggest operation he had ever run. The judge owned the English import Hark-forward, and there were never fewer than twelve race horses in active training, with more brood mares and colts "than you could dream about in one night." The stable kept forty to forty-five men and boys constantly employed. As the boss, Stewart had a house overlooking the stable yard, and this was one slave who called the overseer when he wanted him.

"My bell rang in the overseer's house, the head helper's, and the stable. Besides, I had a boy to sleep en every stall. I was just put right at the head of everything." Once again there was that sense of freedom, false of course, but not entirely. "Nobody could say nothin' to me at all. If I said I wanted *this*, I got it, or must have *that*, I got it, too."

Porter's plantation was a major draw for the Louisiana turf crowd, just as Willie Jones's had been in North Carolina, Andrew Jackson's and Colonel Elliott's in Tennessee, and William R. Johnson's in Virginia—all boasted their own tracks. A racecourse was almost as much a part of the Southern landscape as an oak tree. But in this catalog of elite professionals in America's most elite sport, it is easy to forget that this life and its superficial advantages were mere dreams for most people.

As a reminder of the crime against humanity that took new victims every day, there is the story of Solomon Northup in Louisiana, not far from where Stewart was. A free man, Northup was conned into joining a road show in Saratoga Springs, New York, in 1841. Brought to Washington, D.C., he was thrown into a slave jail, where he was savagely beaten in the shadow of the Capitol and then shipped south to the New Orleans auction block. "Customers would feel of our hands and arms and bodies, turn us around, ask us what we could do, make us open our mouths and show our teeth, precisely as a jockey examines a horse, which he is about to barter for or purchase," he would write later. Like Charles Stewart, this captive ended up on the bayous in the early 1840s, a little more than one hundred miles north of Oaklawn Manor. Unlike Stewart, Northup resisted and plotted against his "master"—and suffered more sadistic beatings. "The crack of the lash and the shrieking of the slaves can be heard from dark to bedtime," he said of the twelve years he spent in slavery before he escaped.[16]

What drove Charles Stewart in his own life under slavery? It was not the hope of escape—since there were examples everywhere of what a desperate hope that was—but it wasn't merely survival, either. It was a sense of freedom in work, in professional fulfillment—an emancipation of his own making. He loved his profession so much and was so good at it that he actually expanded Oaklawn's operations by training for other stables, as he had seen Colonel Johnson do. He took on so much work that he had to set limits. As Annie Porter said, "He was called upon to train horses for this or that gentleman so frequently that he was compelled to establish a system, and undertake so much and no more." In the meantime, he found Porter to be a most judicious judge. Of course, he could have been expected to tell Annie Porter that—and he did: "He was just as open-handed and generous, but he wouldn't stand no foolin', neither, I tell you. Things had to be just so, but there weren't no naggin' nor scoldin'; it was just steady management."

JUDGE PORTER—apparently without giving a hoot, or in any event without campaigning—was reelected to the Senate in 1842. When it came time to take his seat the following March, however, he was in poor health and did not go to Washington. He died in January 1844 at age fifty-eight, bequeathing Oaklawn and its slaves, including Stewart, to his brother James. Describing James Porter, the ever-gracious Stewart said to Annie, "If there ever was a good man walked in shoe-leather, he was one." Stewart continued to pursue a very active racing schedule, following the endless rhythm of the South, "traveling every spring and autumn to one course or another as the horses went to fulfill their engagements." The imported Harkforward stood at the head of the Oaklawn stud, and when a reporter visited in 1847, he found several of his colts to be impressively large.[17]

But it lasted only a few years. James died in 1849, leaving Oaklawn Manor in the hands of his widow, Mary, who continued to live there with their two daughters. At that point, Mary Porter reduced Stewart, said Annie, "to the less glorious level of family coachman." Although he also remained the "general 'boss' of everything in the way of horseflesh on the place," it was hardly the same as running a racing stable. It was, in fact, the end of one of the notable careers in America's first sport. This hard-driving professional had witnessed three decades of expansion, but he had also mellowed, and he went through this passage with his usual grace, his own method of survival. "We just went on peaceful and happy till the war come and rooted every blessed thing up by the roots."

Stewart, about fifty-three when the Civil War came, remained loyal to Mary Porter, just as Austin Curtis had stuck with Willie Jones during the Revolution, when the British would have welcomed him. Every case was different, of course. As for Stewart, Annie said, "He never left his mistress, who was alone on the plantation during the whole period, for a single day." Actually, her two unmarried daughters lived there, too. Mary Porter tried, without much success, to keep the plantation running during the war and for a few years afterward. Along with Stewart, some of the other emancipated slaves continued working there, harvesting the sugarcane, cultivating the seventy-three acres of formal gardens, and helping in the massive brick manor house. It must have taught Mary Porter a lot because she had to work side by side with her former slaves to keep the place barely running.[18]

It was no use, of course. By 1873, most of the African American workers were gone, the cane fields were overgrown, and carpetbaggers showed up at the wrought-iron gate outside the colonnaded piazza of fading Oaklawn Manor. They were wealthy New Yorkers looking for a killing in the ruined South. Mary sold the plantation to them but retained the fabulous French furnishings Judge Porter had installed and the right to go on living there with her daughters. After eight years, however, the three ladies gave up for good. They sold the furnishings to one of the New Yorkers and moved to Europe to live for the rest of their lives— with only their memories of the Bayou Teche, of James and the judge, of the sugary world of Oaklawn, and of the stables and the famous trainer who came from Kentucky.

Stewart stayed in the Franklin neighborhood. He had married again. Annie wrote in 1884: "His third wife, whom he married after he came to Louisiana, is still living, and has three grown children, who are of little assistance or profit to their father." That was her opinion, and that was all she said about it.

Stewart continued working as a servant for other Porter descendants, although Annie did not say which ones or identify her own branch on the family tree. She did say that Stewart remained "a life-long servant and friend . . . the constant, never-failing factotum, adherent, and, as he calls it, 'pendence' of the whole family." She was amazed at how energetic he was, describing him in his seventies as "an extremely active, hard-working man, always busy at carpentering, gardening, shoe-making or 'horse-doctoring,' in which branch of medicine he is a great authority." He was, as always, the self-made man. Right after the New Yorkers got the manor house, Stewart moved to a home of his own, which he built mostly by himself on five or six acres that he purchased and planted with all sorts of fruit trees, vines, and shrubs.

Annie Porter lived not two hundred yards away. She never made clear her relationship to Judge or James Porter, but she said her mother had kept documents that confirmed Charles's story. It was unfortunate that she knew nothing of his profession—of "the names and dates of races and horses"—and thus could not deliver the real story of Charles Stewart to her readers. But nearly a century after his career was over, a historian would list the "Distinguished Men" of the sport in that era. Along with Andrew Jackson and William Ransom Johnson appeared the name Charles Stewart, with no indication that he had been a slave.[19] Stewart himself had made that irrelevant.

Even today, the Pocahontas kid still has a way of hanging around power, if only in spirit. As the twentieth century turned into the twenty-first, the judge's old Oaklawn Manor, restored to its splendor, would be the family residence of Mike Foster, governor of Louisiana.

The jockey Ben and the trainer Manuel with Tobacconist (owned by John Minor Botts of Virginia), painted by Edward Troye. Courtesy of Virginia Museum of Fine Arts Paul Mellon Collection.

·4·

THE EXPANSION
ERA

FROM JESSE TO CATO, THE FREEDOM RIDER

1828–1839

HORSE RACING GREW with the country in the 1830s. From the White House to the Appalachians, from the Deep South to the far North, America revealed itself at the racecourse, and the end of the decade saw the race that would inspire the spectacle that still draws the biggest crowd in American sports.

NEARLY FIFTEEN years after being battered for the last time by Simon and Haynie's Maria in 1815, Andrew Jackson was sufficiently recovered to get back into racing. After he defeated John Quincy Adams for the presidency in 1828, and after his wife, Rachel, died that December, Jackson needed the intense distraction that only racing gave him. It was this president's golf, only more so, and why not? He was in spitting distance of the Washington Jockey Club racecourse, or almost: they did spit a lot back then—his White House was full of spittoons—but not for twenty-two blocks, which was the distance to the track, north on Sixteenth, just beyond Boundary Street (today's Florida Avenue).

Andrew Jackson formed the White House racing stable. It was the first and only time the White House was also a full-fledged professional sports organization, not to mention the only time it used slave jockeys, although other presidents have been known to engage in unusual behavior to relax. Not only did Jackson bring a few of his and his family's best thoroughbreds up from Tennessee, along with some of his slave jockeys, but he stabled a few of his friends' steeds at the White House for the important race meetings in Washington and Maryland. Every morning Old Hickory would go out to check on his horses, and as often as he could, he went up to the racecourse.[1]

Although his nephew and secretary, A. J. Donelson, was directly in charge of the stables and training, the president was always looking over his shoulder. When in 1831 Jackson decided to sell his favorite stallion, Bolivar, Donelson sent the prospective buyer a letter letting him know that it was going to be expensive, that the dam was by Pacolet, the granddam by Truxton, and the next granddam by the best four-miler in the West, although, in the latter case, "The pedigree is mislaid." The president saw that pusillanimous line and immediately scrawled next to it, in bold script, "She was a thoroughbred mare." Donelson wrote to the prospective buyer, "Uncle will sell Bolivar for $2,000. He is much admired. The fever for fine horses is higher here than it is in Tennessee." A few weeks later, the president made a note: "Received of Benjamin Cooper of New Jersey for one fourth part of my stud horse Bolivar the sum of five hundred Dollars."[2]

The president had the Hermitage overseer put three thoroughbreds and three of his black jockeys on the road to Washington in 1832, despite warnings that his sporting habits could foul up his reelection campaign. What the worriers did not realize, however, was that Jackson was determined as usual not to lose any races of any kind. Donelson wrote to the folks back home, "Do not fear the consequences of its being known that the President has consented to have his horses trained and raced if there is a prospect of his winning. I can assure you that injury on this score is imaginary, and has long since ceased to be harmful." By the time the popular president's second term got underway, the White House stable was a well-established part of the professional racing scene. In 1833, the prominent turfman J. M. Selden wrote to Donelson at the White House and asked to borrow a good jockey "called Fox." And the Philadelphia stable owner General Callender Irvine turned his injured Busiris over to the White House stable, in hopes Donelson could get it back into racing shape, which he did.[3]

BUT ONE day in early May in 1834 would be remembered above the others. Jackson, Vice President Martin Van Buren, and Donelson rode out on horseback to watch the final time trials before the spring races. Congressman Balie Peyton was there to clock the nags for the president, as he always did, and, as it turned out, to write the only account of that day. After the thoroughbreds were saddled, "Busiris, an immense animal, and of prodigious muscular power, became furious and unmanageable, requiring two men to hold him for Jesse, Maj. D.'s colored boy, to mount."[4]

"Maj. D." was Donelson, and Jesse—like Austin Curtis during the Revolution and Simon during Jackson's returns from various wars—had a close-up view of history, as did his fellow jockeys. That spring they watched from the backs of four thoroughbreds in the stable of the president of the United States: Jackson's three-year-old gray filly Bolivia, sired by Bolivar; Donelson's five-year-old chestnut mare Emelie; the four-year-old bay Lady Nashville; and the seven-year-old Busiris, sired by American Eclipse—and just now still rambunctious under Jesse.

Suddenly, "Gen. Jackson fired up, took command, and issued orders to everybody," Congressman Peyton remembered. "Why don't you break him of those tricks?" the president shouted at the Army major who was doing most of the hands-on training for the White House at the moment. "I could do it in a week." And he yelled at Peyton, "Why don't you take your position there—you ought to know where to stand to time a horse!" The congressman fell in line. "Nobody," he said later, "ever jawed back at Old Hickory when he was in one of his ways." But Busiris was still acting up—"kerlariping," as Peyton put it. Maybe it had to do with the brutal training regimens favored by many owners and trainers, including Jackson and Busiris's owner, Callender Irvine. To recover from his leg injury, Busiris had been walked ten to twelve miles a day before being turned over to the White House.

Old Hickory was a commanding figure, thin as a stick at 140 pounds, but a tall stick, and he apparently assumed that Jesse was the only other person there who knew what he was doing. "Hold him, Jesse!" the president shouted. A fence separated the president's party from Jesse and Busiris. "Don't let him break down the fence! Now bring 'em up and give 'em a fair start!" Busiris and another nag, probably Emelie, were about to put in a timed workout, but then more trouble broke out. The rotund, five-foot-six vice president, always wrapped in the latest fashion, had ventured from his safe position in the rear and ridden out almost onto the course. Jackson, "flashing his eye from the enraged horse to Mr. Van Buren . . . stormed out" and cried, "Get behind me, Mr. Van Buren, they will run you over, sir!"

The vice president got behind him. But that line—"Get behind me, Mr. Van Buren, they will run you over, sir!"—became a political hit. The story of how Jackson's fatherly protection saved the bumbling "Little Magician," as the evasive vice president was known, was one of the jokes during Van Buren's 1836 presidential campaign, and it was a particular favorite on the Tennessee stumps, where Old Hickory, of course, was a deity. Van Buren won the presidency anyway. (And lost in all the fun was the fact that the fat little overdressed vice president happened to be an excellent rider.)

WHEN THE spring races began on May 7, 1834, Jesse and the other black jockeys, and a few white riders, got to ride for the most powerful audience in the country, as they had since George Washington's day. "The magnates of the land, friend and foe in the political arena, met on the turf in cordial fellowship," said a reporter covering the showery opening day. The *American Turf Register*'s report did not mention whether the president was present, but Donelson's horse Emelie was, winning on the mushy course in straight two-mile heats. The report also did not say who was riding her, nor did it say who was controlling Busiris—was it Jesse?—when he took to the track on Thursday, as the sun reappeared and brought out "such a fashionable reunion as has rarely assembled at any of our courses." Busiris had yet to win a race, but now his fame had "risen by being from Major Donelson's victorious stable." That day he turned in the fastest three-mile heats recorded in the capital in years. His owner, Irvine, was in Philadelphia, and he was ecstatic; he wrote to Donelson, praising him for snapping Busiris's bad luck ("your management has broken the spell"), and adding, "I am gratified in learning that Busiris has contributed to the amusement of yourself and friends." In this case, "friends" was code for the president.[5]

Both houses of Congress adjourned two days later—Saturday was normally a work day—for the last day of race week. The record does not show which of the six presidents—past, present, and future—currently in Washington attended this race: Andrew Jackson, Senator John Tyler, and Congressmen John Quincy Adams, Franklin Pierce, James Polk, and Millard Fillmore. Was Davy Crockett, also in the House, at the races that day, two years before he would die at the Alamo? We know the White House stables were busy that spring. Eight days after the Washington meeting, Donelson's Emelie came in fourth at Timonium, fifty miles up the road in Maryland. Was the 107 pounds that she carried mostly Donelson's Jesse? Was it still another White House slave jockey, weighing less than 97 pounds, who finished third at Baltimore, on Donelson's Lady Nashville?

Certainly Congress must have liked what it saw at the track because that June it appropriated $6,670 for "repairs to the President's house, flooring the terraces and erecting stables." Finished by that fall, Jackson's new stable was quite impressive, made of brick and stone, with stucco on the outside and the interior walls plastered and whitewashed. It had painted window frames and doors, a floor "ingeniously protected against ants," a granary and saddle room, and two rows of facing stalls for about ten horses. The celebrated architect Robert Mills, whose works included the adjacent Treasury Building, measured the brickwork for the stable. We can only wonder who, that same fall, rode Bolivia when she won a $650 sweepstakes at Washington, or when she came in third at Baltimore ten days later. In the meantime Jackson was horse-trading again, selling Bolivia to Colonel John Crowell of Alabama.[6]

NEARLY TWO years later, another spring race galvanized Washington. The press in those days was not yet the president's constant shadow, but on May 2, 1836, a reporter happened to spot "the Old General, mounted on one of his fine greys" at the racecourse. Jackson was watching Pennsylvania, sired by his old favorite Bolivar, "brush" the home stretch in preparation for the contest. Again the jockey was not named, but Pennsylvania impressed the reporter. "My word for it, she is a smart nag." Of course, Jackson himself knew a filly, and he might have been thinking it was one thing to look bright while exercising in the cool of an evening, another to win the upcoming sweepstakes and bring $10,000 back to the White House.[7]

The reporter also reserved a few words for the new Washington oval, which had become notable itself, and for Yelverton N. Oliver, a promoter from Virginia who had recently been named the "proprietor and treasurer" of the new National Jockey Club. Oliver was now in charge of the track, and he had his own ideas about the future of racing and society. Over the next five years Oliver would move the country several steps further toward modern, democratic sports. He started with the surface of the racetrack itself.

Most track operators didn't care exactly how long their ovals were. President Jackson, watching his filly on this one, could remember when close to a mile was close enough, especially if you owned Truxton or Pacolet. But this was 1836, and post-race controversies were starting to bubble up over the actual track distances—twelve feet short of a mile, thirty feet over a mile, and often a lot wider of the mark than that. It was time to nail down the statistics, especially with huge races pitting state against state, section against section, North against South, and increasing amounts of money, press coverage, and pride at stake. So forward-looking Yelverton Oliver actually measured his track, happy to discover it was exactly one mile. The reporter said he also laid on "an entirely new and elastic covering of artificial soil." The filly was whipping home on fake dirt, the sports surface of the future.

The newspaper reporter described Oliver's own stable, located nearby, and his trainer Hope Thompson, who made sure it ran like clockwork. The reporter wrote some silly things about Thompson, describing him as "a fair specimen of God's image in ebony" and "one of the most, if not the most, honest of Africa's tawny sons it has been my lot to meet." A free man was what Thompson was, as well as a strict disciplinarian and a stickler for detail. He might not have been an easy man to work for, but the reporter said Thompson's eyes glistened as he talked about his friend Oliver's eight thoroughbreds and his expanding prospects. Oliver dreamed of moving west, to New Orleans, to build "the most complete and perfect racing establishment in the country."

But Oliver was already creating the future in Washington. He had enlarged the stands—which rose behind the president-on-horseback that early May evening—so that on a good day they could accommodate three thousand Jacksonian Democrats. He put in a food concession, lauded for its "elbow room," as if future Americans might actually want to eat during a sports event. He encouraged women to turn out in force, and their presence would become an Oliver trademark. He played to the rich: in an ad for the $10,000 sweepstakes, he proclaimed, "Here is a chance to bet your thousands." And on the big day, with the place full to bursting and everyone eager for the race, he pulled the politicians, on horseback or in carriages, into the infield. "There was no keeping from the field the

Cabinet, Senate, or Members of the lower House," one reporter noted. "Of all the candidates for the Presidency for many years since, [General William Henry] Harrison alone, was absent."

One paper said it would have saved a lot of trouble if they had all just run around the track for the presidency, which would be decided that fall. "An Olympic trial might have at once settled that vexed question. [Henry] Clay, [Vice President Martin] Van Buren, [Tennessee favorite son Hugh Lawson] White, [Daniel] Webster, [John] Calhoun were all in the field." Jackson himself was not there on this day, so he didn't have to witness the second-place finish of his horse, Pennsylvania. It's impossible to imagine five presidential contenders meeting at the racetrack in any age but Jackson's. After that, the sport would be judged political poison for sitting presidents, not one of them daring to go to the races, although queens of England would.

There was no question about it: thanks in part to Andrew Jackson, America's sport was booming in the 1830s, not only in its ancient strongholds of Virginia, Maryland, and the Carolinas, but across the Gulf states of Georgia, Alabama, Mississippi, and Louisiana, and, of course, in the bluegrass "border states," Tennessee and Kentucky. Before the decade was out, there would be sixty-three official racecourses across the South, not counting all those plantation tracks, with ten in Tennessee and seventeen in Kentucky, the most of any state. In sheer numbers, the black jockeys so dominated the action that one historian would declare they "monopolized the saddle" in the Old South, which was not quite the case. There were plenty of white jockeys in the South. In fact, white jockeys had to work the South to survive, as there were only six racetracks in the puritan Northeast, four in New Jersey, one in Pennsylvania, and the Union on Long Island.

THE MOST celebrated athlete in the country in the mid-1830s was William R. Johnson's white rider, Willis, whose fame was phenomenal. From 1833, when he rode a celebrated racer named Trifle, through that 1836 Washington meeting, Willis was the only rider to be identified in one news account after another. It was far more unusual, almost unheard of, for the name of a black jockey to make print. A good example of this was a Southern preliminary to the next great North-South battle. The preliminary attracted enormous betting, estimated at two hundred thousand dollars, and an audience of five thousand in a town of only eight thousand—Augusta, Georgia. In press accounts, Willis was praised effusively for his ride aboard Argyle, even though he lost to a black rider on a horse named John Bascombe, owned by Colonel Crowell of Fort Mitchell, Alabama. The *Spirit of the Times* referred to the winning jockey only briefly, and not by name: "The noble Bascombe . . . obtained permission from his sable rider and, in passing, bid Argyle 'good bye.'" With that, the reporter also bid good-bye to the black rider. A few lines later, recounting the race in a flight of fancy, the reporter called out to the losing Argyle: "Bring home the noble Willis—his friends may be anxious for his fate."

When Crowell's John Bascombe was entered next in the wildly ballyhooed North-South race on Long Island, it would be with Willis, not his black rider, aboard. Southern owners sometimes were reluctant to bring their black jockeys north, out of justifiable fear that they would escape.[8] And once again, as the latest North-South race approached, the Civil War broke out early in the sporting press:

THE RACE

May 31, 1836. Post match. THE NORTH *vs.* THE SOUTH, Four Mile heats, for $5,000 a side, h. ft. [half if forfeited]. The North to name at the post any horse raised north of Maryland, and the South in like manner any horse raised south of the Potomac.

In this case, the South won the war, and it made Willis a national hero. The press compared him with Sam Day and James "Jem" Robinson, the best in England, whose jockeys were still the American standard of excellence. Within a few years Willis would grow too big to ride, unable to make 126 pounds, but the grateful Johnson, Napoleon of the Turf, and his trainer Arthur Taylor would make him "associate trainer," as they began to call that job.

But if the North-South race was the peak of Willis's fame, it was also the end of his reign as the only rider worthy of mention. The loser, the permanently tiny Gilbert Patrick, immediately became a darling of the press, who called him a bantam, "this game chicken," while his friends around the stables had already given him his future *nom de course*, Gilpatrick. The twenty-four-year-old from Poughkeepsie, New York, was more typical of the successful white boys. Unlike Willis, who rode only Johnson or Johnson-trained entries, Patrick was an independent operator who could negotiate his own terms. As he came into constant demand, from the Union Course on Long Island to the Deep South, he would soon leave Willis far back on the track of fame. It was the independent white boys who gravitated most easily to the top, and along with Gilpatrick the names of John Alcock, Francis "Barney" Palmer, and Joe Laird also began to surface in the press.[9]

AMONG AFRICAN AMERICANS in the sport, the trainers were more likely to be widely known than the black jockeys, even though there were thousands of black athletes riding through those antebellum years in the horse-racing states of Virginia, the Carolinas, Maryland, Georgia and Alabama, Kentucky and Tennessee, Mississippi and Louisiana. One published short list of the country's leading trainers included such whites as Johnson's Arthur Taylor, the sometime White House stablemaster M. L. Hammond, and Simon's old mentor, Green Berry Williams, as well as such blacks as Charles (probably Charles Stewart but possibly "Old Charles" Sykes of New Orleans), "Tawny Sam" (who trained for the New Yorker Robert Tillotson), and Hark, who managed one of the biggest racing stables in the antebellum South at Wellswood Plantation in Louisiana, and whom we'll meet later.[10]

The slave jockeys were not only much less likely to get credit than their free-wheeling white counterparts, but they were also bound to the sporting fortunes of their stables. Bad luck for their bosses limited their careers and—more important—limited their opportunities to escape some of the horrors of slavery. As for the very few who were free, they still faced the omnipresent racism of the day and the various local "black codes," laws severely restricting their rights as citizens. Those realities made the success of many of the African Americans unique as the sport took off in the 1830s. As in the riding days of Austin Curtis, Simon, and Charles Stewart, it was talent and determination that provided them with an escape within the protective world of their profession, and they made the most of it.

It would be hard to overestimate the contributions of the itinerant artist Edward Troye in preserving the memory of those slave athletes. Was it his Swiss birth and English training, the fact that he had not grown up amid slavery, that let him see people as they were? He portrayed slave athletes and trainers just as sympathetically as he did whites, such as Willis in the company of the black trainer William Alexander and their champion Trifle. Troye was the equestrian world's equivalent of the artists who toured the northeastern mill towns painting well-to-do families. Troye worked the horse farms and racecourses, and his main subjects were neither the families in residence nor their black or white stable help. Instead, he painted the triumphant thoroughbreds, whose pictures were a source not only of immense pride to their owners but of encouragement to others to pay for their stud services. There were a few other horse painters, but nobody covered the territory as he did. In his early days, he painted in New York, Pennsylvania, Virginia, and South Carolina. Then he lugged his bolts of canvas, woven in England of Irish flax, and his easel, paints, and brushes through the Cumberland Gap, probably on a pack horse. He worked Kentucky, Ohio, and Tennessee before settling on a well-earned farm of his own in Alabama.

In 1833, a year after he painted Medley with Charles Stewart, Troye portrayed Tobacconist with his rider Ben, who wore his jockey cap, a dark suit, and red stockings; with Ben aboard, Tobacconist had carried home the New Market Plate a month earlier. Ben was the favorite jockey of future Virginia congressman John

Minor Botts, whose Half-Sink plantation sprawled along the Chickahominy River near Richmond, Virginia. In fact, Troye painted "Botts's Ben" three times that autumn, twice with other champions and once with the slave trainer "Botts's Manuel." Some of the congressman's descendants, however, apparently could not live with the memory of Ben's brilliance. According to "family tradition," Ben tended to be heavy, so to get him down to riding weight, Botts would bury him up to his neck in manure and provide Ben with only spring water, all the while enjoying mint juleps himself by the banks of the Chicahominy. Whether true or a fiction of the descendants, the supposedly funny story of the tormented athlete provides a fine metaphor for the tragedy of the black jockeys and the cowardice of the slaveholders.[11]

A year later, Troye parked his palette in Scott County, Kentucky, and captured the black jockey Lew with the equine Richard

The jockey Lew, trainer Harry (in top hat), and groom Charles
with the champion Richard Singleton (owned by Willa Viley of Kentucky)
as painted by Edward Troye. Courtesy of Virginia Museum
of Fine Arts Paul Mellon Collection.

Singleton, who like a lot of nags was named after a human, in this case a luminary of the South Carolina turf. Lew's mount became paintable by defeating the champion Collier, although the latter was so unwilling to run that jockey John Alcock broke an exquisite ivory whip over his neck. The portrait gives us not only "Viley's Lew" but trainer Harry and groom Charles. It was said the leading Kentucky turfman, Willa Viley, had "purchased" Harry for fifteen hundred dollars and then freed him and paid him to continue training his horses. For this portrait Harry wore the standard top-hat regalia of the stable owners, though with bright southwestern touches, such as a green frock coat with twelve brass buttons.

IN THE second half of the 1830s, the racing world was dominated by Boston, one of the thoroughbreds of the century. The quadruped was named not after the city but after the card game called Boston. As the story goes, he was the pot happily collected by a Mr. Nathaniel Rives of Richmond, Virginia, but he seemed a mixed blessing at first. As a three-year-old, Boston would toss his exercise boy, and on the rare occasion he somehow couldn't quite do that, he would throw himself on the ground and start rolling. This could easily kill a boy caught in the stirrups, but from the horse's perspective, it always seemed to get rid of him. A disgusted early trainer recommended two ways of dealing with the colt, that he be "either castrated or shot—preferably the latter."[12]

In his first formal effort, Boston did not impress. In fact, he was "distanced"—so far behind he was ruled out of the race. It didn't matter, as he had no plans to go anywhere, having stopped dead and rejected the pathetic efforts of two jockeys to jump-start him. One of the two was a heavy slave rider named Ned, who was then as-signed the frightening job of breaking Boston once and for all. Ned was supposed to accomplish this while using the horse as a hack, tak-ing people on rides through the streets of Richmond or in the nearby countryside to take in "the scenery"—a concept that suburbs and interstate highways would expunge from American life a century and a half later, along with the scenery itself. The dangerous horse battled the chunky human through that summer of 1836. The human won, breaking the horse in time for the races that fall—although for the rest of his life the animal would lash out his heels when rubbed down, and he would glare and show his teeth at almost any human, and many a horse, who dared approach.

The ferocious animal was turned over to William R. Johnson's celebrated Virginia stable at Newmarket and assigned to Cornelius, a slave who was also one of Napoleon's top jockeys. A satiny chestnut, Boston quickly earned a nickname for the blaze on his face: as he began his patented late charge on the racecourse, the crowd would scream, "Old White Nose!" Standing 5 feet, 3 inches from the withers (the beginning of a horse's back, at the base of the mane), this colt was not unusually tall, but he had an enormous, barreled body, with rear ribs that suggested "the power of a suspension bridge," a stride of up to twenty-six feet, and, most important for the jockey, a smoldering personality. Boston began his career under Cornelius by winning two races, at Petersburg and Hanover Court House. Then Johnson, watching the colt rocket through a workout that winter, finally got interested and began racing the colt in the Johnson colors, rather than in those of Boston's owner.

In his pale blue jacket and cap, Cornelius was suddenly flying on his racer up and down the coast—at Washington, where Martin Van Buren had just moved into the White House, at Baltimore, in south Jersey and north Jersey, and at the Union Course on Long Island. Under Cornelius, from October 1836 through April 1838, Boston won eighteen of nineteen races, all of his victories at three- or four-mile heats, an unthinkable achievement today. Though few know of Cornelius today, in his time he heard the applause of hundreds of thousands. What was life like for this professional athlete? In one way it was like that of many professionals today: a life on the road, rushing from one venue to another with Johnson's stable, and time for little but staying in shape, keeping his weight down, training, and competing.[13]

Union Course, Long Island. The North's biggest track in the mid-1830s, when Cornelius rode there. Courtesy of Keeneland Association.

Cornelius and Boston opened their extraordinary 1838 campaign at the Union Course on Long Island. From published notes by the touring Irish actor Tyrone Power (not to be confused with the later Hollywood actor), we have a glimpse of the North's most important sporting venue at the time. Women were still betting gloves in those dusty days, and surprisingly, so was this fastidious actor, soon to be starring at London's Covent Garden. Power gambled a dozen pairs of French gloves on Trifle and then upped the stakes to nine dozen pairs. These he most happily received the next morning, and he concluded, "It will be my duty henceforth to back Trifle." Cornelius was resplendent in the blue-and-blue silks of Johnson's stable, the greatest sports organization of the day, but Power's notes are a reminder that many of the black jockeys did not have it so good.[14]

"Appointments of the negro jockeys more picturesque than race-like—ill-fitted jackets, trousers dirty and loose, or stocking-net pantaloons ditto but tight, with Wellingtons over or under, according to the taste of the rider; or shoes without stockings, or stockings without shoes, as weight be required or rejected."

In other words, one way for them to make the weight requirement would be to take off their shoes. Power was startled by their riding posture, too—with the jockey crouched over the horse's neck, a style that had begun with the rapid sprints of quarter-racing but would not be fully accepted in America until the end of the nineteenth century. Power wrote, "They sit well forward on the withers of the horses; do not seem over steady in their saddles, but cling like monkeys." While some American jockeys, white and black, rode that way, others retained the more respectable, if ridiculous, English seat, sitting as straight as possible even as the animal lurched forward.

Tyrone Power found a lot to be shocked about. While the English boys used their hands to play their mounts like violins, these Americans, he thought, were way behind. "Their whole sleight-of-hand appears to consist of a dead pull." And they left all the strategy—"their time for lying low or making play"—to be "entirely governed by their masters." What Power did not realize was that the American stable owners and trainers often wanted it that way. Not content to sit back and watch like some English lord, they got out by the rail and screamed their orders at the jockeys. No doubt some English owners and trainers would have done the same if they could have, but their tracks were neither short nor circular, so the jockeys weren't flying by so often. In America, in four-mile heats, the jockeys came around the bend as many as eight or twelve times—and up to twenty times (twenty miles!), as in a five-heat race that Trifle lost to Black Maria.

TYRONE POWER was surprised by something else on his visit to Manhattan, which merits a small detour in our survey: amateur racing by all the young bloods on a public road, a forerunner of the "drag races" that would frighten so many future parents. From Revolutionary days, the most famous speedway in the country had been these five or six miles that paralleled the Hudson River, through what is today Manhattan's upper west side, near Morningside Heights and Columbia University, to "the pretty village of Harlem." Here, Power observed, "about sunset, the amateur of horse-flesh may see done the fastest pace in the trotting world." He decided to try it himself and recalled, "Whirling along this road at the heels of one of the crack-goers of the city, amidst clouds of dust through which the rushing of other vehicles might be dimly made out, and startled by the wild cries used by the rival drivers. . . . I thought it one of the most exciting things I had ever met." His use of the words "vehicle" and "driver" is a reminder that much of the language of the later automobile age was simply borrowed from the horse-and-buggy age.

Midway along the Harlem speedway, as Cornelius might have been able to verify, a legendary African American presided over yet another tradition of American sports, food. This was Cato, whose tavern sat just beyond the dust, between two little rises in the road. Cato might even offer breakfast if it was ordered in advance. "A woodcock and toast as served up by him on these occasions is a thing not to be forgotten," Power wrote. The drinks were even better. This would be a contender for America's first sports bar, if that honor didn't already belong to the ordinaries set up next to the quarter-racing strips a century earlier. In any event: "Cato is a great man, foremost amongst cullers of mint, whether for *julep* or *hail-storm*, second to no man as a compounder of *cock-tail*, and such a hand at a *gin-sling!*" The celebrated Irish thespian was quite entranced by "the practical experiments of this distinguished spiritous professor," and he left "with added respect for the great man."

As FOR Cornelius, he had more races aboard Boston after Long Island. He caught the ferry to Hoboken—a New Jersey refuge from the antigambling law that had shut down racing in most of New York State—where there was not only racing but turtle and pistol matches, and strolling and picnicking in the adjacent Elysian Fields. This was the "rural" retreat of Manhattanites, their first "Central Park." Less than five years later, in the early 1840s, it would also be the site of some games of "base" with newly drawn rules, which would make Hoboken and Brooklyn (where the same gentlemen also played) the twin birthplaces of modern baseball, regardless of what the next century would claim for Cooperstown, New York.[15]

But Cornelius was busy with America's first national pastime at the moment, specifically making sure Boston won his four-mile heats at the Beacon Race Course, next to the Elysian Fields. Cornelius registered two important achievements for black jockeys at Hoboken that Thursday, May 17, 1838. First, he won prominent mention in the national sporting press. The weekly *Spirit of the Times* said Boston was in fine order, "with Cornelius on his back, who, by the bye, has rode him a winning race every time he has started." And then he was listed in the official chart, or summary of the race, as the winning rider. The losing rider, also listed, was the very light-complexioned colored jockey George Nelson.

Then Cornelius and Boston took the steamboat for Camden, New Jersey, near Philadelphia, and another four-miler a week later. Today's athletes should be allowed no complaints. It was hard enough just for the sports reporters to keep up with those athletes, and apparently they didn't always succeed. "We take it for granted," said the sarcastic *Spirit of the Times* after the Camden race, "that the gentleman who went on to Philadelphia expressly to report this race for us is dead and buried without benefit of clergy, for we kept our paper open until eight o'clock this morning, and not a word have we heard of him." But at least the editor could add: "A passenger on board the Philadelphia boat, which came in about 2 o'clock this morning states that a gentleman who saw the race informed him that BOSTON WON EASILY IN TWO HEATS!" In another fast turnaround, Cornelius returned to Long Island for yet another four-miler a week later. It produced the greatest praise of his career.

"'*Pull him steady!*' was again Napoleon's order at the stand," said the *Spirit*, reporting what Johnson himself yelled at Cornelius as he came flying by the towering Long Island stands, with their thousands of spectators. "But at the quarter mile post, Cornelius could hardly keep in check the irrepressible energies of the phenomenon under him." The crowd was thrilled by the sight of Napoleon, his crazy white hair flying like that of a maestro with multiple batons. "*Take the track!*" Johnson screamed. Back at his offices, the *Spirit*'s reporter sat down and wrote, "We have just returned from one of the most splendid races ever made on the American Turf." Boston had run the first three miles in record time and the second-best four-mile heat in America. "Boston had *Cornelius* up, his usual rider, and Jem Robinson or Sam Day could not have brought him home more gallantly." It was a milestone of sorts, the first time an African American had been compared with the greatest riders of the English turf.[16]

Then they ferried again back to Hoboken, where the press detailed their performance against a four-year-old colt named Duane, under a boy named Stephen, possibly the white rider Stephen Welch. This report verifies the fact that black jockeys, whatever their legal status and just like their white colleagues, heard the applause of their fellow Americans in scenes that unfortunately never made the history books. In the second heat, said the *Spirit of the Times*, putting the applause in parentheses, "Duane went up with a rush that sent him clear ahead (Tremendous cheering). Boston sulked for an instant, and then, like the nonpareil that he is, made a dash and regained his place in front (Three cheers more). Again the stout-hearted colt made a brush and a second time he was ahead (A louder cheer yet), but in four tremendous leaps Boston was again in front (Three cheers and one more for Boston). . . . Cornelius took a good strong pull on Boston . . . whips are at work, and the spurs are drove in up to the rowel heads—'Go it, Boston!' 'Hurrah for Duane!' . . . Ten thousand people shout like devils—a cold shiver—a suspension of breath ensues for an instant, and the heat is over. *Boston wins by the length of his nose!* As soon as the horses were taken up and brought back to the Judges' Stand, *Duane's rider fainted* from exhaustion." Cornelius was praised for his tactics. Had Stephen been able to pull Duane toward the end, to save his energy, "precisely such a respite as Cornelius gave Boston, he would have won the heat."

In the excitement, Cornelius's trainer, Arthur Taylor, "chewed his tobacco a mighty deal finer than ever"—engaging in what remains another popular tradition in American sports. For the third and final four-mile heat at Hoboken, a fresh rider, John Hartman, was thrown on Duane. They tore around the turn past the grand-stand, "Cornelius hugging the fence so close as to tear his linen pants," but coming home first by about half a length.

That fall, the black jockey and Boston were off and running up and down the coast again, from Petersburg, Virginia, to Baltimore to Camden, New Jersey, to Long Island to Hoboken. At Hoboken and at the Union Course, Cornelius again made the official charts, with George Nelson and the white riders William Craig and Gilpatrick. Capturing eleven victories in eleven starts in 1838, Cornelius had traveled more and seen more than most Americans ever would. Riding above and beyond slavery, he created for himself a brilliant career, piloting "Old White Nose" for 143 miles before tens of thousands of Americans. He lost only once, in two-mile heats at Petersburg in April 1839, when Boston was "off his foot"—off-balance. Eleven days later, the jockey and his angry steed turned in an appropriate finale, the fastest three miles yet run at Broad Rock, Virginia. With that, Cornelius was replaced on Boston by Gilpatrick, under whom the furious chest-nut would go on for four more years. Altogether, Boston would capture forty of forty-five races, and seventy of his eighty-one heats, an astounding 284 miles of triumph, a little more than half of it under Cornelius.

THE LAST year of the decade also saw the most important horse race of the era, a preview of one of the most celebrated events in sports, the Kentucky Derby. Like the modern Derby, it was half horse race, half promoter's masterpiece. The sporting impresario Yelverton Oliver, last seen revamping the racetrack in the nation's capital, resurfaced in Louisville, where he renovated the Oakland Race Course and announced Kentucky's first nationally important race. If the North-South matches anticipated the development of nationally organized sports on a modern scale, this was billed as a new step in that direction, an East-West match pitting a Virginia-bred horse against a Kentucky foal trained in Louisiana.[17]

It would be a sweepstakes—winner take all—costing two thousand dollars to get in, with a one-thousand-dollar forfeit to be paid by any subscriber who dropped out. To this grand prize the promoter would add his own, throwing in all the receipts from the stands (but not general admissions). Oliver was a modern organizer for America's first sport, thinking of the public first, the rich stable owners second. He also warmed up to the press, luring founder-editors John Skinner of the monthly *American Turf Register* in Baltimore and William T. Porter of the weekly *Spirit of the Times* in New York. These two men also founded modern American sports journalism, a title sometimes mistakenly awarded to *New York Herald* publisher James Gordon Bennett, who had yet to make his important contributions. By 1839, Porter was in the process of consolidating his power, buying out Skinner and covering the race for both publications. His reports turned it into a national event.

On September 30, 1839, an estimated ten thousand people, half the population of Louisville, converged on the Oakland Race Course at what is now Seventh and Magnolia Streets in the city's old section. Two thousand mounted men met in the infield. Others watched from the stands, fences, and tops of carriages, from every tree with a decent branch and every hill with a view. Oliver had learned in Washington how to attract power. Judge Alexander Porter of Louisiana and his old friend from the Senate, the Kentucky hero Henry Clay, showed up early on that radiant Monday. They were joined by several other senators, Kentucky's military, sporting and social leadership, and turf lovers from Ohio, Tennessee, Alabama, Maryland, and Virginia.

Oliver had learned the importance of getting the women, too. From the late eighteenth century, in fact, American track operators had realized that no sporting operation would last long without them. Of course, it would never be difficult to get the horse-loving, sports-loving Kentucky women to the track, or for that matter the women of Tennessee, South Carolina, or Virginia—provided it was worth their while. On that day, eight hundred white women, the "belles" of Kentucky, filled the Ladies Pavilion.

And were they welcome! Anyone searching for the most extreme case of antebellum gallantry could find it in William Porter's description of the "daughters of Old Kentuck" in the *Turf Register*. Although his prose is florid, and through a twenty-first-century lens even grotesque, it seems to reflect the upper-crust white male fantasies of the day. As such, here's the Ladies Pavilion:

> The young miss just from the trammels of school, flush with joy and fears, the budding, blooming girl of sweet sixteen, the more stately and elegant full-blown woman, the dark-eyed Southerner, with her brown complexion and matchless form, the blue-eyed Northerner with her dimpled cheek and fair and spotless beauty were gathered here in one lustrous galaxy. . . . If any demand by what right we allude so pointedly to them, surely we may ask by what right they have to be so beautiful. . . .
>
> There was a reigning belle, in the spring-time of her youth and beauty, with a face beaming with perfect happiness. . . . There comes a bride—and from the East, too. A peep at her face, almost hid by clustering braids of raven hair, displays a belle of an Atlantic city, and ere we have time to ask her name, a lovely blonde sweeps by in a gay mantilla, changeable as the hues of the evening, with a hat whiter than the wing of a dove. . . .
>
> Who can fail to detect the graceful being on our left, in a Parisian hat, lined with violets, whose soft liquid eye and raven braids render her the fairest gem in the brilliant cluster of Western beauties? The flashing eyes of a dark-browed matron from Missouri are roving restlessly over the nodding sea of heads beneath, and the pensive smile of a fair lily, just home from school, has become absolutely radiant as she shakes back, from her open brow, a flood of glistening ringlets, and gazes down upon the multitude with the innocent gaze of a young-eyed seraph.

They just don't make white women like that anymore. And they had another quality that might be missed. They didn't think it proper to get their names in the paper, or as the reporter put it, "Good breeding forbids an enumeration of the distinguished throng of belles." Of course, Porter wasn't as naive as his account makes him seem. He was a tough, eighth-generation New Englander transplanted from Vermont and Connecticut to the cynical environs of New York City publishing. And like Oliver, he had to woo the gallants of the South and Southwest, where racing was happening— and he had to woo the women, both for the sport's success and for the circulation of his newspaper. His prose may have been phony, but it also touched something real. Southern gallantry survives today in pockets throughout the region. It flares up on festive occasions and fairly explodes on Derby day, with its flotilla of belles under broad-brimmed hats and a handy umbrella of Kentucky courtesy.

UNFORTUNATELY, as they still do, the daughters of Kentuck' had competition on the track. If a gentleman liked anything better than a belle, it was a horse. At a quarter to one, the bugle called the entries from the paddock to the track. First to come out was a magnificent light gold chestnut, ridden by the jockey Cato and bred by Daniel Dugger, who ran the Dugger Hotel in Lawrenceville, Virginia. From the beginning Dugger had reason to think his colt would lead a prosperous life, which it did. Unfortunately, Dugger did not.[18]

One day, in August 1837, this very popular hotelier was carving a fowl for his guests as they celebrated the end of the court session. His fortune depleted by his racing habit, he nevertheless could congratulate himself on the fact that things were looking better. His three-year-old colt, as yet unnamed, had won his debut at Lawrenceville that spring and then placed a highly respectable second at Newmarket in a strong field of nine, with entries owned by such powers of the turf as Johnson, Botts, and William Mc-Cargo. Baltimore sportsman John Campbell had been so impressed with Dugger's colt that he paid him five thousand dollars for the foal right there at the track. But where would Dugger dig up his next gold mine? If that's what he was thinking as he sliced the bird, it didn't last long. "Dugger, damn Dugger as a political mentor! Why, he is below infamy and beneath contempt!"

It was "Old Drum"—George Dromgoole, the Democratic congressman and drunk, seated at Dugger's right and doubtless sporting his trademark gold-rimmed spectacles. Dugger was actually Drum's friend but also a supporter of the opposition Whigs. As they passed the decanter—as they did all through those Brunswick County nights—the congressman, hopelessly intoxicated, insulted his friend. Dugger slapped Drum across the face, which knocked him halfway across the basement dining room. He then threw his carving knife at Drum when he tried to get up. And so, a duel was set.

By the rules that were eventually drawn up, Dugger and Drum would shoot for three seconds or until one was "killed, mortally wounded, or so disabled as to be unable to fire." The continuous shooting for three seconds may have been prompted by the fact that the congressman didn't understand how to fire a pistol and the hotelier-breeder couldn't comprehend how to hold one. They would need practice.

Although this may seem like a digression, this duel demands urgent consideration in a study of the lives and times of the black jockeys, as it offers a contrast in the lives and times of the white thoroughbred owners. Certainly the African Americans must have had some laughs over this hilarious tradition that from time to time thinned the European American population. Everybody in Brunswick County figured the two fools would fire a bunch of shots, miss, and pass the decanter happily ever after, as was often the case in duels. Dugger's wife, however, took it seriously. A general's daughter, she suspected Dugger was a coward and reportedly told him that if he didn't fight the duel with the congressman, she would. But Dugger had other nags on his mind. In fact, history records that he had the duel postponed to "settle his worldly affairs," which included going to a race, believed to be the three-mile heats that Cornelius and Boston won at Camden, New Jersey, on October 26.

Six days later, the duelists met on a plateau above the roaring Roanoke. The Honorable Mr. Dromgoole arrived in a carriage, with his second dressed in the French style for a duel: lace ruffles, silk stockings, patent leather pumps. The lowly Dugger arrived in a wagon, with a bed in the back for the victim. The doctor arrived in a gig.

Dugger's second won the right to give the command, which would be: "Gentlemen, are you ready? If prepared, keep silence. If not, speak. Fire! One-two-three, stop!"

They fired from thirty feet. Dugger's bullet went through the brim of Dromgoole's hat, hitting nothing else. Dugger was reported to have been quite disappointed that he had not killed the congressman, especially when he realized that, quite the contrary, it was he who was shot. Dromgoole, aiming for Dugger's pistol or hand, had hit him below the armpit. Well informed at last, Dugger pitched to the ground, his face bloodless, his lips blue. Dromgoole cried, "I regret it exceedingly! I regret it exceedingly!"

Doubtless aided by the legend of the duel, Dromgoole served six terms and reportedly declined an offer to run for vice president with William Henry Harrison because he would have to surrender his decanter. Dugger died three weeks after the duel—almost at the moment that the nag he had sold to John Campbell was winning the two-mile heats at Mobile, Alabama. Newly named Wagner after Campbell's friend James V. Wagner, the colt had been turned over to the training stable of James Garrison of Louisiana. Garrison had put him in the sure hands of "Old Charles" Sykes, whose fame as a trainer was surpassed only by the eternal Arthur Taylor's. Riding Wagner was Cato, a black jockey.

Now five years old, Wagner was absolutely gorgeous. He had "immensely strong" shoulders, a deep, powerful chest, and white hind feet. Like Boston, Wagner had a blaze on his face, although his was not white but a roan swath down the right side. Recently he had been brutally overworked. He had traveled over three thousand miles in 1839 alone, without as much as three weeks' rest, and had been exercising at a gallop for four weeks. Yet his record put him nearly in Boston's category: twelve victories, ten of them at four-mile heats, in fourteen outings.

If Wagner was gorgeous, his main competition, Grey Eagle, with the white jockey Stephen Welch aboard, was something else. When this Kentucky-bred four-year-old was led out to the top of the quarter stretch—the home stretch, or last quarter mile of the track—a murmur from the crowd "was soon lost in a suppressed cheer," then a burst of applause. Trained in Kentucky, too, he was the favored son, but the Kentuckians weren't the only ones murmuring. Lavishly hailed by Porter as "the most magnificent specimen of the American Race Horse that we had ever seen," Grey Eagle had a "sumptuous" front and was a drop-dead silver, which along with his father's handle had inspired his avian name. Fathered by Woodpecker, Grey Eagle had demolished the American record in two-mile heats, running them in 3:41 and 3:43½. But he had been raced lightly, winning only the last two of his four starts, and he had never competed in four-mile heats. He was in that sense still a baby. Spotting a legend in the making, promoter Yelverton Oliver himself had bought an interest in the silver bird from his Kentucky partner, Miles Dickey, before announcing his dream match. Never mind that it wasn't a real, one-on-one match race. Two others, Queen Mary and Hawk-Eye, were also in it, though today they only serve as answers to the antebellum trivia question: Who also ran in Wagner versus Grey Eagle?

But if the two horses seemed reasonably matched, their jockeys did not. Who was Cato? We know almost nothing of his personal life. We do know he overcame his name, which was the cruel joke of slaveholders who named their captives after Roman heroes, such as Caesar and Pompey and Cato. He was not the first African American Cato to do so. One hundred years before this race, in September 1739, a South Carolinian Cato led a slave rebellion, marching to drums and killing all the whites who tried to stop their escape to Florida; the death toll was about thirty whites and more than thirty blacks. The Cato who ran the legendary tavern by the Harlem speedway also made the name his own. Now, this latest Cato, on Wagner, was about to garner the sort of national plaudits reserved for only a very few white jockeys. His friends called him Cate, but his name would be recognized far beyond the stables, albeit often spelled "Kate" in the two national sporting publications. What Edward Troye was doing with his brush, introducing black jockeys and trainers to America in his paintings (which he often exhibited), William Porter would exceed with his two presses, presenting Wagner's rider to a national audience.

"At half-past one o'clock," he wrote in the *Turf Register*, "the order was given to 'clear the course.' *Cato*, called Kate, in a richly embroidered scarlet dress, was put upon Wagner; he is a capital jockey and rode nearly up to his weight, 110 pounds." That meant that Cato weighed nearly the 110 pounds that the five-year-old Wagner was assigned to carry. His "scarlet dress" was a red jacket, his cap was blue, his pants white.

In red, blue, and orange, the jockey Stephen Welch was no Cato. A substitute for another jockey, who had suddenly lost the confidence of his owners, the tiny white boy weighed eighty-two pounds. In order to make the one-hundred-pound burden assigned to Grey Eagle, including saddle and bridle, they had to fill his "shot-pouches," which were pockets attached to the saddle, with thirteen pounds of lead shot. As a four-year-old, Grey Eagle was assigned less weight. Stephen drew the inside post position along the rail, Cato the outside.

The purse they were racing for was not, in itself, very large. Ten stable owners had paid the two thousand dollars each to subscribe, but then six had dropped out, sacrificing the thousand-dollar forfeit fee. That left a winner's purse of fourteen thousand dollars, plus the general admission receipts as promised by Oliver, which would be about another thousand. As usual, this total prize of about fifteen thousand dollars was nothing next to the betting, which had intensified daily in different parts of the country, from New York to New Orleans. Nationally, Wagner was favored by about 50 to 75, meaning a bettor would have to risk seventy-five dollars to win fifty. As it always would, homestate chauvinism drove the Louisville plungers, who dumped immense sums on Grey Eagle to win the first four-mile heat.

Intimidated by the local vote for Grey Eagle's early speed, Wagner's owner and trainer, Campbell and Garrison, had decided not to battle for the first heat, but to let Grey Eagle have it if it came to that—until a huge bet came in from out of town. Acting for a New Orleans gambler, a betting agent staked thousands of dollars on Wagner and Cato, with the Campbell-Garrison team standing to share in the winnings. So they changed their minds and decided to go for the first heat after all.

The race was about to start when, at the last moment, the Oakland jockey club officials took time to dislodge the band members from their fabulous seats just above the judge's stand. Prominent guests were invited to take the band's seats, among them old Henry Clay, Judge Alexander Porter, and the latter's friend (but no relation), the journalist William Porter. The rest of the press was already enjoying its prerogatives: "We all obtained a fine view, not only of the race, but—of the ladies in the stands opposite."

Then: "Go!"

With a shout, and a tap on his drum, the jockey club president sent the horses flying. "Grey Eagle was last off, while Wagner went away like a quarter-horse," William Porter reported in the *Turf Register.* Indeed, like Austin Curtis's and Old Ned's tilts, it was a jockey battle, the difference being that this was an eight- or twelve-mile war, so it called for more strategy. Cato let Hawk-Eye win the first mile, and tiny Stephen Welch held Grey Eagle, back, "tugging with might and main." In the second mile, Cato passed his stable, where the grooms and other riders gave a cheer, which made Wagner take off on his own, bolting like lightning past the stands. This startled Stephen and the other "jocks," as

Porter was already calling them, and they turned it on, too, catching Wagner, until "like twin bullets the gallant gray and Wagner came out of the melee." It was Wagner, then Grey Eagle, past the stands and into the final mile, with nobody watching the Ladies Pavilion.

Oliver had not tamed this track. Coming out of the first turn, it sloped downward all the way around the top of the home stretch, and Grey Eagle caught Wagner on this decline. "For three hundred yards the pace was tremendous. Grey Eagle once got his head and neck in front, and a tremendous shout was sent up." But out of the last turn, where the track slanted uphill along the six hundred yards to the finish, Wagner forced Grey Eagle to the outside and won the heat. Hawk-Eye was distanced—so far behind he was officially out of the race. Queen Mary had barely "saved her distance," finishing with the required distance to qualify for the second heat. But it wasn't nice of Wagner to beat the Kentucky-bred Grey Eagle in Kentucky.

"The disappointment and mortification was so great," said Porter, that as the horses cooled off between heats, the distraught crowd began betting on Queen Mary in the second heat, giving up on their clipped Eagle. But then embarrassment turned to pride, and the crowd went back en masse to Grey Eagle. *Not a Kentuckian on the ground laid out a dollar on Wagner!* They might want to, given his blood, his form, his performances, his condition, "but they *would not* bet against *Kentucky!* Talk of state pride in South Carolina! Why, the Kentuckians have more of it than the citizens of all the States in the Confederacy added together. They not only believe Kentucky to be the Eden of the world, and the garden of the Union, but their own favorite county to be the asparagus-bed of the State!"

These animals were bred for distance. If a horse were ever to attempt a four-mile race today, he would earn a lay-off of at least a couple of weeks, but after forty minutes of cooling off (at other tracks they cooled off for thirty to thirty-five minutes), they were ready to go again. Grey Eagle was judged to be "as fine as silk." No study has been made of Monday's impact on the French glove-making industry, and on the silk factories at Lyons, but as the Kentucky Eagle came out to applause, his "noble bearing and game-cock look" was so impressive "that a cargo of laces, gloves, bijouteries, etc., must have been required to pay the wagers made in the Ladies Pavilion."

He returned the compliment. "After a terrific burst of speed," the silver bird led in the first mile. As if inspired by the cheers "and the tokens of unalloyed gratification exhibited by the galaxy of radiant beauty in the stands, Grey Eagle kept up his murderous rate throughout the entire second mile" and well into the third. Then Wagner made his move.

"*Rowel him up!*" Campbell shouted as Cato passed by, meaning dig into his mount up to the rowel heads of the spurs. Then Cato passed Garrison as the trainer waved his hat at him, near the top of the home stretch, shouting at him to pour it on.

The horses were side by side, no "daylight" between them, jockeys applying catgut whips and steel spurs. It was Grey Eagle by a neck in the third mile, but here Cato's experience told. As Stephen forced him to the outside and appeared to take over the fourth mile, the Kentuckians' roar "made the welkin ring for miles around," and Cato's stable friends, thinking it was now or never, shouted to him, "*Go on!*" But Cato didn't.

Instead, he bided his time, "calm as a summer morning." There was no way he could win, he figured, if he went all out against Grey Eagle just then. Fully aware of his own mount's game, Cato "thought if he could bottle him up for a few hundred yards, there was still another run to be got out of him." So he pulled on his mount, letting him catch his breath. Stephen, meanwhile, was losing his; the jockey was so exhausted that "he rode wide, swerving considerably from a straight line, and was frequently all abroad in his seat." Cato let Wagner go coming into the home stretch of the last mile. It was one of those instants, to be repeated only rarely in the future of sports, when there should have been deafening applause, but there was nothing. Louisville's first national crowd fell silent.

"The feelings of the assembled thousands were wrought up to a pitch absolutely painful. Silence the most profound reigned over that vast assembly, as these noble animals sped on. . . . Both jockeys had their whip-hands at work, and at every stroke each spur, with a desperate stab, was buried to the rowel head."

Cato took a clear lead, but then it was Stephen. "Now Wagner—now Grey Eagle has the advantage. The people shout—hearts throb—ladies faint—a thrill of emotion, and the race is over! Wagner wins by a neck, in 7:44, the best race ever run south of the Potomac." Though shoulders short of that seven minutes, forty-four seconds, Grey Eagle had become the first Kentucky-bred horse to run four miles in the "forties."

Cato had won the race in two straight heats. Minutes later, this African American hero was lifted back onto Wagner and handed Campbell's stakes winnings of fourteen thousand dollars; then, in his scarlet jacket, he paraded the light gold winner victoriously before the screaming ten thousand. In our time, on the first Saturday of May, tens of thousands of Kentuckians sing and weep when the band plays "My Old Kentucky Home," and the stands are flooded with a mass display of Derby emotion that amazes visitors from colder climes. On that beautiful last Monday of September in 1839, Cato rode behind the band as it played "Ole Virginny Never Tire."

OLE VIRGINNY NEVER TIRE
When the work is done in the afternoon
We sweep the floor with a brand new broom
And after that we make a ring
And this the song that we do sing
Chorus: Old folks, young folks, clar de kitchen
Old folks, young folks, clar de kitchen
Ole Virginny never tire.[19]

Did the Virginians and many former Virginians in that Louisville crowd sing along? Had the words themselves, which sound chilling today—a tribute to slave labor—carried their literal meaning, or was it only nostalgia for Virginny, the state that bred the winner of this East-West encounter?

And what about a legend that said that Cato's prize for winning this race was his freedom? It was extremely rare for a slave to win freedom based on merit, since merit only made him more valuable to his "owner." Nor was Cato's winning his freedom part of the general postrace celebration as recounted by Porter, who had the best seat in the house and stayed close to the opposing camps for the next week. But in a tantalizing line, he did say: "Wagner's rider, Cato, had become free about the time of the first race." That was apparently all he knew. He did not say the jockey got his freedom as a result of the race, but rather at about that time. Nevertheless, this was a case of a brilliant rider who did win his freedom. And Porter added, referring to the freed Cato's appearance in a second Wagner–Grey Eagle race to be held in five days: "If he rode the second as well as he did the first, many were the odd twenties and fifties he was promised."

Even before the rematch, and whether slave or free while doing it, Cato had raised the public recognition of these long-ignored athletes by another notch. Although most accounts still left out any mention of jockeys' names, and the charts virtually never included them, Cato's performance forced the *Turf Register* to list him as the winner in its charts, as they had listed Willis three years earlier. More than that, Porter spelled out the jockey's importance. "To say that Wagner was better managed and better jockeyed in this race than Grey Eagle is to express the opinion of every unprejudiced individual who had the pleasure of witnessing it." Which didn't mean that he thought Cato could have beaten anybody: "With Gil. Patrick on his back, Grey Eagle would have won the *second* heat," forcing a third.

Now ALL attention was focused on the rematch, and Stephen Welch's skimpy eighty-two pounds prompted the Grey Eagle camp to look for another jockey. The only one around who was any better was "Mr. McCargo's Archer." William McCargo was prominent on the eastern racing circuit, and Archer was "a very capital rider, with a good seat, a steady hand, and a cool head." But while offering Archer's services, McCargo put out the word that he didn't want to be caught in the middle of this intense rematch with all its possible repercussions. So Grey Eagle's owner and trainer went back to Stephen Welch, "whose only fault was that there was not enough of him!" as Porter said in the *Turf Register.*

From miles around, they turned out for Yelverton Oliver's brilliant second act, thrown together on the strength of the first. It was a promoter's dream. A delightful Saturday at the close of a week that delighted Oliver to the tune of fifteen thousand dollars from general admissions and concessions. A rematch of the two heroes with the same jockeys, again at grueling four-mile heats. From every town within fifty miles they came: from Cincinnati, just across the Ohio River, and from the Kentucky breeding and racing centers of Frankfort, Lexington, and Georgetown. Every last gig in Louisville was requisitioned for the trip to the Oakland club—a ride that was a far cry from one in a New York carriage. "Many . . . call it 'riding' when jolting along in a bone-setter, compared with which riding on a white-oak rail would be fun!" But then: "the ladies turned out *en masse* to grace the scene with their radiant beauty and 'lend enchantment to the view.'"

But another race of two, perhaps three, four-mile heats in five days? At the start, Grey Eagle looked fit, at least on his silvery surface. Everybody screamed as he made a fantastic one-hundred-yard dash down the stretch to take the third mile and then won another stretch battle to capture the first heat. With that, they waved hats and handkerchiefs—"the tumultuous cheers," as Porter put it, "well might have drowned the roar of Niagara!" This time, stuck "with so light and feeble a rider as Stephen," the Grey Eagle camp had saved their speed for the right moments, a lesson Porter said should apply whenever they faced an important contest without "that most indispensable of requisites to success—a suitable jockey." It had taken more than one hundred years to see the jockey's role acknowledged so plainly in print.

Stephen Welch and the newly freed Cato were about to give the famous turf editor "the most game and spirited race we ever witnessed." Another assessment in the press: "A better race was never run in America."

As Cato smacked him, Wagner jumped off from the drum tap for the second four miles, but the two horses were "lapped"—side by side—when they reached the stands the first time around. As the crowd thundered its approval, Grey Eagle pricked his ears and moved ahead, little Stephen bracing him "as well as he was able." Cato again applied catgut and dug in with his spurs, and they flew by the roaring stands a second time, neck and neck. A seven-hundred-yard stretch battle brought them to the stands a third time. "In spite of Cato's most desperate efforts, Wagner could only reach Stephen's knee," and Grey Eagle led going into the final mile.

"Ram the spurs into him!" Cato was ordered, as they entered their sixteenth mile of racing in six days.

"Keep him moving!" Stephen was told.

"Grey Eagle came round the last turn on the outside with his head and shoulders in front, at a flight of speed we never saw equaled." But it was too much for Stephen. With both jockeys close to dropping from exhaustion, "Stephen, poor fellow, lost his presence of mind." As they tore up the home stretch, he "unconsciously yawed his horse across the track, which broke him off stride, while Cato, holding Wagner well together and mercilessly dashing in his spurs, brought him through a gallant winner by a neck."

After another short break and a shout of "Go!" they were off for an incredible third heat to decide it. But with Cato and Wagner ahead after a mile and a half, Grey Eagle "suddenly faltered as if shot, and after limping a step or two, abruptly stopped!" Shouts came from the crowd: "Grey Eagle has let down!"

He had broken down after nine and a half miles of racing that day—seventeen and a half for the week. Almost a colt at four years old, he had injured a joint in the coffin, the main bone in the hoof. Cato pulled up on Wagner, and then he galloped slowly for two and a half miles to take the victory. When they passed their own stable for the fourth mile, the grooms and exercise boys on the roof gave them such a cheer that Wagner took off again. "In spite of Cato's utmost exertions," he ran at top speed for nearly 500 yards, "as if plied with steel and whalebone the whole way!"

Not everyone in Kentucky was thrilled. "We think two such matches in one week the highest of cruelty to the noble animals, and no prospect of gain ought to tolerate it," said the *Gazette*. Grey Eagle's breakdown would lead a popular nineteenth-century

Grey Eagle, one of the most beautiful horses of his day, held by his groom, Milo. This was the largest mezzotint engraving ever made in America. The original, painted by Edward Troye in 1841, was lost in a fire on a Mississippi River steamboat. Courtesy of Keeneland Association.

historian to appeal for an end to four-mile races, the "heroic distance" that Americans kept their thoroughbreds running long after England discarded it as excessive. Until the Civil War, however, they would remain the classic American sporting event.[20]

A month after Cato's historic performances, Edward Troye painted him with Wagner, an image that was reproduced the next spring in the *Spirit of the Times* and again three years later in the *Turf Register*—among the earliest pictures of an American athlete to appear in national publications. "He has a handsome figure," Porter wrote of Cato, "which is set off to great advantage by a very beautiful and costly dress." In return for the horse being named after him, James "Duke" Wagner had given both his friend Campbell and the free Cato the scarlet suit seen in the picture. "Cato's entire dress, boots, cap and all, also a bright scarlet, with gold tassles, epaulettes, and lace; everything about him is a 'neat fit,' so that when mounted he looks 'rayther varmint.'"

In a remarkable moment, the foreign painter and the New York editor joined forces to promote this African American athlete. "CATO (called Cate-O) stands out in pretty bold relief in the picture, as he does in the racing world," Porter noted. He announced to his national audience: "As a jockey Cate-O has very few equals on this side of the Atlantic. He has a capital seat, is very strong in his arms and thighs. . . . His coolness and presence of mind under the most trying circumstances have acquired for him a reputation as a jockey second only to GIL PATRICK."

After Cato's victory, the *American Turf Register* returned briefly to listing the winning jockeys in the race summaries. The charts never indicated who was slave or free, black or white; the statistics treated them all as equals. Other winners at Louisville that fall were given as Madison Powell, John, Miller, Jack, and Archer; in New York: Joe Laird, Abram, Harry, and Jack. As Cato, Cornelius, and others rode their way out of their chains, another group of African origin was making news across America by breaking theirs. In the midst of the excitement over Cato's race,

The combination of Cato on Wagner won the biggest race in Kentucky history before the Civil War. Cato was given his freedom in the midst of the excitement. Courtesy of Keeneland Association.

the newspaper *Commonwealth*, in the Kentucky state capital of Frankfort, was headlining the arrival off the coast of Long Island of a mystery vessel, "The Low, Black Schooner." It had the beguiling Spanish name *L'Amistad* (Friendship), and the newspaper boasted that it would tell "the whole of the particulars concerning the Piracy, Mutiny and Murders on board the Spanish schooner Amistead, which was captured on Monday last and carried into New London, Ct."[21]

Jesse, on Planet, rode for Thomas W. Doswell of Virginia. This Edward Troye painting was stolen by marauding Yankee soldiers during the Civil War but was recovered. Courtesy of a private collection.

·5·

THE SHADOWS *of the*
CIVIL WAR

"CHISEL'EM" AND THE GREAT SLAVE SALE

1836–1862

A s one of the Confederacy's most powerful politicians was fleeing the thieving, drunken Yankee soldiers, Abe Hawkins, one of the politician's four hundred–plus slaves, was making his way north. This slave would ride not only to freedom but to glory as America's top athlete, but he first came to national renown at home in New Orleans.

By the mid-1840s, New Orleans was America's sporting capital, thanks to Yelverton Oliver, the impresario who had renovated Washington's National Course in 1836. That same year, Oliver had hurried off to pursue his dream: to build a racetrack—America's greatest racetrack—in the Crescent City, the westward-looking, anything-goes city of the future. Build it and they will come, somebody probably told him long before anybody dreamed such a thing for the game of "base." Oliver threw together a jockey club, with Judge Alexander Porter as president, and then created the Eclipse Course six miles up the Mississippi and right on the water.[1]

As he had in Washington, Oliver combined modernism with munificence: he created a special surface for the track (a mixture of sand and loam), offered elaborate restaurant fare, and catered to women, whom he knew loved horses and the races even more than their husbands did. Oliver used the first profits from this track to buy the Oakland Course at Louisville as a side operation and to create the 1839 Wagner versus Grey Eagle extravaganza witnessed in the previous chapter. In New Orleans, where his epiphany was quickly seen as a gold mine, two more tracks appeared within a year, the Metairie Course on Metairie Ridge—with its lovely new Shell Road, surfaced with centuries of oyster shell deposits and running along the canal—and the Louisiana Course, hard by the railroad line from the old town to Lake Pontchartrain.

All three courses became the stage of Abe Hawkins and his predecessor, known in the wacky world of New Orleans as "Chisel'em."

The name "Chisel'em" was a corruption of "Chisholm," although the turf records of the day didn't translate it, simply calling the jockey Chisel'em like everybody else. No translation was necessary for the tens of thousands who saw him ride—and who had figured out that Chisel'em was just what he would do to anybody who dared bet against him. Racing records at this time usually named only the winning jockeys. Chisel'em's name appeared again and again.[2]

Chisel'em rode for Duncan Kenner, and their names appear together in the charts and accounts of races as far back as March 1843 at Metairie. Kenner's father, a sugar banker, had died bankrupt, but the son was on a fast climb back to the top. On the backs of hundreds of slaves, he was creating what would become one of the biggest plantations in Louisiana. And on the backs of just a few slaves, he was building a major racing stable, training and racing thoroughbreds for himself and other owners. His flaming foxhunter colors—bright red jacket, bright red cap—inspired his unofficial *nom de course*, "The Red Fox." But things didn't start well for the best rider in red-and-red, at least not when he first appeared in the national press in that March of 1843.[3]

"We never heard public opinion more decided than in condemnation of the jockeyship of *Chisel'em*," noted the *Turf Register*. Chisel'em had stayed too far back with Blue Bonnet, biding his time, so that when he went all out it was too late to catch up. He came in for even more criticism on a cold and windy St. Patrick's Day when he did just the opposite on another gray filly, Music. "All allowed that Chisel'em rode the second heat most injudiciously in taking the track and forcing the running as he did." Still, the crowd seemed to like something about Chisel'em, and the reporters found excuses for him. "We presume the lad was in some manner misled" on Blue Bonnet, the reporter said, and he conceded that Music probably couldn't have won anyway. Other jockeys got it worse. The rider on the chestnut George Martin—"a yellow boy called Isaac"—drew "a severe reprimand" for foul riding, albeit with no official evidence and even though he won.

The generations met at that 1843 St. Patrick's Day meeting. Judge Alexander Porter was still listed as president of the jockey club, and his brother and soon-to-be heir, James, owned Berenice (who finished third but ahead of Chisholm on Music), which meant that Charles Stewart, head trainer for the Porters, was almost certainly at Metairie, too. Stewart must have known Chisholm. The rarefied world of professional sports offered them camaraderie and stories to share, but there was something extra special this time. Waving in the March wind was the white mane of the once and forever Napoleon of the Turf himself, Colonel William R. Johnson. Old Nap, as they now called him. "The arrival of no gentleman but Mr. Clay," declared one editor, "could excite such a sensation in town." And of Johnson's fading fortunes, it was advised that people beware, for it applies equally "to 'Old Nap' of Virginia as to his quondam namesake of France that 'he is never more to be feared than in his reversals.'"

Colonel William R. Johnson, the "Napoleon of the Turf,"
was the dominant stable owner in American racing in the early 1800s.
Courtesy of private collection.

We can only wonder what sort of New Orleans meeting Johnson might have had with Stewart, with whom he never had wanted
to part—in both the horrible and sentimental meanings of parting
then. Given his extraordinary survival instincts, Stewart likely
would have been obsequious; given his monumental ego, privately
he would have considered himself an equally legendary, if largely
unrecorded, figure on the turf. Which, of course, he was. So Johnson was not the only emperor around. This history of great little
jockeys might as well have been entitled "A History of the
Napoleon Complex."

But most likely, Stewart and Johnson would have been just
plain thrilled to see each other again. Theirs was an exotic world of
impossible reunions and of frequent escapes from the straitjacket
of slavery.

Balie Peyton—the former Tennessee congressman who, as a
boy, had gawked at Simon as he defeated Andrew Jackson and who
had seen the jockey Jesse defuse a crisis in Jackson's White
House—was now living in New Orleans as the U.S. Attorney. In
October of 1843, Peyton decided to sponsor America's richest formal purse yet—the thirty-five-thousand-dollar Peyton Stakes,

which was run back home at Nashville. To ride his own entry, Great Western, Peyton engaged Monk, the second-best rider at New Orleans, after Chisholm. Once again travel restrictions on both slaves and free blacks were not about to prevent an important stable owner from fielding one of the best athletes in the country or, for that matter, the trainer who managed his stable. Wade Hampton II was at that Nashville event, too, his Herald to be ridden by Sandy, "who had been brought from South Carolina expressly for that purpose." The white riders John Ford and Francis "Barney" Palmer rounded out the group. The winner: Palmer on the huge Glumdalclitch, named after the giantess in *Gulliver's Travels*, but about to live more happily ever after with a new name, Peytona, in honor of Balie. Incidentally, among other well-traveled jockeys, there is a record of a "Chisolm," possibly the same one, winning in South Carolina in those years.[4]

Along with Chisel'em and Monk, the African American jockeys at New Orleans had such names as Isaac (the unlucky rider above), Frank, Jack, and Remus. But when Barney Palmer, the North's most celebrated white rider, came to town, he stole the press. After he took the three-mile heats on Christmas 1844, the *Turf Register* declared "the jockeyship of Palmer . . . beyond all praise." Granted the reporter might have said this only because he didn't want to waste time thinking up praise, for he added: "We cannot so desecrate Christmas day as to devote any time to the race when a Christmas dinner is before us." In another race, when the jockey named Frank beat Barney, the *Register* said Frank's last three heats were "won cleverly in spite of all that could be done by the finest jockey we ever saw in a saddle." It never did mention Frank, except in listing the winner's name. Not that Barney's talents were ever in doubt. The following spring Barney, on the now-famous Peytona, outran another white boy, Joe Laird, on Fashion, in a North-South race before seventy thousand people at Long Island's Union Course. Then, on Christmas Eve of 1845, hundreds of vehicles jammed the Shell Road to Metairie to see Barney Palmer and Peytona win again. Barney and other white riders found it easier than

African American jockeys to win praise, as would be the case for white athletes for another century and a half. Palmer and the losing white boy, William Craig, were "two as able and experienced Jockeys," drooled the *Register,* "as ever 'set a pigskin' . . . each a perfect picture of success." It was not a question of the top whites (predominantly Irish, Scottish, and English Americans) not being brilliant—they were—but of the other top hyphenated riders, such as Chisholm and Monk, climbing a much rockier road to glory.

A fragment of the statistics from just two years, 1843 and 1844, shows that Chisholm was the leading jockey at the Metairie, Eclipse, and Louisiana Courses: he had twelve victories in races totaling fifty-five miles, the equivalent of fifty-five races today. Monk had nine wins. Of course, for many of the riders, white and black, the difference between winning and losing was not so much athletic skill as brains—strategy, tactics, judgment, timing—and it was all the more true in those races at great distances, where all-out, end-to-end speed was impossible. Chisholm demonstrated this on a filly with the lovely Creole name of Jeannetteau. A reported noted, "Chisel'em, who was astride the winner, managed her with the utmost prudence—never pushing her nor allowing her to drop too far behind—[and] now made play in earnest for the heat." Management was indeed another word for it.

In 1844, the *Turf Register* ran the headline "Best Three Mile Race Run in America!" above its story about the January 5 contest between Chisholm on the little colt Patrick Henry Gallwey and Monk on the favored gelding, Saartin. Chisholm won, but the two finished each thrilling heat side by side ("there was no daylight between them"). Remarkably, the two black jockeys got all the credit in the report by the anonymous "Rambler," although the writer deployed the usual racial epithet to describe the stable help, a level to which the *Register* very rarely descended. It makes for a revealing, and typical, contrast of the times, two black athletes performing to unprecedented applause, outmanaging each other every step, and being featured in a national publication, even as the reporter held fast to the slur of the day.

And now the backers of the favorite's stable sent up their shouts—niggers jumped higher, threw their hats farther, and swore *wusser* than was ever before known. With a slight advantage in the start, Chisel'em rushed for the inside. . . . They were nearly dead locked but on the turn Chisel'em drew just clear. . . . Monk made up before they reached the stand, and they passed it a second time, locked, in 1:53, amidst the loudest cheers and the most intense excitement. . . . [Then] it was manifest that Chisel'em *had* the favorite and he passed the stand a clear length in front, amid prodigious cheers. The shouting was equal to old Kentuck's best, and this time the niggers couldn't jump—they laid down and rolled and yelled. The last mile was run in 1:56½, making the heat 5:40½, and the race the best three-mile heats ever run in America."

DUNCAN KENNER was so proud of Gallwey and Chisel'em that he had their picture painted—by the peripatetic Edward Troye, of course. It was probably in 1845 that he invited the celebrated portraitist to Ashland, the Kenner plantation on the east bank of the Mississippi, or the Upper Coast, as they called the spectacular, mansion-lined shore between New Orleans and Baton Rouge. Troye found himself in one of the most magnificent estates of the South, a natural paradise of songbirds, orchards, gardens, and swaths of velvet lawn. As was the case at the Porters' Oaklawn, Ashland's thoroughbred stable had become as important as the cane, at least sentimentally. The private track was a wonder. Just over a mile long, it was behind and about ten acres east of the manor, so isolated that a group of departing guests once got onto it by mistake and circled it endlessly, thinking they were on the way home.

Kenner's riders apparently used the upright English seat still favored by the American turf establishment. A visitor commented that "these little fellows sat their horses so well" one would think they were "young gentlemen out training"—until they went around the turn and he could see their faces were black. But it was not merely their deportment that marked them as professionals; it was also their ethics. As Kenner's daughter, Rosella, put it later, "The youngest negro rider connected with my father's stable would have scorned to take advantage in riding a race."[5]

But painting jockeys on horses actually bothered Troye. Although his pictures of dismounted riders were masterful, he had been embarrassed to discover that, for some reason, he couldn't draw them astride, and eventually he refused to try, always showing the horse riderless unless the patron asked. The artist remained at Ashland for weeks, painting a number of horses, sans jockey. In the case of Gallwey, however, Kenner asked. Perhaps it was because Chisel'em had become a New Orleans legend in his own time, much better known, for example, than the horse, whose name would not even appear in the American Stud Book. So for the first time in a dozen years, Troye put the rider on the horse.

NEW ORLEANIANS pretended to love their slave jockey. Indeed, they were said to be deeply concerned when a track accident almost cost him his career. It happened at the new Bingaman Course that Yelverton Oliver had helped Adam L. Bingaman of Natchez, Mississippi, create at Algiers, just across the river from New Orleans. This course was close to the ferry, making it easily accessible to the general public, which was quite important because Oliver, then feuding with the local turf aristocracy, had announced it would be "preeminently the people's track." He charged only fifty cents admission, half the usual fare, and offered bull and bear fights, too. But it was for a horse race that Chisholm appeared on March 26, 1847. The weather had cleared the night before, so that Friday dawned cool and clear, with a bracing northwest breeze, a fine omen for Chisholm's mount in the three-mile heats, Kenner's Night Breeze. Toward the end of the first mile, however, Night Breeze kept trying to bolt.[6]

"At last, a stirrup leather gave way in one of her attempts, and she threw her jockey, the famous Chisel'em, with violence. He fell directly at the foot of the winning post. Medical gentlemen who were at hand think that he is not seriously injured, though his escape was a narrow one," the *New Orleans Picayune* reported.

"The feelings of all were pained." But the thousands who turned out on Saturday were delighted to find the jockey back on the job, aboard Kenner's Louisa Jordan. "It was gratifying to see how he had recovered." By his talent, courage, and charisma, Chisholm forced the press to accord him the same treatment that top white jockeys got. He was the only jockey mentioned in a long new report on several races that Saturday—"prudently" holding back Louisa in the first four-mile heat and then challenging Fanny King in the second, even though he lost his race. Afterward, he became known as "the jockey with a scar."

Not long after Chisholm's accident, a Mr. Ivy sold a fourteen-year-old slave jockey named Jim to the owner of a racing stable. Within two weeks the child was riding on the same Bingaman Course in the grueling four-mile heats. He was flying through the third and final heat, the twelfth mile, when the horse stepped into a bad spot, throwing Jim. It killed him. The crowd was shocked. "We have seldom seen so much distress and sympathy manifested by a crowd," said the *Picayune*, "as was excited by the sad end of poor Jim." The reporter's comment shows the privileged place that slave jockeys sometimes held among the delusions of that society. "His handsome face and intelligent features, together with his fine qualities as a jockey, had made him many warm friends."[7]

ABE HAWKINS was the next jockey to conquer New Orleans. He was known just as Abe in his racing career, but he would become the second best known Abe in the country, the other residing in the White House.

Of the thousands of antebellum black jockeys, many, of course, had the same first name. For example, long after the White House Jesse—the one who calmed the agitated Busiris—there was another Jesse, who navigated the racer Planet for Thomas W. Doswell of the Bullfield Plantation near Richmond. There were other Abes, too. One with the family name Speck had gone north from Kentucky and married an Indian. Their son George, a chef at a restaurant on Saratoga Lake, invented America's first snack, the Saratoga chip, later somewhat better known as the potato chip. This apparently inspired him to adopt the name George Crum, a slightly bigger deal, perhaps, than George Speck.[8]

Abe Hawkins may have come to Louisiana from Mississippi, since it was said he was originally a slave of the Natchez-based Adam Bingaman. He was very black and had the fierce, burning eyes of someone who was going somewhere. He may have earned his first mention in the national press at the Metairie Course in April 1851—but for the wrong reason. "A negro boy named Abe, who rode Hiddlestone, was ruled off the track, for plain, positive and palpable dishonesty—in plain terms, 'throwing off' a race which he had already won, by sawing his horse around," noted the *Picayune*. This certainly doesn't sound like the later Abe, famous for his honesty and professionalism, but if it was, perhaps it served as a lesson. Also, if this was indeed Hawkins, Bingaman must have loaned him for this race to T. B. Poindexter, the owner of Hiddlestone and lessee of Metairie. Poindexter was in the process of transferring control of the course to the future king of New Orleans racing, Richard Ten Broeck, a gambler who was originally from Albany, New York.[9]

Three years later, according to one account, Bingaman sold Abe to Duncan Kenner for $2,350—and the jockey was launched on his extraordinary career. Hawkins's career began with one of the most celebrated series of races in American history, a series that opened on April 1, 1854, with the Great Post Stakes at New Orleans. An estimated hundred thousand dollars was wagered on the race in New York City. And twenty thousand people crammed the Shell Road getting to Metairie. The Eclipse, Louisiana, and Bingaman Courses had faded, but Ten Broeck, who could out-promote even Yelverton Oliver, had gilded Metairie, improving the track and enlarging the stands, which on that day saw four thoroughbreds parading to the post.[10]

Lexington, with a young Creole rider named Henry Meichon, and Lecomte, with an increasingly prominent slave jockey named John, were the best in the field. Each colt was an undefeated son of Boston (whose feats were chronicled in the previous chapter): Lexington with three wins, Lecomte with five. As it happened, black trainers had played a major role in their development, and there are worthwhile tales to tell.

LEXINGTON WAS bred in Kentucky by Dr. Elisha Warfield, who originally named him Darley, after the English foundation sire Darley's Arabian. Then in his seventies, the doctor decided he was too old to be racing horses himself, so he leased Darley to "Burbridge's Harry," the former slave trainer of the Burbridge family of Kentucky. Or rather, the doctor leased Darley's "racing qualities," as they put it then, which meant that Harry could train and race him at his own expense and collect any winnings, but he wouldn't own the horse outright. Racing rules prohibited a Negro, free or slave, from entering a horse on his own, so Darley would run in Warfield's colors—light blue cap, white jacket. But when it came time to post the $100 entry fee for Darley's debut at age three, Harry could raise only half. So the doctor threw in the other fifty dollars, on condition they split the purse if Darley won, which he did. It was $1,700.[11]

When Darley's second race came up, Warfield offered the same deal, but this time Harry said no. After all, Warfield still owed him $850 from the first race. And with Darley now the favorite, Harry had no trouble borrowing the entire entry fee for the second contest, so he told the doctor, as one report put it, that "he knew nothing about no halves." Darley won again, adding $1,300 to his earnings.

But Harry ran into a more serious problem with his lease. Before the second race, Warfield had sold Darley out from under him to Ten Broeck and three Kentucky partners. This was quite proper, since, after all, Warfield owned the animal, but the buyers figured they also should get a $1,300 discount, since they were the legal owners when Darley won the second race. But the purse had gone to Harry, and he plain refused to fork it over, which, of course, was equally proper, since he had leased the horse's racing qualities and paid the entire entry fee. The lessee-trainer absolutely refused to budge—and he won. Under their contract with Warfield, Ten Broeck and company were forced to pay the full amount for the colt—who would become, in the eyes of many even today, America's greatest horse. The price was cheap: $2,500. Ten Broeck renamed the horse Lexington, and to prepare him for that April 1 Great Post Stakes, he sent him down to Adam Bingaman's training stable at Natchez, under the white trainer J. B. Pryor.

THE OTHER favorite horse, Lecomte (named after a Creole sportsman, Auguste Comte), had been bred by T. J. Wells at Wellswood and was saddled by Hark, the head trainer there. The modern turf historian John Hervey calls Hark "the most successful colored man in his profession," but that obscures the fact that he was among the best of all trainers, white or black. The operation he managed in Rapides Parish included a training track that was a marvel, and like Duncan Kenner's in Ascension Parish, it boasted one of the few full-mile private courses at the time. Hark and his assistants were even busier than the trainers at Ashland because Wellswood was also the leading stud farm, or breeding center, in the state.

A few of the countless other late-antebellum black trainers were Anthony, who managed Captain William Minor's stables in Louisiana; Jack Richelieu, Balie Peyton's trainer (the staff also included Holcombe, the stud groom, and Jack Rosseau, the workout jockey); and Stuart and Cornelius, who trained for Wade Hampton and Richard Singleton, respectively, in South Carolina. "I presume no one in the last thirty-five years of attending the Charleston Races but recollects 'Old Cornelius,' " wrote John Irving, who was secretary of the South Carolina Jockey Club in those years. "He was in South Carolina what 'old Charles' was in Virginia—a feature in the crowd upon a race field." Hampton once tried to get Singleton to hire Cornelius out to him. "He would be very useful to us," Hampton wrote, "& might be advantageously employed for himself." Hercules, another prominent South Carolina trainer, was frequently hired out by the Sinkler family. Not to forget Ansel Williamson, who began with T. B. Goldsby, of Selma, Alabama, and had a spectacular career that stretched well beyond the war.[12]

THE RESULTS of Louisiana's April 1 Great Post Stakes were sent to New York City by the newfangled telegraph. The New York gamblers who had bet so much money on this race were big fans of the wire, since as soon as the flash came over, they could rush out and bet on the race with some ignoramus who hadn't gotten the news yet. One kindly editor advised "the knowing ones" not to try that stunt because it could backfire. "A Telegraphic communication is no more to be depended upon, under such circumstances, than 'the big dog under the wagon!'"

This time, anyway, the telegraph got it right: Lexington won, his little Creole rider, Henry Meichon, so exhausted he had to be lifted off. Lecomte finished four lengths back. And Abe Hawkins? He was nowhere in sight. Abe's Arrow finished behind the "distance" pole in the first heat; in other words so far behind he was disqualified, an even worse showing than Gilpatrick's Highlander, who was not "distanced" until the second heat.

T. J. Wells, Lecomte's breeder-owner, blamed the loss on the light jockey. He agreed to take on Lexington again—but only if, as he put it himself, "Kenner's boy—Abe—could be reduced to within three or four pounds the proper weight to ride him." Obviously, Hawkins's reputation hadn't been hurt by Arrow's loss. Being sought after was something he would get used to; even more important, he would learn how to deal with it. A week later, a doubtless starving Hawkins was down to eighty-nine pounds, and he was aboard Lecomte as the rich red chestnut again faced Lexington, the "blood bay" who was more red than brown, with Meichon again riding.

It was a wildly ballyhooed rematch that more than lived up to the hype. In the first heat, Lecomte and Abe won by knocking no less than six seconds off the world's best four miles, with a time of

7:26, Abe using neither whip nor spur. Between heats Ten Broeck replaced Meichon with a new boy, but after he was dressed and the bell had rung to saddle them for the second heat, the substituted jockey "was reclaimed by his owner." So Meichon rode again, mortified by the whole thing. In the second heat, they battled all around the course until, in the fourth mile, just as Lexington threatened to take over the race, somebody, perhaps a Lecomte backer, supposedly shouted to the Creole boy:

"Pull up! The race is over!"

And the inexperienced Meichon, already shaken by nearly getting kicked out of the race, actually did, until a newspaper reporter at the rail shouted, "Go in and win!" Lexington fairly flew to make up time, but he was still four lengths behind Lecomte at the finish. The race was wildly debated. Lecomte's backers said that Lexington had indeed faltered in the backstretch of the fourth mile, but that nobody shouted anything at him. In any event, trying to "rein in our pen to fit our space," the *New Orleans Picayune* said it was satisfied "that we have witnessed the best race, in all respects, that was ever run, and that Lecomte stands proudly before the world as the best horse ever produced on the turf."[13] Accolades have never been in short supply in the racing world, and this particular one would be debated endlessly, some feeling Lexington's shorter career was still the greater.

As for Hawkins, he came back the very next day on Arrow to defeat Gilpatrick and Little Flea in the fastest three-mile heats yet, eclipsing Chisholm's and Gallwey's times a decade earlier. Abe was now so well regarded that Ten Broeck, according to a story told by his enemies, secretly secured the jockey's services from Kenner— this time to ride Lexington against Lecomte in another match race for five or ten thousand dollars. Ten Broeck then reportedly tied up Gilpatrick's services, leaving Lecomte without an adequate rider. Understandably, Lecomte's owner, Wells, turned him down. Several months after Lecomte's record-breaking victory over Lexington, there was a grand ceremony in which Governor Hebert himself presented two medals to the winners, creating a rare moment: the governor gave a medal of gold to Wells and one of silver to a slave, not to Abe Hawkins but to Lecomte's trainer Hark, master of racing operations at Wellswood.

LEXINGTON WAS brought back to Metairie on April 2, 1855, to try to break Lecomte's world record of 7:26 for four miles. But it would not be attempted against Lecomte and Abe. Instead Lexington raced against the clock under Gilpatrick—and demolished the record by another six seconds plus, with a time of 7:19¾. This record would stand for nineteen years, until it was bested by Lexington's grandson Fellowcraft at Saratoga.

This threw Abe Hawkins and Lecomte into a final race against Gilpatrick and Lexington on April 14, 1855. It was their first real match race, with no other entries, and it stirred up more excitement than did American Eclipse versus Henry in the first great North-South race in 1823. People from all over the country converged on the Shell Road to Metairie, which had become a giant picnic, a forerunner of the twenty-first-century tailgate party, but with coaches and carriages of all sorts. Their occupants watched the races from these vehicles in the infield, while others jammed the stands on the other side of the track, along the home stretch. As Creole dancers, minstrels, and purveyors of drinks and exotic birds worked the infield, every tree around the course sprouted railbirds, somewhat removed from their native habitat, the rail, but happy to have even a glimpse of the biggest American sporting event anybody could remember. It was the Super Bowl of the nineteenth century.

When the drum was tapped to start the race, something happened that almost never did in a four-mile heat, where strategy was everything: Abe and Gilpatrick flew off at top speed on these two sons of Boston, Gilpatrick grabbing the lead. Abe would have none of that and tried to reclaim it into the first turn, but Gilpatrick and Lexington fought him off. Abe rode in the futuristic, if still unappreciated, crouch, his butt in the air; Gilpatrick rode in the upright English seat. They did the first quarter mile in a blistering 25½ seconds.

"Suicidal! They will walk home!" grumbled the old-timers.

They were right, too, as far as Lecomte was concerned. Lexington sailed on, while Abe's mount became so exhausted the horse nearly collapsed—and was withdrawn from the race after the first heat. Lexington had beaten Lecomte's record for four miles against another horse in 7:23¾. For years after, people argued about which horse was superior, but Lexington and Lecomte would not meet again.

In fact, Lexington was going blind and would never race again. In six victories (including the race against time) and one loss—winning in thirty-four of forty-two miles raced—he had collected $56,600, third only to Peytona and American Eclipse in total winnings. Far more important, however, was his fabulous career as a sire. After Robert Alexander of Kentucky bought him from Ten Broeck in 1857, the blind legend of Woodburn Farm would surpass even Glencoe as a progenitor, standing to this day as his country's leading father of champions, leading the annual list of top sires for a record sixteen years.

Lecomte finished his career with sixteen wins and five losses (the races totaling ninety-eight miles, the wins fifty-six). The year after the final showdown with Lexington, Ten Broeck purchased Lecomte and brought him to England, which took him out of the hands of Hark. The first American stable owner to invade the thoroughbreds' motherland, the New York Dutchman also brought to England the white jockeys Gilpatrick and John Ford and an outstanding black trainer, the tall Bill Bird. It would be said later that neither Abe nor Hark could have gone to England because, as slaves, they would not have been permitted to leave their states. But since many slaves crossed state lines for races, it would be more accurate to say that they would not have been permitted to leave their owners. For his racing colors over there, Ten Broeck modestly chose the crimson and white stripes of the American flag, with blue cap and white stars. And he flamboyantly announced that Lecomte would take on any English horse for ten thousand dollars—only to be told that such match races had become quite old-fashioned in

England. He would have to be satisfied with entering him in a normal club race. Lecomte lost by twenty lengths in the Warwick Cup and died of colic a month later.[14]

IN THE late antebellum decades, hundreds of local black jockeys continued to dominate the action in the South. At the same time, a small number of well-publicized whites ranged the South as freelancers for the biggest stables; this was the only way for them to make a living, since antigambling forces were holding back Northern racing. For the moment, sports became an equalizer in an unequal society.

It was not only talent that leveled the field, but the rules. There had to be rules if the sport was going to be legitimate. The South Carolina Jockey Club required that if any rider "shall presume to cross, jostle, strike or use any foul play" and then win the race, the purse would be denied to "the master, owner, or person employing such rider." The color of one's skin had nothing to do with it. And equal participation often meant equal recognition, at least by those who were close to the sport. In 1858, Dr. John Irving listed a few of the athletes who had donned Wade Hampton II's colors—blue jacket, red sleeves, blue cap: "His riders have been Willis, Gill Patrick [Gilpatrick], Craig, Stephen Welch, all white Jockies. Among the most distinguished of his black Jockies have been Lewis, from Kentucky, Fed, Jim Gloster, Sandy, and George, from Virginia. The celebrated [white rider] Joe Laird, Fashion's jockey, with Daniel were once in his stable."[15]

Rising above their slave status, black jockeys were thus seen as distinguished professionals by turf leaders like Irving, who for years was the secretary of the South Carolina Jockey Club. Earlier, in the 1840s, the doctor made no distinction between blacks and whites when he praised a trend throughout the country toward proper uniforms as a mark of professionalism.

> Every occupation *has*, and *must have*, a distinctive dress—
> a jockey no less than any other professional man. . . .

Who has not seen a superb animal . . . mounted by a dirty little specimen of humanity, in his short sleeves, ragged trowsers and shoeless feet? These liveries of a young country are rarely to be met with, it is true, now-a days; yet they will, from time to time, be seen unless some measure be adopted by common consent of all our clubs throughout the country to banish them from our courses. We propose that the dress of the English Jockey be adopted. Can any thing be more appropriate, more beautiful, than his silk jacket and cap, his buckskin breeches, fitting snugly to the thigh and knee, and with a neat and light top boot completing the outfit?[16]

Abe Hawkins, the slave jockey who wore Duncan Kenner's red-on-red, was extraordinarily lucky, of course, developing a much lauded career and hearing the applause at one of America's most famous races. Denied the far greater rewards that freedom would have offered such talent, he at least enjoyed a professional life beyond the dreams of most whites, let alone slaves. Just the atmosphere of his racing life must have been marvelous, centering as it did on Kenner's lovely track and the hilarious New Orleans scene. Yet he would be described later as an extremely serious man. "Solemn" was the word the press used more than once, seemingly mystified by the man. This solemnity was a mixture, if the reports are to be believed, of intensity and melancholy, and it should have been understandable. After all, Abe Hawkins had only to look around him to see how the other 99 percent of Ashland's 473 slaves (the count by 1860) lived. And died.

Like other plantations, Ashland had a horrible mortality rate, with nearly 55 percent of its children dying before they were seven years old. In Craig A. Bauer's *Duncan Farrar Kenner*, a biography of the planter, the author writes that the children not only were often victims of whooping cough, pneumonia, cholera, and gastrointestinal disorders, as were free children, but they got minimal care in the plantation nursery, as they were watched over by older sisters or elderly slave women. At fourteen, the children joined the work force. This was also common among urban white and free black children, but slaves, of course, had it far worse. Sugar plantations were more labor intensive even than cotton and other agricultures—the cane workers labored from sunup to sundown six days a week through most of the year, on Sundays during grinding season. One Christmas Eve at Ashland, they worked until midnight grinding the cane, and then they continued in the fields on Christmas Day. The most common punishments were extra or obnoxious work, whippings, confinement in stocks, or, rarely on sugar plantations where all the workers were needed, being sold.[17]

Clothes were generally handed out twice a year on the plantations, a typical allotment being four pairs of pants, four shirts, and one or two pairs of shoes a year for the men, four dresses or the material to make them for the women. The slaves were allowed to keep small gardens, which, as Bauer reports, "they worked enthusiastically into the night," and they were allowed to raise poultry and hogs, thus raising money "to buy little comforts, such as tea and clothes," although Kenner insisted on a cut of their profits. They had to sell their chickens to him for twenty cents each; he resold them for thirty cents.

As for that landmark of the antebellum South, the racecourse, it may have been an escape route for many of America's first professional athletes, but it was also the venue of the biggest public slave sale in the years before the war. One winter afternoon in 1859, Duncan Kenner might have spotted a front-page classified ad in his *New Orleans Picayune* for the Georgia event.

GREAT SALE OF PLANTATION NEGROES
The undersigned will sell at Savannah, Georgia, on the third and fourth days of March next, Four Hundred and Forty valuable Plantation hands.

Terms—One-third cash, balance on one and two years' credit.

J. BRYAN, Savannah[18]

An advertisement in the *Savannah Republican* five days later moved the sale up a day, to the following Wednesday, and provided more detail:

> *LARGE SALE OF NEGROES.*—Upwards of four hundred negroes of both sexes and all ages are now quartered at the Race Course, in charge of Capt. J. Bryan, of this city. The sale will commence Wednesday next and probably continue for some days. This is probably one of the largest lots of negroes ever offered in the state, and it therefore presents many inducements to purchasers.[19]

So the Savannah Race Course sale was set to start on March 2, 1859, and it provides a stunning example of the experience many of the slave jockeys were able to avoid. The seller was Pierce M. Butler, heir to both a cotton plantation on St. Simons Island, Georgia, and a rice plantation just across the intracoastal waterway—as well as to more than four hundred slaves. Butler was an absentee planter, a resident of Philadelphia—and now a victim of the Crash of '57. He was struggling to get out from under massive debt as the Wall Street collapse dragged into 1858, and the decision to liquidate some of his holdings and sell his slaves was a financial one, plain and simple.

Two decades earlier, Butler's then-wife, Fanny Kemble, an English actress and fierce opponent of slavery, had lived there and filled up a diary with her observations ("I am very sorry to hear today that Mr. O——, the overseer at the rice island . . . had one of the men flogged very severely for getting his wife baptised"). At one point she took a moment's consolation from the fact that the slaves lived as families and as a community. "The slaves on this estate are not bought and sold, nor let out to hire to other masters," she wrote, "and members of one family are not parted from each other for life and sent to distant plantations in other states."[20]

But Butler had to ask himself which was more important: his four hundred–plus workers whose tragic lives had been described so affectingly by his English wife, or his own financial well-being? Fanny was not there to advise him (they had divorced a decade earlier); nor did he waste a lot of time thinking it over. In early 1859, Butler turned to the Savannah slave trader Joseph Bryan, a former naval captain, to handle the details. One big advantage of using a trader, of course, was his knowledge of the labor market. Bryan knew that the owners or operators of the rice, cotton, and sugar plantations were always on the lookout not only for help but especially for expertise. From their first arrivals, African Americans had been contributing talents the whites desperately lacked, a contribution that slave sale ads had been underlining for more than a century. One of Bryan's ads headlined Butler's slaves as "long cotton and rice Negroes" and then added: "A GANG OF 460 NEGROES, accustomed to the culture of Rice and Provisions; among whom are a number of good mechanics and house servants." The "mechanics," or skilled workers, included coopers, carpenters, shoemakers, and blacksmiths. Those talents would nearly double the price of a slave: a man who was valued at nine hundred dollars without a trade could easily bring sixteen or seventeen hundred dollars if he was a passable cooper or blacksmith.[21]

Bryan ran his ad in major newspapers across the South, from the Richmond *Whig* and Charleston *Courier* to the Memphis *Appeal* in Tennessee, from the Vicksburg *Southron* in Mississippi to the Mobile *Register* in Alabama. It was on February 23 that it hit the *Picayune*'s front page, aimed at the big Louisiana planters like Kenner, Thomas Jefferson Wells, and Mary Porter.

Another advantage of using a trader was anonymity, which protected the distinguished owner from being associated with the slave trade. What would Pierce Butler's friends in tony Philadelphia think about his abandoning his family's longtime employees to unknown horrors? Nevertheless, even as his name was kept out of the papers, Butler decided to risk attending the sale. After all, what were the odds Philadelphians would show up at a slave sale on the Georgia coast? He even planned a gesture of love and friendship to his slaves once the auction was over and they had stepped down from the auction block. Attending seemed to be no risk at all.

Unfortunately for Butler, he hadn't counted on Horace Greeley, publisher of the *New York Daily Tribune*. Greeley sent one of his investigative journalists, Mortimer Thompson, to infiltrate the sale as a buyer and then file a report. When it was published, the story covered an entire page of the *Tribune*. Detailing the horrors, Thompson struggled openly with his emotions as a mere journalist and helpless witness. He almost couldn't stand it. More than once, Thompson said, he wanted to hit somebody, anybody. And with a passion long since missing from the press, the *Tribune* topped Thompson's report with headlines that dripped sarcasm:

AMERICAN CIVILIZATION ILLUSTRATED . . .

MR. PIERCE M. BUTLER
CHANGING HIS INVESTMENTS . . .

MR. BUTLER GIVES EACH CHATTEL
A DOLLAR.[22]

For several days before the racecourse sale, Thompson reported, the Savannah hotels filled with "negro speculators from North and South Carolina, Virginia, Georgia, Alabama, and Louisiana. . . . Nothing was heard for days in the bar-rooms and public rooms but talk of the sale, criticism of the business affairs of Mr. Butler, and speculations as to the possible prices the stock would bring. . . . The buyers were generally of a rough breed, slangy, profane, and bearish, being for the most part from the back river and swamp plantations."

Down the coast, foreshadowing a horror of a later age, the African Americans were separated into groups and put into boxcars for the seventy-mile trip to Savannah. A neighboring planter's son watched some of them get on the train. As soon as each group reached Bryan's "slave pen"—one of the many fortified private jails built in the major Southern cities to hold the victims of sales or those who had been caught after escaping—they were taken to the racecourse three miles from town and nearly surrounded by woods. The last group from the plantation reached Bryan's jail in Johnson's Square on the Friday before the coming sale on Wednesday and Thursday. At the track they were housed in the sheds used for carriages on race days—"huddled pell-mell," said Thompson, with boxes or bundles of scanty clothing, and tin dishes and gourds.[23]

Their food was "rice and beans, with occasionally a bit of bacon and cornbread." There was no bench or table. The captive African Americans "sat and slept on the bare boards" or on their huge bundles, "when not restlessly moving about or gathered into sorrowful groups, discussing the chances of their future fate." All wore "an expression of heavy grief." Some "were sadly trying to make the best of it"; some brooded, "their chins resting on their hands, their eyes staring vacantly and their bodies rocking to and fro. . . . [F]ew wept, the place was too public and the drivers too near, though some occasionally turned aside to give way to a few quiet tears."

Their clothes told another story. They were somehow superior to everything around them, their vivid colors and variety pulsating with life and often with humor.

> They were dressed in every possible variety of uncouth and fantastic garb, in every style and of every imaginable color; the texture of the garments was in all cases coarse, most of them being dressed in the rough cloth that is made expressly for the slaves. . . . There was every variety of hat, with every imaginable slouch, and there was every cut and style of coat and pantaloons . . . with a general appearance of perfect looseness that is perfectly

indescribable except to say that a Southern negro always looks as if he could shake his clothes off without taking his hands out of his pockets.

The women, true to the female instinct, had made in almost every case some attempt at finery. All wore gorgeous turbans, generally manufactured in an instant out of a gay-colored handkerchief by a sudden and graceful twist of the fingers. . . . There was occasionally a more elaborate turban, a turban complex and mysterious, got up with care and ornamented with a few beads or bright bits of ribbon. Their dresses were mostly coarse stuff, though there were some of gaudy calicoes; a few had earrings, and one possessed the treasure of a string of yellow and blue beads.

The little children were always better and more carefully dressed than the older ones, the parental pride coming out in the shape of a yellow cap pointed like a miter, or a jacket with a strip of red broadcloth round the bottom. The children were all sizes, the youngest being fifteen days old. The babies were generally good-natured, though when one would set up a yell, the complaint soon attacked the others, and a full chorus would be the result.

There were about thirty babies, and some of the African Americans remained in the carriage sheds for more than a week. All were there for at least four days before the sale. That allowed the buyers and brokers in the hotels to go out to the track to inspect them between ten in the morning and two in the afternoon, with the aid of a sixteen-page sale catalog that Bryan had prepared. Each African American had a number. The historian Frederic Bancroft would later list a few of the catalog entries:

99—Kate's John, aged 30; rice, prime man.
118—Pompey, 31; rice—lame in one foot.

345—Dorcas, 17; cotton, prime woman.
346—Joe [Dorcas's child], 3 months.

The captives bore the inspections in silence, the reporter Thompson noted, or "in some instances with good-natured cheerfulness—where the slave liked the appearance of the proposed buyer and fancied that he might make a kind 'mas'r.'" One father—Number 5, Elisha—tried to get "a benevolent-looking middle-aged gentleman" to buy himself along with his wife, Molly, his son, Israel, and his daughter, Savanda. "Look at me, Mas'r," the father said, within earshot of Greeley's spy. "Am prime rice planter . . . do carpenter work, too, little." Elisha told the man that his wife was a good rice hand, too, and had her come forward. As Elisha spoke more rapidly, desperately trying to save his family, "Molly advances, with her hands crossed on her bosom, and makes a quick, short curtsy, and stands mute, looking appealingly in the benevolent man's face." The father pointed out Israel, too, and three-year-old Savanda, "who stood with her chubby hand to her mouth, holding on to her mother's dress, and uncertain what to make of the strange scene." The benevolent gentleman found a better bargain elsewhere.

Thompson said the African American women responded to the horror with supreme dignity, rising above it through sheer willpower. "The women never spoke to the white men unless spoken to, and then made the conference as short as possible. And not one of them, during the whole time they were thus exposed to the rude questions of vulgar men, spoke the first unwomanly or indelicate word, or conducted herself in any regard otherwise than as a modest woman should do; their conversation and demeanor were quite as unexceptionable as they would have been had they been the highest ladies in the land."

A VIOLENT rainstorm broke on the Wednesday of the sale. It shrouded the racecourse and rendered it practically inaccessible by horseback or foot, thus restricting the attendance mostly to actual buyers, "who had come long distances and could not afford to miss the opportunity." They hired carriages. "If the affair had come off in Yankee land," Thompson joked, "there would have been a dozen omnibuses running constantly between the city and the Race Course, and some speculator would have bagged a nice little sum of money by the operation. But nothing of the kind was thought of here, and the only result was to the livery stables, the owners of which had sufficient Yankeeism to charge double and treble prices."

Buyers found the slaves crowded into the grandstand's upper hall, which was about one hundred feet long and twenty feet wide, Greeley's man noting that "the close confinement indoors for a number of days and the drizzly, unpleasant weather began to tell on their condition." Then, out of nowhere, a man whom the slaves all knew materialized, a man who might be able to save them at the eleventh hour. They must have been startled to see him. "This morning," Thompson reported, "Mr. Pierce Butler appeared among his people, speaking to each one and being recognized with seeming pleasure by all."

They must have been hoping against hope. Thompson went on: "The men obsequiously pulled off their hats and made that indescribable sliding hitch with the foot that passes with a negro for a bow, and the women each dropped the quick curtsey which they seldom vouchsafe to any other than their legitimate master and mistress. Occasionally, to a very old or favorite servant, Mr. Butler would extend his daintily gloved hand, which mark of condescension was instantly hailed with grins of delight from all the sable witnesses."

One advertisement had promised that "the negroes will be sold in families." But as Thompson reported, "A man and his wife were called a 'family,' their parents and kindred were not taken into account; the man and wife might be sold to the pine woods of North Carolina, their brothers and sisters be scattered through the cotton fields of Alabama and the rice swamps of Louisiana, while the parents might be left on the old plantation." As Thompson noted, Butler's and Bryan's decision to sell the slaves "in families"—"that is to say, a man would not be parted from his wife, or a mother from a very young child"—profited them, "for thereby many aged and unserviceable people are disposed of, who otherwise might not find a ready sale."

Double doors at one end of the upper hall led to a smaller sales room, which was open on one end to a rain-fogged view of the empty course. The desks of the "entry clerks," who recorded the sales, stood on a platform about two and a half feet high, with room also for the auctioneer and the slave or slaves for sale. Surveying all this was the bespectacled Captain Bryan, in a yachting hat, looking both fierce and nervous, his movements sharp and jerky. His auctioneer was a Mr. Walsh, a large man, carelessly dressed, whose florid face was perhaps "natural in a whisky country" but also blistered and peeling, so that he looked "as if he had been boiled in the same pot with a red cabbage."

At eleven in the morning, with about two hundred buyers present, the sale began.

Thompson reported: "The wind howled outside, and through the open side of the building the driving rain came pouring in; the bar downstairs ceased for a short time its brisk trade; the buyers lit fresh cigars, got ready their catalogues and pencils, and the first lot of human chattels are led upon a stand, not by a white man, but by a sleek mulatto, himself a slave, and who seems to regard the selling of his brethren, in which he so glibly assists, as a capital joke."

As listed by the catalog, the first family brought out was:

Name	Age	Remarks
1. George	27	Prime Cotton Planter
2. Sue	26	Prime Rice Planter
3. George	6	Boy Child
4. Harry	2	Boy Child

The buyers were asked to offer not a price for each person, or for all four members of the family together, but an average price for the four. The bidding started at $300 and rose to $600, or $2,400 altogether. The winning buyer, however, had not understood the bidding, so he would not take George and his family. They were sold again on the second day, for an average of $620, or $2,480.

Thompson sketched the buyers:

> The Georgia fast young man, with his pantaloons tucked into his boots, his velvet cap jauntily dragged over to one side, his cheek full of tobacco. . . . His ready revolver or his convenient knife were ready for instant use in case of a heated argument. . . . White neck clothed, gold-spectacled, and silver-haired old men . . . ignoring, as a general rule, the men but tormenting the women with questions which, when accidentally overheard by the disinterested spectator, bred in that spectator's mind an almost irresistible desire to knock somebody down. . . . And then all imaginable varieties of rough backwoods rowdies. Those of your readers who have read "Uncle Tom"—and who has not? [it first appeared as a newspaper serial in 1851]—will remember with peculiar feelings Legree, the slave driver and woman whipper. That that character is not overdrawn or too highly colored there is abundant testimony.

The strangest buyer, though, was the one who was always in the middle of it whenever anything was going on, "a rich planter," it would seem, "with forty thousand dollars where he could put a finger on it." Catalog and pencil in hand, he darted here and there across the grandstand hall, "talking confidentially to the smartest ebon maid, chucking the round-eyed youngsters under the chin." Passing the double doors, he occasionally bid for a large family yet for some reason never had any luck. His bid was always so low that somebody would immediately raise him twenty-five dollars, at which point "the busy man would ignominiously retreat." Thompson, describing himself, was never unmasked. Personal safety had helped decide him to go incognito, "not desiring to be the recipient of a public demonstration from the enthusiastic Southern population, who at times overdo their hospitality."

Thompson wrote about a fifteen-day-old baby and her mother, Daphney. The baby had been born on Valentine's Day, and Daphney had spent six or seven more days confined to a sickbed in a shed. Then she had been shipped in the freight car to Savannah with the family—her husband, Primus, their three-year-old daughter, Dido, and the infant. At the racetrack, she carefully wrapped a large shawl around the newborn and herself, which prompted remarks such as: "What's the fault of the gal? Ain't she sound? Pull off her rags and let us see her."

Because of Butler's and Bryan's bidding system, as Thompson sarcastically reported, "it was very considerate of Daphney to be sick before the sale, for her wailing babe was worth to Mr. Butler all of a hundred dollars." Yet there in the Savannah grandstand the family sold for $625 apiece, or $2,500 for the four.

Number 319, a twenty-three-year-old, was put on the block alone. "Jeffrey being a likely lad, the competition was high. The first bid was $1,100." A young man finally bought him for $1,310. Jeffrey went to the buyer, "the big tears standing in his eyes and his voice trembling with emotion," and told his story, how he and Number 278, Dorcas, had fallen in love back home. He asked the man to buy Dorcas when she came to the block the next day. Jeffrey went to the hall and brought back Dorcas, and the prospective buyer, after inspecting her, "crowns Jeffrey's happiness by making a promise that he will buy her if the price isn't run up too high. And the two lovers step aside and congratulate each other on their good fortune."

But the next day Jeffrey would learn, as Thompson reports: "*Dorcas is not to be sold alone*, but with a family of four others. Full of dismay, Jeffrey looks to his master, who shakes his head, for although he might be induced to buy Dorcas alone, he has no use for the rest of the family. Jeffrey reads his doom in his master's look, and turns away, the tears streaming down his honest face. . . . Dorcas is sold, and her toiling life is to be spent in the cotton fields of South Carolina, while Jeffrey goes to the rice plantation of the Great Swamp."

Thompson continued: "In another hour, I see Dorcas in the long room, sitting motionless as a statue, with her head covered with a shawl. And I see Jeffrey, who goes to his new master, pulls off his hat and says [here Thompson's "dialect" is somewhat reduced], 'I'se very much obliged, Mas'r, to you for trying to help me. I knows you would have done it if you could . . . but it's . . . very . . . hard'—and here the poor fellow breaks down entirely and walks away, covering his face with his battered hat and sobbing. . . . He is soon surrounded by a group of his colored friends."

The two-day sale at the racecourse involved 429 victims—men, women, and children—grossing $303,850 for Butler. The lowest price was for Anson and Violet, "a gray-haired couple, each having numbered more than fifty years; they brought but $250 apiece." When the sale was over, baskets of champagne were brought out, and the customers were invited to partake, on Bryan's tab.

Outside, on the grounds, a large group of the African Americans got another surprise as they were preparing to leave. Pierce Butler reappeared and was "solacing the wounded hearts of the people he had sold from their firesides and their homes, by doling out to them small change at the rate of a dollar a head. To every negro he had sold, who presented his claim for the paltry pittance, he gave the munificent stipend of one whole dollar, in specie." The silver dollar wasn't all Butler offered, "he being provided with two canvas bags of 25 cent pieces, fresh from the mint, to give an additional glitter to his munificent generosity." And had Thompson not proved so careful a reporter, his closing detail would seem hard to believe. "As the last family stepped down from the block, for the first time in four days the rain ceased, the clouds broke away, and the soft sunlight fell on the scene." And that Thursday night, he noted, not a steamer left Savannah, "not a train of cars sped away from that cruel city, that did not bear each its own sad burden of those unhappy ones." It was midnight in the garden of evil.

MOST SLAVE sales were not huge events that might wind up in Horace Greeley's New York newspaper. Individual exchanges, or the odd sale at a farmer's market, or at estate and barn auctions, were far more common, and even more tragic, if possible, precisely because they were such quotidian affairs. A story is told about that towering figure of the turf Balie Peyton, who happened by an auction mart one day on a visit to his Tennessee estate, Station Camp, near Gallatin. The postbellum account of this incident may have wallowed in the paternalism of the day, but it caught some of the truth.[24]

> His attention was called to an aged colored woman already on the block, and for whom some trifling bid had been made. The gray hairs, rounded shoulders and above all the copious tears of the old creature at once melted his tender heart. An advance bid was made, and the slave became his property. . . . In a few moments an old, decrepit negro man was seen hobbling up to the crier's desk, and with his arrival the announcement was made, "this negro is the husband of lot number so-and-so, just knocked down to Col. Peyton, how much am I offered to start him?" There stood the old veteran of many a hard day's toil, doubled up with age, tottering upon his crudely fashioned staff, hat in hand, surveying with a timid glance the surrounding assembly, the very picture of loneliness and dread. At last his eye caught that of the handsome, radiant features of the Colonel, and such an expression of hope beamed from his ebony-hued complexion, that said in its own peculiar language, "Mars kernel, buy me, too, to go 'long wid de old ooman."
>
> Everyone noticed the mute appeal, and its effect upon the Colonel, and from that moment the bidding began to be lively, evidently based upon the belief that

Col. Peyton would have the old man conte quid conte, and so it was, for though the bids went $50 better each time, the Peyton blood was aroused, and had it cost him his entire estate, as he said afterwards, "I was determined to have Old Caleb." Old Caleb was a famous character, very pious and religious; his influence among the negroes of Sumner county was unlimited, and although the price paid for him and his wife was far in excess (specially Caleb's) of their value at the time, it turned out to be most fortunate purchase the Colonel ever made. For years, the old couple lived at the homestead, performing such light labor as they could, but principally by their upright conduct and sound advice always being given to the colored folks in the country.

But the great rice, cotton, and sugar planters, and their "negro brokers," and the owners of the horse farms weren't the only ones trying to purchase slaves. Far more often than has ever been acknowledged, former slaves tried to purchase the freedom of loved ones left behind. On at least one such occasion, the heroic efforts of free African Americans to buy relatives out of slavery involved Duncan Kenner himself. His brother George apparently had an affair with a unnamed slave woman for years before he was married, at which time he freed her and four of her children, perhaps in payment for her silence. The former slave family moved to St. Louis, where it transformed itself into an American success story, working hard at washing clothes and finally amassing a nice income and several thousand dollars' worth of property. And they now offered Kenner two thousand dollars for the three children who had remained behind at Ashland. One of them happened to be one of Kenner's assistant horse trainers, however, and Kenner said he would part with him only for a sum equal to all the mother's property. Determined to rescue her son the trainer, the woman offered twenty-five hundred dollars for him. Kenner announced that the price was thirty-four hundred dollars, which the trainer could help pay by working at Ashland for another three years at fifteen dollars a month.[25]

But then the mother, indomitable in life, died. With that, Kenner, who was a longtime state legislator and highly influential, went so far as to get himself appointed executor of her estate, controlling her minor children's shares. But it was not over, because one of the free children, Alexander Kenner, was gifted with his mother's courage. When he became an adult and was living in Louisiana again, he approached Uncle Duncan (who would hardly have acknowledged any familiarity) and requested his share of his mother's estate. Legally or illegally, the planter refused. So the young man actually sued Duncan Kenner—and, even more amazingly, won. He then offered the entire settlement to buy his brother William out of Ashland. Duncan Kenner refused again. But this time William himself also rejected the offer. Like Charles Stewart, he apparently found himself more secure where he was. William remained at Ashland even as many other slaves were fleeing the plantations during the Civil War.

To THE moment of war, and even beyond, the Duncan Kenners of the South brought their thoroughbreds and black jockeys to the sporting field. One Northern travel writer, John Milton Mackie, so admired both racers and riders in Charleston that he casually suggested the black jockeys "like the steeds . . . must have been bred specially for the race course." This was just as wide of the mark as a statement by the next century's commentator, who notoriously suggested that black football stars had been "bred" to have big thighs. Mackie's statement was also a reminder of how deeply ingrained racing was, even as war loomed.

On a bleak New Year's Day in 1861, winter racing began in New Orleans when Kenner's colt Sid Story took the five-hundred-dollar sweepstakes. A week later, the Savannah Race Course—the site of Butler's 1859 slave sale—opened for a full four days of races.

By then, South Carolina had seceded and would be joined within weeks by Mississippi, Alabama, and Georgia. Despite this, Confederate Charleston, South Carolina, and Mobile, Alabama, went ahead with their spring race meetings, in February and March, respectively. Racing, after all, *was* the South. Antigambling crusades had long since chased the thoroughbreds out of the North and had shut down all but one track up there, with a few exceptions—such as the Fashion Course at Newton, Long Island, which was mostly for trotters, and Saratoga, which was almost entirely for trotters.

Of all the jockey clubs that operated the Southern tracks, Kenner and company were the most stubborn. After Louisiana seceded on January 26, 1861, the Metairie course stayed open. Kenner and others had recently overhauled the showplace again, adding a wonderful brick-and-iron grandstand, the first in America, and the slave jockey Abe Hawkins was back, winning the single event on April Fool's Day. The next day he was flying Kenner's red-and-red colors aboard Panic, perhaps named to ridicule the war fears. Kenner, now a member of the Confederacy's Provisional Congress, didn't seem worried: he probably figured if worse came to worse and the Federals really came after him, he could just jump on one of his thoroughbreds and outrun any Yankee nag in sight. Especially if his mount was Panic, although a turf reporter said Panic's chances on that April 2 were "strengthened by the fact that he was ridden by Abe." The bay son of Glencoe defeated the gray Lightning in three-mile heats, overtaking him and then outracing him in a neck-and-neck stretch run—"as fine and gallant a struggle as was ever witnessed," a reporter said then. It was one of Abe's most memorable wins ever, a reporter would still be saying six years later.

Ten days after Abe Hawkins and Panic prevailed, the rebels answered Abe Lincoln's famous question—"Shall it be Peace or War?" At four-thirty in the morning on April 12, Confederate shells exploded over Fort Sumter in Charleston Harbor. That and the Northern response ended antebellum racing in the Deep South, except for Kenner and his friends. Even after Lincoln ordered a blockade of the South, including the mouth of the Mississippi, even after the Yankees seized Ship Island, halfway between Mobile and New Orleans, and even as they prepared to capture New Orleans, Kenner and company staged another race meeting, albeit the last one at the greatest racetrack of the South—and therefore of the country. The first and last winner in those five defiant days in December of 1861 was the horse called Panic.[26]

"One . . . two . . . three . . ."

A year had passed since Fort Sumter. It was April 24, 1862, and all thoughts of racing had been pushed aside by battle. An Englishman, a schoolteacher standing in front of a classroom of squirming New Orleans children, was counting the city bells in his proper British accent, which sounded even more clipped than usual.

"Four . . . five . . . six . . . seven . . ."

They sounded very much like the prearranged alarm for the arrival of the Yankees. Twelve bells if by river—that was the warning. Twelve in a row three times if the Federal fleet had breached the two forts on the Mississippi that were the last line of defense for the Crescent City.

". . . Eleven . . . twelve."

That was it. The elderly English gentleman simply put on his hat, said good-bye to the children, and left to see what he could learn in the streets.[27]

Duncan Kenner was in Richmond, Virginia, for the Confederate Congress when he heard about the Federal occupation of New Orleans, but he quickly rejoined his family at nearby Ashland. One day he and his former head trainer, George Graves, were out riding with a neighbor when the Federals docked at the plantation to arrest Kenner. Tipped off, the leader of the Louisiana turf simply mounted the four-year-old Sid Story to make a fast escape. Sid, apparently a Yankee sympathizer, refused to budge. Kenner switched to the neighbor's horse and got away.

Graves ran up the staircase to tell Kenner's wife, Nanine, who immediately did what every former reigning belle would have done: she hid the silver. Actually, it was the minimal tableware,

forks and spoons, the best having been carted to the nearby residence of a man who was in debt to Kenner, on the theory that he
would therefore protect it. But now the slave who had driven the
cart told this to the arriving troops, who later recovered the silver
after allegedly beating the hiding place out of the debtor. Everything was happening so fast. Some of Kenner's other slaves directed the troops to the wine supply beneath the floor of a big
pigeon house—then they helped drink it, supposedly leaving a
number of drunken European and African Americans decorating
the plantation.

The troops invaded Graves's house, where the Troye paintings had been put for safety's sake. Rosella, Kenner's daughter,
who spent a lot of time there, would write, "I can remember peep-
ing under the curtains that shaded and screened the upper gallery,
and seeing below a soldier busy in cutting with his penknife an oil
painting from its frame. It was the picture of one of my father's
race horses, and a good painting." The soldiers stole several of the
Troyes, including the picture of Patrick Henry Gallwey with the
jockey Chisel'em. It turned out to be a Yankee habit. Toward the
end of the war, when they raided the Bullfield estate near Richmond, they cut several of Thomas Doswell's Troyes from their
frames, including that of Jesse on Planet. Later these were found
in an outbuilding, thrown on a pile of refuse and covered with
dirt, but they were just about perfectly restored. But Troye's picture of the beloved Chisel'em, the only known portrait of the
jockey, has been missing ever since, perhaps one day to turn up in
somebody's attic. As for Chisholm himself, he had become too big
to ride, but he had stayed at Ashland and was there when the Yankees docked.[28]

The Ashland invaders looted more than pictures of horses.
Kenner had sixty blood horses at the time, his most valuable mov-
able property. Just as African American grooms had hidden the
thoroughbreds of patriots from British raiders during the Revolution, Kenner's grooms were able to hide a few mares in the woods.
The troops got the others, apparently including the Yankee-

sympathizing Sid Story—but not including Whale, who had only one friend, as he used to demonstrate at the races. "Whale and Abe were bosom friends," wrote historian Harry Worcester Smith, who interviewed Kenner's descendants.

> When the race was about to start, Abe would move over to the side, far away from the other horses and wait there for the signal. Whale would stand quiet and patient but no man could hold his head or touch him or speak to him except Abe. But at the tap of the drum Whale would spring forward "like an arrow from the bow." He was a powerful animal and never lost a four-mile race. . . . Whale was in the stable when the federals came, and they were so impressed by his fine appearance that they made up their minds to take him above all the other horses. But Whale was a horse of uncertain temper, and just as often as the bluecoats mounted him just so promptly he threw them off until they finally gave him up and he was left at Ashland.[29]

In that night of crisis, a slave took over the manor house, an ex-Kenner jockey named Henry Hammond.[30] A light-skinned mulatto from Virginia who had gotten too big to ride, Hammond had become Kenner's coachman and manservant. With Ashland's white men under arrest, Nanine Kenner took a pistol that she had hidden from the troops and gave it to Hammond, who was now in charge. He ordered the field foreman and other slaves to protect the house while he sat with his pistol at the door of the upper hall. The next day, *sans père*, the Kenners went into exile, moving deeper into Confederate Louisiana—at one point traveling through Mary Porter's and Charles Stewart's territory on the Teche—to safe haven in a series of temporary homes. Although freed at last by the Federal raid on Ashland, four of the remaining five house servants joined the retreating family. All over the South and "West," African Americans faced similar choices, which must have often been reduced to an issue of which way was safest. At Balie Peyton's Tennessee farm, that postbellum report said, "When the Federals occupied the country, the best friends the family had were the negroes, and, through persuasion and trusty allegiance to the Peytons, save them much annoyance and loss from incursions upon the farm by the troops, and caused them to be held in high esteem instead."

Back at Ashland on the Mississippi, George Graves, freed by the Yankees, proceeded to manage what was left of the estate, saving it from the complete ruin that overtook so many abandoned plantations. As the field help drifted away, the slave force of 473 was reduced to 125 free employees, so Graves diversified the labor-intensive sugar operation. As Bauer points out, he converted a thousand acres of mostly sugarcane to more than half corn, about a quarter cotton, and only eighty acres of cane. Meanwhile, the fugitive Duncan Kenner was all over the South, attending Confederate Congresses and advising rebel commanders. His devotion to the cause was informed by the fact that this son of a bankrupt planter had more slaves than anyone else in those Congresses (only 160 planters in the whole South had more than three hundred). One of Kenner's slaves, the former jockey who had guarded Nanine with his pistol that night, had hooked up with him again and was at his side as he crisscrossed the Confederacy. After the Union Army began its long siege at Vicksburg, Mississippi, in 1862, Kenner and Henry Hammond would sneak through Federal lines downriver to get back to Louisiana. At least once, failing to find a ferry, the former great white planter and the former black jockey crossed the river in a skiff, their horses swimming alongside.

In the midst of the Federal takeover, Abe Hawkins disappeared from sight, but a good place to look for him might have been in Kentucky, since he would turn up on a Kentucky horse two years later and resume his magnificent career. Confirming itself as the new Race Horse Region for all time, Kentucky staged twenty-six days of racing in 1862 while supplying many of the owners, horses, and jockeys for an effort to revive racing in the North, far from the battlefields. There were twenty-four days of Northern racing that year, a schedule split among New Jersey, Pennsylvania, New York, Rhode Island, and Massachusetts. In 1863, as the Confederates surrendered to Grant at Vicksburg and lost their northernmost encounter at Gettysburg, both on the Fourth of July, the North's new racetrack operators acted as though the war were over. That year's twenty-two racing days included an impressive meeting at Paterson, New Jersey, where the fugitive Duncan Kenner's Panic, now owned by George Wilkes, editor of the new *Spirit of the Times*, proved he still wasn't panicking. He did finish last, however. But the most spectacular new racing by far was at Saratoga Springs, which is where the next part of our story takes us.³¹

They're off at Saratoga! An engraving from an 1865 Matthew Brady photograph. The shamrock porthole in the grandstand is a symbol of the track's Irish American founder, John Morrissey. Courtesy of author.

*A Civil War jockey identified as either "Brown Dick,"
who was known after the war as Ed Brown, or the slave rider named John.
The jockey rode for R. A. Alexander's Woodburn Farm in Kentucky,
where he was painted by Edward Troye.
Courtesy of Virginia Museum of Fine Arts Paul Mellon Collection.*

.6.

FREE *at* LAST?

THE OTHER ABE AND THE CIVIL WAR

1863–1866

O N AUGUST 3, 1863, ensconced in the wicker chairs lined
up along Saratoga's towering piazzas, the Vanderbilt crowd
had come for the waters and the races, but they still had time to
leaf through Horace Greeley's *New York Daily Tribune*. Greeley
featured two stories at the top of page one.

"THE SIEGE OF CHARLESTON" told how the black
Fifty-Fourth Massachusetts Infantry had launched an almost suicidal attack on Fort Wagner, gateway to Charleston Harbor. Under
a torrent of fire, the black troops were determined to reach the
parapet of the fortress. "Sergeant-Major Lewis H. Douglas [Dou-
glass], a son of Fred. Douglas, by both white and negro troops is
said to have displayed great courage and calmness, was one of the
first to mount the parapet, and with his powerful voice shouted,
'Come on, boys, and fight for God and Gov. Andrew,' and with
this battle cry led them into the fort."[1]

The *Tribune* continued: "But above all the color-bearer deserves more than a passing notice." Actually there were two, and

Greeley's man at the front focused on these black noncommissioned officers.

> Sergt. John Wall of Co. G carried the flag in the first battalion, and when near the fort he fell into a deep ditch, and called upon his guard to help him out. They could not stop for that, but Sergt. William H. Carney of Co. C caught the colors, carried them forward, and was the first man to plant the Stars and Stripes upon Fort Wagner. As he saw the men falling back, himself severely wounded in the breast, he brought the colors off, creeping on his knees, pressing his wound with one hand and with the other holding up the emblem of freedom. The moment he was seen crawling into the hospital with the flag still in his possession, his wounded companions, both black and white, rose from the straw upon which they were lying and cheered until exhausted they could shout no longer. In response to this reception the brave and wounded standard-bearer said: "Boys, I but did my duty; the dear old flag never touched the ground."

In the battle, the Fifty-Fourth lost nearly half its men, including their leader, the white abolitionist Colonel Robert Gould Shaw, but it had won an even more important propaganda war. Greeley's other big front-page story was a furious warning by Abraham Lincoln, doubtless inspired in good part by the black soldiers at Fort Wagner:

> The law of nations and the usages and customs of war permit no distinction as to color in the treatment of prisoners of war. . . . To sell or enslave any captured person on account of his color . . . is a relapse into barbarism and a crime against the civilization of the age. . . . For every soldier of the United States killed in violation of

the laws of war, a Rebel soldier shall be executed, and for
every one enslaved by the enemy or sold into slavery, a
Rebel soldier shall be placed at hard labor on the public
works, and continued at such until the other shall be
released.

ABRAHAM LINCOLN[2]

A few hours after reading about the black heroes at Fort Wagner that Monday morning in August 1863, the Saratoga crowd witnessed a black athlete riding to glory, winning the first event in
modern national sports as we know them today. His mount was the
filly Lizzie W. The jockey was an escaped slave named Sewell, with
only one working eye.[3]

"We shall not soon forget the lurid light which glowed in the
one eye of the contraband who rode her," wrote the almost frightened editor George Wilkes in his *Spirit of the Times*. Thousands of
slaves had escaped north across the lines of the invading Yankees,
and the Union general Benjamin "Beast" Butler had dubbed them
"contraband." This one, Sewell, had just launched the Saratoga
Race Course for John Morrissey, America's retired undefeated
boxing champion and Manhattan's most notorious gambling house
operator. "Notorious" meant that everybody loved him but nobody could say so. A sporting impresario in the mold of Yelverton
Oliver and Richard Ten Broeck, Morrissey had leased Saratoga's
1847 race grounds to throw a full-scale thoroughbred meeting for
his friends and clients, "Commodore" Cornelius Vanderbilt, the
steamboat and railroad king, and his Manhattan cronies.

Unlike such earlier climaxes as the North-South races, the August 3 Saratoga meeting was not merely a national moment but the
first in a series of national moments, annual contests on a circuit
that already included New York, New Jersey, and Pennsylvania,
and that would soon expand. It was a preview of an enormous transition that would occur after the Civil War, when racing would
shrivel and almost die in the South, only to expand in the North,
attracting not merely the rich and the privileged but all classes of

people. What made this race meeting national, really, was the audience. Unlike Race Week in the antebellum South, it was not simply a regional or even sectional tradition; Saratoga had become far and away America's leading popular resort, its gargantuan hotels (the Union's sixty-seven-yard dining room sat one thousand) filled with crowds from north, east, and west even at the height of the war, not to mention a few horsey Southerners, whose numbers would multiply once the fighting was over.

Even more important than the fans who attended the contests that day was the far bigger audience of newspaper readers, who found "the Saratoga Races" a break from the war news. Indeed, the races were the most prominent nonwar news in the New York papers, especially in James Gordon Bennett's *New York Herald*, which noted in 1863: "With the advantages which Saratoga possesses, in easy and convenient access from the Canadas and all parts of the Northern and Western States, we have no doubt that this meeting will in future years be one of the best patronized and most successful of any in the North." And the *Spirit of the Times* sporting weekly splashed Saratoga across page one, while setting a permanent precedent by listing the names of Sewell and all the other jockeys in the races. The fact that all this was illegal in antigambling New York State hardly mattered, for the popularity of the sport had often shielded it from the laws and rules of the day, just as it had protected many black jockeys from some of the rules and horrors of slavery. Besides, recent New York legislation had provided a loophole that allowed racing for the improvement of the breed.[4]

Little is known of the personal life of Sewell, the eighty-seven-pound (maximum), one-name, one-eyed athlete who inaugurated the new age—except that the reference to him as a "contraband" would indicate he came from the South. Naturally, he got no credit for his effort in the win, another report simply kissing him off as "the darkey Sewell." The two-horse opener, the first contest in modern American sports, was a battle between a black and a white athlete as Sewell and Lizzie W. defeated young Billy Burgoyne and a colt named Capt. Moore. That same week Sewell would follow up his victory with two more to take top jockey honors—not that they were distributing jockey honors—and he would be back to collect more. The first winning trainer was also an African American, and he literally towered over the jockeys. It was Bill Bird, home from training in England for Richard Ten Broeck. Bird saddled all save one of the winners in that historic meeting— and he had a remarkable career ahead.

Among that initial Saratoga band of nine to twelve jockeys (the riders of three entries were not named), the African Americans were a minority. There was another rider identified simply as Jesse, but there were several Irish American boys, too ("boy" still simply meaning jockey). And back on the scene at last was another Irish boy: Gilpatrick, somewhere between forty-five and fifty-one years old. Could his rival in the celebrated Lexington-Lecomte series be far behind?

Where, indeed, was Abe Hawkins?

On May 14, 1864, the phenomenal jockey burst upon the western racing scene in St. Louis. Somehow he had found his way to the Bluegrass State, for he was now aboard Rhinodine, then owned by the Kentuckian John Harper. It was Hawkins's debut outside the South and the beginning of his reign as a great athlete on the national circuit. In the featured four-mile heats, noted the *Spirit of the Times*, Rhinodine was piloted by "the able and veteran jockey Abe, who used to ride for Duncan F. Kenner in the South and steered Panic to victory over Lightning in the race at three-mile heats." The lineage of thoroughbreds also creates a lineage of great athletes. Abe's Rhinodine was a son of Cato's Wagner. And although the war and slavery were still far from over, they were not very relevant on this bright new day for Hawkins. He was up against his old nemesis, Gilpatrick, and Robert Alexander's "own boy"—possibly "Alexander's Dick," who would one day enter sports history on his own. Hawkins beat them in straight heats.

Four days later during that same St. Louis meeting—again against Gilpatrick and another great white jockey, John Ford, plus four others—Abe demonstrated why many Southerners rated him better than Gil. Indeed, Abe's performance reminded the sporting writer Joseph Cairns Simpson, who was there, why this jockey "never had a superior in inducing a horse to make the greatest effort he was capable of." After Abe won the first mile heat, a witness said, the other jockeys ganged up on him, combining to trap him in a pocket. Undaunted, Abe got his mount, Sue Lewis, to go along with his improvised strategy. He moved to the track's harder outside, which favored speed, and assumed his American seat, in contrast to the rigid English styles of Gil and Ford.⁵

"Crouching over the mare's neck, knees pressed firmly against her shoulders, a clear space between him and the saddle, specks of froth from between the closely set teeth flecking the intensely black visage, he seemed the very incarnation of frantic energy, inspiring the animal with his intense resolution to win; the heat was gained by three-quarters of a length," wrote Simpson. Gil and Skedaddle, a better horse, won the next three heats and the race, but in that second heat Abe had demonstrated his exceptional skill to a knowing bystander. Robert Alexander, the master of Woodburn, was standing with Simpson 120 yards from the finish line. "As Abe rushed by so close to us that an outstretched hand would have touched him, Mr. Alexander exclaimed, 'I have seen all the best jockeys in Europe; not one of them is nearly the equal of that old darkey.'"

Three weeks later, Abe made the Northern scene in America's first derby, "the Jersey Derby," at Paterson. This track was ten miles west of northern Manhattan, above the rolling Passaic River. A "derby" is simply an annual race for three-year-olds, but everybody was aware that this was America's first serious attempt to reproduce the traditions of the English Derby at Epsom, the world's most famous race. And it was by far the best thing American sports had to offer in that war year of 1864. "Next to the war and the state of the country," said a reporter, the Jersey Derby was the talk of Manhattan—at businesses, out on the town, and "in the saloons and drawing rooms of the fashionable avenues and squares."

This scene of the Northern home front never makes it into the Civil War histories because it complicates things; that front refuses to behave as historians want it to, what with its explosion of sporting events even as the far-off cannons roared. Just as Grant's bluecoats were closing in on Petersburg, thousands of other Yankees marched on Paterson, cramming the morning trains and the fine turnpike up from Hoboken. "The Erie Railroad carried vast numbers of people in immense trains of cars," one reporter noted, while another observed the "splendid display of fast teams, buggies, barouches, tandems, four-in-hands, etc., mixed up with the humbler vehicles ordinarily met with on the Jersey roads." The fanciest turnout was probably the four-in-hand of Leonard Jerome—banker, part owner of the *New York Times*, a founder of Saratoga Race Course, and future grandfather of Winston Churchill. It may be that seeing Abe in action that day was what prompted Jerome to bank on him later.

What a turnaround it was for Abe Hawkins, who had been riding for his "master," Duncan Kenner, only three years earlier. Kenner's slave sat on one of the finest thoroughbreds of the land before seven to ten thousand Yankees. Here he was, suddenly a de facto free man and facing his old rival, Gilpatrick, the boy from Poughkeepsie. After more than two centuries, the sport's human athletes were not only free but about to be famous on a regular basis. It started with the *Spirit of the Times*, which lavished attention on the pilots in the first American derby, albeit still obsessed with the fact that the black jockeys tended to be black. It was a strange attitude that would characterize white journalism through the next century and beyond. There was a real admiration for the talents of the African American riders, yet it came with disclaimers in the form of references to their race—irrelevant, albeit helpful to future historians trying to identify them.[6]

Here, then, mounted for the Derby, were "the dark and solemn face of Abe, bent over the lofty crest of 'Tip'" [the colt Tipperary], Sewell, "another of the dark division and looking ominously out of his one eye," and "the fat and sooty countenance of Bill Bay with a broad grin on it." There may have been other black riders among the nine. Several Irish names stood out, among them Gilpatrick and Billy Burgoyne. With the reawakening of Northern racing, the sport had become more racially balanced. Rather than, as in the South, a few outstanding white riders among the black majority, here was a sizable contingent of white, especially Irish, riders with a new influx—just starting—of black jockeys, either from the North or on their way from the South or the border states.

Hawkins's debut in the North was a knockout. He didn't win, but he did extremely well to come in second in the Jersey Derby— for the winner was Lexington's best son, Norfolk, who would never be defeated. Norfolk was accompanied by the outstanding black trainer Ansel Williamson. Hawkins did even better to out-finish Gilpatrick, since Gil was aboard Kentucky, Norfolk's nearly as great half-brother by Lexington. It was the only race Kentucky ever lost. And then Abe commandeered the meeting, winning four of the next eight races. For all the praise he had won back home, Hawkins must have been startled when, in the first of those races after the Derby, the applause reached a new level as he navigated Fleetwing against the chestnut Aldebaran, Burgoyne up.

"Abe, the great rider of the South, was on Fleetwing," the *Spirit* reported, and leading in the two-mile heats. "Past the quarter Aldebaran came with rush and got neck and neck with the leader." Under this threat, Abe responded by not responding, by simply ignoring Aldebaran and Burgoyne, as he pressed Fleetwing just a little more, demonstrating the cool attitude that would become his trademark across the country. "Old Abe, as unmoved as if the other had been a mile off, threw away no powder in fireworks [but] soon shook Aldebaran," capturing his first race in the North to the roar of thousands.

"Old Abe." Along with "Uncle," the paternalistic prefix popularized by *Uncle Tom's Cabin*, "Old" was a relic from slavery days. However, with this rider, perhaps it was inspired partially by the fact that another Old Abe was sleeping in the Lincoln bedroom, or nervously scanning telegrams to the War Department. The jockey's family name, Hawkins, would never surface in the press.

Here was another oddity of that transitional age: the scattering of first names of recent slaves in the charts of Northern race results—Aaron, Charlie, Frank, John, Richard, and many more. And this didn't count all those in the hundreds of races at the majority of tracks, such as those in Illinois, Missouri, Ohio, Kentucky, and Tennessee, which over the next few years still would not publicly identify their jockeys by name. Why did they continue to use only their first names? Partly it was a holdover from slavery. The rarefied world of horse racing had exempted many of them from the subcrimes of slavery, such as general restrictions on travel and making money, but it didn't necessarily extend to them the rights and liberalizing trends of the outside world, either—among them the dignity of a surname, as jockeys remained beholden to their not particularly enlightened bosses. At its worst, the profession that once, in brief and shining moments, represented something like freedom now occasionally looked a little like slavery.

But there was another, less dark reason, too. The first names that sprouted in the race results at Paterson, Saratoga, and a few other courses were also the professional names of these jockeys. A single name did not mean anonymity. On the contrary, these recent slaves discovered something new in their lives—public praise. It started with Abe, whom the press decided to love from the start. "Fleetwing went into the next mile all life, Abe, his rider, nursing him nicely," said Bennett's *Herald*. Wilkes's *Spirit* summed him up rather more lavishly: "To extraordinary patience and judgment, Abe adds marvelous strength and skill. With a clip of the knees and thighs that incorporate him with the horse, and arms that never tire, he always has his colt right by the head and directs unremitting observation to what the others are doing. His sagacity is greatly relied on by the gentlemen who know him."

Solemn. Extraordinary patience and judgment. Sagacity. In the North, Hawkins was acquiring not only freedom but a public persona, albeit an almost melancholic one. Perhaps he had seen

184 • FREE AT LAST?

more than the reporters had. For the first time, we even hear from Hawkins himself and discover he had a speech impediment. The *Spirit:* "After the first heat, he was questioned as to how it lay between Fleetwing and Aldebaran. With a flash of the dark melancholy eye from beneath his pent brow, he replied: "I can b-b-beat him anywhere.""[7]

The stammer hardly affected his ego. Later, one of those who had asked him the question remembered the answer a little differently: "I c-c-can l-lick his head off!""[8]

ABE HAWKINS wasn't the only major figure in racing who stuttered. William Riggin Travers made himself famous for it. President of the racing association at Saratoga, where Abe was about to perform, Travers was a jokester who turned his impediment into a weapon and a small gold mine. Whenever reporters relayed one of his jokes, they would try to reproduce his stutter in print. Not only did this not offend Travers, but he encouraged it, constantly seeking out reporters to tell them another story, which in turn publicized Travers and all his works, from the Saratoga Association to the New York Athletic Club, of which he was also an early president.

"These yachts belong to Wall Street brokers," a friend told Travers one day as they strolled by a marina at Newport.

"Where," Bill wanted to know, "are the c-customers' yachts?"[9]

He and E. Berry Wall, the "King of the Dudes," met a lady coming from the park one day, having tried Saratoga's Congress Spring.

"Lovely water," she said. "I've just had four glasses."

"Then, Madame, p-pray do not let us detain you."

Having helped inaugurate America's first derby, Abe would now do the same for its first Travers Stakes, which today is the country's oldest major sporting event. But the Civil War made these strange times, indeed. Three days after intense fighting at Petersburg, Virginia—where tons of gunpowder blew up under rebel defenders and Yankee attackers, and where members of a black division were either cut down in action or murdered as they tried to surrender to the rebels—three days later, Abe Hawkins helped baptize the nation's newest sporting venue, which today is its oldest professional sporting grounds.

The Vanderbilt crowd had been mightily pleased the year before by Morrissey's experiment on the 1847 Saratoga grounds, so they formed the Saratoga jockey club and built a new track across the street. But the railroad and Wall Street gang preferred the less leisurely and more businesslike term "Saratoga Association." Few were gentleman jockeys anyway, and as they plotted their postwar empires, they had no time for such civilized Southern pursuits, so local "racing associations" began to replace "jockey clubs," though some organizers kept the old term.

The country's first modern sports facility exceeded even the dreams that Yelverton Oliver had realized in Washington, Louisville, and New Orleans. This track's surface looked level but wasn't. It ascended and descended, just as Louisville's had, but with far more precision, the rate of the slant calculated to the fortieth of a foot per rod. And as Abe may have noticed as he flew through its first race in August 1864, the curves were banked, too. The surface under Abe was a careful composition of loam and clay. Of course, Abe didn't spend much time looking at it—although, unfortunately, he did have a few seconds more than Gilpatrick. Having had no chance against Lexington's famous son Norfolk in the first Jersey Derby, Abe also had no chance against his half-brother Kentucky in the first Travers. Still, the *New York Tribune* cited "Abe's determined efforts" as he and Tipperary came in second before the inaugural crowd of five thousand.

That October he traveled halfway across the country again to St. Louis, where they loved him. Only when this visiting celebrity was in a race did the Laclede Association bother to list the jockeys' names. Saluted as "that artist of consummate skill and craft," Abe helped the public to see the importance of the jockey, even when he didn't seem to be doing anything other than sitting on the animal. To the horseplayers that meant he was *about* to do something spectacular. After a one-mile heat, the St. Louis bettors suddenly abandoned the favorite. "The shrewder portion, noticing that the dark sage of Louisiana, Abe, had made no use of [the filly] Caroline Richings, put their greenbacks upon her." It was betting Abe on Abe, since by 1864 greenbacks were already imprinted with a picture of Abraham Lincoln, and once again it paid.

Abe had replaced Gilpatrick as the favorite of the press, getting much more ink. Thanks largely to Abe, newspaper readers began to get a precise idea of a top rider's tactics. He would "save" his horse. "Old Abe, with a fast hold of his horse's head, as usual," said a report on the three-mile heats at St. Louis, "pulled him well together and saved him for an effort further in the race." He would keep an eye on the other horses. "We think that Abe speedily detected" that the pace was harder on the other horse. He would know when to keep racing and when to pull back. "Abe kept Red Oak going and soon had a clear lead. . . . Rounding the turn, Abe wisely took a pull on Red Oak." He had now captured audiences from Saratoga to St. Louis. "The dark sage's" two-length victory over the favorite thrilled the Missouri crowd, one reporter noted. "The riding of Abe was the theme of unbounded praise."

While Hawkins was in St. Louis, a band of rebel guerrillas raided Robert Alexander's Woodburn Farm in Kentucky, where Lexington was early in his reign as the leading sire. Alexander was having lunch as the rebs took their pick of the stable. They grabbed five horses, the guerrilla leader taking Asteroid (who with Norfolk and Kentucky completed the triumvirate of Lexington's fabulous three-year-old sons). Fortunately, about a week later the guerrilla leader returned Asteroid for three hundred dollars. The following February, in 1865, thirty reb guerrillas attacked Woodburn, capturing fourteen trotters but by some miracle leaving Lexington and other thoroughbreds in their separate barns. Union cavalrymen encamped at Lexington went after them, unhappily shooting the stallion Bay Chief out from under the guerrilla leader and forcing the guerrilla-mounted sire Abdallah to run so far it killed him. With that, Alexander shipped Lexington and his thoroughbreds to Illinois and Ohio for safekeeping through the end of the war.

The rebels' return of Asteroid in October had made it possible for his portrait to be completed—by none other than Edward Troye, who had not shared his Southern patrons' secessionism and had moved to Kentucky. One of his best works, it shows the courtly former slave Ansel Williamson, last seen at the Jersey Derby and dressed here in the portrait regalia of the antebellum trainers. As a slave, Williamson had trained the great racer Brown Dick for T. B. Goldsby of Alabama, who then sold Ansel to A. Keene Richards of Kentucky, who sold or loaned him to Robert Alexander. Ansel stayed with Alexander, whose formidable sire Lexington had made the place a trainer's dream, at least between rebel raids. What stories he could have told, and doubtless did. The groom in the painting is unidentified.[10]

Kneeling by Asteroid is one of his slave jockeys, believed to be either John or the later celebrated Dick, who was then about fourteen years old, locally famous for being fast on his feet and doubtless a close student of Williamson's. Born in Fayette County, Kentucky, Dick was seven years old when Alexander bought him and brought him to Woodburn Farm. The boy soon acquired the nickname "Brown Dick." As the historian Alexander Mackay-Smith has suggested, this may have been Ansel's doing, inspired by his former fleet-footed champion. In any event, the kid quickly became one of Woodburn's top riders, and within two seasons he was a regular on the big Northern courses, riding from slavery into legal freedom but staying with Alexander all the while. In the early racing records he was Dick, or Alexander's Dick, or Dick Alexander, but before he was finished he would be Edward Dudley Brown, one of the most successful and richest independent trainers in the land.

For the moment, Dick could only admire the two veterans at the top of the heap, Gilpatrick and Abe. Or as they put it after those St. Louis performances the previous October, "Abe and

Gilpatrick." Stretching from slavery days across the Civil War and into the postwar era of expansion, theirs was the first famous long-running rivalry in modern American sports. Riding up fast behind them was another black and white pair: Billy Burgoyne—who had made a name for himself "second only to those of Abe and Gilpatrick," the *Spirit* said—and Sewell, whom the press soon rated right there with Billy. But for the moment, the two elders stood alone at the top of the nation's sports establishment, especially since John Morrissey refused to come out of retirement, leaving a gaping hole in boxing, and baseball was very far from getting organized nationally.

Abe had outfinished Gilpatrick in the first Jersey Derby and then dominated that inaugural Paterson meeting. But Gilpatrick had won against Abe when they next met at Centreville on Long Island and then took the first Travers and beat Abe again at Saratoga. But Abe had come back to star at St. Louis in the fall of 1864. Around and around they went, as they would continue to do.

IN A SENSE, Duncan Kenner was also going around and around. The biggest slaveholder in the Confederate Congress had not given up. In early 1865, appointed Envoy Extraordinary of the Confederacy, Kenner slipped into New York City and aboard a steamer to London. There, it was said, Lord Palmerston told him Britain would consider recognizing the Confederacy if France would, which encouragement sent Kenner off to Paris. There, it was said, the emperor assured him of French recognition if Britain made the first move. By the time that Kenner got back to London, however, Sherman had marched through Georgia. Palmerston had a simple and final reply to Kenner: "It is too late."[11]

As America celebrated the end of the war, the Irish American and the African American were back at it, but Kenner's (now definitively) former slave was still the press's favorite. Even as he lost the opening race at Paterson in June, Hawkins was singled out: "Coming up to the homestretch . . . the clever colored rider Abe, on Luileme, stole a march upon the favorite." By now the press not only respected him but loved him, and pretty much him alone. As they prepared for the next race that day, the second Jersey Derby, the editor who presided over the entire sport, and had modestly retitled his paper *Wilkes' Spirit of the Times,* made his way on foot down the steep Passaic bank to the stables.

There, he wrote, he ran into a white man and a black man.

> We meet face to face with two of the hardest and finest-cut "old files" on the American turf. Close behind the cheery, frosty visage of [trainer-owner] Colonel [Philo] Bush comes the dark, thoughtful countenance of Abe, the jockey sage of Louisiana. His bronzed and solemn phiz relaxed into a broad grin of pleased recognition, and then we "foregather," as the Scotch say. Abe was taciturn as usual, glancing the white of his eye at the listeners on either hand. He told us he was going to ride the gray colt Richmond in the Derby, and added nothing to that information, but we thought there was a great deal of eloquence in what he did and didn't say. The magnates of the turf fill the public eye, but to us Abe, albeit small and shrivelled, is a mighty man. The former are much like some giant or magician of the olden time, who set the populace agape, but really transacted his marvels by the agency of this little necromancer who followed humbly at his heels.

Color-obsessed as he was, George Wilkes showed Hawkins the sort of respect the jockey had only rarely experienced from whites in the South. Just as, a century ago, the American victory after the Revolution had loosened the grip a bit on African Americans, the dawn of Reconstruction after the Civil War would bring a few seconds of racial decency to white America. Of course, the black jockeys still had the additional comfort of knowing that the only colors that counted in those turns around the track were the ones on their backs. And now, in the red and white emblazoned on his scanty

FREE AT LAST?

torso, Abe Hawkins snagged the second Jersey Derby and "was much applauded" by the vast postwar crowd.

But shriveled? He was small and thin, meager even for a jockey, but nobody had ever called him that before. Was something wrong? If so, it was not likely that Abe would make it public.

He was the stable owners' favorite, too. The hilarious William R. Travers himself now secured his services to ride the fabled Kentucky, in which Travers had acquired an interest, in the two-mile heats at Paterson on that same opening day. It would be easy to see Travers and Hawkins liking each other.

"W-would you ride Kentucky?"

"Y-yes."

More likely Travers would be calling over the reporters to tell them a story like the one about the time he and a friend were strolling past the Union Club in Manhattan. The man asked if the men he could see through the windows, enfolded in their giant luxurious chairs, were habitués of the club.

"No," said Travers, "some are s-sons of habitués."

ABE WON on Kentucky, of course, in that 1865 Paterson meeting. Then in August he won four more at Saratoga, in the midst of a gigantic postwar celebration at the Springs. It was the country's biggest party, and it lasted for six weeks—a whirl of banquets and balls, with Ulysses S. Grant and several other generals on hand, not to mention the three New Yorkers with the tallest piles of money in the country, Commodore Vanderbilt, William Astor, and Alexander Stewart, inventor of the modern department store. With the blowout at Saratoga, sports—which is to say horse racing, still the only national sport—leaped to New York's front pages, replacing the dried-up rivers of news from the front. After a trotting (or harness racing) "carnival" in July, there were fifteen thoroughbred races over six days in August, including the second Travers, the first Saratoga Cup, the Saratoga Stakes, a "hurdle," a now rare four-miler, and a spectacular six-horse contest that went to seven one-mile heats—and the press covered every inch.

So Abe was not the only victor. Gilpatrick won five during the same meeting, including the Saratoga Cup, although his fifth was a "walkover," meaning he was unopposed and had only to walk his colt (this time it was Gil on Kentucky) around the course to collect the winnings. And Sewell beat both Abe and Gil in the Travers, becoming the first African American to win that venerated fixture. But the excitement that the two veterans delivered was something else. The *Spirit* captured it in a report on a minor race of two-mile heats:

"The display of jockeyship was very fine. Gilpatrick was quiet as usual, but his spurs were never out of Arcola's sides. Abe was all legs and arms. His whip curled all around Fleetwing, he shook him up with the bit in the English style. . . . There never was a colt that could stand more driving than Fleetwing; there never was a more resolute driver than Abe. Inch by inch they gained. . . ."

But Gil still won that heat, and the next. He used the still prevalent English seat with a slight American modification, the beginning of a crouch. Abe, more bent over, was known for a firm hold on the head yet an appearance of complete comfort. "He sat a horse with ease, and rode with remarkable judgment." A Saratoga morning is perfection, yet Hawkins improved upon it. "The chestnut horse Rhinodine was a great favorite with Abe," a turf authority would write, "and we do not remember anything finer than his early morning gallops before the Saratoga Cup."

By that Saratoga summer of 1865, this thoroughly modern athlete had learned something Gilpatrick hadn't, something his speech impediment didn't restrict in the slightest: talk to the press. One reporter wondered why Abe hadn't made a run for it in those two-mile heats and then added: "But Abe is a good judge, and he told us between the heats that it was very hard work for Fleetwing to run on such ground." He built a reputation for being friendly with reporters, trainers, and owners, always keeping it at a high professional level, never the showboat. Not that George Wilkes, the *Spirit of the Times* editor, wouldn't have minded a little showboating. Wilkes seemed to sense that Hawkins could contribute something new to the exploding phenomenon of national sports:

he could be a "star," although the word had not yet been minted for that use, or he could develop an "image," which was even further from coinage. Wilkes took to calling him "the Black Prince," or some version of it.

Abe Hawkins became—not merely the first African American athlete to win lasting popularity in both the general and sporting press—but the most beloved athlete in America. He was the second best known athlete, after Gilpatrick, but still, after all those years Gil had acquired almost no public persona, no "image" at all. A master technician, he just won races, and apparently would go on doing that forever. On the other hand, Hawkins became an intriguing enigma and a figure of enormous dignity, although it sometimes displaced as little as eighty-seven pounds.

He had something else that was lacking in many of the other athletes—not to mention their bosses: a combination of brains and leadership ability. When the chestnut Fleetwing faced Burgoyne's bay, Captain Moore, in three-mile heats on the fourth day of racing during that Saratoga blast, the public was told that "a grand council and 'pow wow' had been held at Fleetwing's stable between young Bush, Old Abe and [trainer] Uncle George and after much cogitation, it had been decided to make the race a cracker from the start and, if possible, cut down the bay." And they did, demolishing Captain Moore, and more than that: "Fleetwing has added immensely to his reputation by this race." This joining of minds to produce valuable results, Hawkins knew, was what the sport was about at its highest level. And the raves kept coming. When Abe and three-year-old Baltimore edged Gilpatrick's filly in another contest, at a mile and a half, Bennett's *New York Herald* marveled on page one, "The run for the last fifty yards was most brilliant, 'Old Abe,' the rider of Baltimore, by his masterly skill landing him a winner by a neck."

Having supplanted New Orleans as America's sporting capital, Saratoga offered a "great display of fashionable ladies, who seem delighted with the capital racing that takes place." The *Herald*'s man added, "The ladies' stand is the most beautiful of its kind in the country." Actually there was no ladies' stand; the women had simply taken over the grandstand. And they were dressed grandly, indeed: decked out by the ateliers of Lyons in postwar splendor. The painter Winslow Homer sketched them swathed in yards of fabric. It wasn't easy to outdress the jockeys, however. "Gilpatrick in the orange and crimson of Mr. Hunter, mounts the bold Kentucky, whose fine appearance and grand air impress the ladies," fancied a male covering the Cup. "Abe, resplendent as some prince of Ethiop, in the green and gold of Mr. McGrath, vaults into the saddle of the red horse Rhinodine. Young Burgoyne, in the corn color of Mr. Watson, springs up on Captain Moore, and away they go . . ."[12]

While Homer was catching the carnival in the grandstand, photographer Matthew Brady and his men, also home from the front, captured the action in front of it. Another artist was on hand at Saratoga, exhibiting a portrait of Lexington: the ubiquitous Edward Troye. Among other diversions was the de rigueur ride to the lake, the only place in the world where you could nibble the treat

As sketched by the great Winslow Homer,
the Saratoga crowd watched Abe, Gilpatrick, and other standouts
at the 1865 season celebrating the end of the Civil War. Courtesy of author.

concocted by the black jockey Abe Speck's son, George: "shavings of potatoes."

However, neither Abe nor any of his African American friends would have been allowed in the Saratoga grandstand that summer—if they had wanted to be—despite the fact that black athletes and black trainers were providing much of the talent, and black grooms much of the labor, behind the biggest national sports festival yet. This might sound like a modern observation, the modern response being, "That's the way things were." But Horace Greeley's was not as lazy as the modern mind. This imbalance was exactly the objection of his *New York Tribune*, far ahead of its time then and now, and the *Tribune*'s special correspondent was not going to let this pass without front-page comment. Noting that America was still too pessimistic about what human beings could accomplish, the correspondent—sounding like Greeley, the future presidential contender, himself—had this to say: "I should mention as a symptom of this era, when the capacity of the human races [is] to be demurred, that half of the jockeys are the blackest Africans, and I have yet to learn that their color interferes with their fitness for this most responsible business. One of them, who passes by the soubriquet of Old Abe, is highly spoken of as a judicious jockey. The same democracy of feeling does not extend to the spectator's galleries, for an addendum to the Programme says: 'Colored persons not admitted to the stand.'"[13]

Certainly there were no "colored persons" in Homer's renditions of the Saratoga grandstand. Judging from the need to ban them, however, there must have been a lot of African American spectators on the grounds, in addition to the many black jockeys, trainers, and grooms. A later program, for a day at the races in 1868, carries no addendum banning African Americans.[14]

The *Tribune*'s observation—that about half the jockeys were black—also indicated a slight increase since the wartime meetings. More African American riders were making their way to New Jersey and New York, joining those already there. As was already becoming commonplace, first names dotted the cards in 1865: they included Albert, who was one of the best of the newcomers, Erastus, Tommy, and Ephraim, and in 1866, Dick, Archy, Aleck, Alexander, Alphus, and Rock.

Greeley's *Tribune* was not the only journal to observe the hypocrisies of racial barriers following the war. *Wilkes' Spirit of the Times* got a question from a reader about the supposedly more gentlemanly sport of harness racing. "Has a Negro a right to drive?" the reader asked. Apparently, an African American, or African Canadian, had tried to enter a trotting race at Hamilton, Ontario, in 1866. The reader wrote: "There never has been instance in the West where they permitted one to drive; and when he got into the wagon or sulky, the public hooted him down." The reader then made a bet with somebody that even if the black driver had driven and won, he couldn't have been declared the winner for betting purposes, because "in all gambling transactions, customs make the rule." And then he went home and sat right down to write George Wilkes's paper, asking if it agreed. It didn't.[15]

"You have lost your bet," the editor answered. "Custom has nothing to do with it. A man has as much right to employ a negro to drive a trotter as to ride a racehorse, and if a negro did drive and win, the owner of the horse would have just as good a right to the money as he would if [the celebrated white driver] Hiram Woodruff had driven. Does any man with a pennyweight of brains think the less of Charles Littlefield or Gilpatrick because they ride against Abe or Albert or Alexander's Dick?"

But Greeley, or his man at the Springs, had still more to say after watching Abe beat Burgoyne's Captain Moore in three heats totaling nine miles, and black or white had nothing to do with it. He didn't like what human beings were doing to these animals. A newcomer to racing, like most others in the North, where for the most part it had been banned for six decades, he was aghast at what was happening to Abe's and Burgoyne's mounts, especially "the tremendous pressure upon their poor bounding flanks after two terrible miles at the top of their speed," which left their speed "visibly slackened" as they finished the third mile. He noted that this was followed by "forty minutes spent in cooling and washing and scrubbing down the poor panting beasts" before they would start yet another three miles. Then he added: "One cannot but reflect upon the cruelty of spurring these beautiful animals into a foaming and exhausting speed as a matter of sport. Perhaps it is necessary that the speed and bottom of our stock should undergo such severe ordeals, much as students are fitted to fatal tasks that great thinkers may be reared, but one cannot grieve that such excellence is attended with so much cruelty."

The *Tribune* grieved alone, however, as "Fleetwing, ridden by Old Abe, came in at a canter." Of course, many questioned whether all this was ever about improving on nature. As one commentator pointed out, "Anybody who supposes that this species of amusement has anything to do with the improvement in the breed of horses is capable of believing that prizefighting has for its object the improvement of the breed of man."

Whatever the object, Abe and Gil continued their battles through the fall of 1865, Hawkins adding the featured St. Leger Stakes and another at Paterson in the fall, while Gilpatrick took four there. Next year would be different.

A WARM, hazy April day comforted the once-supreme and now-revived New Orleans Jockey Club as it opened its 1866 season. In the two-mile dash, said a local paper, "the superior skill of *Rousseau's* rider showed itself, and he seemed fairly to lift his steed ahead." The winning athlete, in purple, was none other than "the renowned jockey, Abe, a black boy, formerly owned by Col. Kenner (for twenty years) and who still clings to his old master now that he is free. He is probably the best rider on the continent, is a dwarf in size but well formed and 'knows the ropes like a book.' We make these remarks for the benefit of strangers, for all frequenters of the Southern turf know Abe."

What the reporter did not understand was that the North knew him now, too, and the idea that this famous former slave was still clinging to Kenner was merely a magnolia-and-moonbeams fantasy. June found Hawkins back in New Jersey, where the New York press was kept busy following both America's Derby and the efforts of African Americans to organize politically.

MEETING OF THE COLORED MEN
A meeting of colored people, Rev. John Peterson presiding, was held last evening, at their church in Sullivan-street, for the purpose of discussing the best means to be employed to secure to the colored people the right of suffrage.

The June 6, 1866, *New York Times* also reported, in the very next column, exactly adjacent to that notice, "The veteran Abe, by long odds the best colored jockey in America, was on Richmond, as he had been when he won last year's Derby." Before the year was out Abe would finally prove that he was not only the best colored jockey in America but the best jockey—period.

The race just before the 1866 Jersey Derby was not a bad start. Abe and Richmond beat three white boys, the up-and-coming Charlie Littlefield, Patsy Hennessy, and Gilpatrick. Then came the Derby itself. Storm clouds hung low over what the *Times* called "the great three-year-old event of the American turf," although the *Herald* conceded that New Jersey's grand moment had not yet acquired the importance of the English Derby. Abe was on Merrill. Gil was on King Lear. Also in the nine-horse field were three more comers: Dick, the young black rider (about sixteen) from Kentucky, not yet known as Ed Brown; Bobby Swim, a white boy from Missouri; and Albert, on Enchantress.

To go straight to the Derby finish, the *Times* reported that Remorse, with McClary up, "came with a rush through his horses, cut down Ulrica and Enchantress, and made a determined effort to reach Merrill, but Abe stalled off his challenge and won one of the most exciting races ever witnessed." Like the rest of the general press, the *Herald* was more color-conscious than the sporting papers, which had known for years that color had nothing to do with it. "It required all the cunning of that artful darkey Abe," said Bennett's man, "to bring the colt just under the string."

The jockeys had plenty of fun. America now had its first regular sports calendar, and everyone went down the new turnpike to Hoboken for the next race meeting. There, trainer Bill Bird had a hell of a horse to show Abe and young Dick. He was a powerful six-year-old named Climax, and Bird had Abe put him through a two-mile workout, an easy run that was supposed to be done in four minutes. But Climax, as usual, cut loose and couldn't be held back, breezing the distance in 3:48½. "When he was stopped, Abe had no feeling in his hands and arms, and declared that he wouldn't ride him for less than $100, win or lose," noted the *Spirit of the Times*. It didn't sound like the mild-mannered Abe of old, and it was also a tip-off to how much money he was getting. Finally, Bird got Dick, "a strong and resolute rider," to board him for the two-mile heats, and they put a chain bit on the horse, but even then Dick couldn't keep Climax anywhere but way out in front. Hawkins was riding the gray Loadstone.

"The Black Prince set to work on Loadstone with catgut and steel. . . . Nevertheless, the heat was not in doubt, the gray could not overhaul Climax. . . . It was a great triumph for Bird, and as for Dick, the young rascal grinned excitingly over the defeat of 'Uncle Abe.'" Hoboken was never good luck for Hawkins. The next day, when everybody thought Loadstone and Abe had edged out Richmond, with Dick up, in the first two-mile heat, the judges said it was too close to call, that the heat was dead (hence, the term "dead heat"), and Knightbridge, with Patsy Hennessy aboard, went on to take the race.

When a reporter showed up, Hawkins snapped: "Y-you must win by two lengths here or else they c-can't see it!"[16]

Next came the third Travers Stakes at Saratoga on July 24. Saratoga thought the Travers, not the Jersey Derby, had become the most important three-year-old event in America. Which was the greater prize was a matter of debate. It didn't matter this year, since Abe and Merrill won them both. But Abe's biggest 1866 victory was yet to come.

———

HAWKINS WAS at the moment better off than Duncan Kenner, but Abe had not forgotten his former "master." Many years later the trainer James McCreery would remember: "I met the great Negro jockey Abe . . . who I saw reduce for five days to scale one hundred pounds, and his food I doubt was a pound a day. . . . He always dressed nicely and used clean language." In addition to Hawkins's manners and professionalism, McCreery recalled something else about him.

> He succeeded very well, rode and won many races, es-
> pecially at Saratoga. One day at Saratoga Abe saw in the
> race paddock a gentleman whom he recognized as com-
> ing from New Orleans and a friend of Mr. Kenner's. He
> sought out an opportunity of speaking to him and said:
> "I know, Sir, you are from New Orleans and are ac-
> quainted with Mr. Duncan Kenner. I hear he has gone
> back there. Do you ever see him?"
> "Yes," the gentleman replied, "I see him rather often."
> Then said Abe, "When you see Marse Duncan, will
> you please give him a message from me? Tell him I have
> ridden a great many races here in the North and have
> made right smart of money. It is all in the bank and it is
> his if he wants it, because I am just as much his servant
> as I ever was."
> The gentleman returned to New Orleans, met
> Mr. Kenner and gave him Abe's message. Mr. Kenner said:
> "Are you going back to Saratoga?" "Yes I am." "Then,"
> said Mr. Kenner, "look up Abe and tell him I thank him
> very much for his offer; that I do not need the money; and
> add that my plantation has been restored to me and that
> Ashland is as much his home now as it ever was, and when
> he wishes to return there he will be welcome."[17]

This and many of the other glimpses of Hawkins in the press challenge a later story from a prominent sporting editor, who claimed, speaking of a man Abe often rode for: "Mr. McGrath looked out for Abe's pecuniary interests, the latter being little more than a child in relation to anything but horses."[18]

Abe was just the sort of gold mine H. Price McGrath would try to control and claim credit for. In their New Orleans days, McGrath was a partner in the wild city's biggest gambling joint, on rue Carondelet, not far from Kenner's town house. When the Federals took over during the war, McGrath moved to St. Louis, then to New York—with a few prison stints in between—finally hooking up with the retired boxer John Morrissey, becoming a partner in the latter's gambling operations and an official at Saratoga. McGrath soon owned one of the best horses in the country, Tipperary, and was indeed helping introduce the North to Louisiana's best rider. Abe had come in second on Tipperary in the first Derby and in the first Travers. But he rode for many others, spoke his mind, set his price, and generally demonstrated both the independence and intelligence that put him above and beyond McGrath's grasp, mental as well as financial.

ON SEPTEMBER 25, 1866, in the stands high above the new Jerome Park, sat the nation's savior, General Ulysses S. Grant. Given his services, one newspaper thought that his initials could have stood for United States or Union Saver Grant, Unshackle Slave Grant, Unabated Siege, Unadulterated Saltpetre, or Use Sambo Grant. He was presiding over the opening of America's next major sporting venue, inspired by Saratoga and built in Fordham, New York, near what would become Jerome Reservoir in the Bronx. Leonard Jerome, seeking to become the sportiest man in New York and pretty much succeeding, had unloaded half a million greenbacks on the place, along with some strange designs.[19]

The grandstand, which in one of its several sections managed to contain the large and tainted corpus of William "Boss" Tweed—and nine thousand others that day—was perched high on a hill above the course. The Anglophile Jerome had the track laid out in

This Harper's Weekly *engraving of the 1868 season opening day at Jerome Park in New York did not identify the jockeys, but the best of both black and white jockeys competed there. Courtesy of author.*

a figure-eight, apparently not wishing to ape his lowly fellow Americans with their uninteresting ovals. These might democratically offer all a view of the whole proceedings, but they were otherwise quite tedious. Besides, the general and everybody who was anybody could see everything from the clubhouse hill.

"The moment has at last arrived for the horses to start," reported the breathless scribe for Greeley's *Tribune,* "and as they are led out on the course, with their parti-colored jockeys, clad in all the colors of the rainbow, there is a universal cheer from the throng."

No American athlete had ever seen such a day as this. Abe, Albert, Gilpatrick, McMahon, Foley, and J. Gray paraded to the post for the first race before the eyes of Grant and twenty to twenty-five thousand others—or at least before the eyes of those who could see. America was still decades ahead of the time when more progressive authorities would decide that blacks and whites could not compete together, and nearly a century ahead of the day when it would be proclaimed, erroneously, that Jackie Robinson had just "integrated" American professional sports. They had been "integrated" for two centuries when Abe and Albert and Gil and the others rode their thoroughbreds to the post.

The press was there to document the opening. Greeley's man: "A tap of the drum, a wild cheer, the jockeys apply whip and spur, the horses stretch out their long necks, like pointers seeking game, there is a general cry from the multitude: 'They are off, They are off. . . .'"

The *Times:* "Sweeping round the foot of the bluff on which the Club House is situated, the horses were lost to sight. . . . Abe, on the favorite, now began to creep up, but reserved his final effort until they had fairly entered the straight, when he shot past his horses. . . ."

Hawkins, or as another witness put it, "the solemn face and figure of Abe," won the mile-and-a-quarter dash. Or to put it into perspective, the conqueror of Lexington, the greatest Southern jockey until the Yankees arrived, the victor in the second and third Jersey Derbies and third Travers, had now added the opener of the biggest day yet in modern American sports.

After the race, many in Jerome's paradise then retired to "the refreshment saloon." Here they found that "such choice beverages as lemon-soda, lager, Bourbon, and S.O.P. could be had at fair California prices—also, lunch." Those Americans knew how to take a lunch, as the *Times* made clear. "Jolly little picnics pervaded the place—atmospheric vapors became laden with congenial cognac, gay old rye, cool claret, bully Burgundy, cold biscuit, appetizing tongue, cut chicken, apple pie, old and lively cheese, every thing that appetite could crave or experience suggest—not to forget champagne and cigars."

But as they were drinking their lunch: a commotion.

> The word was passed that GEN. GRANT was coming down the hill, then that he was on the track, then that he was inside the course fence . . . and as the modest General came to the steps of the grand stand, Dodsworth's

Band struck up "See! The Conquering Hero Comes," while the people rushed to see, and the others clapped their hands in unisonic demonstrations of delight. . . . The great concourse of people who had waited patiently about the stand until he should appear gave him three hearty cheers, which he acknowledged courteously and then turned to be presented to Mme. RISTORI, who, under the skillful convoy of the great GRAU, was in attendance. We did not learn whether the conversation was in Italian or French, but the result was that GRANT accepted an invitation to attend Mme. RISTORI's performance of *Mary Stuart* this evening, which so affected GRAU that he at once telegraphed the fact to all the newspapers in the country.

Ulys had not brought his wife, Julia, to the track.

Parked about the grounds were vehicles of a luxury Americans had never seen before. The *Herald* spotted "stanhopes, broughams, four-in-hands, landaus, barouches, sulkies, double teams. . . . Here is a four-in-hand modeled at Auteil after the example set forth at Longchamps, brought over three thousand miles of ocean highway without a stain on its tuckered surface at a cost of $8,000."[20]

The next race was the feature of the day, the Inaugural Stakes at four-mile heats. With General Grant now up in the clubhouse section trying to watch—"but the fact is that he cannot move without somebody bellowing after him"—along came "the jockeys in the colors of their chiefs. Charles Littlefield, in the famous coin color and crimson sash of Mr. Hunter, mounted *Kentucky.* Young McClarry, in the canary of Mr. Watson, sprang into the saddle on *Onward.* The Black Prince of Riders, Abe, looking more than commonly solemn, backed the old mare [Idlewild] in the blue jacket and white cap of Mr. Alexander. And Sidney Smith in the new broad blue and white stripe of Mr. Jerome took *Fleetwing* to the post."

As the *Times* put it, Idlewild, who had beaten Abe's and Lecomte's four-mile mark of 7:26½ by a quarter of a second, now had the advantage of Abe himself—"that consummate artist in the saddle . . . and her numerous backers felt assured that all that jockeyship could effect with her would be done." But her nine years told, and she faded in the fourth mile, finishing too far behind the "distance pole" to qualify for the next heat.

The unusual result was that Hawkins would be the only jockey to ride two horses in the feature. Leonard Jerome himself, the man of the hour, made the call. His own Fleetwing had not done much better in the first heat, finishing third, so Jerome dumped his jockey, Smith, and replaced him with Abe, whom he had seen in action for three years now. As a turf authority would say of Fleetwing, "We have seen that renowned horse come very near losing a race with a lot of duffers, solely for want of Abe to get him out." Naturally, every serious bettor in Jerome Park noticed the switch. The *Spirit of the Times* said, "Abe is the only rider that has ever got *Fleetwing* thoroughly out, and when he appeared in the blue and white stripe, the faces of those who had laid odds [against Fleetwing] fell."

The switch didn't work, though, as even Abe couldn't make up the difference against Kentucky in the next heat. Abe did collect the thousand-dollar second-place money for Jerome, who immediately set about buying Kentucky. To celebrate his new purchase, Jerome had Kentucky's portrait painted right there on the spot. The short, robust artist, his blue-gray eyes sparkling, his neat beard bristling, was, of course, Edward Troye. Jerome also lifted his twelve-year-old daughter, Jennie, onto the illustrious son of Lexington; it was an experience she never forgot and may well have described, in later years, to her son, Winston Churchill.

The next day, there was more racing at Jerome Park—as well as a glimpse of the future in Philadelphia. There, thirty thousand people showed up as the home team Athletics met Brooklyn's Atlantic Club "for the championship of the United States." The game started well. A reporter noted, "The betting all day before the game commenced was very brisk. The Brooklyn men came out with plenty of money and fairly bluffed their opponents off in betting." The crowd got a little unruly, though. "CRANE was next to the bat but before he had a chance to strike, the game was stopped to allow the crowd to be cleared from the left field. Fully half an hour was taken up in the effort, but as soon as the crowd were put back on one side they pushed up on the other." The police couldn't control them, so they finally decided to postpone the game.

At Jerome Park Hawkins went on to win the next big feature, the inaugural Jerome Stake, with Watson "pulling Abe nearly out of the saddle, so that at last he gave him his head." With that win, Abe crossed back over the Hudson to Paterson, New Jersey, to beat his black colleague Albert in the autumn opener there, with "a very fine piece of riding—a patient and masterly effort," as one reporter would put it. As for Gilpatrick, that year he won three races at Paterson but none at Saratoga and none at Jerome Park.

By now Gilbert Watson Patrick and Abe Hawkins had confirmed their position as the first two great athletes of modern American sports, which had dawned with these postwar meetings. At this moment, the end of 1866, Hawkins stood at the top, judging from his performances that year as well as the decisions of stable owners, the commentary of experts, and the judgment of the betting crowds. If the enormity of the voyage he had made from slavery days to 1865 threatened to overwhelm him, he seemed to have developed a consistent strategy to keep that monster at bay: to do his job, to take his profession seriously, to keep quiet unless it served some professional purpose but to not be afraid to speak up when it did, and to be, as by all accounts he unfailingly was, both loyal to his employers and correct in his manners.

To be loyal and correct may not seem like the proper strategy for someone who had seen what Abe Hawkins had, but then who would be qualified to judge? In any event, it was clearly his strategy. And if his and Gilpatrick's extraordinary accomplishments before hundreds of thousands of cheering Americans over the years have gone unnoticed by historians to this day, it is hardly the fault of the athletes or their fans.

When the news finally came that "Old Abe" had died, it was a shock to the sporting weekly *Turf, Field and Farm*. The obituary on

May 4, 1867, was brief but considered important enough to be second item on the editorial page—after a commentary on general news entitled "The Situation in Europe," which dwelled on threatened hostilities between France and Prussia. When the editor got to the subject that really interested the readers, he said of Abe: "For a quarter of a century, his name has been familiar to those who take an interest in equine contests." After Hawkins directed Lecomte to his victory over Lexington and later found his way north, his name became known to countless thousands more. The editor, with the usual obsession about color, continued, "All who have attended meetings on the turf in various parts of the United States for the past fifteen years will remember his swarthy face, his thoughtful air and his light figure."[21]

A week later, the other sporting weekly, the *Spirit of the Times*, waxed sentimental about some of the late Abe's post-Lecomte moments—prevailing over Panic, threatening Norfolk in the first Jersey Derby, winning with Fleetwing when nobody else could have, galloping through a lovely Saratoga morning aboard Rhinodine. Like Austin Curtis, the late Abe Hawkins was honored with a prominent obituary in the establishment press—not only once but twice. In fact, he did Curtis one better, by getting to read it himself. Shortly after the above two obituaries ran, the *St. Louis Republican* ran a slightly different story: "A Race Rider Reads His Obituary And Is Delighted."[22]

As it turned out, "the great American jockey 'Abe'" was feeling much better. "Abe owes his recovery from his severe illness to Duncan F. Kenner, his former master, who in the hour of sore affliction attended with parental care to the wants of the supposed dying freedman." The trainer James McCreery said later that in late 1866 or early 1867 Abe had come down with "consumption"—tuberculosis. Was that why he had looked "shriveled" when he won the Jersey Derby in June of 1865? Had the wasting away already begun? After his 1866 triumphs, which finally knocked Gil off his perch, Hawkins had returned, sick, to Ashland, where the equally indomitable Kenner was plotting his return to power, both as a Louisiana planter and on the American turf. For a while, Hawkins apparently felt well enough to plot his own return at the Buckeye Jockey Club's spring meeting in Cincinnati, which opened on May 27, 1867, three weeks after he was pronounced dead.

But less than two weeks later, on June 8, the *Turf, Field and Farm* had to run yet another item, its crude language suggesting that the editors were exhausted by their own fiascoes:

> OLD ABE DEAD AT LAST.—We resurrected Old Abe last week, but send him to the charnel house again this week. A dispatch from Cincinnati informs us that he was taken with a relapse during the Buckeye Meeting, and sank rapidly into the cold embrace of death. Having read his obituary himself and enjoyed it much, he could seek the mysterious shadow land with greater satisfaction than a majority of persons do. We are now assured that the death of the celebrated jockey is no longer doubtful. . . . It would appear that in the first heat of his contest with Death, Old Abe successfully jockeyed his formidable opponent, but in the second heat was distanced by the grim phantom. Peace to his weary old bones.[23]

Peace to the weary old editors, too. Abe really had died this time, and at least with a smile on his usually solemn face. Like those of Simon, Cornelius, and Chisholm, his had been one of the most remarkable of any American athletic careers of any period. Not even counting the antebellum years—such as his victories aboard Lecomte, Arrow, Whale, and other Southern champions—Hawkins, in just a fraction of his career since 1864, had won twenty-five races totaling seventy-nine miles, many of them the country's most important events. His best tribute, in the end, was that first obituary in *Turf, Field and Farm*, edited by the great turf authority Sanders D. Bruce. It said of Abe Hawkins: "As a rider and jockey, he had no equal in the country. . . . He was a master in his profession. . . . The death of Old Abe is an irreparable loss to the American turf."

He is said to have been buried by the Ashland training track, under a live oak tree.

Oliver Lewis rode Aristides to victory in the inaugural edition of the Kentucky Derby. Courtesy of Kentucky Derby Museum.

·7·

THE AMERICAN
SPECTACLE

"THE ORANGE-CLAD BOY"

AND THE KENTUCKY DERBY

1867–1878

F REE, THE BLACK jockeys would soar to startling heights—so startling to the white establishment that it would soon no longer accept them at the top. Slave and brilliant in an athlete was one thing; free and brilliant was quite another, a clear and present danger, a blatantly democratic threat. The black jockeys began to pose that threat in the postwar years as America's only truly national sport exploded, staging spectacular competitions (including the first Kentucky Derby in 1875), inaugurating even bigger and better venues, entertaining vast crowds of workaday urban Americans—becoming, in short, an industry.

At about age twenty, Dick, the recent slave, commanded Kingfisher in the 1870 Belmont Stakes at Jerome Park. Spotting a sneak attack at the finish, Dick responded with a cut of the whip to go under the string first by half a length. The Belmont is the oldest of the three races that would be dubbed America's Triple Crown (after the English Triple Crown, which by then already existed and consisted of the Derby, the St. Leger, and the 2,000 Guineas). This first jewel of the American triple was named for August Belmont, banker and president of the Jerome Park racing association, a group that expansively entitled itself the American Jockey Club, although it was merely a New York City–area jockey club, albeit the richest in the country. White riders had won the first three editions of the Belmont: Gil won the inaugural in 1867 on Ruthless, Bobby Swim the second on General Duke, and Charley Miller the third on Fenian. Charley was not to be confused with his lesser-known namesake, who was helpfully described in a footnote to one race chart: "The C. Miller who rode CORSICAN was a colored boy."[1]

Dick, the Belmont's first African American victor, had by then been riding for five years in the North; one of his notable early victories was in 1866 when he rode the powerful Climax and demolished the mounts of Abe, Albert, and three white boys. Dick continued riding for the powerful combination of Robert Alexander, his former slave master, and trainer Ansel Williamson until 1867,

The jockey Joe Colston, painted by Edward Troye,
holds the reins of the great Enquirer, owned by Abe Buford
of Kentucky. Courtesy of a private collection.

when Alexander died and his nephew, Daniel Swigert, took over Woodburn Farm. When Dick won the Belmont it was under owner Swigert, who by then had established his own stable under a new trainer, Raleigh Colston, who, by developing Kingfisher, became the first African American to train a Belmont champion. As for Dick, the jockey was getting chunkier and couldn't make the weight for the Travers in the summer of 1870, so they put the white Charley Miller on Kingfisher and won. Dick would switch to steeplechases, which typically allowed loads of 145 pounds, and by 1874 he started training for Swigert under his legal name, Ed Brown.

Later in the summer of 1870, Kingfisher would be bested by Enquirer at another new track, Monmouth Park in New Jersey, which had opened to siphon more of the New York masses who couldn't get enough of peace and sports. Enquirer was piloted by the Kentuckian Joe Colston. The horse's owner, Abe Buford, was so delighted with Enquirer's role in helping to baptize America's newest sporting facility that he had Enquirer's picture painted by the apparently immortal Edward Troye. Mercifully, Troye was spared the agony of attempting to draw Colston astride, instead showing him holding Enquirer by his bridle, a white bulldog at his feet.[2]

Enquirer, as the painter noticed, had a bunch of white spots on his reddish-brown rear, having once enquired into a nest of wild bees, and he ran like they were still after him. As a two-year-old, he ruined the debut of the soon-to-be-legendary Longfellow and would end his career by capturing the first Kenner Stakes at Saratoga, Joe Colston up. But why "Enquirer"? It had nothing to do with that bunch of bees. Owners, long aware of the importance of tradition in sports, were always naming something after something—so this champion was named after the great Cincinnati newspaper, Longfellow after the living poet, and the Kenner Stakes after the late Abe Hawkins's old "master," Duncan Kenner. Kenner, by the way, had bounced back. He had restored his sugar plantation and was now a regular at Saratoga Springs, holding fast to his high silk hat and the airs of a Southern "gentleman," as if nothing had changed.

Poor Joe Colston must have had his hands full with his employer. Abe Buford was an officer at the Battle of Buena Vista in 1847. Having dubbed his Versailles, Kentucky, farm Bosque Bonita (Pretty Forest) in memory of Mexico, he set about making life a haunted bosque for his Bluegrass rival, Robert Alexander, over at Woodburn Farm. Once, when Buford defeated a Woodburn horse at Lexington, he "lay down in the middle of the track and wallered like a dog," it was recalled.

"He hollered so loud everybody on the grounds could hear him. 'I beat Alexander! I beat Alexander!' I don't reckon anything did him any more good."[3]

In the Civil War, he became a Confederate cavalry general, riding with another mental case, Nathaniel Bedford Forrest, one of the future Ku Klux Klan founders. Apparently it ran in Buford's family. Abe's younger brother Tom thoughtfully appealed a Kentucky court decision against him by shooting and killing the judge, after which Abe spent much of his Bosque Bonita racing winnings trying to defend Tom, finding peace at last by committing suicide. Just like Dick, Joe Colston could have told some stories.

THE BLACK jockey known simply as Albert was just a baby, three months old, when he was purchased, along with his sick mother, by David McDaniel of Virginia for $150. By 1871 he had beaten the two best boys around, Gilpatrick and Abe Hawkins, and had won at Hoboken, Paterson, Saratoga, and Jerome Park. But like Dick, he had gotten too big for flat racing and switched to the popular steeplechase racing—the jumping events.[4]

Albert was dark-skinned, "as black as the ace of spades," said a New York reporter, as white as the joker. As Albert might have noticed yet again when he was riding at Saratoga one Friday in July 1871, the pot wasn't really melting. The hotels were full of the news, arriving in urgent telegrams from Manhattan, about Irish Catholics attacking both Irish Protestant marchers on the Orangemen's July 12 holiday and the marchers' protectors, the police and the army.[5]

"A general war is impending," screamed one of the telegrams.

"Fighting in Fifth Avenue. . . . The Eighth Regiment fired on," the reports said.

Albert's own reaction, if he had one, has not been located, but the piazza population was panicking. It was estimated that three-quarters of them were from the New York area. "Men rushed about the piazza shouting the terrible announcement and there was a rush of pale-faced people to the telegraph office. . . . The . . . word 'horse,' which had been all day the absorbing theme, seemed to have disappeared from the vocabulary." One count of the dead in the Orange Riot put it at forty-six civilians, two soldiers, and one policeman.

But the Irish fighting wasn't the only ethnic confusion. Absorbed in their front pages, the wicker-chair set also read of the Franco-Prussian War of 1870–1871, noting that the German forces were withdrawing from the neighborhoods north and east of Paris. In New York, there was a mass meeting at the Germania Assembly Rooms, which had nothing to do with Germany. The meeting had been organized to plan a celebration of Italian unity, and it featured the reading of letters from the Hungarian Club, an Irishman, and a Cuban organization, all applying to join in the festivities.

Nor did the ethnic flashes stop there. On one front page, adjacent to "The Saratoga Races," was a bulletin that an Indian chief had been sentenced to death by the military in Texas. Another bulletin, next to the betting pools on the second race, brought the latest on Chiefs Satanta and Big Tree, who had been captured at Fort Sill and sent to Austin. They had just escaped, freeing themselves from their shackles "by gnawing the flesh from their hands and feet, but were discovered and shot dead." The New York papers also took note of the upcoming Saratoga lacrosse match "between the champion red men of Canada and the champion white men of the world."

Neither could a reader ignore the updates about a white man traversing Africa in hopes of learning more about the black man's continent, unaware that he would only run into another white man. Or, as the latest from London put it: "Dr. KIRK, of Zanzibar, writes that Dr. LIVINGSTONE is still in the country west of Tanganyika, and the Arabs there count him a resident. In that region no ill-feeling is manifested toward him. He is moving slowly but safely, and will leave no doubts in the geographical problem, whether Lake Tanganyika is the real head of the Nile, or if it empties by the Congo."

ALL THIS was Albert's world in 1871. He must have had some interesting thoughts about how the world was changing, and how it wasn't. Here was a former slave, still working for the Virginian who had "bought" both him and his mother, entertaining some of the wealthiest ladies and gentlemen of the land. In July, on the day of one of the big steeplechases, "many of the ladies wore the brightest of colors, elegantly arranged, and sported the Club collar and killing necktie. Others were encased in tight-fitting jackets of velvet, blue and black, skirts of deep scarlet silk, and in their hair were golden trinkets of unique design and elegant finish." The steeplechase itself was the highlight of any race day, "exciting interest by its romance and novelty among ladies and outsiders as well as among those not pecuniarily interested." At one point, a "tendril of beauty," said the *Herald*, "jumped upon the cushion seat, and shouted, with bubbling eagerness, 'Oh Tammany, can't you win? Why can't you win?'"

But the chestnut Tammany would lose to one of the great jumpers of the era, Oysterman, not only on that July day but again four days later, both times with Albert riding and the tendril's bubbling notwithstanding. On yet another day, in August 1871, as the exquisites in the grandstand urged them on, Albert and Oysterman led the way "over the ninth, tenth and eleventh obstacles, which were a hedge, a water jump and a hurdle"—finally winning by two lengths.

The romance of the steeplechase was all in the stands, however. For Albert and the other riders—who were often owners as well, this being the branch of the sport where the gentleman jockeys not only survived but thrived—it was extremely dangerous, as they rode unprotected and unhelmeted. Four days later, for instance, Oysterman was doing all right in the hurdles, but another horse hit a barrier and threw his rider. In another event, the jockeys turned into acrobats: "The animals sped along merrily, causing any amount of excitement among the spectators, even the ladies sharing in the enthusiasm of the moment. The rider of *King John* was thrown over his horse's neck as the leap on a wall and a ditch near the judges' stand was made, but the little jockey quickly recovered and resumed his saddle amid wild cheering. *Astronomer* made a similar miss and disabled his rider, when another jockey leaped upon the startled horse and finished the race. *Milesian* also threw his jockey, who imitated the rider of *King John*."

We have a few words from Albert himself. They appeared in the *Commercial Advertiser*, a New York newspaper. The interview by Melville Landon began with a note that readers, then as now, could appraise for themselves. "Major McDaniel, who is a plain, blunt old Virginian, fairly worships the boy, who in turn looks upon the Major as the very Caesar of the track." The reporter asked Albert how long he'd been with the McDaniel.

"Don't know. Reckon it's going on twenty years," Albert replied.

"But Albert, you're not twenty years old."

"Well, I'ze done been with Major Mac all my life. Sometimes down in Virgin, and sometimes up at the Paterson track—then over to Nashville and Memphis."

Albert probably had no choice but to stick with his employer once freedom, if that's what it was, arrived, and he had no choice but to act as though he liked it. As Landon concluded: "Like Artemus Ward [the humorist], whose daughter had been singing the 'Mocking Bird' for three weeks, Albert thought he should like it—living with the major."[6]

What the journalist missed, however, was that Albert had reclaimed his family name, and, more than that, by his extraordinary talents he was making it famous. In the official charts of the races, as published by the *Spirit of the Times*, his family name now suddenly appeared alongside those of the nation's other top equestrian athletes. It was Welch. Albert Welch. First on Oysterman on July 13, first on July 17, first again in August: Welch, Welch, Welch. For Albert it was a small step toward full recognition and equal consideration in a world where he was now technically free—but we have no record of how he felt about it.

THE TOP jockeys at Saratoga that summer, including Albert Welch and Bobby Swim, were among the first Americans to be dubbed "stars," or rather "star athletes," the word as yet being employed only as an adjective (it would be a century before journalists would start overusing it as a noun). As Landon reported, "Belmont and Harper have been figuring for the star jockeys for the Kingfisher-Longfellow race tomorrow." The "race tomorrow" was the 1871 Saratoga Cup, "the grandest race which has ever or will ever take place on this continent, and a race on which will be staked untold thousands."

Exaggerating was perhaps America's real national pastime in those years. At one time, "the greatest race ever" only occurred every decade or so, but now it seemed to come every year as the exploding country felt its muscles. For the Saratoga Cup, the celebrated white jockey Bobby Swim would ride Longfellow. Kingfisher would be guided by Jake (also called Billy) Palmer, an exercise boy on Long Island, where August Belmont's Nursery

Saratoga Race Course, the leading sporting venue in the country, as it appeared in 1874 in an engraving by Albert Berghaus for Leslie's Illustrated Newspaper. *Courtesy of author.*

Stud was located. The contemporary records are not clear on whether this Palmer was white or black, but to Belmont, who had purchased Kingfisher after the colt won the Belmont Stakes with Dick in 1870, it did not make much difference.

"Who is to ride the Fisher?" Landon asked Belmont.

"Why—Jake, the smartest boy in the world."

"Who's Jake?"

"Jake is an Island boy. . . . I got him pardoned out of the House of Correction. Don't you know Jake? . . . Jake . . . is the brightest boy on the track. I've got twelve different boys, most of them from 'the Island,' but Jake can steal them all poor. He has the best whip, the best spurs, and is sure to steal the best place on the track."

Belmont made it clear that Palmer knew how to win teammates and influence trainers. "Jake divides with the boys, and they like him," Belmont said. "Last summer he stole two pet chickens from my trainer, and the next day the little rascal presented him with one of *his own chickens all dressed!*"

The natty August Belmont, his white hat and silver feather attracting attention in the grandstand, was quite the little rascal himself (it went with his side job of chairing the national Democratic Party), but there was nothing this power broker could do once the white flag dropped and Jake and Bobby took off. Longfellow flew by Kingfisher like an arrow, turning in the fastest American mile yet—1:40—on the way to capturing the two-and-a-quarter-mile Saratoga Cup, to the applause of ten thousand spectators.

After the race, the reporter Landon asked Longfellow's owner, "Uncle John" Harper, "Who have you got training this $60,000 worth of horse?" Harper replied, "Oh, my darkey boys take care of him—they're good boys. I raised 'em, too—on the farm with the horses. The boys like the horses, and they get on well together. I bought old Jake [not the jockey] there for $1,500 from Dr. Shelby in Kentucky, but I think *as much* of him as I do of Longfellow."

After the race, said the *Spirit of the Times*, "'Uncle John,' as he is universally called . . . tottered along, leaning on his cane and shouting directions to the negro boys who were grooming the victor."

Despite cantankerous Uncle John's reluctance to share the credit, Longfellow did have a professional trainer. He was an African American named Mose.[7]

The Old South hadn't died in the racing stable, which had become a cocoon that now hid its occupants from an outside world of newly won rights—just as it had once shielded them, if only temporarily, from the external horror of slavery. In the stable area behind the main course at Saratoga, the Old South still ran thick as molasses. The *Herald*'s man peeked in on Thomas W. Doswell's stable very early one morning in that summer season of 1871, unwittingly providing a sample of what the black jockeys had to take:[8]

> The happiest specimen of the black group was the orange-clad boy of yesterday that rode Ecliptic to victory. The bright costume had gone. Barefooted and with clothes considerably the worse for wear, "toted" all the way from Virginia and lacking much of the picturesque, he lay half asleep, with his head in the doorway of his "master's" stable and feet elevated upon a water pail just beyond. It looked as if he had offered the white-worn bottoms of his feet as a flag of truce not to be awakened, and his expressions denoted that he was satisfied and enjoyed the hallucination of being comfortably undressed in bed.
>
> Life to the young contraband that instant was pleasant and seemed to have been arrested, in his case, not exactly as it was in the Palace of the Sleeping Beauty, for I discovered but little picturesqueness in his slumbers, and I did not believe any beautiful young princess would ever want to wake him with a kiss.
>
> The dull waiting silence brooding in the atmosphere was soon broken. The phantasmagoria of sleeping jockeys, rubbers and stable boys was changed to a scene of activity. A remarkable looking black hero, with his wool spread thin and fine over his skull, reminding me of the crisp black moss which grows on rocks,

emerged from Buford's stable, and showing his rows of white teeth, twinkling a pair of bright eyes and looking as if he wished for breakfast, this veteran placed his huge hands to his mouth in a conch shell shape manner and spluttered out a noise like the monotonous clank of gig wheels. It was the stablemen's "reveille to the morn." Then my orange-clad boy of yesterday was wide awake, and soon all was excitement.

Once again the traditional press wallowed in the crime of the day. The man in the orange uniform had a name, of course. It was Gibson, as the official charts reveal, though they do not give first names. The historian wants to repeat it. Gibson. There it is at last, in the ancient "stats," listed with the other champions of his day. A name, attached to the highest honors of his profession.

THE BLACK jockey John Sample rode Longfellow in the next year's "greatest race ever," or the greatest pair of races, since there was a rematch. To quote the *New York Times* headline on the second race, it was "The Greatest Contest in the History of the American Turf."

The first confrontation was on July 2, 1872, with forty thousand working people converging on shiny new Monmouth Park in New Jersey. To be sure, there was the usual smattering of aristocrats, some arriving by special railcar from the South and also from the Philadelphia area, some rolling in by luxurious carriage from northern Jersey. But most of them were laborers, especially rail and oil workers, and salesmen and store clerks; more than half reached Monmouth by steamboat and train from New York City. Of course, by this time horse racing wasn't the only American sport, but the second national pastime wasn't doing particularly well that day in 1872. On a Brooklyn baseball field, the hometeam Atlantics were back at it against the New York Mutuals, but the game drew only three hundred people. The nine-city National Association of Professional Base Ball Players, formed only the year before, was already on its way to falling apart.

The star athletes that day were "Uncle John" Harper's John Sample and David McDaniel's new boy, Jimmy Rowe. The crude McDaniel was not shy about advertising his biases, having christened a black filly Black Slave (her dam, Greek Slave, had been named for whites in the same predicament), but at least he was quite catholic in his exploitations. Jimmy, for example, was white. When McDaniel spotted him in Richmond five years earlier, the boy was ten years old, working at a newsstand, and exercising horses for the Exchange Hotel's livery stable. So here was another in the ancient American tradition of competitions between a black and a white athlete—such as that "boy of Chamberlaine" against Thomas Cocke in 1677, that anonymous "sable rider" and Willis, Cato and Stephen Welch, Abe and Gilpatrick, each time meeting on equal terms.

Jimmy's mount, the chestnut Harry Bassett, was the heavy favorite, at about two to one, according to the strange new betting machines from Paris. At about the same time that bookmakers arrived at American tracks, in the early 1870s, pari-mutuel betting arrived as well—though many today think pari-mutuel betting, which has become the standard, was a twentieth-century innovation that improved on bookmakers. The first system of organized betting on American racing, however, was neither the pari-mutuels nor the bookmakers but the "pool" system. The latter system still existed, so bettors had three ways to lose their money.

Only big spenders could afford the old "pool sales," which were auctions. The only way to get a bet down was to bid—that is, shout—for a ticket on your favorite horse. Constantly having to top other offers, you might have to bid—scream—three hundred dollars to get the ticket on Longfellow, while someone else would have to roar "One hundred!" to get the ticket on the less-favored Harry Bassett. The total pool, or the amount bid on all the entries, divided by the highest bid on each, would reveal the odds on each horse. That same total would go to the holder of the winning ticket, minus a 3 percent commission for the auctioneer. To accommodate all those who wanted to bet, the latter would "sell" as many of these pools as he could, at the track and at a local hotel on the nights before the races. Henry James, the precious Bostonian who was horrified when things started getting too American and who therefore became the idol of American Literature professors, was of course shocked by hotel auction pools, like one he saw at Saratoga Springs. "A noisy auctioneer, in his shirt and trousers, black in the face with heat and vociferation, was selling 'pools' of the races to a dense crowd of frowsy betting-men." (Henry would flee to England but would make frequent triumphant reappearances in American book-review sections.)[9]

Another betting system—bookmaking—had been in action as early as 1840 in England and soon crossed the Channel to France. There was no bidding with bookmakers. They simply offered tickets—redeemable slips of paper—of various amounts to bettors, at whatever odds the bookmaker chose to offer at that moment, take it or leave it.

About 1868, a Paris perfume seller, Pierre Oller, decided to leave it. Quite unsatisfied with the odds he was getting from the French bookmakers, he invented a third system of betting. It was something of a combination of the old pool sales and the bookmakers. Like the latter, he sold tickets to all comers, but what was new was that everybody paid exactly the same amount for a ticket, no matter for which horse and without regard to the odds. Thus the total amount bet on a horse was really a mutual bet, a *pari mutuel*. As in the old auction pools, the total amount wagered by all of Pierre's customers, divided by the total bet on a horse, would reveal the odds on the nag. And all the holders of the winning ticket, those who came up smelling the sweetest in Pierre's *parfumerie*, would split the money in the total pool, minus a commission for Monsieur, *bien entendu*. The French racetracks lost no time in copying the idea. And they installed simple adding machines to keep a running tab on both the total pool and the pools on each entry, thus providing the odds.

Et voilà! Le pari mutuel!

Introduced at Monmouth Park, the French machines took democracy to a frightening new level, just as the French Revolution had (*Mon dieu!*). When would it all end? Monmouth offered absolutely anyone a ticket on any horse for five dollars (the standard price at the beginning), which clearly implied that ordinary Americans had a right to gamble, just like rich Americans and poor Frenchmen (*Quel scandale!*).

"It is somewhat astonishing," said George Wilkes' *Spirit of the Times*, the sporting weekly, "to see how rapidly these pools are increasing in public favor," proving "that a much larger part of the community is interested in horse racing." Most that day bet their five dollars on Longfellow. So now everybody was throwing their money around while, in the side action, the tobacco magnate Louis Lorillard laid a thousand dollars on Longfellow. Naturally, wide-open gambling increased the pressure on athletes, who—it was widely assumed, often correctly—were available for purchase. One man walked up to Longfellow's jockey with a fifty-dollar note. "You win," he said, "and you get this." John Sample merely smiled, and then he went on to take the two-and-a-half-miler by an astounding margin of nearly two hundred yards. "Longfellow is now crowned king of the turf," crowed the *Times*.

Harry Bassett and Longfellow reconvened in the Saratoga Cup, Rowe and Sample up again. "Never, perhaps, in the racing history of the Saratoga or any other track has such a scene been witnessed." As the saying went then, "there was no daylight between them" for the whole two and a quarter miles. Nobody paid much attention to the third horse, John Morrissey's Defender, or its rider, a man pushing sixty with the odd nickname Gilpatrick. Nor did many notice that when the horses got off, Longfellow twisted his near forefoot, bending the plate, or horseshoe. Rowe and Bassett kept inching ahead, Sample and Longfellow kept catching up, finally moving in front by a head after the first mile, the crowd going wild. "The men are hoarse with shouting, and the ladies shout with them." It was Bassett by a head going into the backstretch for the last time when suddenly Longfellow faltered— lurched. Did some old-timer there remember Grey Eagle?

"Longfellow's beat!" Morrissey shouted.

But the black jockey John Sample "called on him," somehow pulled even with Bassett, the pair hitting the two-mile mark faster than any horse had run two miles anywhere in the world. Down the stretch they came, "at a pace unknown on the Saratoga track," Sample whipping Longfellow, the big animal responding, but then faltering again, in terrible pain, his plate (though nobody knew it) doubled over and embedded, his forelegs spreading. "The excitement knows no bounds," said a reporter. "The policemen endeavor to make the people keep their seats but without avail." Standing in his stirrups, Sample flogged Longfellow. Again the animal responded and closed on Bassett. And with Longfellow fighting, wobbling, fighting, they went under the string together, but with Harry Bassett the victor in a record 3:59.

"The colored jockeys and trainers yelled like maniacs, tumbled over one another, and fought to get to the judges' stand," said the white *New York Times*, sounding like the *Turf Register* at New Orleans three decades earlier, and like the British visitor at an American quarter race a century earlier. Longfellow limped to the judges'

John Sample on Longfellow leads Jimmy Rowe on Harry Bassett in this Currier and Ives portrait of one of the great thoroughbred rivalries of the century. Courtesy of Historical Society of Saratoga Springs.

stand, too, on three feet. Later the *Spirit*'s correspondent found him in his stall. "He stood in his box, holding the foot on its mangled edge, and as each visitor came, he would turn his large eyes upon him and then drop them to his foot, as if asking sympathy for his misfortune. Old John Harper sat leaning on his stick, with the big tears trickling down his face."

Longfellow never raced again. He and Harry Bassett, Sample and Rowe up, would be portrayed by—guess who? The popular engravers Currier and Ives.

THROUGH THE 1870s and early 1880s, the big stakes events in Maryland and New York were not dominated by African American jockeys, but by the English. Led by such immigrants as Norwich-born George Barbee, they all but owned the second-oldest jewel in the future triple crown, the Preakness Stakes, which was run at Pimlico Race Course, near Baltimore. The unusually short (even for a jockey), unusually powerful Barbee won it three times, starting with its inauguration in 1873, plus the Belmont Stakes, plus back-to-back Travers, racking up an exceptional winning rate of 27 percent in some 490 races in this country. So perhaps the Irish and the Scots weren't Britain's best horsemen, after all; maybe it was the English, especially if they hailed from Yorkshire, where a man once bragged to his first-born son: "My boy, I must tell thee that I was never done in a horse deal but once, and that was by a Scotchman who throwed me off my guard by saying grace over a gill of whiskey."[10]

In Yorkshire, where "the women fry ham all day, and the men drink ale and talk about racehorses all night," Cyrus Holloway was put in the hands of a horse trainer at age ten. When his four-year indentured apprenticeship was up, this York-born slip of a child—he could get down to eighty-four pounds—went to America, where in the late 1870s he wound up winning the Preakness twice and the Belmont once. His compatriot, Lloyd Hughes, did even better than Barbee in America's most renowned sporting events, tripling in the Preakness and doubling in both the Belmont and the Travers from 1875 to 1880. Then there was England's George Evans, who also claimed an early Belmont, and the sensational Billy Hayward, one of the first to come out, taking the Saratoga Cup as early as 1868. Thus, the English riders were much favored by the big Northern stables, where they reinforced the white boys who had supplanted Gilpatrick at the top, notably Bobby Swim and Jimmy Rowe, winners of two Belmonts each.

The greatest stage of the black jockeys at this time was Kentucky, especially Lexington—until May 17, 1875, the day the focus suddenly shifted slightly to the west, to Louisville.

"TODAY WILL be historic in Kentucky annals as the first 'Derby Day' of what promises to be a long series of annual festivities, which we confidently expect our grandchildren a hundred years hence to celebrate in glorious centennial rejoicings."

The confidence of the *Louisville Courier-Journal* would prove justified, to put it mildly. Now, 125 years hence and going into the twenty-first century, the Kentucky Derby is still one of the most moving public gatherings in America, in or out of sports. Its phenomenal on-site crowds of well over 150,000 people—something baseball and football and basketball can't dream of—still stand as one as they try to follow the local folks to the strains of "My Old Kentucky Home," a heart-tugging few minutes worth the race itself. At a venue almost void of physical charm, in a sport almost dead, one of the most magical moments in sports is still created around—what? An idea? A tradition? Hype? The best the sport can offer? Better to leave it a mystery. At the same time, however, as the Derby enters a third century, it is many furlongs behind the original in one aspect: the representation of African Americans in important roles.

The first Kentucky Derby—foreshadowed by the 1839 Kentucky sweepstakes matching Wagner and Grey Eagle—began modestly. It was certainly no more impressive than America's first derby, day eleven years earlier in New Jersey, with its huge New York crowd, raving press coverage, and guaranteed participation by the major stables. Yet it held considerably more promise than that 1864 derby in Paterson. Unlike New Jersey and New York, Kentucky knew right away that it had bottled something precious, something that it had always possessed, its identity. It was—and to those who look closely, still is—symbolized by the women of Kentucky, not only in the way that the states of the Old South crowned their reigning belles, but in the way that nation states coined a national woman, in the way that America, in eleven years, would put one on a pedestal in New York Harbor, even if she would spend the rest of her stone cold life trying to get down, proving that she wasn't from Kentucky. When the *Courier-Journal*'s rival, the *Louisville Commercial*, reminded everybody, "Kentucky is proverbial the world over for its beautiful women as well as fine horses," the compliment was graciously accepted. And when the women turned out in force that Monday, they were really more than a measure of commercial success; they were the most important part of the event. Kentuckians saw not only their new derby but especially the women there as a rare and valuable expression of statewide unity and pride.

"Until the close of this first day it has been the wont of our people to refer with glowing enthusiasm to the extraordinary aggregation of beauty which congregated at the Gray [sic] Eagle–Wagner contest of thirty-five years ago," said the *Courier-Journal*. "It would seem that no impulse, in the long interval since, so served to draw together the people of Kentucky; but we now have another great event."[11]

That first Wagner–Grey Eagle event had drawn about ten thousand people; so did this one. And just as editor William T. Porter had waxed on about the beauty of the ladies watching Cato ride Wagner to victory over the Kentucky-bred Grey Eagle, the *Courier-Journal*'s man at the first Kentucky Derby couldn't stop once he had started on their daughters. He led off his report with the crowd, with the results of the race taking a back seat.

> It was made up of every element; but *place aux dames et demoiselles* before the pen shall treat of another feature. It is much, indeed, when attention and admiration may be

diverted from the prime object which has gathered a great assemblage together, but not the Derby itself, with its absorbing interest and excitement, will linger as long in the minds of the spectator there, as the brilliant array, arranged in dazzling groups and lines, from the outermost limit of the stand full a hundred feet to the black mass beyond, which marked the half space set apart for the men, and in its serried parallels stretching up in twenty tiers back to the outer railing. Blondes and brunes there were, stately beauties and petite, matrons and maids, in such bewildering number as to daze the eye, except that the cumulative effect was striking and even glorious to such a degree as may not be seen twice in a lifetime. We dare assert that the most glowing description given to this feature of yesterday's gathering cannot be too extravagant to adequately picture the panorama, constantly shifting with its varied and brilliant colors, during five hours of the day. There were a thousand women there, each exemplifying in her own enchanting face that

> "Loveliness, ever in motion, which plays
> "Like the light upon Autumn's soft, shady days,
> "Now bare, and now there, giving warmth as it flies
> "From the lips to the cheeks, from the cheeks to the eyes."

Obviously, it was hard on the frontier. To this day, no great sporting event attracts as large and enthralled an audience of women as the Derby does. And only a Bluegrass belle could appreciate the compliment, quoted on that first Derby Day, that a passing horse trainer once paid to "a high-bred Kentucky girl" when he exclaimed, "By George, she looks like a thoroughbred Glencoe filly." After all, she was likely to know that the imported Glencoe was an incredible "filly sire," the progenitor of 481 children, of whom an astounding 370 were daughters, a good many of them champions.[12]

The ten thousand at the first Kentucky Derby were also inaugurating the Louisville Jockey Club and its new track on the old Churchill family land, to be dubbed Churchill Downs a decade later. "The stand is second in size only to Saratoga and will seat 3,500," the *Courier-Journal* boasted. The prices ranged from ten dollars to watch the finishes from the quarter (home) stretch to a dollar for the grandstand to fifty cents for the "field stand," or bleachers with not much of a view. Within a few years, admission to the vast infield, circumscribed by the track, would be free of charge, "both to people and wagons," and home to about two-thirds of the crowd. While the grandstand and quarter-stretch crowd represented "social life," one reporter noted, "the swarm of free visitors typified popular (including negro) life."[13]

Reviving one of Yelverton Oliver's dreams, M. Lewis Clark, grandson of the explorer William Clark, had organized the new Jockey Club, but the loudest presence, with his white hat and red ties, was the flaming Irishman H. Price McGrath, who had been John Morrissey's former partner at Saratoga and Abe Hawkins's self-proclaimed protector. McGrath was now loudly lording it over his home state. If there was something going on, McGrath was in the middle of it. Born poor, he was after success with a vengeance, and he was now creating a Kentucky racing stable and stud farm of his own, discreetly named McGrathiana, its manor house modeled, with equal modesty, after Saratoga's cavernous United States Hotel.

"For two and a half cents I was denied an education," said the bitter McGrath. As a boy, he had given a dime to a wealthy neighbor and asked him to bring home a spelling book from the city. Returning without it, the rich neighbor gave the boy his dime back, explaining, "The book cost twelve and one-half cents." Still trying to get that two and a half cents out of the rich, McGrath flew his green and gold on two entries in the first Derby, Chesapeake and Aristides. They were the favorites, too.[14]

"A dense, pushing and vociferous mass of excitable gentlemen" mobbed the little stands where the English-originated auction pools were underway. Next to them, in the enclosure reserved for the

"Paris Mutuals," as the new pari-mutuels were called by the local paper, the betting went on "in the quiet manner that this system appears to effect." Perhaps, since each pari-mutuel ticket was democratically priced at five dollars, there was nothing to talk about; only plenty to worry about as the nervous buyers considered their options. Today vast lines of anxious bettors line up for their moment of truth at the pari-mutuel windows in uncharacteristic silence, as if they are about to make their confession. This religious silence is almost total at the automated machines, where they don't even have to talk to the priest at the window. Gone forever is the sweaty display of humanity that so shocked the effete Henry James, the shouting, shoving, shirt-sleeved auction pool crowds. But through the rest of the nineteenth century, the old yelling crowd and the new queues of pari-mutuel bettors coexisted at the Kentucky Derby and elsewhere. There was also plenty of side betting. "Cigars, champagnes, silk hats and suppers were won and lost ad libitum."

On that first Derby Day, a single ticket in the auction pools on either Chesapeake or Aristides was bid up to $105 (then as now, two horses entered by one owner were bet as one, a "stable entry"). McGrath's strategy was to use his little red sprinter Aristides as a mechanical rabbit to exhaust the others, leaving the durable Chesapeake to run them over; if McGrath had any side bets with individuals, he had his money on Chesapeake.

Opening the day's entertainment was a three-quarter-mile sprint by a field of six of all ages. The English rider Billy Lakeland, on Bonaventure, staved off another white boy, Bobby Swim, on Hutchinson, to win the inaugural dash in front of the one thousand white belles with the best seats in the house. But when fifteen three-year-olds—thirteen colts and two fillies—pranced out on the track for the second race of the day, the very first Kentucky Derby, the preeminence of the black jockeys at Louisville was obvious. It was pretty much an African American parade to the post, with William Henry on Chesapeake, Oliver Lewis on Aristides, and black riders on most of the others as well; the white jockeys, Lakeland, on the filly Ascension, and Cyrus Holloway, on Enlister, were a tiny minority. Faced with incomplete records, most historians have guessed that Lakeland was the only white rider, resulting in countless regurgitations of the impressive but erroneous line: "Fourteen of the fifteen jockeys in the first Kentucky Derby were black."[15]

So there they were, pounding down the stretch toward the belles, Oliver Lewis pulling with all his might on Aristides so Chesapeake could take over, but Aristides refusing to cooperate, wanting to run. And in the spirit of Willie Jones, and Andrew Jackson, and the Napoleon of the Turf, Price McGrath didn't just sit in the clubhouse and watch. Let a man who was watching tell it: "Lewis, on Aristides . . . seemed to take a pull on his horse, expecting Chesapeake to come in and take up the running, but where, oh where, was Chesapeake? . . . Fortunately for the favorites, McGrath was near the head of the stretch, and taking in the position of all at a glance, waved his hand for Lewis to go on with the good little red horse and win if he could all alone." Aristides "dashed under the wire the winner of one of the fastest and hardest run races ever seen on a track. The time made, 2:37¾, is the best for the distance ever accomplished by a three-year-old with 100 lbs. up."[16]

Here, then, are the horses and their jockeys, the first five in their actual order of finish, the rest listed simply as "also-rans" in the next day's reports and the earliest official records.

THE FIRST KENTUCKY DERBY, MAY 17, 1875

Entry	Jockey
Aristides	Oliver Lewis
Volcano	Howard Williams
Verdigris	Dick Chambers
Bob Wooley	William Walker
Ten Broeck	Monroe Kelso
Grenoble	James Carter
Bill Bruce	M. Jones
Chesapeake	William Henry
Searcher	Raleigh Colston Jr.

Ascension	William Lakeland
Enlister	Cyrus Holloway
McCreery	Dick Jones
Warsaw	Peter Masterson
Vagabond	James Houston
Gold Mine	Cornelius Stradford

For the $105 ticket on Aristides in the auction pools, a bettor got $495. Along with the winner's purse of $2,850 for the first Derby, Aristides's owner got a $1,000 sterling silver punch bowl to add to the wonderful awfulness of McGrathiana. The winning trainer was none other than Ansel Williamson, the former slave who had also captured the first American derby at Paterson, New Jersey, in 1864 and had joined McGrath after Robert Alexander died.

What happened to some of the black jockeys who rode in the first Kentucky Derby? Oliver Lewis got a place in history—and no footnote, at that—although he would be denied acknowledgment by most sports chroniclers of the next century and a quarter. Along with the most historic victory in American racing, Lewis and Aristides nearly added the Belmont Stakes at Jerome Park in June 1875, despite the fact that McGrath was just using his little red as a rabbit again. This time, knowing his colt, Lewis pulled even harder than he had in the Derby—pulled and pulled, in fact, until the crowd finally shouted, "Let go that horse's head!" Lewis didn't let go, though, and McGrath's Calvin, with Bobby Swim up, won as intended, the owner collecting thirty thousand dollars in bets. McGrath did prefer the more experienced Swim, so it was Bobby who rode Aristides to victory in the important Jerome and the Withers Stakes in New York. Lewis was said to have become a bookmaker in later years, and he was on hand to watch the 1907 Derby.

The third-place pilot in the first Derby, Dick Chambers, took the other important trophy of the six-day inaugural meeting, the Louisville Cup on Thursday, May 20, and before a much bigger crowd than had attended the Derby on Monday. For the Cup, elegant carriages filled the infield and the crowd totaled 15,000 to

20,000. "Mrs. Grundy's Louisville Letter to the New York Graphic" allowed as how, when they were liberally toasting the Cup winner, Balankeel, and his owner, they forgot to include somebody. "The jockey, who was as black as coal, should have come in for his share of refreshments." It was nice of Mrs. Grundy to notice, but she didn't bother to mention Chambers's name. A white gentleman jockey, however, did come in for his share of the refreshments the next day, when an undying American sports tradition had one of its early enactments. President Clark formally presented Trigg Moss with the Gentleman's Cup, for his victory on Misfortune, "and completed the ceremony by pouring the champagne over his head."[17]

African American jockey Raleigh Colston Jr., who navigated Searcher in the first Derby, would become a very prominent trainer and the owner of the third-place finisher in the 1911 Derby (deservedly named Colston). His father had trained the 1870 Belmont Stakes laureate, Kingfisher.

WILLIAM WALKER would turn out to be that first Kentucky Derby's most celebrated name. A son of slaves, he was born in 1860 in Woodford County, Kentucky, the records disagreeing on whether it was at John Harper's Nantura Stud or on Abe Buford's Bosque Bonita farm. Billy was already riding at Jerome Park by the time he was eleven, under contract to an owner named Wood Stringfield, and he claimed a stakes victory at thirteen. In a sign of great things to come, he won the admiration and affection of M. Lewis Clark and the Louisville crowd the day after the first Derby. In a race that day, Billy Lakeland, on the outside, had moved toward the rail, crowding one horse against another and forcing Walker's mount, Excel, to run against the fence, "tearing away several palings and nearly throwing his rider." It happened in full view of the crowd. "It was a perilous moment for Walker, half off of his horse and crowded against the fence, but he was a gallant lad and riding a gallant horse, and although his leg was severely bruised, with true nerve he recovered and started off after the leaders," the

Commercial reported. Billy closed a gap of nearly two hundred yards to come in second by only half a length.

The *Courier-Journal* said Billy had the women swooning when the fence palings were torn off "and the little black rider was pulled from his seat. There went out to him from every woman's throat a suppressed cry of sympathy and alarm, while the men held their breath in suspense. But the brave mite of a lad clung to the main and saddle while his horse plunged for a moment, then he was in the saddle again, with teeth set and torn clothing and bruised limb." When Excel finished a close second, "there were plaints from every female throat that he was not adjudged the race for his pluck and his rider's bravely unsuccessful fight against misfortune. President Clark never found himself so little favor with the fairer kind as when he announced officially that Excel was only second in the contest. And, indeed, it was a beautiful bit of skill on the part of rider, and speed on the part of horse, which really won them the race, whatever the record." It was a publicity windfall for the new kid at the track. The fifteen-year-old was such a hit that he was brought out for a special ceremony in front of the crowd the next day.

It may well have been the greatest public honor yet for an African American athlete. The *Commercial* described the scene. "Walker was notified to ride Excel up to the judges' stand, and President Clark, in the name of the association, presented him with a beautiful silk purse containing $25 as a mark of merit for the bravest riding ever done on the turf. Seated on his gallant steed, the jockey raised his cap in acknowledgement, and with a modest thank you, sir, galloped away around the turn. . . . There were hundreds on the grounds who would willingly have contributed to the purse had it been generally known that the presentation was intended." The *Commercial* dubbed Billy "the bravest jockey of them all."

On the last day of the meeting, the *Courier-Journal* noted that the horse Big Fellow, "let out by Billy Walker, his judicious rider" scored an upset "amidst the wildest cheers" of his backers, adding

that Walker "deserves much credit for his skill and judgment."
Once again, it was the black jockeys forcing the press to recognize
them. Obviously Billy was not merely the beneficiary of racial paternalism, or, more accurately, maternalism. But it was also true,
from before the days of Austin Curtis, that these athletes had long
since achieved the status of hero, even if it was not yet trumpeted
in the press every day. In fact, the *Courier-Journal* took a moment
to declare them heroes, a declaration doubtless inspired by Billy's
riding and incidentally a reminder of how common the American
seat had become. "The jockey on the winning horse is a hero," said
Kentucky's leading newspaper in 1875, "and he knows it. He lays
low on the pig skin. His knees press hard upon the shoulders of the
animal. His boots are pushed to the heels in the stirrups, and his
whip ruthlessly cleaves the zephyrs. Amid the roaring of the assembled thousands, his short, sharp 'Hoop-la' can be heard, urging
the thoroughbred on to glory."

The seventeen-year-old Billy Walker was on Baden Baden for
the third Kentucky Derby in 1877, a time when transportation by
horse was definitely the way to go. Labor trouble tied up the eastern and midwestern rail lines, leading to rioting in Chicago, terrorism in the Pennsylvania coal fields, the destruction of railroad
property around Pittsburgh, and the hanging of eleven "Molly
Maguires," the labor activists, or agitators, depending on whether
you worked on the railroad or owned it. But Dan Swigert's stable
wasn't having any labor trouble, at least not with this jockey.
Walker's contract paid him just $15 a month, but that was consid-
ered a good deal at the time, what with the perks that included
travel all over the East, the applause of thousands, and such
bonuses as an extra $50 for winning the Derby (Swigert got
$3,300). What few people knew was that Walker was also saving,
and scrimping, and quietly investing in real estate.[18]

Swigert, the former manager of Robert Alexander's Woodburn
Farm, had an up-and-coming trainer, Ed Brown—the Alexander
jockey formerly known as Dick, who was now literally making a
new name for himself. So for the second time a black jockey and

black trainer had won the Derby. Of course, this winning combination dated far back into the antebellum South and had been seen in thousands of races, but with the Dick-Colston combo taking the 1870 Belmont, then Lewis-Williamson taking the inaugural Kentucky Derby, and now Walker-Brown the third Derby, the black contribution to America's first sport was shining on a national level. Billy Walker was also developing a very healthy ego.

The Manhattan plutocrat William Astor bought Baden Baden and sent him to Monmouth Park, where he won the 1877 Jersey Derby with Walker. As Billy would remember it years later, Astor engaged him to ride all the colt's races that season, but when Astor was in England Walker's trainer dumped him for a recently arrived Newmarket boy, Tom Sayers (son of the famous English boxer). Astor cabled the trainer to countermand the switch. But Billy, already temperamental, refused. Would they never learn? He would have added the Travers, which Baden Baden won under Sayers.

Billy's career also included a number of memorable trips aboard one of the also-rans in the inaugural Derby, Ten Broeck, named for the New Orleans impresario.[19] In the years following the 1875 Derby, Ten Broeck became a legend: he lowered Fellowcraft's four-mile mark to 7:15¾, and the mile to 1:39¾ (among other records), and he won five of eight starts at age three, all but one at age four, and all of his races at age five. In 1877, the Congress of the United States even adjourned to catch a glimpse of Billy and Ten Broeck in a race. Not that it was anything new for the government to halt for a horse race. When John Tayloe, famed for his beautiful residence, the Octagon House, and his blooded horses, entered his steeds at the Jockey Club meetings, the halls of Congress emptied. At the track laid out in a field north of the city, as William Plummer wrote back in 1803, "persons of all descriptions, from the president and chief officers of state, down to their negro slaves . . . collected together, driving full speed about the course, shouting, betting, drinking, quarrelling and fighting."[20]

It is unlikely that then-President Jefferson unwound quite that much, but he did go to the track. Nor did anything stop members of Congress from getting to the races on big days in the Jackson administration in the 1830s. And while, by 1877, the puritans had permanently frightened sitting chief executives from venturing near a horse race, the House of Representatives did adjourn on October 24 for just that reason. The Senate didn't have to adjourn since it wasn't in session. An estimated half the population of Congress actually turned out, too, riding up to Baltimore and across Druid Hill Park to Pimlico, where ten to fifteen thousand ordinary voters were on hand as well.

The great attraction was a triangular match featuring the country's three greatest thoroughbreds at the time: Kentuckian Frank Harper's Ten Broeck, ridden by Walker; George Lorillard's Tom Ochiltree, George Barbee up; and brother Pierre Lorillard's Parole, under another white rider, named Barrett. Billy's beautiful bay Ten Broeck, with a star on his face, was far and away the favorite, but the animals did not follow the script. Ten Broeck and Walker paraded in front for two miles, only to discover Parole and Barrett whizzing by in the final half mile, outclassing the favorite by five lengths.

But it was another Ten Broeck outing that everybody in Kentucky remembered, a match against a famous California mare, Mollie McCarthy, on the following Fourth of July in Louisville in 1878.

"I hear you are going to throw this race," the president of the Louisville Jockey Club, the legendary M. Lewis Clark, said to his former favorite, Billy Walker. "You will be watched the whole way, and if you do not ride to win, a rope will be put about your neck, and you will be hung to that tree yonder"—he pointed to the tree opposite the judges' stand—"and I will help to do it."[21]

The eighteen-year-old tried to get out of the race, but Clark wouldn't let him. Throughout the first four-mile heat, the other jockey kept pinning Billy and Ten Broeck to the outside rail, which, of course, was nothing new to Walker. "Finally, I just got tired of his fouling," he said, "and I ran into the mare and knocked her out of the way." Mollie, exhausted, was distanced in that first heat and reduced to walking home, turning the ballyhooed East-West (or rather West–Far West) match into a failure that depressed Clark even more. His claim that Walker had been planning to throw the race was disputed by everybody in sight, including Ten Broeck's young black trainer, Harry Colston, the most convincing evidence being that Billy himself had a big bet on Ten Broeck. Apparently he didn't just scrimp and save to build up those Louisville real estate investments.

Isaac Murphy was one of America's first modern sports stars, known for his talents as well as his good looks. Courtesy of Keeneland Association.

.8.

THE RISE *of a* STAR

IKE MURPHY, "PROUD OF MY CALLING"

1861–1896

WHEN I WON, it was all right, but when I lost, and when not on the best horse," Isaac Murphy grumbled, "they would say, 'There, that nigger is drunk again.'" It was a bitter end to one of the greatest careers in American sports.

He was born Isaac Burns, on David Tanner's Pleasant Green Hill Farm in Fayette County, Kentucky, near Lexington. Guesses at his birth year have ranged from 1856 to 1864, with most early sources agreeing on 1861, and on New Year's Day. As luck would have it, Isaac was free. He was the son of James Burns, a bricklayer who enlisted in the Union Army at nearby Camp Nelson, on the Kentucky River, probably in mid-1864, when free African Americans began reporting to Nelson for training. Burns died there, in circumstances that have never been clear. His widow moved in with her father, Green Murphy, a bellringer and auction crier in Lexington, where she raised Isaac and a sister, making her living by doing laundry for several families. One of her customers was Richard Owings, who operated a racing stable with James T. Williams. Taking the very brief measure of the boy, Owings introduced him to Williams, the active partner, and Isaac was off to the races.[1]

He was put to work as an exercise boy, breaking yearlings, or vice versa. His first trip to the ground turned out to be an auspicious disaster: the thrower was a future threat in the first Kentucky Derby, Volcano. Next, with his mother's and grandfather's encouragement, Isaac became the pupil of Eli Jordan, a leading black trainer, who would later offer a hint for those who could not fathom this jockey's near perfection, how he became, as another authority put it, a machine. It went back to his work habits, instilled by his mother or grandfather and perhaps inspired, too, by his soldier father.

"Isaac was always in his place, and I could put my hand on him any time, day or night. He was always one of the first up in the morning, ready to do anything he was told to do or to help others. He was ever in a good humor and liked to play, but he never neglected his work, but worked hard summer and winter. *He never got the big head.*"[2]

At age fourteen, weighing less than ninety-five pounds, Isaac Burns rode his first race. It was at Louisville, five days after the first Derby, in 1875. Not only did one chart of the results call him "Barns," but he finished last, in fact was distanced, on Lady Greenfield. He was in good company, though, the other losers that day including Oliver Lewis and Bobby Swim, not to mention Billy Walker, who became Isaac's friend and would later say he taught him the rudiments of riding. In the summer of 1876 at Lexington, young Burns and the filly Glentina beat a two-year-old with a future, Baden Baden, and by September he was riding, and winning, as "Murphy," in honor of his grandfather. It was not going to be easy, however.[3]

In the spring of 1876, a black jockey named Ringo had been viciously jeered by a Lexington crowd for getting off to too fast a start on a three-year-old named Bazar, who, if he hadn't been tired so quickly, might have beaten Bobby Swim and four-year-old Aristides. "Look at that d——d nigger," said one man, "he running the life outen Bazar." Obviously, "damned" was the unmentionable word for the *Louisville Courier-Journal,* which ran the report on its front page, adding that the other riders "no doubt cursed the blacky who engineered Bazar for his folly as heartily as any of the crowd in the grand stand."4

But as the sport was rapidly expanding along with the rest of the country, good young jockeys, black or white, moved up very fast, and not only on horseback. Amazingly, less than a year after he became a Murphy, Isaac was making his national debut in the North, at mid-Victorian Saratoga in 1877, where he must have been astounded by the wealthy crowds that crammed Broadway and the enormous, end-to-end hotel piazzas. Isaac may well have heard of two major news items while at the Springs. Jews had been banned at the Grand Union Hotel, perhaps the biggest hotel in the world, in the country's first major anti-semitic scandal. The talk of the day, it was splattered across the *New York Times* and other papers. Isaac doubtless would have had his own opinion of the news, if he had had any time to pay attention to it. He would have also heard the other big news story: pool sellers had been banned by the state legislature in Albany in a fallout from the shocking sums that the Manhattan pool rooms had made off President Rutherford Hayes's disputed election. As laws long since had been mere technicalities at racetracks, the pool sellers thrived at Saratoga, not that this jockey was interested. Unlike Billy Walker, he didn't bet.

Newcomer Murphy rode into the Saratoga spotlight aboard the bay gelding Vera Cruz and against the giant Tom Ochiltree, the great George Barbee up—the same combination that Billy Walker, riding Ten Broeck, would encounter at Pimlico that fall, when the government stopped to watch. Here, Murphy and Barbee were neck and neck down the stretch, until the black kid surprised the crowd and "came home like a hurricane" to win. The late rush would turn out to be classic Murphy.

Before the year was out, Murphy also captured the Kentucky St. Leger at Louisville, the Breckinridge Stakes at Pimlico, and a

November encounter at Jerome Park, all on Vera Cruz. But the next year at Cincinnati, he drew a suspension—and blood, they said—for hitting a rival jockey with the butt of his whip. Isaac denied it, saying the other rider kept crossing in front of him, until his own mare, Classmate, got knocked to her knees, "but I soon pulled her together and was back in the race." It was "another boy, Link Gross," he said, who hit the plaintiff across the face after being jostled by him.

"Blood squirted on my shirt," Murphy said. "The officials looked at my shirt and disqualified Classmate. They also fined me $25 and suspended me for one year." In fact, he was reinstated several months later, after Gross, according to Murphy's friend and lawyer, L. P. Tarlton, admitted his guilt.[5]

THE TEENAGER took two giant steps in 1879. He was working for several owners now, including his original patron, Jim Williams, but especially for J. W. Hunt Reynolds, who presided over Fleetwood Farm in Kentucky. Reynolds would be his main employer for the next several years, and Mrs. Reynolds, refined and sympathetic, took a special interest in him, becoming another important role model, a molder of character and manners. Reynolds employed Eli Jordan, too, so Murphy was doubly grounded at Fleetwood. It was there that he climbed aboard perhaps the most important horse of his career, Falsetto. The superstitious said that Falsetto had something to do with the fact that Fleetwood's corn came out that year in Reynolds's colors, red and white. When Murphy leaped on the colt's back in the spring of 1879, he was still packing his winter weight of 130 pounds, way too much for anything but a light workout on an unraced three-year-old with only three weeks of training. It was an early example of the weight problem that would plague Murphy for the rest of his life. Nevertheless, he was told to put the colt through a strong mile. Falsetto, the son of Enquirer, overdid it, turning in a 1:49, impressive under the circumstances but frightening to Jordan, who eyed him sharply for several days, worried that he would break down from the test.

Then it was good-bye to spring training and off to the races again—specifically, the 1879 Kentucky Derby. Isaac drastically slimmed to less than a hundred pounds by May 20. At the start of the race, a colt named Lord Murphy charged to the front, but after a mile the other Murphy was flailing his whip and moving faster, on Falsetto, than anybody else; the other black jockeys in the race included Alonzo Allen, Link Jones, and John "Kid" Stoval. The Lord, under the white jockey Charlie Shauer, held on, with Isaac second by a length. A month and a half later, Isaac made up for that with what he would call "my most successful day's ride," taking all four races on the Fourth of July card in Detroit, including one on Jim Williams's gelding Checkmate, eventual captor of forty-one races (among them the Saratoga Cup, Murphy up).

But Isaac's first giant step happened two weeks later at Saratoga, when he rode into the national limelight on Falsetto in the 1879 Travers, deflating Belmont Stakes laureate Spendthrift under the white jockey Edward Feakes—and perhaps equally important for his career, being interviewed in the *Spirit of the Times.* To be quoted at length in a national publication was extremely rare for any athlete, few of whom, in any event, could have handled it with this precocious eighteen-year-old's aplomb. It also gave America an extraordinary look into the mind of one of its greatest athletes.

The interview occurred right after Falsetto's victory. "I spoke with Murphy, who rode him," said "Albion" (*nom de plume* of the *Spirit*'s racing writer). "He is a bright youth, and although his winter weight was over 130 lbs., he can, under the reducing process, ride at 105 lbs." He was under 118 for that Travers. "I inquired of him what were his instructions in the race."[6]

"I had no instructions, except that I was to win the race."

"With such instructions, do you not think you laid away rather far for the first mile?" The Travers was a mile and three-quarters, and Albion thought Murphy had held Falsetto too far back for too long—for a whole mile. Isaac replied by giving him and the country a lesson in advanced jockeyship. As quoted in Albion's stilted sentences, the youngster came off as all work, yet full of confidence and exceptionally bright and articulate indeed. His plan had been to turn the Travers into a race down the stretch.

"Well, I don't know, sir. I wanted a waiting race. I thought Spendthrift was the horse I had to beat. I did not know about Harold [who would finish third], but I believed that my horse could win from either of them if I could get the race put upon a brush down the homestretch." So he laid back, not only to conserve Falsetto but to hide from Spendthrift and Harold. "I kept away from them to keep them from becoming alarmed. I was always in striking distance, and you know when Spendthrift went away on the backstretch, I was ready for the move."

"Yes, that is true, but why did you go up to Harold and Jerricho at the half mile, and then fall away again?"

"I did not care for Jerricho, but while I thought Spendthrift was the dangerous horse, I wanted to go up to Harold to see how he felt"—in other words, to check him out, to see how he looked—"so I tapped Falsetto with the spur one time, went up to them, felt of Harold, found him all abroad, sprawling over the course, and saw he was out of the race, and I fell back to keep Feakes [on Spendthrift] from thinking I was at all dangerous." Of course, the Travers-day crowd didn't know that he was just feeling out Harold, so when he dropped back to go into hiding again, the cry went up:

"Falsetto is beaten! Spendthrift wins!"

To most spectators, a race was just a hell-bent rush from end to end, but to this new kid—who was suddenly seeming like a fabulous judge of pace—that 3:09¼ was all the time in the world. He turned moments into something almost like leisure, racing up, dropping back, feeling out the competition, adapting tactics, and keeping a sharp eye on his colt. He missed nothing that was important to know.

"Is Falsetto a free mover?"

"No, sir, not generally. He does not run on the bit." In other words, he did not usually grip the bit, the steel part of the bridle inserted between his teeth, and take off on his own, with no help needed from the jockey. But this time he did, "and ran better on it than I ever knew him. He held it till I hit him with the spur the first time. . . . He turned it loose as soon as he felt it, and never took hold of it again." The colt was turning the race over to the jockey, who of course preferred it that way. And Murphy continued his ruse, waiting patiently until the final turn. There he spurred Falsetto one more time and slipped to the inside of wavering Harold. It was a move that actually called for several split-second decisions.

"How did you get between Harold and the pole on the turn?"

"I didn't intend to go up on the turn, but when we started toward the stretch, Harold was tired and unsteady, and he leaned away from the pole and gave me room to go in. I thought it better to run for the position than to have to run around him, so I jumped at the chance and went up between him and the rail. I steadied my horse here for a moment to compel Harold to cover more ground on the turn, and beat him good, for he was very tired." Having beaten Harold on the turn, Murphy explained, as if all these decisions were being made over minutes instead of fractions of a second, "I laid there a little while and kept touching my colt with the right spur, to keep him from bearing out to Harold, and also to make him hug the pole." He knew his Falsetto. "He is a long strider and is inclined to lean out on the turns." So, Harold was out of it, an exhausted third. "Just before we got to the stretch I left him and went off after Spendthrift."

Falsetto shot past Harold "with such masterly ease," said Albion, "that the whole grand stand absolutely groaned with excitement." He tore into the stretch "as if propelled with the power of a steam engine," but the engine was Murphy, chasing Spendthrift.

"Where did you catch him?"

"Just after we got straight into the stretch."

"Did you have to punish Falsetto?"

"I kept the spurs pretty busy on him until I got to Spendthrift. Here Feakes drew his whip, and Spendthrift refused to respond to it, so I stopped and let Falsetto come along, but I kept urging him with the reins. He moved so strong that I did not have to punish him any more."

"The people fairly went crazy" as Falsetto took the lead, Albion said. As always, a huge block of that Travers crowd was jammed against the rail. "Yell followed yell as the mighty son of Enquirer and Farfaletta came with a mighty flight of speed toward the surging masses of humanity." Falsetto won by something less than three lengths. "I cannot undertake to describe the scene which followed. The air was rent with shouts of joy. Stable lads threw hats into the air."

"What is the best horse you ever rode, Murphy?"

"Falsetto is the best."

"How many races have you won this year?"

"I have had thirty-five mounts, and have won twenty-two, and made one dead heat." The kid was keeping careful track, and he was feeling expansive at the moment, as the cheers of the crowd echoed in his ears. "I had pretty good luck on the Fourth of July. I had four mounts at Detroit and won them all."

Albion gave him a tremendous boost: "Murphy is one of the best jockeys in America. He is very observant (as the above conversation shows) during the progress of a race, keeps a sharp lookout for danger, is quick to perceive the weak points of an adversary, and prompt to take advantage of them. He has a steady hand, a quick eye, a cool head, and a bold heart."

It was a triumph, too, for the black trainer, who considered this his best horse to date. "I was politely received by his trainer, the veteran Eli Jordan," wrote Albion. "'Old Eli,' as he is familiarly called, is very proud of Falsetto, and well he may be, for a better colt is rarely met. He deserves great credit for the skill he displayed in bringing his favorite to the post in perfect form. I declare that I never saw a more perfectly ordered horse. His flesh was firm, his action perfect, and his spirit and temper were both thoroughly preserved." Or as Jordan himself put it, after ordering a groom to lead Falsetto out in front of the stable for the reporter: "Now, sir, there is he. Pick out the bad point."

After his first giant step—capturing the Travers and national publicity—Murphy took another one of a different kind three weeks later, just before the Kenner Stakes at Saratoga Springs. By now the tradition of "pulling" a horse to let another prevail—as McGrath had tried and failed to do with Aristides in the first Kentucky Derby but managed in the Belmont—was frowned upon. Indeed, a new rule called for a "declaration to win," of all things. But just before the Kenner, where Murphy would again race against Spendthrift (this time under Billy Hayward), the teenager was reportedly offered enough to buy a Bluegrass spread for himself—if he would just pull Falsetto. It was a wholly credible report because a big bettor could earn an enormous amount from a Spendthrift victory. But when the Kenner Stakes arrived on a bright August day, Murphy won again. This time, he did more than just succeed in a big race.

He once gave some advice to another black jockey on the way up. "Stoval, you just ride to win. . . . A jockey that will sell out to one man will sell out to another. Just be honest, and you'll have no trouble and plenty of money." In 1882 Kid Stoval would win both the Spinaway and the famous Alabama Stakes at Saratoga.[7]

"JUST BE honest, and you'll have no trouble and plenty of money." In a profession that was rife with corruption, that was Isaac Murphy all over, to the point where he personally, by maintaining that example of incorruptibility at the top, contributed to the survival and success of the whole sport. Perhaps more than anything else, he was a man in total control of himself, off the track and on. Like Abe Hawkins, he was quiet, unsmiling, unshakable—a Sphinx, they would call him. It was as if he knew things others did not, which, of course, he did—not only those terrible things that every black man in America knew but others, such as how to ride a horse as nobody else could, black or white, and with almost frightening control. Trainer Jack Joyner would label him "the best judge of pace I ever saw."

"The black machine," one startled horse owner called him after witnessing Murphy's skills. As the *Courier-Journal* told the story, in 1885 stable owner Jack Chinn, in St. Louis with his horse

Ban Fox, asked Murphy if he could beat Bankrupt over six fur-longs, or three-quarters of a mile. Bankrupt was winning every-thing in sight.

"What can your horse go the distance in?" Murphy asked.

He was told 1:14½.

"If he can do that, I can win . . . because Bankrupt can't do it. I have watched the horse closely, and I believe if you head him off, he is a quitter."

The next day Chinn gave Murphy his instructions for the race. He was to do the quarter in 24½ seconds, the half in 49, the race in 1:14½. At that rate, in the jockey's opinion, Ban Fox would be sure to head off Bankrupt, who would quit. Chinn stationed himself at the quarter and his trainer at the half, and they were off. Bankrupt jumped to the lead by two or three lengths over Ban Fox, but the emotionless Isaac just sat there, straight up in his English "seat."

"Coming by me," said Chinn, "Bankrupt was still well in front and that black machine sitting on Ban Fox was sitting like a log. I glanced at my watch. It was just :49 to the dot. In the last quarter he closed up on Bankrupt, passed him and came under the wire an easy winner. I looked at the time when it was hung up. It was just 1:14½."[8]

It wasn't a fluke. "I tried him out many times," Murphy's friend, Billy Walker, recalled years later, "and he rarely missed guessing how fast he was going. That is something not one in ten of the present-day jockeys can do. . . . That is the reason one sees a trainer continually 'waving down' riders during a trial."[9]

While Murphy was bursting like a comet on the national scene that year, a certain legend was still going strong. Gilbert Watson Patrick—Gilpatrick—won a mile race at Baton Rouge in 1879. But three years later, at about age seventy, he succumbed to pneumonia after catching a cold at Jerome Park. Other jockeys died young. George Lewis, the black jockey who won the 1880 Kentucky Derby on Fonso, suffered fatal internal injuries in a spill three weeks later at St. Louis. He was seventeen.

———

IN THE meantime, where, in all of Isaac Murphy's success and athletic perfection, was love? It was a question that rarely occurred to journalists of the day, when celebrities were known mostly for their talents—and in most cases they actually had to have some to be celebrities. For instance, little was known of Billy Hayward's or Bobby Swim's private lives, just as before them the public had been satisfied merely with reports of Gil's and Abe's unending professional triumphs. Besides, what sort of life could a professional athlete have when he spent so much of it on the job? It was about this time that the *New York Sportsman* devoted two full columns of tiny type to all the rides of twenty-six-year-old Cyrus Holloway over the past dozen years, an amazingly full *curriculum vitae*, then concluded, a little sadly, "Cyrus is not married." But it encouraged the young man: "being a man of steady habits, he no doubt soon will find a companion for life, thus following the example of his countrymen— Hayward, Barbee, Evans, Hughes, etc."

Isaac Murphy didn't wait. In 1882, at twenty-one, he married the former Lucy Osborn. She was light-skinned, with reddish-brown hair, and was a beautiful woman. A year later they purchased a home in Lexington for five hundred dollars, a modest but solid Italianate house, with a hipped roof boasting one large corbeled chimney in the front and another in the rear, Flemish stone courses in the walls, a brick parlor bay window, and inside, a sign of plans to keep moving on up, an Italianate octagonal newel post. They became members of Lexington's first black Baptist church. Isaac and Lucy Murphy settled in quickly and made big, if undefined, plans for the future. Isaac ran an ad in the *Kentucky Livestock Record* in March 1883.

"I will make engagements to ride in the stakes for the coming racing season at Lexington, Louisville, Latonia, Chicago, and Saratoga. I will be able to ride at 110 (possibly 107) pounds." It worked, too. Among many other prizes, Murphy added the mile heats at home in Lexington, the Woodburn Stakes at Louisville, the Illinois Derby at Chicago, and the Grand at Saratoga. He and Lucy were going to do very well indeed.[10]

THE YEAR 1884 was another watershed year for the world. In England, modern terrorism began with an attempt to blow up the London Bridge and, almost as bad, the *Times*. In America, Republican candidate James G. Blaine's nomination for president infuriated the splintered Mugwumps, who then helped turn Grover Cleveland into the first Democratic president in twenty-eight years. And the nation's capital had finally, after thirty-six years of interrupted construction, completed its obelisk in memory of George Washington. Before they topped the monument off with an aluminum pyramid (the largest block yet cast from that then rare metal), the pyramid was exhibited in Washington and New York, where visitors would ask if they could step over it, so they could say they stepped over the Washington Monument. And it was a year that transformed the life of Isaac Murphy, who also stepped over an important peak, in fact several of them.[11]

Isaac started by almost not winning the Kentucky Derby in May. He was supposed to ride Buchanan, but having tried to steer the horse at Nashville the year before, he had had quite enough of that chestnut. Widely reviewed as a bad actor, the thing had bolted, run off, and generally refused to participate. Murphy insisted he wouldn't board him again, but the Louisville Jockey Club said he would, or be suspended for the entire meeting. The jockey gave in, and once more Buchanan was "fractious" at the start, as the chart would put it, but by then Murphy knew his animal. So he "saved ground" for three-quarters of a mile, and only then called on the rambunctious one, who suddenly broke into gigantic strides and delivered the Derby by two lengths.

Buchanan's African American trainer was none other than the lanky Texan Bill Bird. For Bird, an animal with an attitude problem was nothing. He had trained Ten Broeck's horses in England more than a quarter of a century earlier, had saddled Saratoga's inaugural champion, and had once had to deal with Crickmore—not only the turf editor H. G. Crickmore but the quadruped named after him. This colt's problem: He was a picky eater, or so everybody thought. But Bird knew that he wasn't really a gourmet at all; he

was a gourmand. He liked to eat, period—and his only requirement was the one common among gourmands: quantity.[12]

On a Saturday at Saratoga in 1881, Bird slipped a friend one
hundred dollars and told him to bet Crickmore in the Windsor
Hotel Stakes.

"But your horse is running against Hindoo, and he ain't been
beat," the friend was quoted as saying. Trained by Ed Brown, two-
year-old Hindoo had won seven straight.

"When Crickmore eats four quarts of oats, he can beat any
horse. He ate four quarts last night. Bet that hundred."

Trainer Bird's horse had trainer Brown's horse for dessert. The
Murphy-Bird combination was followed by another successful
African-American duo in the next year's Derby, with Erskine Hen-
derson aboard the chestnut Joe Cotton, trained by the conditioner
Abe Perry.

In 1884, Isaac Murphy's career began evolving very fast, but he
had some challenges. Perhaps most important, his mentor, trainer
Eli Jordan, died that year. He still had Lucy for encouragement
and guidance, but he had lost the anchor of his professional life
just as he was taking off.

A month and a half after the Kentucky Derby, the sport expanded yet again, with the inauguration of Washington Park in
Chicago and the new American Derby, the latest, most spectacular
version of what had become America's most loved sports feature. After the Jersey and Kentucky versions, derbies had begun sprouting up
all over, attracting the most promising three-year-olds just coming
into their racing years. States and cities saw them as wonderful pro-
motional gimmicks. "Take me out to the racetrack," was what most
Americans were asking, and they would make a day of it at the Tennessee, Ohio, California, Texas, and Illinois Derbies, not to mention
the St. Louis, Chicago, Crescent City (New Orleans), Detroit, and
Tijuana Derbies, plus many more (a number of which Isaac would
capture during his career, including the Kentucky, Latonia, Brooklyn,
and Illinois Derbies). But now came the biggest of them all for the
next few decades: the American Derby at Washington Park. Headed

by General Phil Sheridan, the Chicago group could guarantee a giant metropolitan crowd, which would produce the sort of news that enhances reputations and a horse's value, and much higher purses as well. For example, Murphy and Buchanan had collected $3,990 for stable owner William Cottrill, of Alabama, in the Kentucky Derby. But at Chicago—where Murphy showed "rare judgment and a cool head" in grabbing the first American Derby by just six inches—he and his mount, Modesty, picked up $10,700 for Ed Corrigan, a major Kentucky breeder and investor in western racetracks.

With fame came familiarity. They started calling him Ike in the press.

What few knew, however, was that Ike and the great white jockey Jimmy McLaughlin were both victims of brutal "flipping"—crash dieting. Jimmy was a muscular white boy with a handlebar under his nose, but like a lot of other jockeys he tended to be more than muscle. He had been forced to drop seventeen pounds for that 1884 Kentucky Derby that Murphy won. As for Murphy, he had been "flipping" since his late teens. From his frequent between-meetings weight of 130 to 140 pounds, he had to deflate to 110 for his 1884 Derby and to between 118 and 122 pounds a few years later, when the Derby's weight limits were raised.

Unlike athletes in other sports who had to bulk up, jockeys had to bulk down. It wasn't a scientific diet. They mainly just stopped eating, but they could also throw on heavy clothes and exercise to sweat it off. One later jockey said he would spit a lot. He claimed he could spit off half a pound in a day. In a way, flipping was the early jockey's variation on what would later be recognized as bulimia, the eating disorder characterized by compulsive overeating followed by self-induced vomiting and often accompanied by depression. In the jockey's case, it was hardly overeating but rather more like normal eating during the winter or on long layoffs, followed by career-driven weight loss—and probably accompanied by depression as well. Some of the jockeys in old group photographs look wan or angry, especially next to those who seem perfectly content and who perhaps had less of a weight problem.[13]

By 1884, Isaac Murphy's handsome face had become something of a national icon—"like a Sphinx carved out of ivory . . . familiar on every racetrack in America," said the *Louisville Courier-Journal.* "An elegant specimen of manhood . . . strong, muscular, and as graceful as an Apollo," said Walter Vosburgh, a turf official who saw him often. "He sits in his horse like a centaur." Yet Vosburgh understood what Murphy was going through. On a regular basis, that classic starved visage would inflate to a puff ball, and back again. After Saratoga's 1885 meeting, for example, a reporter noted, "Ike Murphy is a sick man. . . . His stomach is all out of order. He has been traveling back and forth from Saratoga a great deal, and besides he had to reduce to ride Bluewing."[14]

CHISELED OR PUFFED, Murphy caught the eye of a flamboyant, transplanted Californian—Elias "Lucky" Baldwin—and the pair would team up for the next several years, winning lots of races and making tons of cash. However, the curly-haired, mustachioed Baldwin was the opposite of the late Eli Jordan. Baldwin was loud, licentious, and loaded. "Lucky" had struck it rich on Nevada mining stock, including a piece of the Comstock Lode, and with that he had created a racing and breeding empire on sixty thousand acres of Los Angeles County. It was laid out with lakes, vineyards, orchards, bridges, rustic homes, and a three-mile avenue divided by a row of pepper trees and bordered by eucalyptus. He styled this golden empire Rancho Santa Anita, after one of his two daughters, and the name and a few relics of the estate have been preserved at modern Santa Anita Race Course. Yet like a lot of Californians, he felt he had to prove himself in the East. It was Lucky Baldwin who had sent his western champion, Mollie McCarthy, to Kentucky in 1878—and to defeat at the hands of Billy Walker on Ten Broeck. In 1884 he decided to invade the East personally and throw around some of his estimated twenty million mid-1880s dollars, but what got him noticed at first was that he kept throwing it at women.[15]

At Saratoga Springs, only ladies were allowed in Lucky's luxurious coach, "and only the prettiest who applied," noted the social historian of Saratoga, George Waller. "When the spirit moved him, he selected only blondes, or only brunettes, as his passengers, and whirled them off to the race track to watch his horses run and see him win or lose anywhere from $5,000 to $50,000 on a single nose."[16]

In 1884, neither Baldwin nor anybody else could help but notice the star jockey Isaac Murphy, who soon would have a lot to do with Lucky's noses. That season George Lorillard put him, profitably, on his white-faced Monitor, a.k.a. "Old Baldy." Ed Corrigan, who had first call on his services, even named a horse after him, and he got paid back right away, the two Isaac Murphys earning him $3,505 in the 1884 Kenwood Stakes. So Lucky Baldwin decided to move in on this star athlete, too, paying Corrigan $1,500, and Murphy himself $1,000, for the jockey's services in the second American Derby in 1885. It was worth it: Murphy and the three-year-old Volante returned $9,570 to Baldwin in 2:49½. Of course, it was in the betting that Lucky and the others made their real dough. In one Saratoga outing, with Volante and Murphy a huge favorite, 1 to 20, a small bet would have paid a few cents; the only way really to make anything on the pair was to lay, say, $40,000, on them, as Mike Dwyer did. With that investment, the wiley Brooklyn merchant stood to profit by some $2,000. He lost.

Murphy's most riveting successes in 1885 were for Ed Corrigan on the great champion Freeland, dueling neck-and-neck with Miss Woodford, the first thoroughbred to amass more than a hundred thousand dollars in winnings. Murphy and Freeland beat Miss Woodford two out of three times at Monmouth Park in late August, prompting the rich Miss's co-owner, Phil Dwyer, to bet Corrigan twenty thousand dollars that Freeland couldn't beat her again—on Dwyer's home turf, at the Brighton course in Brooklyn. For the rematch, owners Phil and his brother Mike—a couple of Brooklyn butchers who had invaded the thoroughbred world—called on Jimmy McLaughlin to pilot their great mare. McLaughlin was in the middle of his four-year reign as the nation's top jockey (as measured by total wins), which lasted from 1884 to

1887. He took the Belmont Stakes an incredible six times in seven years and the Travers four times, feats not to be equaled until Eddie Arcaro rode into the picture half a century later. The 1885 rematch of Freeland and Miss Woodford was so thrilling it inspired a ditty, "Ike Murphy's Ride." With apologies to Longfellow and Paul Revere:

> You know the rest in the books you have read
> How McLaughlin kept the brown mare ahead,
> Till Freeland came with a sudden dart
> At the finish, and Isaac proved too smart
> For the Dwyers' jock; how at last
> He nailed him just as the post was passed
> Oh, I tell you it was a close-run race,
> And it gave to Murphy the pride of place.[17]

By 1887, Murphy was probably America's best-paid athlete, earning well over twelve thousand dollars, which was his fee from Lucky Baldwin, who now had first call on him. That was a huge amount for first call, which meant that the stable owner could count on Ike's availability for any race. An owner who paid him for second call would be guaranteed Ike's services if Baldwin wasn't using him at the moment—and if Ike chose to ride for him. The jockeys could always turn down an owner and not ride at all, which, of course, rarely happened. With fees from others added for second or third call, Murphy's total salary was between fifteen and twenty thousand dollars. This would have to be multiplied many times over to be translated into twenty-first-century dollars (though there is no reliable multiple for making an accurate conversion to a modern figure). Of course, Baldwin himself earned hundreds of thousands of dollars off Murphy over those years. In 1886, Lucky had made three-quarters of Murphy's fee in just a few minutes, as Isaac took his third straight American Derby, on Silver Cloud. Baldwin also cashed in nicely on Murphy's trips aboard Emperor of Norfolk, who won twelve times in 1887.

That year Isaac bought seven acres on the north side of what would become East Third Street in Lexington and built a larger home, for ten thousand dollars. The Murphys were looking ahead, with plans for the obviously brilliant Isaac to become an owner and trainer. In 1888, he bought a colt named Barrister as something of an experiment and sold him for four thousand dollars; he made a start on a small stable of his own, registering his own colors—black jacket, red cuffs, white belt, and red cap with green tassels. Meanwhile, he exercised his considerable talent for living as well as riding in style. It was said he often surprised Lucy with diamonds and had more than a few gems himself. Murphy dressed to kill, and to enhance his great looks he hired a young white boy as a valet (not unusual for a star athlete: John L. Sullivan had a valet as well). Isaac Murphy had only to show up to outclass everybody in sight.[18]

Sports writers took to calling him "the colored Archer," after his contemporary, Fred Archer, the king of the English turf. Archer had become famous in this country when he helped make Pierre Lorillard and Iroquois the first American winners of the original Derby, at Epsom Downs in England. But Murphy's friends said Archer should have been called "the white Murphy." As for Ike himself, he was not inclined to go to England, as many of his fellow Americans were starting to do.

"It would be a disadvantage to any horse I rode, for they [are known to] combine against our white jockeys over there, and they would beat any horse I rode, sure."[19]

This was pure Murphy, expressing it in his usual professional way, putting the horse before the jockey, and his job before his ego, but with an edge this time, as he pointed out that America wasn't the only place where black riders would have it tough.

By 1888, Lucky Baldwin was not the only American who had reason to believe that Jimmy McLaughlin was no longer the country's top rider. That year a letter to a sporting editor insisted it was Murphy, "who in spite of his name," as the writer helpfully put it, "is neither Irish nor Hebrew, but a darky" (clearly the pot wasn't melting yet). For the past six years, Murphy's admirer said, "he has won over 38 percent of his mounts . . . while Mr. McLaughlin has won less than 35 percent, and Garrison less than 31 percent." Young Edward "Snapper" Garrison was a great white rider famous for his high crouch, halfway to the modern position. He was even more celebrated for his frightening final rush, the "Garrison finish." While it was true that Ike had not ridden as often as Jimmy or Snapper, the letter-writer decided this was "easily accounted for" by the fact that Murphy had more trouble making the weights.[20]

The "flipping" that Murphy, McLaughlin, Garrison, and many others went through was dangerous enough, but it was sometimes compounded by a little drinking—a bit of champagne as a "stimulant"—before a race. Murphy was accused of losing one race on Emperor of Norfolk in 1887 after he had drunk champagne, but a witness said it was the Emperor who was "not himself." The next year Murphy was down to 123 pounds and back in Chicago with the Emperor for a shot at yet another American Derby. His streak had ended at three the year before, when his friend Tony Hamilton, a terrific black rider from Charleston, South Carolina, broke it on a horse named C. H. Todd. And now once again, in 1888, that contest in the Windy City was a typical American championship, with four blacks and three whites vying for the nation's top sports prize.[21]

The African Americans that day were Murphy, Tony—the black press was trying to call him "the Black Demon"—Hamilton, Kid Stoval, and Isaac Lewis (born in Bourbon County, Kentucky, and victor in the 1887 Kentucky Derby, on Montrose). The white riders were the great Fred "The Flying Dutchman" Taral and two boys named Armstrong and McCarthy. When it was over, Ike had paid back Baldwin's guarantee again, and then some. His fourth and final American Derby victory was worth $14,340. But let's not forget the horse. "I consider Emperor of Norfolk the greatest horse I ever rode," Murphy said later. "He was a wonder. . . . Outside of his qualifications as a race horse he was a great animal to ride. He ran as well in the ruck as in front, and when called on never failed to respond."[22]

In that same year, the stakes were raised, literally, with the in-auguration of the richest annual American sporting event yet. It was dubbed the Futurity because the organizers called for the entries to be nominated even before they were born. Hundreds of hopeful owners had paid entry fees for mares whose offspring would be nominated, plus fees for the offspring themselves, plus forfeit fees for any no-shows, and finally starting fees—to all of which the organizers added ten thousand dollars. With this event, big money officially entered American sports (though it had long been there in the form of side wagers): the first Futurity paid an unheard-of $40,900. It was staged by the Coney Island Jockey Club, a pretty layout along Ocean Avenue, with fine restaurants, shade trees and lovely lawns, right off breezy Sheepshead Bay. Brooklyn was never so beautiful.

Among the fourteen jockeys, McLaughlin, Taral, and Murphy were the best known in New York. Ike was supposed to have slimmed down to 112 to ride Princess Bowling but was listed at 114. The other African Americans included Isaac Lewis, George "Spider" Anderson, Tony Hamilton on Salvator, and a new star, Shelby "Pike" Barnes from Beaver Dam, Kentucky, who was on the favorite, Proctor Knott. It was a sprint for two-year-olds, six fast furlongs, the equivalent of three quarter races by Austin Curtis and Old Ned a century earlier.

On this day, Murphy did not win. It was Proctor Knott and Salvator who battled it out at the end, waiting until they were in front of Coney Island's packed and pretty grandstand, with its touch of tudor beams by the beach, before making their moves and grabbing the lead together. From their tiered little perch, topped by a Turkish cupola and gilded horse weathervane, seven judges in bowlers were riveted by the finish, in which Proctor Knott and Barnes held off Salvator and Hamilton to win by half a length.

It was a fabulous year for Barnes, who had the most wins in 1888, which made him the national riding champion. Barnes was also the first jockey to rack up more than 200 wins since *Goodwin's Official Turf Guide* had begun keeping records three years earlier.

(Various publications kept more or less reliable records prior to that.) Barnes had 206 victories in 1888, more than twice as many as white runner-up George Covington, with 95. The black jockey "Monk" Overton was third, with 93. For those who argue, sometimes convincingly, that percentage is what counts in measuring a jockey's ability (if not the money he brings the owner), Barnes also led the front-runners in that category, winning a sensational 32.9 percent of his races. Dropping farther down the list, McLaughlin had 72 wins, Snapper Garrison 71, and the highly selective Murphy 37. Murphy's low position on the list is a reminder that his fame rested on his rarely equaled mastery in a relatively small number of races—which often included the biggest events on the calendar—his intellectual superiority, his management of the press, and his great popularity.

That same band of powerful black jockeys, most of them from Kentucky or the South, had begun to throw fear into New York's white establishment. They did not dominate that capital of American racing—they were merely a very strong minority—but they were clearly as good as the top white riders in the East. A year earlier, in 1887, *Harper's Weekly* had exaggerated the number of black jockeys who had ridden in the postwar North but thought it spotted some great white hopes at the new Brooklyn Jockey Club track by Gravesend Bay (the great white hope would become a famous theme in boxing). "The professional jockeys some years ago were Southern Negroes, and with the exception of a few cross-country riders of Irish parentage, monopolized nearly all the mounts. Today it is very different. With McLAUGHLIN, GARRISON, LUKE and [Andrew] McCARTHY—a quartet equal to any in the world—there is but little doubt that if a horse has got it in him to win, he will have to do it when either one of them is on his back."[23]

Meanwhile, the great black hopes kept coming to New York. "Colored Jockeys Show the Way," shouted a *Herald* headline on September 20, 1889, trumpeting a day in which African Americans had won all six races in Brooklyn. The report was a mixture of admiration and racial slurs hard to comprehend a century later, yet it is revealing of what those athletes had to overcome. It began, "If a composite photograph had been made of the jockeys who rode the six winners at Gravesend yesterday afternoon, it would have been as black as Erebus. There wouldn't have been a single light in it, unless the camera had happened to catch Hamilton with his mouth wide open, displaying the pearly white teeth which form the only relieving feature on his coal black face." The next paragraph reflected the country's obsession with color. "The sons of Ham outrode the children of Japhet with a vengeance, for not a single white boy was successful in guiding a winner past the judges. It was a field day for the dusky riders, and they forced their Caucasian competitors to take positions in the background."

The winners were Barnes (twice), Hamilton (twice), Murphy, and Spider Anderson. The first three and Isaac Lewis also chalked up five seconds in the six races. For the year, the black jockeys also looked pretty good in the statistics. Pike Barnes became the national champion for the second consecutive year, with 170 wins, Hamilton was third best with 113, and Anderson was ninth with 91—on a list of 56 jockeys. Choosy Murphy was way down—fifteenth—on this list, but had the most impressive percentage among the heavy hitters, 29.7 (58 wins). Indeed, while his total number of races was rarely impressive, his winning percentage almost always was, especially considering that his "resume" was a list of many of the most important and hard-fought showdowns in the sport. It was a career, above all, of quality.[24]

THE FOLLOWING year, 1890, took Isaac Murphy to the pinnacle of his career—and a start on a bitter road downhill. In May he made the jaunt over to Louisville and became the first jockey to double in the Kentucky Derby—where it was Corrigan's Riley, Murphy up, an Irish trio if there ever was one, as somebody noted. And a rainy day it was, too, the first one for the Derby. And though it was also the richest to date, it was worth only $5,460, a reminder that Churchill Downs was still very far from achieving its dreams.

A second Derby win might have been the highlight for most years, but not this one. Murphy was back home in Lexington that spring when bigger money entered the picture again. He got a telegram asking him to come ride for James Ben Ali Haggin in the East, although it was only as far east as Brooklyn. Haggin was not at all from the Mysterious Orient, as a lot of people doubtless thought; he was a Kentuckian who had picked up his middle names from his grandfather, an officer in the Turkish Army. Haggin's own career was exotic enough, though: he had struck it rich in the California gold rush, but as a lawyer, not as some dumb farmer sitting on the ground with a frying pan. He had acquired gold, silver, mining, and especially real estate holdings and was turning his Rancho Del Paso near Sacramento into the world's biggest thoroughbred breeding center. At the moment, however, Ben Ali was invading Sheepshead Bay.[25]

The month of June found Murphy stealing the Suburban Handicap by a neck on Haggin's fabulous steed Salvator. But this turned out to be only a prelim to a bigger race on June 25 at Sheepshead Bay, which would rank with Wagner–Grey Eagle, Lexington-Lecomte, Longfellow–Harry Bassett. Like those, it was a historic black-white encounter, although nobody thought of it that way at the time. "The imperturbable Murphy," exhibiting his fine English seat, "well down in his saddle and straight as a dart," the *Spirit* said, was again on the chestnut Salvator, whose record was 14-9. His rival, and his junior by ten years, was Snapper Garrison, commanding the reddish brown Tenny, 13-7. The race would go right to the wire, and in fact, this pair of jockeys helped invent the term "grandstand finish," which Webster's dictionary traces to the 1890s. The *Times* once noted "Garrison's inordinate desire to ride a grand-stand finish, in which respect he is very much like Isaac Murphy. . . . Garrison wants to win by a nose or an eyelash, if possible, as that satisfies best the vanity which is the dominating feature of this young man's make-up."[26]

And the *Tribune* said of Murphy's style, "He has a penchant for gallery finishes." When Ike had a mount he knew was superior, his strategy was often to "lounge along in the rear of the field till he strikes the homestretch and comes in range of the clear vision of admirers in the grand stand." Then he would move up and poke his horse's nose in front of the leader's. "He proceeds to hold it there in a most artistic way till both horses pass the judges. It is the height of Murphy's ambition to ride such a finish." The trouble with this, complained the *Tribune*, was that it often cost Murphy the race, at the expense of the owner. Ike denied it. "It is hard to be told you ought to have won further off when I had to hold my breath to win as I did."

The run was a mile and a quarter. Poking his white face in front, Salvator first tied or broke (the watches disagreed) the record for a mile (1:39¾), then for a mile and an eighth (1:52¾), until suddenly, at the top of the home stretch, came the Garrison finish. The furious Ichabod Crane was spurring his animal and switching his switch from one hand to the other. Murphy was a horse whisperer, famous for cajoling them; Garrison was a whipper, notorious for beating the hell out of them—but it, too, often got results, such as now. "The way Tenny came up with his flying rival in the last 100 yards was a miracle, perfectly stupendous," said the *Spirit*. But let poet Ella Wheeler Wilcox call the finish, as Snapper Garrison and Isaac Murphy thundered down the track:

> One more mighty plunge, and with knee, limb and hand
> I lift my horse first by a nose past the stand.
> We are under the string now—the great race is done—
> And Salvator, Salvator, Salvator won![27]

But had he? John Hemment, the Coney Island Jockey Club photographer to the rescue, with a forerunner of the modern photo finishes. The *Spirit* had earlier made "a strenuous appeal in favor of the adoption by racing associations of the aid afforded by photography in registering an immutable record of the positions in a close finish." Hemment's immutable picture caught it all right: Isaac, in Haggin's orange jacket and blue sleeves (except that it didn't catch the colors) and hardly leaning, the winner by a head; lanky Snapper, crouched, hugging, his back noticeably more arched, but to no avail. Murphy looked the picture of "superb coolness and judgment of pace," as somebody called him, above it all, seeming to ignore the furious Snapper. As one reviewer of that fabled contest said of the unflappable Isaac Murphy, "No man with a touch of heart disease should ever back his mounts."[28]

Less than two months later, on August 12, the cardiac patients braced themselves for the rematch, as Salvator met Tenny in the Junior Champion Stakes at the beautifully rebuilt Monmouth Park, which had opened on the Fourth of July, 1890. Testifying to a bright future for American sports, Monmouth lured more of the New York masses and immediately became the new capital of American sports, with the longest racecourse in the country at one and three-quarter miles. The patients needn't have panicked: it was Ike and Salvator by four lengths. With that, the authoritative *Spirit* concluded, "About the immense superiority Isaac Murphy

Ike Murphy, in his upright English style, beats the lanky Snapper Garrison, in his high crouch, in one of the greatest races in American history, at the Coney Island Jockey Club on June 25, 1890. This photograph by John Hemment might be considered the first of a "photo finish," although it was not an official track photo. Courtesy of Keeneland Association.

shows over the majority of the jockeys at the present day, especially in match races, there can be no room for doubt." Like Abe Hawkins, Murphy seldom smiled in public, but he gave the gift that day. "It was no wonder that Isaac Murphy's quiet countenance beamed as he trotted back to the paddock. He had won the Junior Champion Stakes . . . but above all he had ridden the best horse of the decade, if not the century, on the American turf, in the race [Salvator versus Tenny] which was the supreme climax of a grand career."[29]

Two weeks later, they had a celebration to fete the mighty Salvator and all his triumphs. James Haggin's increasingly well-to-do trainer, Matt Byrnes, threw a clambake at his home, Chestnut Grove, near Eatontown, New Jersey, on August 24. "The Salvator Club," they called the gathering, but there was plenty else to celebrate, too, such as the gorgeous new Monmouth track with its 660 acres of grounds. "The champagne ran in streams and rivers," said the *Spirit*, but it was all "a feast of reason and a flow of soul." Present were "half the judicial and political 'somebodies' of New York," but there was no question who the "somebody" was among

This celebration of Salvator's victories was held at Matt Byrnes's home near Eatontown, New Jersey, on August 24, 1890. Some suspected that Murphy, third from right, may have had too much to drink at the party. Courtesy of Keeneland Association.

the six men (five whites and one black) getting their picture taken on Matt's fence. As usual, Murphy was the most elegant figure in the viewfinder, in his derby, his double-breasted, velvet-collared chesterfield coat, and his fashionable pointy boots. He was the only man there with a fine long riding crop (was that the silver-mounted whip the Salvator backers had just given him?), the only one with his legs neatly crossed, fastidious.

But in control at that moment? The question would arise a few days later. For now, at least, it seemed that Isaac Murphy could handle it at the top in a way that some of his rich employers could not (such as Ed Corrigan and Lucky Baldwin, whose less than exemplary behavior is reviewed below). George "Spider" Anderson hadn't been able to handle it, either, when he showed up at Pimlico to ride a horse called Buddhist in the 1889 Preakness.[30]

"'Spider' Anderson enlivened matters before the races began by striking a colored coachman named James Cook over the head with a loaded whip, cutting him severely," reported the *Herald*. Jockey's whips were often loaded with lead for balance, so they made good weapons, too. The cause of the altercation isn't known, but Cook worked for former Maryland governor Oden Bowie, who had the only other horse in the race, Japhet, so perhaps Cook had just offered Spider an opinion about the upcoming Preakness. In any event, the eighteen-year-old star jockey lost his cool—and Cook would have none of it. Nursing a nasty cut, Cook immediately called in the authorities, who got a judge, and they set up a little court right there at Pimlico. First things first, though: it was decided to let Spider ride in the Preakness before rendering a decision. The jockey certainly didn't need to use the whip on Buddhist, who romped home, enriching his Pittsburgh owner, S. S. Brown, by $1,130. That, and the fact that Bowie got $200 for practically walking home second in the two-horse Preakness, may have had something to do with the fact that Cook decided not to press charges after all.

The first African American to win the Preakness, Spider would go on to take the important 1891 Alabama Stakes at Saratoga. The above minor incident notwithstanding, he "became well known for

George "Spider" Anderson was the first black jockey to win the Preakness Stakes at Pimlico Race Course in Maryland. Courtesy of author.

his integrity, his cleverness and his general success," according to the contemporary *American Turf*, published before the century was out. Later, losing the battle of the scale, Anderson would switch to steeplechase riding.[31]

Two DAYS after the bubbly clambake at Matt Byrnes's house, Isaac Murphy reappeared at the new track in the mile-and-a-quarter Monmouth Handicap, on Haggin's outstanding mare Firenzi. Before the race Ike dropped by the fabulous new iron grandstand to pay a visit to Lucy, who was accompanied by his valet, and they had the waiter bring them a refreshing glass of imported Apollinaris water. Then he was off to battle—and disaster. Not only did Isaac Murphy finish seventh in a field of seven, badly handling the familiar and highly regarded Firenzi, but he had trouble dismounting; he was dazed. Monmouth Park suspended him from riding there. The *New York Times* was aghast.

"A popular idol was shattered at Monmouth Park yesterday. That Isaac Murphy, who has always been considered the most gentlemanly as well as the most honest of jockeys, would have made such an exhibition of himself as he did was past belief. He rode Firenzi in the Monmouth Handicap, and that he did so was alone the reason for the ridiculous way in which she was beaten, finishing last in a field of horses that she should have defeated with but little trouble."[32]

What happened? The *Times* said it probably started with the "gang of politicians" at the clambake. "Loading a car and themselves up with liquor," they went to Matt's, where the liquor was "the largest part of the affair. . . . Although Mr. Byrnes kept his head clear, Murphy there laid the foundation for yesterday's exhibition." At the race, the jockey was slow in weighing in and failed to show up "until sometime after the bugle call." As the horses came down the stretch, people started to realize Ike wasn't behind because he was pulling his horse—he was just trying "to keep himself straight in the saddle." When the race was over, "what strength he had was gone, and he fell out of the saddle in a heap on the track. Then, for the first time, the crowd realized what was the matter and that it was an animated champagne bottle instead of the peerless jockey, Murphy, who had been riding the mare. It was a shock to everyone." An assistant helped Ike back on the horse. "That the crowd was pained at the exhibition Murphy had made of himself instead of being angered was shown by the fact that he was not hissed when he rode back to the paddock."

What was that drink Ike had sipped with Lucy? The valet said it was only Apollinaris water—so did the waiter, so did the café cashier. Everybody got into the act. What was Apollinaris water anyway? It bubbled, didn't it? The London company itself weighed in: "The statement published elsewhere of the Apollinaris Company, of London, England, effectually refutes the false charges brought against this popular beverage, and conclusively proves that it is purely a natural mineral water." When Murphy weighed in before the race, track official Walter Vosburgh was standing right by, and he said he certainly would have noticed if there had been anything wrong with Ike, but he didn't notice anything. What about that clambake? Didn't they look drunk at Matt's party—wasn't Ike in a daze? The fact that it had been held forty-eight hours before the race seemed not to discourage the gossipers, or the *New York Times*, for that matter.[33]

Vosburgh had his own explanation: flipping. He said Murphy had been reducing fiercely, getting from his winter weight of close to 140 pounds down to 110 to ride Salvator in the big June match against Tenny. Ike would ride only thirty-eight times that year, again apparently because he had trouble making the weights. Now it was nearly September, and Murphy had probably been starving himself for months. Vosburgh's argument, plus the potential lingering effects of the clambake, made a strong, if circumstantial, case for the cause of Ike's collapse.

Murphy himself had his own excuse. He was convinced, according to his lawyer, that he had been drugged, and he would go to his death convinced, which probably kept suspicions alive for years. Who could possibly have slipped a mickey into the Apollinaris? The valet? The waiter? The cashier? Certainly not Lucy!

In any event, two days later, on August 26, when Haggin brought Salvator out on Monmouth's fancy new straightaway, and he beat the clock to set a new world record of 1:35½ for the mile, it was the white jockey Marty Bergen aboard. A friend in need, trainer Matt Byrnes said his horse would have run it in 1:33 if Murphy had been up, but Murphy was momentarily out of commission. He began seeing a New York doctor, and late that year he told a Lexington reporter, "I can't say definitely I was poisoned . . . but something suddenly got the matter with me and I have never been well since."[34]

THE FOLLOWING January, 1891, Isaac seemed to be feeling completely well again, and he and Lucy gave an enormous party at their home in Lexington, by all accounts a delightful all-day shower for the jockey Tony Hamilton and his bride. It opened with a sumptuous lunch that stretched into a buffet dinner, all blessed with champagne, of course, and served nonstop from the Murphys' dining room, parlor, and library. At eight, dancing began, highlighted by a "Jockey Quadrille," according to the *Lexington Transcript*'s account of the fete, the social event of the year for black Lexington. Among the many guests were two other Derby champions, Billy Walker and Isaac Lewis, and another great black jockey, Tommy Britton.

Flipping or not, Ike was back in form that year, with more than one hundred mounts. A record crowd, somewhere over twenty-five thousand, jammed the 1891 Kentucky Derby, a "crowd . . . so great that locomotion was almost impossible. The inner field presented one mass of humanity from the head of the stretch nearly to the quarter pole." The pools, run by just one or two auctioneers, had been banned, forced out by the large flock of bookmakers. But the French pari-mutuel machines were still available, and the price of a ticket had been knocked down from five to two dollars, which became the standard for a bet on the ponies for the next century. That record crowd didn't get much of a race, though, what with only four colts out there. The three black riders finished in front: Murphy came in first on Kingman, then Alfred "Monk" Overton, "the best left-handed whip that ever sat in the saddle," then Robert "Tiny" Williams, who would win the 1891 Travers. Last was Tom Kiley.[35]

It was Murphy's third Derby victory, a record until Earl Sande equaled it on Gallant Fox nearly four decades later, in 1930. Ever the analyst, Ike would have been the first to admit that the Kentucky Derby was still not the big time in the 1890s, and that his three weren't much to write home to Lucy about. Buchanan had turned in a most pathetic 2:40¼ for the mile and a half, Riley a disgraceful 2:45 in a field of just six, albeit in the mud, and Kingman a 2:52¼ in a field of four, the most leisurely of all the Louisville classics, "The Funeral Procession Derby." But, of course, the best athletes took what they could get, and they knew that over the long run showing up was more than half the battle. By showing up, Murphy was the first to take two Derbies in a row and to help register another black jockey-trainer victory, Dudley Allen having brought Kingman to the post. As the lead partner in the winning Jacobin Stable, Allen also became the first African American owner of a Derby champion.

So Ike was again the hero of the Bluegrass, having just showed how he became "the greatest jockey on the American turf," said the *Courier-Journal*. "His reputation for honesty and integrity is a matter of great pride among turfmen."

He finished 1891 with a modest 32 wins (putting him eighteenth on a list of forty-six top jockeys) but with a very strong 28 percent winning rate. Still, in the next few years he rode less and less, never again doing better than his six wins in forty-two races in 1892. Something was obviously wrong, and a friend noted that Ike showed "the wear and tear of a sick spell." In 1892, he was reduced to riding for Frank Ehret's stable, known for its cock fighting. Ehret refused to book him on good mounts in New York, favoring the white rider Sam Doggett. Not everybody agreed with Ehret's choice. "The action of the Ehret Stable in putting up Doggett in preference to Murphy caused some surprise," the *Sporting World* declared. "It appears that the stable has an opinion that the 'colored Archer' is at a disadvantage on a two-year-old." Murphy tried to get out gracefully, to make the transition to owning and training.

Isaac bought some two-year-olds in 1893 and maintained a small stable, which happened to boast the country's most famous athlete. Seeing their world shrink, the Murphys began consolidating, too, selling that first five-hundred-dollar home for two thousand dollars. He descended a few more steps in 1894. First, he costarred with his old mount Freeland, he of "Ike Murphy's Ride," in something even worse, a "horse play," or "historical picture," called "The Derby Winner." Featuring seven thoroughbreds, it played the West, including the Grand Opera House of St. Louis, and eventually Murphy's hometown. One report sadly described the human star as "Isaac Murphy, the whilom great jockey," who had been "selected as a drawing card to pilot Freeland once more in the fierce contests upon the stage." Worse still, if possible, the jockey who had captured five of Kentucky's famous Latonia Derbies was suspended in 1894 for being drunk at Latonia on a horse named Myrtle. A reporter rushing to his defense said, "He might have taken a drink for courage" and then got dizzy because he had not eaten a proper meal.[36]

Ike was back east for the summer of 1895, but he had only twenty mounts at the major tracks that year, with a pallid record of two wins, one second, and seven thirds. That November, at his home track of Lexington, he rode and won his last race, on a horse called Tupto. "The clever way in which he nursed that famous quitter and landed him a winner was enthusiastically applauded," someone said, but Murphy himself wasn't applauding. After his Lexington race, he spoke with Broad Church, the veteran racing writer for the *Spirit of the Times*, who had admired him for a dozen years and who thought his problem really was the bottle. Church wrote, "When in his prime he was the peer of any jockey in America. But, for reasons pretty well known, he lost his grip several years ago and he himself appeared to be cognizant of that fact, although he essayed to ride at odd times. At the Lexington fall meeting I had quite a talk with him, when he appeared a bit sad over the drift of events in connection with himself. 'I think I will go down to New Orleans,' he said, 'and maybe I can make a reputation once more. I am disgusted with the way they treated me in the East during the summer. When I won it was all right, but when I lost, and when not on the best horse, they would say, 'There, that nigger is drunk again.' I tell you, I am disgusted and soured on the whole business."

A FEW months later, at 1:30 A.M. on Wednesday, February 12, 1896, Isaac Murphy died at his home, reportedly of pneumonia. He was thirty-four or thirty-five. Upon his death, commentators continued their speculations on the cause of the famous jockey's decline. In fact, far into the next century, lung diseases would be common among jockeys, whose crash diets, intensive exercising, and sweat baths would reduce their resistance to infection. Surprisingly, the *Spirit of the Times* missed this. "He might have remained one of the leading jockeys until the time of his death had he not been addicted to drink," it insisted. "His drinking propensities in a large measure brought about his ruin and his early death." It failed to consider those years of "flipping" and the eventually hopeless war against weight, which so often left Murphy weak and sickly and drove so many from the sport, among them Jimmy McLaughlin, forced out by the scale at age thirty-one.[37]

More than five hundred mourners paid their respects to Lucy at their home. The African American Masons (Sardis and Lincoln Lodges) and the Bethany Commandery of the Knights Templar escorted the funeral cortege, which was so long it had to circle the cemetery, where the crowd gathered in the snow. Ed Corrigan sent lilies of the valley. So did Ed Brown, the slave jockey formerly known as Dick. The "Flying Dutchman," Fred Taral, sent a wreath. Tony "the Black Demon" Hamilton and Robert "Tiny" Williams sent a large horseshoe of flowers. They knew that the century had lost one of its greatest athletes.

"As a judge of a two-year-old, he was second to McLaughlin," said the *Spirit*'s obituary, which was brief and stingy, "and as a judge of pace he was only surpassed by [Billy] Hayward." But after his Firenzi suspension, he "never after regained his former good standing. In 1892, he rode six winners in forty-two races; in 1893, four in thirty races; in 1894, no wins were to his credit, and in 1895, he scored one win in twenty trials." (*Goodwin's Turf Guide* gave him two wins.) Murphy's own accounting of all his rides was 628 victories in 1,412 starts, or an incredible 44 percent winning rate. A much later check of the incomplete records put it at 530 wins in 1,538 outings, for a still terrific 34 percent rate. Murphy's record rate and stunning achievements in classic individual races, along with his athletic and cerebral fireworks, cannot be compared with the records of the next century's greatest jockeys. It was a different time and a different place. The later jockeys could compete in thousands more races throughout the year across the country. How to compare a 44 percent rate with Bill Shoemaker's 21.8 percent when the Shoe won 8,833 of 40,350 races? Who is to say how those earlier athletes would have fared today?[38]

Other obituaries stressed Murphy's integrity as much as his accomplishments. In one, his lawyer, L. P. Tarlton, said that the first time Isaac was put on a "dead" horse in a betting scam, he didn't realize it at first, but when he figured it out, he blew up—at the horse. He "punished it so severely as to destroy its future usefulness." Ashamed, Murphy told Tarlton about it later, "with regret, if not mortification," and from then on, whenever he was expected to take a fall, or suspected it, "he would simply return the colors and refuse to ride." But what if he was the target of an outright attack in the middle of a race? That was when the other jockeys saw an entirely new Isaac Murphy. Several crooked jockeys tried it once at Lexington. Murphy, who had been warned that some kind of a fix was on, was moving up in the middle of a big field of at least eleven horses. As part of the scam, the leader intentionally opened the inside for two others and then moved to push another jockey—the one who would anonymously tell the story—into Murphy. At the same time, two more horses, also part of the scam, crowded in on Murphy from the outside, pushing him toward the storyteller and a certain crash.

"In a flash, Murphy catches the drift and swings his right foot into the neck of the horse closing in on him. This throws the horse off stride back into the other one, and in that instant we went out of the jam. If he hadn't done it . . . my horse more than likely would have gone down, and there were eight more coming behind that would have trampled me. . . . But the funniest part was the boy never reported his horse being kicked by Murphy."[39]

His annual income from riding must have hovered around $20,000 over several years, but one obituary said he had been too generous and spent his last years "deeply depressed by a burden of debt," with little to bequeath to Lucy. Not so, according to the *Thoroughbred Record*, which reported that he left an estate of $30,000, with no more than $5,000 in debts. The *Spirit of the Times* put his estate at $125,000 and noted that he left a wife but no children to share in the estate. Whatever her inheritance, Lucy still faced Isaac's medical bills, and apparently she did not manage her finances well. Rather than stay in the big house alone, she quite sensibly moved in with her mother several blocks away, but for a while after Ike's death, according to an elderly resident, she went to the considerable expense of hiring a carriage every day to visit Ike's grave and decorate it with fresh flowers. Later it was said that she was finally forced to sell her diamonds and that, at the worst moments, she lived in near poverty.[40]

But other prominent racing figures of the era had closing chapters even more unfortunate than Isaac Murphy's. In England, Fred Archer's first-born child, a son, died after only a few hours in January 1884. After the birth of his daughter in November, his wife died. He began betting heavily, and badly, and he had to reduce his weight drastically to ride. Paranoid and suicidal, he shot himself in 1886. The fading Ed Corrigan's business tactics included convincing the mayor of Chicago to crack down on rival Garfield Park and to ignore his own Hawthorne track, which was in any event safely outside city limits. On September 6, 1892, hundreds of Chicago police raided Garfield. They were loading jockeys, still in their silks, into paddy wagons when one of the stable owners, Jim Brown, resisted arrest. He shot and killed two officers before they killed him. Thanks to Ed Corrigan, Garfield closed forever.

At about 9:45 A.M., on July 1, 1895, the same year his former jockey died, Lucky Baldwin was in a San Francisco courtroom. He was answering a breach of promise complaint by one of his young lady friends, Emma Ashley, when she pulled out a revolver and fired at Lucky's head, "taking off several of his curls," according to the *New York Times*. Baldwin had a forthright response to Emma's complaint. Having been shot at and wounded by another young lady years before, having fought off an earlier breach of promise suit by his seamstress, having separated from one of his four wives at a cost of one million dollars, having promised Rancho Santa Anita, valued at ten million dollars, to his daughter "if she married to suit him," only to see her elope with her second cousin, Lucky's official answer to Emma was, as the *Times* put it, "one of the most extraordinary on record, but which showed a remarkably clear appreciation of the moral light in which he should be viewed. In effect, it was that no woman with a reputation to lose would have anything to do with him."[41]

Isaac Murphy shines in the context of his times, and ours. Eighty years after his death, when this champion had been totally forgotten by his own country, a Kentucky journalist, Frank Borries Jr., led a campaign to recapture his glory. As a result, in 1967, Isaac

A chiseled Ike Murphy, perhaps the most charismatic athlete of his day and one of many who had to "flip" to lose weight. Courtesy of author.

Murphy's body was reinterred in Man O'War Park, near Lexington, in a ceremony that featured Eddie Arcaro as the guest speaker. Arcaro, the winner of five Kentucky Derbies, looked across nearly a century and saw "a man of great integrity and class. He was a man who, if we lived at the same time, would have been a good friend of mine." Seven years before he died, Murphy himself had tried to sum up his contribution in a statement to a Lexington newspaper. It revealed the qualities that Arcaro liked—integrity and class—which is to say the statement was not really about Isaac Murphy at all. A model of modesty, the epitaph that the jockey imagined for himself was a tribute not so much to himself as to his profession: "I am as proud of my calling as I am of my record, and I believe my life will be recorded as a success, though the reputation I enjoyed was earned in the stable and saddle. It is a great honor to be classed as one of America's great jockeys."

*Tony Hamilton, aboard Pickpocket in 1893, wears the flaglike silks of
C. A. Brown—blue jacket and red cap with stars.
Courtesy of Keeneland Association.*

·9·

THE GREAT
BLACK HOPES

WILLIE SIMMS AND THE GAY NINETIES

1890–1900

As the Gay Nineties opened, the black jockeys sat poised to share in the applause and profits of America's most popular sport. Their hard road across two centuries was at the gates of glory. Before the Civil War, when racing was concentrated in the South, they had dominated it by their sheer numbers. They had not escaped slavery, but they had in a sense defeated it—earning for themselves the satisfaction of seeking their personal best, belonging to a recognized profession, making a living and traveling the land when it was supposed to be impossible, and enjoying the camaraderie of associates and the cheers of America's biggest crowds. More than that, they had created for themselves a measure of freedom, a larger measure than that known to many whites. And if enforced anonymity was one of the obstacles to progress, some had even conquered that, among them the champions Austin Curtis, Simon, Ben, Cornelius, Cato, Chisholm, Monk, and Abe Hawkins.

After the Civil War, however, the least of every Southern capital's worries was its weedy old racecourse. The sport was dead in

Dixie. Yet some of the black jockeys staged an almost miraculous comeback. A few reappeared in the North, half a country away, where racing, reborn, quickly became America's first truly national sport. Thus, the cross-country performers Sewell and Hawkins, Albert and Dick, never lost a beat between slave and ex-slave.

And while the black jockeys would never again dominate racing as they had in the South, a talented band of them continued to do so in what Americans still called the West: in the final Race Horse Region, better known as the Bluegrass state, and at New Orleans, where racing was revived. The Black jockeys won half of the first sixteen Kentucky Derbies against the best white riders of the day. And on contract with the big stables, the best made sorties into the East and North, scoring on the great new tracks being built in New York, New Jersey, and Chicago and competing with their old rivals, the Irish Americans, and a new wave of professional English boys.

"All the Best Jockeys of the West Are Colored," read a headline on a *Spirit of the Times* report from Kentucky in 1890. The report qualified it only slightly: "Nearly every prominent jockey in the West is of the colored persuasion." The prominence of the black jockeys in the West was a frequent theme that year. The *Spirit* noted in March that Pike Barnes, who had been working in California for Lucky Baldwin, was returning to New Orleans and would soon be "the king bee of jockeys on the Western circuit." In the meantime, Harry "Chippie" Ray was the top rider in the Crescent City. But he didn't stay for long. When the Haggin stable's trainer, Matt Byrnes, wired Ike Murphy to come to Sheepshead Bay for that fatal 1890 season of Salvator and Firenzi, he fired off another telegram to Chippie Ray, telling him to come east as well.[1]

Who rose to the top in the West when Murphy and Ray were away? More black jockeys. Writing from Covington, Kentucky, home of the Latonia course, the *Spirit*'s correspondent noted, "Those that have earned and attained [the] most prominence are colored, some of them, like [Alfred] Overton, Hollis and [Tommy]

Britton being very black, and some of them, like Steppe, [Robert] Williams, and [Alonzo] Allen being bright mulattoes." They still had to read through the white reporters' obsession with shades of black, but as for the jockeys: if those six westerners were good, two of them were terrific. The leftie whipper "Monk" Overton would set a long-remembered American record in 1891 by grabbing six out of his six races at Washington Park in Chicago (noted in the records throughout the following century among "Remarkable Riding Feats"). He would appear in eight Kentucky Derbies, never winning but coming in second once and third twice, and he would stretch his career across the decade, collecting the Kentucky Oaks in 1900. "Tiny" Williams would claim the American Derby in 1892, but he would also make spectacular strikes far from the West, grabbing the Travers at Saratoga and, as late as 1898, the Queen's Plate in Ontario.

Fifteen of the country's best riders posed at the Coney Island Jockey Club in 1891. Front row (left to right): Fred Taral, Tony Hamilton, Tom Kiley, Marty Bergen. Middle row: Isaac Murphy, Willie Simms. Standing: Charles Littlefield, George Covington, Miller, Taylor, Pike Barnes, Billy Hayward, Chippie Ray, Lambley, Tiny Williams. (Some first names not known.) Courtesy of Keeneland Association.

If the best in the West tended to be African Americans, they also tended to leave, and the *Spirit* worried, if only for a moment, about this drain. "The East has already gobbled up so many of the crack Western jockeys that there is a dearth of real good jockeys out this way."

As of 1890, then, a group of African Americans, not just the occasional star, was moving into the upper ranks of racing, and it was happening in no other American sport. "Colored riders have made themselves felt in recent years," the *Spirit* noted. "Murphy, Barnes and Hamilton rank with the very best, and it is at least possible that Ray, in time, will be as able as the three named. There are other colored riders, such as Anderson, Stoval, and Fox that are both competent and successful."

Among those named, Murphy was about to peak, prematurely, with Salvator and Firenzi at Sheepshead Bay. But Pike Barnes, the 1888 Futurity and 1889 Travers laureate and the national champion in both of those years, was hardly going to be satisfied with "king bee on the Western circuit." He would head East to add the 1890 Belmont Stakes, among other items. Tony Hamilton, already an American Derby and Brooklyn Handicap winner, was at the door of an extraordinary career of more major stakes wins. Preakness winner Spider Anderson would pretty much wrap up his highlights with the 1891 Alabama and Monmouth Handicaps. Kid Stoval was about done, too, having appeared in six Kentucky Derbies. He had also just won Churchill Downs's Kentucky Oaks, which would be captured in the next three years by Hollis, Britton, and Ray, in case anyone thought the black jockeys did not still rule the Bluegrass.

"In the colored ranks are to be found jockeys of the most sterling honesty and integrity," the *Spirit*'s writer said, "and it is unfortunate that the same cannot be said of all white jockeys." In fact, along with talent, honesty and integrity would turn out to be their most important weapons for survival. If the black jockeys had a better reputation for integrity, which they did, the explanations were several, but fairly simple. More of them had come up the hard way, which built character. Fewer had been exposed to the temptations of easy money, which weakened character. They had a lot more to lose. For them, any trouble was big trouble. If they were caught in a scam, they had reason to fear worse punishment than whites and would also find it harder than whites to get another job. For example, Chippie Ray had aroused suspicion among the New Orleans authorities by substituting for other jockeys (and winning). Later that spring, he was actually suspended in Kentucky and Tennessee for contract jumping. The *Spirit* rushed to his defense. "It is a pity in these days when crude and bungling jockeys are so numerous that Ray 'is on the ground,' for he did some great work early in the season." The reporter said Ray's infraction wasn't nearly as bad as losing by pulling a horse. Many jockeys had been suspended for that recently but were already reinstated—"yet Ray, so far, has been left out in the cold." He would soon be back, though.

The 1890 writer lavishing praise on the black jockeys said he wanted to recognize "thorough ability combined with thorough honesty . . . without regard to race, color, or previous condition of servitude." This was one of those rare moments in history when one group of citizens once had been actual slaves, so that their struggle now was much different from everyone else's. It was on a higher plane, its goal not merely success but freedom. It made them heroes.

BUT THREE social developments of the day threatened to halt the rise of the great black athletes in the only sport where they were already turning heads. The first of these phenomena was an ugly one, which did not yet have a name. It was the mounting onslaught of prejudice, public insults, barbarisms, exclusions, denials of education and medical care, violence, torture, lynchings, abrogations of rights, legal restrictions, formal separation—all of which would be dubbed "racialism" only in 1907, and "racism" only in 1936. The latter coining, the neat codification of the problem, would become a powerful weapon, a real political triumph, but it would not become available until far into the twentieth century.[2]

Things were getting worse for African Americans. Of course, they had known the worst racial oppression for nearly two and a half centuries before the Civil War. But the end of slavery, the ratification of the Thirteenth, Fourteenth, and Fifteenth Amendments, and Reconstruction, which sent many blacks to state legislatures and Congress, had promised something like freedom and opportunity. As it turned out, a promise to blacks was viewed as a threat by many whites. As soon as it dawned on Northern whites that freedom for African Americans was not theoretical, many of them were horrified. They met the threat with a late-century rise in racial prejudice, including a campaign of vicious public slurs in the very best of newspapers. The South met it with a reign of terror, of mob murders, race riots, and lynchings. A congressional report for 1866–1868 showed that 373 freed slaves had been killed by whites. After 1867, the Ku Klux Klan initiated its own program of death and destruction, with the encouragement of Southern Democrats; Klansmen attacked and killed not only blacks but many white Republicans, followers of the party of Lincoln. The less organized violence was just as bad. The number of lynchings of African Americans, mostly in the South and West, would hit 85 in 1890, peak at 230 in 1892, and average about 150 a year until 1900.³

By the 1890s, the white majority, North and South, had begun to institutionalize its fear of sharing and its resultant hatreds. The South enacted discriminatory local and state legislation, replacing slavery with a rigid system of segregation, which had the same goal: the reduction of African Americans to a menial, still unarmed working class. State restrictions of civil rights, especially the right to vote, were accompanied by Jim Crow ordinances, which segregated African Americans in public life. Much of the North was doing the same on the local level, the frightened whites walling themselves off as more African Americans arrived from the South. It was a hypocritical response that would be repeated often during the civil rights era: liberal white Northerners staunchly opposing slavery and segregation until it appeared that they might have to share their neighborhoods and towns with blacks. This growing general nastiness, with its underlying threat of violence, augured new but not better days for America's experiment in interracial sports.

The second development that affected the black jockeys, and changed their world, was the mass African American migration from the South. The escape from the hopelessness of sharecropping and from rural violence led them first to the nearest cities. By 1880, six cities in the South had black majorities: New Bern and Wilmington, North Carolina; Montgomery, Alabama; Charleston, South Carolina; Petersburg, Virginia; and Savannah, Georgia. Four American cities had more than thirty thousand black residents: New Orleans, Baltimore, Washington, and Philadelphia. And with the African American influx, two had more than doubled in population. Indianapolis had grown by 121 percent and Kansas City by 116 percent.

The African American exodus from the South began in earnest in 1879, when thousands headed west, especially to and through Kansas. It led to the strangest paramilitary adventure of the day. To help prevent the South from losing its cheap black labor, a band of white terrorists, led by a former Confederate general, James Chalmers, blockaded the Mississippi and threatened to sink any steamboats that carried the 1879 migrants away from the South and the border states. Caving in, the steamboat companies left the migrants stranded at riverports and refused to take on any more of them, until the U.S. Army broke the ban.

The later migration north was more dramatic. Between 1880 and 1890, when the exodus was still in its early stages, Washington's black population expanded by 65 percent, to more than seventy-five thousand, which made up the biggest urban black community in the country. Baltimore was next, with more than sixty-seven thousand African Americans. Chicago's black population was only sixteen thousand, but that represented an increase of 121 percent. The trip from Southern farm or town to Northern city was a daunting passage, and whites seemed as frightened by it as blacks. In New York City, where the black population jumped by 86 percent in the 1880s, the *New York Age* was soon complaining about the "loud of mouth, flashy of clothes, obtrusive and uppish southern Negro." Worse, blacks were seen as a "threat to law and order." In one massive shift, African Americans had become city dwellers. This alone shrank the pool from which black jockeys might be drawn. Struggling in a big city, a young African American was not likely to find his way to a horse's back, let alone a racecourse. In only a few generations, charity campaigns would be organized to take African American kids to the countryside to show them what a horse's back looked like.[4]

Along with intensifying racial pressures and the displacement of the black population came another phenomenon: big money. Whether the money was coming or going, black jockeys were likely to get the worst end of the deal. It was nothing new. In slavery, some great black riders had carved out extraordinary lives for themselves against all odds, riders like Simon and Charles Stewart, who managed to make good money, and Stewart and Cornelius and Monk, who traveled the country. But many more, like the "sable" boy who defeated the great white Willis at Augusta, got a lot less for their talent, and no credit. The white riders, from Sam Purdy to Barney Francis to Gilbert Patrick, had always been free to build careers for themselves as independent operators and to negotiate the best possible retainers. In the biggest antebellum North-South matches, starting with American Eclipse versus Henry, it was the white jockeys who got to ride, even if it meant dragging Arthur Taylor out of retirement while Charles Stewart was right there at that Long Island track.

While black riders were now free to wheel and deal as well, the white riders were much freer, especially in the giant New York market. They not only faced fewer obstacles, such as bigotry, but they enjoyed far more advantages, such as free publicity in the adoring press, which saw them, as indeed it always had, as the great white hopes. In the Gay Nineties, the press found the white boys increasingly entertaining, even as newspapers stepped up their racial attacks on blacks. Not only could Fred Taral wheel, deal, and command twelve thousand dollars for first call, and eight thousand dollars for second, but he could also create a valuable cloud of publicity for himself, running around with John L. Sullivan while folks laughingly dubbed them "Big and Little Casino." That hilarious world, which generated news, interest in the sport, and job offers, was not open to black jockeys.

A few African Americans confronted big money head on and won spectacularly. One was Albert Cooper. He was the first trainer of Domino, the horse of the 1890s, who was owned by Foxhall Keene, son of the Wall Street manipulator James R. Keene. In the time-honored fashion of dumping African Americans when the money was getting big, Cooper was replaced by trainer Billy Lakeland, the former jockey, before Domino's racing career began. One reason given was that Domino's legs might have been damaged by the fast trials that Cooper put him through, but the switch also seemed proof of a widely circulated ditty that Cooper liked to recite. The subject: what happens when the money hits several figures, with lots of zeros. "A naught's a naught/And a figger a figger/All for the white man/And none for the nigger."[5]

Cooper not only exposed the racket, but beat it. He was one of several black trainers who owned their own stables, and he had a little yearling, Hyderabad, that he had bought for $350. Hyderabad showed such amazing speed, "Foxie" would recall, that the elder Keene bought him for $30,000, a vast sum, just to keep him out of Domino's way. It was a huge score for Cooper, but not for the Keenes, as Foxie admitted. "*Hyderabad* was a bad buy. All he ever did for us was to fall down in the Futurity, causing his stablemate, *Domino*, to trip over him." Domino won anyway, Fred Taral up.

Big money also made it tougher for the small owners and trainers to survive. In Kentucky, this weakened the black jockeys' base, since the small stables traditionally schooled most of the African American kids. In the good old capitalist tradition, a few giants pushed everyone else out of the way. One was Milton Young, who bought McGrathiana, near Lexington, and expanded it to two thousand acres, with more than a hundred broodmares. Another was Keene *père*, who expanded Castleton Farm, also near

Lexington. Then there was James Ben Ali Haggin, who eventually transferred his California stud to Kentucky, bought Elmendorf Farm, and expanded it to nearly nine thousand acres.

In fact, native son Haggin dealt the Bluegrass one of its worst blows when he pulled out of Churchill Downs for good after winning the 1886 Derby. That year, Haggin had brought a gang of friends who planned to back his Ben Ali heavily, but when they arrived for the race, they discovered that, as a result of a licensing dispute, there were no bookmakers at the track. Informed of Haggin's rage, a track official supposedly said, "To hell with him anyway." Haggin pulled out his stable the next morning and headed back east. Other major owners joined him in boycotting Churchill, too. After a few seasons this began to tell. In seven of the ten years starting in 1891, the Derby had fields of five or fewer. And all of that decade's derbies employed only thirty-three jockeys, at least twelve of them black. Of that dozen, several rode in more than one Derby; Monk Overton in seven, for example, and Tiny Williams in five. It dramatized what the *Spirit of the Times* called the dearth of young black jockeys on the way up.

GIVEN THE setting, it is nothing short of astounding that the black jockeys were able to perform so brilliantly in the early and mid-1890s. From 1889 through 1892, *Goodwin's Official Turf Guide*, which gave the records of the prominent riders, would list at least ten to fifteen African Americans out of a total of thirty-seven to fifty-six jockeys a year—I say "at least" because, happily, the jockeys were never identified by race, either in the official race listings or in the records. The above figures represent only those who were known to have been African Americans. Doubtless a few others on the list were black, as were many lesser, or lesser-known, riders who did not make the list at all. In mid-decade, from 1893 through 1898, the number of known African American riders on the list continued to range from a fifth to a fourth of the total.

New York City, with its several racetracks, was still the capital of American sports. And while on any given day the black riders there were almost always outnumbered, four of them would share the pinnacle of their profession with the likes of veteran white jockeys Snapper Garrison, Fred Taral, Martin Bergen, and Sam Doggett, and then with the great white riders who followed them, such as Lester Rieff and Harry Griffin. The four black jockeys who carry us through this decade are Anthony Hamilton, Alonzo "Lonnie" Clayton, James "Soup" Perkins, and the best of them all, Willie Simms.

WHEN Tony Hamilton captured the American Derby in 1887 and the important Brooklyn Handicap two years later, only to be subjected to the racial taunts of the *New York Herald*, he responded by leaping onto Potomac and grabbing the richest sweepstakes yet run in America—at least since the days when Austin Curtis was riding and tobacco plantations were the stakes. It was America's greatest sporting event of the moment, the third Futurity, worth $67,675— and these were 1890 dollars—to August Belmont.

In that same year, 1890, Tony avenged himself again and again with at least four other stakes wins in and around New York City, including the inaugural Toboggan Handicap and a second straight Monmouth Oaks. He was the fourth-leading jockey in the country that year, with 123 victories, and he had the best winning percentage by far among the leaders, a stunning 33.2. Of the fifty-six riders listed in the official records, at least twelve were black.

Hamilton was back on Potomac in 1891 to collect the rich Realization Stakes at Sheepshead Bay, the judges, luckily for him, ignoring a photograph that showed Montana's head in front. That $30,850 went to the increasingly fancy Brooklyn butcher Mike Dwyer. For 1891, Hamilton was the number-two jockey in the country, with 154 wins, versus 197 for a white rider named H. Penny. The only one who topped Hamilton's winning percentage of 33.7 was Monk Overton, with 34.6. Of the nine riders with a hundred or more wins, four were black (Hamilton, Overton, Simms, and Tiny Williams).

Hamilton experienced a dip in his career from 1892 into 1894, but soon after that he started getting back to his old form, riding for white trainer Billy Lakeland, who was still working for the

Keene stable. South Carolina–born Hamilton worked well with Lakeland, an English immigrant. As a jockey, Billy had won the Louisville Jockey Club's 1875 inaugural, ridden in the first Kentucky Derby, and seen it all. He had worked side by side for two decades with the top black jockeys, and perhaps this had something to do with Hamilton's success under him. Reporting on Hamilton's comeback, the *New York Times* mixed praise with racial slurs in a sentence that was more revealing of white attitudes than the reporter knew. "The once popular and successful jockey seems to be able to ride better for 'Billy' Lakeland than for anyone else, and the trainers assert that this is due to the fact that Lakeland knows more about languages than Prof. Garner ever dreamed of in the wilds of Africa, and so is able to hold successful converse with Hamilton."[6]

Perhaps it was a case of Billy's British English meeting Tony's South Carolina English, and neither of them quite understanding New York English. In any event, it was yet another example of how the white general press was far more prejudiced in reporting on the black jockeys than was the white sporting press, since the latter knew how good they were and how important to the sport. It was also revealing of the widening chasm between provincial Northern whites, who had not met very many black people, and arriving Southern blacks, who were much more sophisticated on that score, having encountered plenty of white people. It took an Englishman to cross the chasm.

Racial slurs from leading newspapers notwithstanding, Hamilton entered 1895 targeting a couple of New York's most prestigious races—the Brooklyn and the Suburban Handicaps—which were vastly more important at the time than the Kentucky Derby, the Belmont, or the Preakness. These were two of the city's great handicaps. To level the competition in these races, the official track "handicapper" assigns different weights to the horses, the loads increasing according to their records and presumed abilities (and, in some cases, age, the older horses generally lugging more poundage). The Brooklyn was first in mid-May, with one of the most powerful lineups yet. Hamilton, aboard Hornpipe, was facing none other than Isaac Mur-

Tony Hamilton takes the laurels as the Suburban Stakes winner at the Coney Island Jockey Club in 1895. Courtesy of Keeneland Association.

phy, who had less than nine months to live. Murphy's horse was an even better four-year-old, the chestnut Lazzarone, a fact which the official Gravesend handicapper noted by assigning 105 pounds to Hornpipe, 114 to Lazzarone, which must have been brutal for Ike to make, unless he was so sick at this point that he was already there. They were off, and in old Murphy fashion, the dying Ike staged a sensational late run—they once dubbed it the "Murfinish"—but it was Hornpipe by a little more than a neck.

"Won cleverly," said the official chart of the race, which never made references to anybody's ethnic background. Hamilton had added eight thousand dollars to the cash reserves of the Keenes. A month later it was the equally prestigious Suburban at the other Brooklyn course, Sheepshead Bay. But this time it was Hamilton on Lazzarone, and it was Lazzarone by a length and a half in another sensational finish. "A clever race," said the chart. The following spring, in 1896, Hamilton took the Metropolitan, on Counter Tenor, becoming the only black jockey ever to win all three of those celebrated New York handicaps, albeit in two different years.

ALONZO "LONNIE" CLAYTON was a boy wonder: the youngest jockey at the time to win the Kentucky Derby. Born in Kansas City in 1876, when African Americans were getting out of the South, he followed a brother into the profession. He was only about twelve years old when he hooked up with Lucky Baldwin's stable in Chicago as an exercise boy, not that twelve years old was an unusual age for exercise boys, black or white. In fact, it was perfect. Young, light boys for young horses. By age thirteen, he was riding in the East, and by fourteen he was competing before the throngs from New York City at Morris Park, the beautiful new track in Westchester County. He won the Jerome Stakes on Picknicker, carrying 125 pounds, a good portion of it being lead in his saddle (suggesting the origin of a less elegant phrase). The boy had to make 108 pounds to board two-year-old Azra for the Champagne Stakes.

The next year, 1892, Lonnie was aboard Azra again for the best birthday present anyone could ask for: he had just turned fifteen when Azra made him the youngest rider ever to win the Kentucky Derby. All of the Derby jockeys that year were black, but it was not much of a horse race, as was typical of the decade. For one thing, there were only three contestants, and the other two (with Tommy Britton and Monk Overton up) were a stable entry, owned

Jockey Alonzo Clayton had just turned fifteen when he won the Kentucky Derby in 1892. Courtesy of Keeneland Association.

by Ed Corrigan. Lonnie and Azra also scored victories in the Clark at Churchill Downs and the Travers at the Spa.

Clayton became one of the great riders of the New York circuit all through the 1890s, but he rode all over the country, doubling in the Kentucky Oaks in 1894 and 1895 and then returning to Saratoga to add the Flash Stakes. In three other Kentucky Derbies, he was "in the money," finishing second in 1893 and 1897 and third in 1895.

JAMES "SOUP" PERKINS was born in Kansas City but was raised in Lexington, the cradle of so many in the sport. James's mother died when he was very young, but he had the comfort of a big family, with four brothers and two sisters. Their father worked with trotting horses and proved quite the role model, as four of the five sons got involved with horses. Little Soup grew up on Thomas Street, if you can call exercising horses at age ten growing up. But Thomas Street was just a hop, skip, and a jump to the racetrack, and as kids who have grown up near tracks will tell you, the place was a playground, with wide-open spaces, strange hiding places, fences, trees, stables, water, and eye-popping horses, not to mention crazy old men to chase you away.

But why "Soup"?

"He'd come home for lunch," his younger brother Walter said. "When he'd go back to the track, the other boys would ask him, 'James, what did you have for lunch?' He'd say, 'Soup.'" And so they started calling him "Soup." The boy got an even earlier start than Lonnie at winning, scoring at Latonia at age eleven in 1891. Eleven? It was extremely young, but that was racing—and it had been for more than two centuries. Of course, at that time, eleven-year-olds, white and black, worked on farms and in factories, too, so why not on the backs of thoroughbreds? At thirteen, he won five of the six races on the card one day at Lexington. At the ripe age of fourteen, Soup won Kentucky's important Latonia Oaks, then took the train to New York, where the *Times* pronounced him "the best lightweight jockey of the West." He sort of proved it by

292 • THE GREAT BLACK HOPES

riding five of the six winners on one card again, this time at Saratoga.[7]

Soup started a fabulous 1895 by winning Lexington's classic, the ancient Phoenix Stakes, aboard Halma. Four days later he was on Halma again in the Kentucky Derby—it was the last Derby run at a mile and a half; the distance would be a mile and a quarter after that. The fifteen-year-old claimed Louisville's classic before a crowd of twenty thousand, tying Lonnie Clayton as the youngest Derby winner ever. Nobody knows whose birthdate fell first, but Lonnie did have an excellent view of Soup—from behind. Perkins won in 2:37½, and Lonnie was third. The white rider Willie Martin was second, and Monk Overton fourth. To describe the winner, the local reporter reached for his racial palette. "Proud and happy was little 'Soup' Perkins, a smile splitting his orange-colored face as he returned to the jockey room." But Soup was used to it, and he would overcome it. We hear from Soup himself, albeit in the reporter's typical stilted translation.

"It's the first Derby I ever rode, and I'm mighty glad I won it. . . . I had an easy thing of it. I never let go Halma's head, and I believe he could have gone the mile and a half in 2:35 easy. I was instructed to get off and go along all the way. I had to hold him clear to the finish. There was no place in this race when I could not have gone away from the field as I pleased, and I felt safe. Halma could have gone six miles further and beat such horses as these. This was the last mile and a half race to be run in Louisville, and I'm proud to have been the winner. All I had to do was to sit still and hold him."[8]

New York City might treat him like an adult, but Kentucky knew he was just a neighborhood kid, albeit a *wunderkind.* "A proud and happy boy was little Soup Perkins," said another report, noting that his family had come over from Lexington and "almost carried him on their shoulders in their pride and joy." This Louisville reporter had his paints ready, too, but he also had nothing but good things to say. "The chocolate-colored face of 'Soup'

Perkins, as he is familiarly called, is familiar to all race-goers. He is one of the remarkably successful jockeys for his age and has the additional merit of being able to ride as low as ninety pounds. According to his own statement yesterday, he is 'going on sixteen' and doesn't remember exactly when he did begin his training as a jockey, but thinks he must not have been over ten or twelve years old when he began his career in the saddle."[9]

Lonnie Clayton and Monk Overton were quoted, too, the reporter noting, "Bright-faced little Lonny Clayton was a little cast down by his defeat. He pointed sadly to his saddle, the back of which was split wide open. 'Just as we came into the stretch for the first time . . . my saddle slipped way up on Laureate's back, and I had to ride out in that way. It may have made a difference in the result, and it may not. I had no instructions, and my idea was to lay with Halma unless the pace was too slow. I hardly think my horse could have beaten Halma to-day.'" Overton said of his mount, Curator: "He went all right at first, and up to the seven-eighths, I thought I had a chance for the place [second]. But when we straightened out on the old back stretch, about seven-eighths from the stand, he had enough. I had no instructions, and all I had to do was whip." Both their remarks reveal the complete responsibility that was often given to the riders.

Halma added a couple of footnotes to Derby lore. He was the first black colt to win it, and he was the first winner to sire a Derby winner, Alan-a-Dale, who took the classic in 1902 with the black jockey Jimmy Winkfield up.

Soup and Halma went on to win the Clark Stakes at Louisville. Before he was through, James Perkins would be America's leading rider in 1895, with 192 wins. The white rider Harry Griffin was next with 187, the black jockey Jerry Chorn third with 179. Brother Walt said Soup was very generous with gifts to his family and also liked to gamble. "He particularly liked to shoot craps." His career was quick as a gambler's winning streak, a flash, a few years near the top—but such a bright spark that it lighted

James "Soup" Perkins steals the spotlight from some of his fellow jockeys.
The jockeys from left are Tommy Knight (star on jacket), S. Koper,
James Connely, unknown, and Soup. Courtesy of Keeneland Association.

the sport in mid-decade. His brother Will Perkins, on the other hand, was a marathon man, carrying the family name far into the future. A fine trainer, Will Perkins saddled six horses for the Kentucky Derby through 1925, two of them, John Finn and Song of John, finishing third.

WILLIE SIMMS and Fred "the Flying Dutchman" Taral were the greatest two American jockeys of the century's last decade, and among the nation's top few athletes in any sport. Born near Augusta, Georgia, in 1870, Simms got into racing for maybe the best reason ever given: he liked the colors of the jockey uniforms he saw at country fairs. Or so it was said. There must have been more to it than that, though, when he set off without his parents' permission for New York.[10]

At age twenty-one, and under 105 pounds, Willie Simms began his conquest of famous stakes at Saratoga, winning the 1891 Spinaway on the filly Promenade. He wound up the fifth-leading jockey in the country that year, and he rose to number two in 1892. That fall Pierre Lorillard, who lorded it over the seven-thousand-acre Tuxedo Park in Orange County, New York, and the fabled Rancocas Stud at Jobstown, New Jersey, signed Willie for what was said to be $12,000 for 1893—"a very big retainer for a boy like Simms," as the *Sporting World* newspaper accurately observed. Lorillard himself must have got wind of it, though, because the next day the paper lowered the amount to $10,500 and attached a warning to Simms, lest it go to his head. "After he will lose a few swell bets for the master of Rancocas, he may receive a vacation." It was still a big fee, more than 25 percent better than the $8,000 that another stable paid for the strong white rider Sam Doggett. Still, he was worth the money, and whoever got first, second, or third call on Simms's services was lucky, indeed. In that 1893 season, on Commanche, he took the Belmont Stakes, which alone was worth $5,310 to the Empire Stable. Moreover, he was the year's national riding champion, with 182 wins, well ahead of John "Skeetz" Martin with 154, and Doggett with 134.[11]

So Willie Simms was officially the best there was in the country's biggest sport. The next year, 1894, produced a marvelous competition with the Flying Dutchman, as Simms and Taral dueled for the honors of New York. Most of the press only had eyes for the "rosy-cheeked" Taral, who did have a pleasant air about him, as seen in one old photograph in which he is smiling contentedly among his colleagues, black and white. It was the year the Dutchman drew a bead on an unprecedented feat, the conquest in one season of all three of New York's great spring handicaps, the Metropolitan, the Brooklyn, and the Suburban. Methodically, Taral won the Brooklyn, on Dr. Rice, and the Metropolitan, on Ramapo. Methodically, Simms beat Taral to win a second consecutive Belmont Stakes, on Henry of Navarre. Then came the third big handicap, the Suburban, and Taral's big chance. He was on

Ramapo again. The race lured at least twenty thousand to the Coney Island oval by Sheepshead Bay. As for Willie, if he loved racing's sartorial rainbow, he must have been agog as he rode to the post on that boiling first day of summer.

"The ladies braved the heat in their latest gowns. The green foliage on the lawn . . . the silks worn by the jockeys, and the grand specimens of horseflesh on the track all added to the picturesque scene. . . . In the throng were doctors, lawyers, actors, journalists, composers, politicians, gamblers, men about town, pugilists, Chinamen, some Indians from Buffalo Bill's Wild West Show, an army of touts. . . . They stood shoulder to shoulder, and cheered Ramapo and his clever rider."[12] The *Times* reporter was also inordinately interested in the colors, not of the jockeys' silks, but of the jockeys. As the dozen steeds pranced to the starting line, he spotted four-year-old "Sport, with the dusky Thompson" and Banquet with "the coffee-colored Sims [a common spelling then]." Soup Perkins was also among the dozen riders, but most of the others were white. The order of finish: Taral, Simms, Thompson. "Taral's Victory Gives Him a Triple Crown Such as No Other Jockey Has Ever Yet Won," shouted a headline, the article calling it "a record for all other jockeys to aim at in the future," although a quarter of a century later a different triple crown would carry far more prestige. In August, Simms would be the man of the moment, taking a remarkable five out of six races at Morris Park and then coming back a week later to do it again. By the end of 1894, the quiet Georgian concluded his second straight year as national champion. Another black jockey, James Irving, was ranked fifth. Taral was seventh, Hamilton eighth.

As the top athlete in the country's top sport, Simms was also making big money. The Brooklyn meat-monger Mike Dwyer, the politician Richard Croker, and then Phil Dwyer had first, second, and third call on his services, respectively, in 1895. That, with extra fees for winning, brought his income to about twenty thousand dollars a year, making him one of the wealthiest jockeys in the country, and it was all his. He never married; he just saved and in-

THE GREAT BLACK HOPES • 297

vested in real estate, although he did treat himself to an estate back home in Augusta, with a modern gymnasium, a riding stable, and a tallyho drawn by six magnificent horses. It would have been a nice place to hang around, but his employers were so happy with him they decided to take him to England, which everybody thought of as the sport's mother country—and which, of course, it was. England meant money, too, and, probably just as important to the Dwyers and Croker, polish.[13]

When he traversed the Atlantic, Willie Simms changed his sport, all over the world and forever, but that was not clear right off. What he did was introduce England to the natural American riding style—short stirrups, rider crouched over the horse's neck and withers—the same aerodynamic style that had been shocking English visitors to this country since the eighteenth century. The style was inspired by the short, fierce Colonial quarter races, in which crouching and clinging definitely beat getting knocked off the animal. It was employed, too, by American Indians on the horses they acquired from the Spanish. English visitors had noticed it most often on black riders, but the slave-holding congressman John Randolph had used it in his own quarter-racing days, earning him one of the first comparisons of the crouching jock with a monkey on a horse. One tourist thought that Duncan Kenner's black jockeys rode like Englishmen, but at least one of Kenner's riders, Abe Hawkins, crouched. Gilpatrick probably crouched to some degree as well, since when he went to England they found his riding style atrocious, although it was never claimed that he introduced the crouch over there. Lanky Snapper Garrison adopted a high variation of it, whereas Ike Murphy sat bolt upright like a proper Englishman. In the mid-1890s, a new white kid out of Indiana, Tod Sloan, was clinging like a monkey on the American tracks and in short stirrups, although he had no choice with the stirrups, since his legs didn't go any farther. Indeed, by this time, the officially incorrect, or at least highly un-English, crouch was on its way to acquiring a slightly dignified title at home, "the American seat."

Was England ready for it?

No.

Was England ready for a black rider?

No.

Was England prejudiced?

"The sight of him taking Eau Gallie to the start of the Craw-furd Plate on April 16 induced ridicule and derision," a later English turf authority wrote of Willie's debut at Newmarket. But as the writer added, "Simms silenced the mockers in the time-honoured way: he won. In his slipstream toiled the cream of English jockeyship, including Morny Cannon, Sam and Tommy Loates, Fred Allsopp and Walter Bradford—the five leading riders in the table."

Simms might have recognized he was in trouble in a place where they spelled it Crawfurd and Allsopp. "Prejudice was hard to overcome. In four months Simms secured only 19 rides (four wins, four places) and he recrossed the Atlantic to resume his Classic-winning habit. . . . Nevertheless, a beach-head was established." Two years later the white boy Tod Sloan, who crouched even more, would cross the water and be accused of turning jockeyship into "monkeyship." But he was not covered with racial hatred and, more important, turned in a fabulous winning record, so that the English were finally dragged, kicking and screaming, into the American seat. And many historians would later conclude, erroneously, that Toddy had invented the "modern riding position" first used on the Colonial race paths and on the Indian prairies.[14]

Following his not quite excellent adventure in Britain, Simms did not have enough of the year left to win the 1895 riding championship, and he had to cede it to Soup Perkins. That made black riders the national champions for three years in a row, and counting Pike Barnes's consecutive titles (1888–89), they had worn the crown for five of the eleven years since *Goodwin's* started keeping annual records on the jockeys. On his return from England, Simms had gone back to Morris Park in Westchester County, New

York. He won the Jerome Stakes on Counter Tenor and the Champagne Stakes on the bay Ben Brush. The two-year-old Ben Brush had begun his juvenile season as the property of Ed Brown, the former slave rider named Dick, who now owned a highly regarded training stable. After Ben Brush won five straight, Brown sold him to Mike Dwyer, who watched him conclude the year with seven straight. Knowing a piece of horseflesh, butcher Mike opened 1896 by fielding his prodigy in Louisville's May classic. It was Willie Simms's first Kentucky Derby.

The shiny Twin Spires of Churchill Downs were a long way from Newmarket, where spectators the previous spring had ridiculed and derided the lone American black jockey. Parading with Simms to the post for the 1896 Derby, which finally had attracted a decent-sized field of eight, were five other African Americans: Soup Perkins, Monk Overton, Tommy Britton, Tiny Williams (riding Ulysses for owner Ed Brown), and none other than William Walker, a veteran of the first Derby, now in his fourth and last.

Though Churchill Downs had installed one of those newfangled starting gates then being tried out around the country, they certainly weren't going to use it for the Derby, which was too important. Instead, Jack Chinn held "the old flag, flat-footed and unaided," and when he dropped it, it looked as though Willie was thinking too much about England, or the beautiful colors, or something, because Ben Brush stumbled, nearly tossing Willie before the screaming thousands. Dwyer's colt looked totally out of it, but Simms found his American seat again and then urged his little bay into an incredible drive—fighting off John Tabor on Ben Eder to win a blazing finish by a nose. It was the first time the winning colt was presented with a collar of roses—white and pink, tied with white and magenta ribbon—although it would be 1925 before a sports columnist would dub it "the run for the roses."[15]

New York was next. Would Simms win his third Belmont Stakes? The second August Belmont was risking an heirloom on this thirtieth running of the classic named for his father. He would give the victor the bowl that August I had earned with Fenian in the third Belmont Stakes: a giant Tiffany acorn held aloft by three silver stallions, with Fenian on top. Actually, Belmont hoped to present this wonder to himself, by winning with three-year-old Hastings. But Phil Dwyer stood to gain a lot more in the way of prestige if he could display that trinket. There had never been many of them hanging around his sides of beef in the butcher shop. And Phil not only had the three-year-old Handspring, who had beaten Hastings in the Withers Stakes. He also had Willie Simms (the Dwyer brothers were operating independently now, and each was using Simms).[16]

In spite of all his accomplishments, Simms was not too well known by the white public in New York. The *Times* said of the crowd on another big race day that they "generally knew of but two jockeys, Garrison and Taral"—then as now acting as if the press had nothing to do with the ignorance of their audience. Not only did the big papers sometimes disparage black jockeys, or give them no coverage at all; the general press also took no note whatsoever of the black fans, who must have quietly rooted for "their" jockeys. Unless they lost, of course—this was racing, after all. They and the sport's professionals, white and black, knew Simms, and none better than "the Western crowd" that had come up to New York from the Bluegrass that spring for the Belmont.

"In their opinion," said the *Times* one day, referring to the Kentucky crowd, "Sims was the greatest jockey on earth, because he had won the Kentucky Derby. A boy or horse that does that is always for the year the greatest on earth, no matter what the horse or the boy may be. That is the sort of patriots they are out that way. It is a mighty good characteristic. It also saves a lot of fault-finding with jockeys." That Bluegrass chauvinism would be just as intense more than a century later. So on that particular Tuesday, in early June 1896, "the greatest jockey on earth" and three white riders—Taral, Doggett, and Harry Griffin—waited for the starter to drop the flag.

They were off! More or less. It was an "outrageous" start, said the *Herald*, with horses facing every which way as the flag fell, but Handspring jumped to the lead and kept it, although no thanks to Simms. Astoundingly, he seemed to be using all his strength to restrain his mount. Dwyer had made a mistake. He wanted this so badly he had micromanaged his jockey, instructing him to hold back at all costs until the final three furlongs. And Simms did, to everybody's confusion.

At the head of the stretch, Simms finally let go, and Handspring sprang. Just as suddenly, though, exhausted after being choked for a mile, Handspring drifted toward the outside rail. Simms dragged the colt back inside, where Hastings caught them with two furlongs to go. Simms found something extra in his colt and squeezed in front again, but Hastings and Griffin, his jockey, extended themselves, too, reaching Handspring's shoulder. The Belmont, then a mile and three-eighths, turned into a sprint. "A chorus of almost demoniac shrieks" rose from the crowd, said a reporter. With one last and supreme effort, Griffin lifted Hastings. August II repossessed the family silver by a neck, and it would become the permanent Belmont Stakes trophy, the prize still awarded today.

In a noble moment for an owner, Dwyer took the blame— "Dwyer Says Orders Beat His Colt," read a headline—and vowed he would "never again give orders to a jockey." In itself, that was something of a tribute to Simms. He had failed to acquire a third Belmont, but with his previous two, he would remain the last African American to wear that jewel for more than a century.

THE FOLLOWING month Simms was a witness, and so was Lonnie Clayton, as Tony Hamilton rode into a brick wall, and not in a steeplechase. Suddenly, not only the *Times* was after Tony, so was the sport's new authority, its first effective governing body.

For two and a half centuries, America's leading sport had been a loose collection of jockey clubs, or racing associations, operating independent tracks. As the sport was part traveling circus, the big stables moving from one track to another, the clubs sometimes coordinated their schedules and regulations. Once, after Chippie Ray got suspended for contract-jumping, the *Spirit of the Times* reporter noted, "The youth has not yet been reinstated by either the Louisville and Memphis clubs, and I assume he will not don the colors for anybody East or West until such reinstatement is effected."

By the 1890s, the chaotic, big-money New York–New Jersey area cried out for organization. It had several tracks serving the same market, among them three in Brooklyn—the Coney Island Jockey Club's course ("Sheepshead Bay"), with the biggest crowds in the country, and its close neighbors, the Brooklyn Jockey Club's course ("Gravesend") and Brighton Beach. Plus there was the new Morris Park in Westchester County, the still newer Monmouth Park in New Jersey, and the Queens County Jockey Club's planned Aqueduct track on Long Island.

Pierre Lorillard had brought an illusion of law and order to this mad scene in 1891 when he organized the regulatory Board of Control, which included the big track operators and a few important stable owners. But its authority and rules had been promptly ignored by smaller tracks and stable owners, who found it amusing to be deemed "outlaws" by the big boys. When the bookmaker Fred "Gus" Walbaum launched winter racing at his Guttenberg track in Jersey, right across the Hudson from Manhattan, the board outlawed it, meaning that no stables that raced there could compete at the big board-approved tracks. As one reporter put it, "the Guttenbergers laughed and went on making money." And both board-sanctioned owners and outlaws were among the winners at Saratoga, when Walbaum took over that mecca in 1892.

Lorillard's laughed-at Board of Control was succeeded in 1894 by the Jockey Club. It was not a jockey club in the original sense of an association of stable owners, would-be gentleman jockeys, who operated a local racecourse. Rather, it was a group of big stable owners who intended to run the entire sport, at least in its most important location, the New York–New Jersey area. Instigated by

James R. Keene, the Jockey Club limited its membership to fifty. Seven served as directors, or "stewards," including chairman John Hunter, August Belmont II, and Keene himself. After a year, Belmont II took over and served as chairman through 1924, carrying on in the tradition of his late father as one of the founding fathers of modern American sports.

Like the Board of Control, the Jockey Club gave itself the power to outlaw tracks and stable owners, banning them from club-approved tracks until reinstated. Like the board, it was widely ignored. There were more than twelve hundred "outlaw" racehorses at one point. Unlike the board, and to its credit, the Jockey Club was more interested in the survival of the sport than in protecting certain individuals, so its authority was increasingly accepted as it set about licensing jockeys and trainers, rewriting rules, setting schedules, and publishing the American Stud Book, a listing of genealogically acceptable thoroughbreds.

The American metropolis cried out for policing, too. As many as sixty bookmakers would set up their stands inside the "betting ring," which was usually on or near the lawn in front of the clubhouse. This menagerie had driven away the old auction pools and the original pari-mutuels and was happily processing hundreds of thousands of 1890s dollars. Each bookmaker would hand out his own stylized tickets—"pasteboards"—collectible the next day. Others operated off-track. And professional bettors, or "commissioners," were another breed, placing wagers for anonymous big spenders. In one sense, little had changed from the days when a Southerner might bet a plantation on the talents of a jockey like Austin Curtis, except that the Northern capitalists were wagering cash to demonstrate their masculinity, one Wall Street john soon earning himself the handle "Bet-A-Million" Gates. It was a breeding ground for scams, fertilized by the fact that stable owners, trainers, and jockeys were among the plungers.

But why was Tony Hamilton, in July 1896, suddenly targeted by the most powerful authority in American sports? His Metropolitan

Handicap win notwithstanding, "Hamilton has been under suspicion all the season on account of his erratic performances in the saddle," said the *Times*. The issue finally reached the Jockey Club president. "One of the last things August Belmont did before his departure for Europe was to give Hamilton a severe but friendly talking to about his performances, a bit of kindly advice." It must have been an interesting scene, the sport's new caesar, one of the richest men of New York, delivering a warning to a lone black athlete.

Hamilton's problems started at Brighton Beach on July 23, a Thursday. In a minor contest with only two other entries, white jockeys up, Tony was on the favored Hornpipe, and he led as expected to the half. Then "the cripple Mirage," as the *Times* described the horse, sailed by and won easily. A reporter called Hamilton's an abominable ride, and it was not a good day, either, for Billy Lakeland: he owned Hornpipe, bet him, and told his friends to do the same. After that showing, Lakeland and his friends naturally put their money elsewhere.

Hornpipe ran again on Saturday. The favorite this time was The Dragon, under Tod Sloan. Also in the race were Willie Simms, Lonnie Clayton, and Doggett. But who should come whipping past Sloan at the half, leading the field of eight in a driving finish before Brighton's new steel grandstand, but old Tony Hamilton, brilliant again. Too brilliant, actually. That extraordinary victory on the same nag two days later convinced the Brighton Beach stewards that he must have thrown Thursday's race. They suspended him for the rest of the meeting and turned the case over to the Jockey Club for possible revocation of his license to ride. The rumor around the track was that he had pulled Hornpipe on Thursday and then gone all out on Saturday, both times for the benefit of some bookmakers. The *Times* went screeching after him, wildly throwing one bomb after another.

"Hamilton, the colored jockey, who has been doing a lot of in-and-out riding this season, which performances have been variously accredited to the too free use of opium, to overindulgence in gin, and to downright rascality, will now have a chance to rest, to sober up, or to take a lesson in honesty, whichever he may need most."[17]

Billy Lakeland, the English trainer-gambler and Hamilton's friend, was no help either. He was asked how Hornpipe could have metamorphosed in two days from a pussycat into a tiger, but "Lakeland said that it completely baffled him. So Hamilton, it was agreed, must know something about it, and it was decided that the race tracks would be very much better off without his presence than with it. Hamilton was, therefore, put where he can do no more damage to the turf for some time to come."

Perhaps the *Times* forgot that this was the jockey who had won the American Derby, the Futurity, New York's three great handicaps, and much else. The paper then declared that the Jockey Club should ferret out the bookies, if they were the culprits, and rule them off the track forever. That might have been a little difficult since, as the *Times* had pointed out a few years before, the assistant secretary of the Jockey Club himself, a man named Hanlon, could be seen "rushing around the [betting] ring backing horses and then rushing back to the clubhouse lawn and holding conferences with the men who act as Stewards." In any event, the *Times* concluded that dishonest bookies "are far more culpable than this ignorant, muckle-headed negro, who has been punished by having his means of livelihood taken from him."

Exculpation, insult, racial slur, sympathy—all in one sentence. What a country!

It was mostly slurs. In the adjacent column, the *Times*'s list of also-rans in the sixth at Brighton included a two-year-old long-shot named Little Nigger. It would have been excused as a minor epithet at the time, a figure of speech, but it still indicated a broad racial attack, a casual way to say that no quarter would be given. Even as the *Times* expressed sympathy for Hamilton's plight, it switched to the plural, "Revoking the licenses of thick-headed negroes will not suffice to do the business at all."

It was as if the white Northern editors did not consider Negroes to be fellow Americans. While the black jockeys had often won respect and confidence in the South and Midwest, where they had always been part of the scene, as the early turf authority Charles Parmer once pointed out, they "were never popular in the East, either with owners or the public." He meant the white public. "The former didn't know how to handle them, and the . . . throngs along the rail looked upon them as curiosities." The white railbirds and editors, however, did seem to notice the African Americans as they reached the cities in increasing numbers and, in this one realm of sports, apparently meant to stay on top.

For once, a black jockey had made the headlines of a major newspaper, even though it wasn't the headline he would have wanted. Blared the *Times:* "Hamilton May Not Ride." With Belmont off to Europe, Tony was called before the imperious James Keene and the other powers of the Jockey Club, who would decide on revocation of his license. It was a frightening prospect, and there's no way to know how even-handedly Hamilton was treated, but on another occasion a black jockey accused of some transgression had figured out a way to deal with the stewards—sucker them. The stewards come off as major bigots in this story, recounted by Keene's son, Foxie, who was a versatile athlete himself and quite the rage among the aristocrats but, like his father, a bigot.

Just before the jockey appeared, according to Foxie, chairman Belmont told the other stewards that the proceeding should be made as formal and impressive as possible to scare the kid into telling the truth. "The negro was then summoned, and Mr. Belmont, with awful majesty, raised his gavel and brought it down on the top of his desk.[18]

"Bang! 'What is your name?'

" 'John,' was the quavering answer.

"Again the chairman's gavel fell. Bang! 'Your last name?'

" 'Williams, sir.'

"Bang! 'Residence?'

"The negro," the younger Keene wrote, "looked helplessly around." Keene didn't realize that it was a stupid question, since most of the jockeys lived on the stable grounds.

"'He means where do you live,' prompted Algernon Daingerfield.

"'Ma home is whar ma hat is,' grinned John Williams. 'Ah'm a flat-footed, no-account loafer, an' a crap-shootin' son of a bitch.'

"Under cover of the roar of laughter that wrecked the last semblance of dignity, Mr. Keene [Foxhall's father] whispered to his nephew, Daingerfield, 'Buy me that nigger, Algy, I like him.'"

No John Williams has been located in the records. But Foxhall's story, however much embroidered for his pals, is a reminder that African Americans had been using their wits to survive since the days of self-denigrating Charles Stewart and sarcastic Simon. And the fact that Foxie would feel comfortable advertising his ignorance as late as 1938, when his memoirs were published, would have been a reminder that the African Americans would need their wits for the foreseeable future. Whether the other Jockey Club stewards were as barbaric as the Keenes is subject to doubt.

The Jockey Club did continue to license black jockeys, whereas interracial baseball failed at the start. In 1884, Moses Fleetwood Walker had signed on as a catcher for Toledo, becoming not only the first black player in the major leagues but the last until Jackie Robinson. By the following year, integrated baseball was over and the first all-black team was organized. But the interracial sport of horse racing—still a much bigger draw than baseball, and still the national pastime as far as the crowds were concerned—continued to offer up great black stars for the public to applaud and the white press to insult. And as it turned out, the *Times* had to put a black jockey in a headline again a few days later: "Hamilton All Right."[19]

Tony had been questioned at length by Keene and other Jockey Club stewards and then exonerated—completely. His suspension at Brighton was lifted. He had done nothing wrong. The

Times was mortified. "With this slap in the face," it said, "the Stewards will probably take no further action no matter what strange things may happen in racing." Whatever the facts of this case, and Foxie's supercilious story notwithstanding, the Jockey Club did not openly treat black jockeys any differently from white jockeys. Like the sporting journals, its public stance seemed far less prejudiced than that of the catcalling general press—because the Jockey Club knew its sport and knew the contributions of the black jockeys.

As the decade wound down, Willie Simms, having won the Belmont Stakes twice, entered the Kentucky Derby in 1898. He was on Plaudit, who like Ben Brush had been purchased from Ed Brown by a rising power on the turf, in this case John Madden, of Fayette County, Kentucky. Unfortunately for Willie, not only was a colt named Lieber Karl the heavy favorite for this Derby, but he would be ridden by the great white pilot Tommy Burns, whose 277 victories that season would make him the leading rider in the country. Liking their chances, the wife of Lieber Karl's owner, J. W. Schorr, went ahead and purchased the most expensive floral design in Louisville to hang over their winner when they were quite finished with the running part. Unfortunately for Tommy and the Schorrs, Willie won the

A triumphant Willie Simms after winning the 1897 Suburban aboard Ben Brush. Courtesy of Keeneland Association.

Derby for the second and last time, by a nose. Research has not un-covered what Mrs. Schorr did with her floral design.

Simms is the only rider ever to bat 1.000 in more than one ap-pearance in racing's most famous event. Afterward, he went up to Gravesend and added the Preakness Stakes, which had been shifted from Pimlico to Brooklyn. So while Tony Hamilton was the only black jockey ever to win all the handicap triple crown classics, Willie Simms was the only black jockey to win all the (later more celebrated) three-year-old triple crown classics.

And just beyond the far turn, the twentieth century would dis-cover an African American rider who was a match for any on the all-time list, black or white. In the face of intensifying pressures, this athlete of the new century would go far beyond where his pre-decessors had been and would succeed when almost all other black jockeys were finding the doors closing. He would create for him-self a strange and exotic life, an adventure that could be described only as "fabulous" in the original sense, resembling the most imag-inative of fables.

Jimmy Winkfield was winner of back-to-back Kentucky Derbies in 1901 and 1902. Courtesy of Kentucky Derby Museum.

.10.

THE FALL *of* AMERICA'S FIRST STARS

JIMMY WINKFIELD AND THE

LAST OF THE GREAT BLACK JOCKEYS

1900–2000

JIMMY WINKFIELD GREW UP in Chilesburg, Kentucky, about eight miles from Lexington. He would never forget watching the thoroughbreds dancing along the white-fenced roads and wishing he was riding them. In 1896, the year Isaac Murphy died right there in Lexington, the year Willie Simms won his first Derby over at Louisville, Jimmy was fourteen. "I was going to school at nights and driving a carriage for some white folks during the day. Saturday we would all go to the race track. I used to play marbles with the stable hands between races, and I got to know the people there. One day in the spring of '97 a man offered me a job at Latonia for $8 a month and board. I was rich."[1]

Winkfield told his story to Roy Terrell of *Sports Illustrated* many years later. "I galloped an old mare that year that won five races, and each time she win, the owner gave me $5 and the jockey $5." He would sometimes switch into racetrack syntax, a bit of Southern English: "Each time she win." "That horse run a hell of a race." Anyway, Jimmy said, "Next spring Bub May hired me for

$10 a month and board. His daddy was mayor of Lexington, and in the summer of '98 they took some horses to Chicago, to Hawthorne [racetrack]. That's where I rode my first race." It was a disaster. Sixteen-year-old Jimmy was on a nag named Jockey Joe. He was also in a huge hurry to be great. So right from the start, instead of heading straight ahead out of his number-four post position, with maybe a slight slant toward the inside to make it a shorter trip, he cut the other three off, and they all collapsed on the ground, including Jockey Joe. "I took him for the rail," was how Jimmy explained it, "right across, in front of the three inside horses—and we all four went down. So the stewards had me up, and they asked me where I been riding.

"'I jus' rode,' I told 'em.

"'Ain't you never rode before, boy?' they asked me.

"'No, suh,' I said. So they looked at one another for a while, and they put me afoot for a year."

Jimmy had to wait a year to get his first win, at Hawthorne on the filly Evan Stock, which he followed up with thirty-nine victories at a little track across the border in Roby, Indiana, where a cold autumn wind blew off Lake Michigan. "It was so cold," he would recall, "that your hands froze on the reins." On the other hand, Jimmy was getting about as hot as he could get. Getting a three-year contract from Bub at twenty-five dollars a month, he went downriver to the New Orleans Fairgrounds, becoming the number-three jockey there in the spring of 1900. Then Bub hired him out to J. C. Cahn to ride the 7 to 1 Thrive in the 1900 Kentucky Derby. As Winkfield remembered it, the turn-of-the-century Derby crowds had the same problem they do now. "They'd walk twenty miles to get there, and then couldn't find a place to sleep."

Winkfield came in third in that Derby, earning three hundred dollars for owner Cahn, who paid him twenty-five dollars for the race. "Usually, I didn't get anything extra unless I won . . . and then only five or ten dollars." It still wasn't much money, but it would keep getting better.

In fact, things were getting so good for Winkfield and other black jockeys that it led to a "race war" that August at Chicago's tracks. It was a minor affair, but a troubling sign of things to come. "A race war is on between the jockeys at the local tracks," the *Thoroughbred Record* reported. "Jealous because of the success of so many colored riders, the white boys . . . have taken desperate measures to put their rivals out of business." The war led to several incidents at Chicago's Harlem Track, the paper noted. "Winkfield, one of the most successful of the colored boys riding at Harlem was crowded against the fence, bruising his leg." His horse cracked a couple of ribs. "Horse and rider escaped luckily at that." The black jockeys fought back. "The colored lads, becoming convinced that they were badly used, retaliated and the next day took a hand in the rough tactics. . . . The officials, who are aware of the jealousy, have done all they can to adjust matters and keep peace among the boys but have not yet succeeded in preventing accidents."

In 1901, Bub May sold Winkfield's contract to Patrick Dunne, and Jimmy became one of the top riders in the country, picking up extra fees on 161 wins. For the Kentucky Derby, he was aboard His Eminence, the best horse of the day, a bay son of Falsetto, grandson of Enquirer. "I got him away in front and stayed there. Was nothin' to it." He got a five-hundred-dollar bonus.

Only Isaac Murphy had won back-to-back Kentucky Derbies when Winkfield got tapped for the 1902 edition by stable owner Thomas Clay McDowell of Kentucky, a great-grandson of Henry Clay. McDowell was fielding two colts, Alan-a-Dale and The Rival. The former had terribly gimpy legs, so weak they usually trained him pulling a sulky (a harness-racing seat), tossing a boy into the saddle only when Alan-a-Dale had to be galloped fast. But Winkfield, who was often that boy and who also exercised The Rival, knew that weak-legged Alan was much faster. But how was he going to get picked for him when McDowell's other rider would be a well-known white boy from the North, Nash Turner? As Jimmy recalled, "Nash was a good jockey, pretty famous by then, and he was a white boy, so he was going to get his pick"—unless Jimmy could help it. Which he thought he could. After all, he was the exercise rider for both colts.

"For a month I pulled Alan-a-Dale in workouts. I never let him go better than 2:11 for a mile and a quarter, and all the time I galloped The Rival at about 2:09. So when Nash came down on the mornin' of the race, naturally he pick The Rival."

Winkfield never stopped calculating. Like all great competitors, he knew not only his opponents but the lay of the land. He knew the Churchill Downs oval was blanketed in the off-season with a protective layer of sand, which was pushed to the outside when the racing season began. So when the front-running Alan-a-Dale started to bobble on those legs past the half, and the favorite, a horse named Abe Frank, caught up to him on the outside, Jimmy moved out and forced Abe into the sand, where he just about stopped dead. Alan-a-Dale wobbled and bobbled on, until he was caught by the other two, The Rival and Inventor, Tiny Williams up. Again Jimmy escorted them to the edge of the sand pile, which didn't stop them but slowed them. He might have gotten in trouble with McDowell for doing this to his own stablemate, but he managed to avoid that by pushing Turner and Williams into the sand together.

Jimmy Winkfield aboard Alan-a-Dale, winner of the 1902 Kentucky Derby. Courtesy of Kentucky Derby Museum.

So gimpy Alan-a-Dale won by a nose, pulled up lame past the finish line, and never raced again. "For a long time," Jimmy told Roy Terrell of *Sports Illustrated*, "people keep asking me how come the second half of that race so slow. Well, I tell you why it was slow. I was ridin' four horses."

Nash Turner had a different version, in which he was just a decoy. "Switching me to ride The Rival caused Mr. McDowell to win the Derby," he said. "I was put on the worse horse so as to confuse the other boys." This did agree with Winkfield's account in one respect; namely, that it could be taken for granted that Turner would get the better mount. Nash said he hung back through most of the race, and the opposition stayed with him, "thinking I had something up my sleeve," which let Alan-a-Dale set his own pace. "When I made my move on The Rival after straightening away for home, they realized that the horse was all out, and the other boys set sail for Alan-a-Dale, but Winkfield had gotten too much of a lead on them. If I had been on Alan-a-Dale, the result might have been different, for [Monk] Coburn and Williams would have chased me hard all the way."[2]

Jimmy Winkfield became the second jockey in history, after Isaac Murphy, to win back-to-back Kentucky Derbies. McDowell gave him a thousand-dollar bonus. He gave the same amount to Turner for coming in third.

ONLY MURPHY had won three Kentucky Derbies, however, and nobody had won three in a row, when Winkfield was tapped for the 1903 edition. He was now an authentic star, especially in the Derby-daffy Bluegrass, or as the *Courier-Journal* put it, "a colored boy but one of the great race riders of the world." His mount, Early, was the heavy favorite. A clean-cut, rangy colt, Early "looked the part of a winner all over," said the Louisville paper. When he was in the paddock, being saddled for the race, "his demeanor was quiet, though when the saddle was adjusted, he opened his eyes wide, took a long look at little Winkfield, and, as if realizing what was expected of him, stepped out of the paddock and down in front of the stand in the parade, as daintily as if he were walking on eggs."

As usual, the horses lined up for the start of the race under the instructions of the starter, Jake Holtman. Jake seemed nervous that day, but it was understandable. He had the worst job in racing, constantly subject to the crowd's abuse when the horses did not get off properly or had to be restarted again and again, which could take several minutes. That day he must have been more jittery than usual because he was using a starting machine for the first time in the Derby. It was a primitive contraption, consisting merely of a narrow elastic tape, webbed and about four inches wide, that stretched across the track between two iron arms. When the starter pressed a button, the arms threw the webbed barrier outward and upward, out of the horses' way. If a horse broke prematurely and snapped the tape, an assistant starter would simply tie the loose ends back together, and they would try again.[3]

"I want you boys to stand up to the barrier and not to break until I give you the signal," Jake shouted, within earshot of the *Courier-Journal*'s man. "I don't intend to take any monkey business, and the first one of you that gets gay will be set down for the meeting!" Jake didn't care who the riders were, or that the Louisville press had dubbed one of them, Winkfield, "one of the great race riders in the world." When a horse started acting up, he snapped, "Landry, I have told you that I won't stand for any foolishness, so bring that colt up to the barrier and stand there!" Another, Bad News, lived up to its name by trying to get a running start, and his jockey caught hell. "You are learning how to ride awful fast for a stable boy, Davis!" Just as all the horses were perfectly aligned at last, Winkfield turned Early just a bit, just enough so that, as the *Courier-Journal* observed: "a beautiful start was spoiled. 'You little nigger!' yelled Mr. Holtman, whose patience had been thoroughly aroused by this time. 'Who told you that you knew how to ride? You are not down at New Orleans now, so come on and get in line!' These and similar other remarks were hurled at the riders by Holtman in rapid succession until their heads were buzzing."

Then: "Biff! Bang! 'Let her go!' yelled the assistant starter. . . .
The barrier was raised, and the race was on. As starter Holtman
walked down to the judges' stand after he had sent the field away,
he remarked: 'Gee, but ain't I glad that it is over."[4]

Jimmy may have spoiled a beautiful take-off for everybody
else, but he got the best start for himself when they had to redo it.
He pushed Early early, heading for an unprecedented third
straight Derby—which would make him more popular than ever
among the big gamblers who had laid vast amounts on him and the
colt. But as Jimmy pressed the winded Early down the homestretch, they were caught from behind by the chestnut Judge
Himes, who—as "the crowd rocked and bowed before the storm of
wild, bewildering sound"—won by less than a length.

In Louisville, black jockeys made the headlines a little more
easily than elsewhere, and Jimmy got a big one all right—top of
the page—but not the one he wanted: "Ill-Timed Ride by Winkfield, the Great Jockey, Responsible for the Result." It was not a
pretty report. Right after the race, the *Courier-Journal* interviewed
the winning jockey, Illinois-born Harry Booker, "an obscure little
white boy hardly graduated from the stable ranks," who had nothing but the old slur for Winkfield. As he caught Early in the
stretch, Booker said, "Winkfield turned around at me and laughed.
It was then that I was sure that I did not have a chance. That nigger, I was sure, was trying to make a sucker out of me. I thought
that he wanted me to come up to him so that he could draw away. I
knew that I had all the others beat off, so I just went on. I passed
Early. 'I have got that nigger beat,' I said to myself, and then I
went to the bat. Winkfield could not catch me. That is the whole
story." So all in the same newspaper Jimmy got "The Great
Jockey" in a big headline and the published slurs from Holtman
and Booker. There was nothing cut and dried about America.

One reporter came up with a grim simile to describe how bettors took Early's defeat. When Judge Himes and the others were
led past the grandstand back to the stables, "the tremendous crowd
greeted the victor like the sad thousands watched the funeral train

of the assassinated President McKinley as it wended its way from the Capitol to Canton. Near the roof of the stand there were sobs and sighs and tears. Below, on the lawn, the warm blood froze in the veins of men who had bet their thousands on Early." As for Jimmy, he had a few more races that day and did well, prompting the press to declare that "his effort on Wain-A-Moinen was brilliant, and his ride on Cogswell was as pretty an exhibition of judgment as his mistake in the Derby was fatal." But the Derby was everything, and Jimmy had lost it all by himself.

Everybody blamed Winkfield, including Winkfield. A reporter said that in the jockeys' room, Jimmy's voice broke and tears welled in his eyes as he said, "I made my run too soon. . . . I wanted to win for the boss, and had I followed instructions, I would have won." Years later Jimmy told how he might have scored a historic third straight Derby, even after wanting it too much and coming on too soon. It was the unethical solution. "When that boy come to me at the sixteenth pole I could have fouled him a little; I was such a favorite they'd never have disqualified me, not in that race. But I let him go, and he won."

It was Winkfield's last Derby. A startling fact: he was the first and last black jockey to win it in the twentieth century. He also had the distinction of never finishing out of the money in four straight appearances: third, first, first, second. Now he got a shot at a bigger prize, the 1903 Futurity at Sheepshead Bay, which could push him several notches up on the national list, where he stood fourteenth at the end of 1902. He would start getting great mounts if he could win the richest race in the country, worth $36,600 to the winner, or more than seven times the Derby's value. So he agreed to ride Minute Man for John Madden, who would soon develop his fabulous stud farm near Lexington. The favorite turned out to be High Ball, owned by Winkfield's other neighbor, old Bub May, who had a talk with Jimmy one day, presenting him with one of those pesky ethical decisions.

"He come to me . . . and offered me $3,000 to ride his colt.

"'I'm riding for Madden,' I told him.

THE FALL OF AMERICA'S FIRST STARS • 319

"'Well,' he said, 'there's $3,000 here if you change your mind.'

"So I changed my mind. At the last minute, I told Mr. Madden I'd got mixed up, that I'd already promised Bub May I'd ride for him."

Twenty-one-year-old Jimmy called it changing his mind. What it was was jumping contract (the behavior that got Chippie Ray suspended), even if it was only a verbal contract. "'Course I didn't fool Madden a minute. But I rode High Ball, and we got left at the post and finished sixth. The Minute Man was third." Madden's two-year-old might well have done better under the brilliant Winkfield. The winner was Hamburg Belle, and Madden, a burly former boxer, was steaming. "After the race, Madden he come up to me and said, 'Winkfield, I don't like to be double-crossed. If you're not going to ride my horses, you're not going to ride for anybody.'" Madden could enforce it, too, not only in Kentucky, where he was expanding his operations, but in the East, where he was a consultant to such potentates as the transit tycoon W. C. Whitney, who had taken over the Saratoga course. Indeed, Winkfield's mounts dropped drastically, from 391 in 1902 to 223 in 1903.

"So that winter, when I got a chance to go to Russia, I went."

To Russia?

ACTUALLY, it wasn't such a crazy idea. Jimmy was merely joining the stream of American jockeys, white and black, who had been seizing opportunities to go abroad since Simms had done it eight years earlier. In fact, the very best were leaving. Tod Sloan, with his "negro crouch," as one later British historian put it, had already become a great star in England, a notorious playboy, and the subject of a newspaper poetry contest. The winner:

> Of Toddy Sloan now let us sing,
> Whose praises through the country ring,
> Undoubtedly the jockey king,
> Proclaimed by everybody.[5]

The American kid was also a famous spoiled brat and prima donna, which was not illegal, and a gambler on his own mounts, which was. In 1900, he got caught in a jockeys' cabal to fix races. Apparently thinking the rules were the same over there as over here, or more likely trying to plead ignorance, he told the English Jockey Club, "I understand it is quite legal for a jockey to bet on his own horse." The Jockey Club responded by denying his applications for a license every year for the next fifteen years. But other white Americans followed him to glory in England.

Lester Rieff actually did become the jockey king, topping the English list in 1900 with 143 wins and winning the Epsom Derby in 1901. Younger brother John, who could get down to 4½ stones (63 pounds), competed in England as well. Like Sloan, though, they had a shadowy reputation and were accused of involvement with American gambling syndicates. When Lester lost his license after the Jockey Club accused him of throwing a race, they went to France (John would return to England and win the Epsom Derby twice).

Danny Maher crossed the water, too, to represent Pierre Lorillard, who promptly died, leaving Danny free to ride for the Brits. He won the original Derby three times, and after another win, he was congratulated in the weighing room by the horse's owner, King Edward VII (Danny managed to blurt out, "I have at last achieved my ambition"). Danny Maher went so far as to become a Brit himself, but he didn't forget his Irish immigrant parents back in Hartford, Connecticut. He didn't just buy them a drink; he bought them a whole saloon. Like Maher, John Henry "Skeetz" Martin vanished from the list of top riders in America after 1900 and also became an English star.

Others Yanks, almost all of them white, went to France, Germany, Austria, Italy, Spain, and Czarist Russia. Winnie O'Connor, the leading jockey in America in 1901 with 253 wins, and Joe Ransch, leader the next year with 246, both disappear from the American list in 1903. Why? Because that year they were among the best riders in France. Many of the Americans stayed abroad. At the end of 1904, O'Connor said, "I have had the best season I have ever had . . . and I am greatly pleased at my treatment. I shall never again ride a season in America." There was a noticeable shift by the American exiles from England to the Continent. As the *Courier-Journal* put it, "In former years, England was the Mecca for American riders, but the fate of the Rieff brothers has made a lot of the talent steer clear of Britain's shores, and sunny France and icy Russia have been the spots most sought." While those two countries attracted the most Yanks, every racing power on the Continent had some, including Tommy Meade in Germany, old Fred Taral and Clyde Van Dusen in Austria, and Dick Waugh in Italy.[6]

Most left because they were getting too heavy to ride at home and wanted to prolong their professional lives. A Russian turf authority visiting the United States said in 1904, "In all European countries, the scale of weights is higher than here, and this is especially true in Russia." The Yanks' great success, ironically, also brought them another weight problem. "So much are they superior," the *Courier-Journal* pointed out, "that some of the countries have legislated against them, to the extent of giving an allowance to the home talent." In Austria, horses with Austrian jockeys got to carry seven and a half pounds less.

But weight was never a problem for Jimmy Winkfield. Many years later his daughter would say that he had been threatened by the Ku Klux Klan before he departed, but that was not the motive for leaving that Jimmy's interviewer quoted him as giving. As reported by Terrell, Jimmy made it clear he would not have joined the exodus had he not jumped contract on Madden to try to get the favorite and then faced the consequences.[7]

"I left," Jimmy said with a chuckle, "because I got too smart for my pants."

American jockeys didn't just grab their saddles and get on the boat, however. They had to have a contract. Winkfield got his from another Lexington acquaintance, Jack Keene (no kin to James R.), who trained a stable of horses in Poland and Russia for various owners. As a result of a doping investigation in Moscow, Keene and his best jockey over there, the American Carroll

Mitchell, had been suspended from racing. Keene asked Winkfield to go over, both to ride and to take care of the operation until he could join him. Winkfield went first to Poland, where Keene's horses were in training. "They gave me a book so I could learn Polish . . . and I rode two winners on opening day." Keene did not show up until several years later, but in the meantime Jimmy got a job riding for an Armenian oil tycoon, Michael Lazareff, who owned most of the horses in the Keene stable and was the leading owner in Poland.

"I went to Moscow," Jimmy said, "and won the Emperor's Purse that year, worth about 50,000 rubles. . . . We really cleaned up." A correspondent in Russia said Lazareff cleaned up to the tune of 300,000 rubles, "of which Winkfield won the biggest part." As a result, the correspondent said, Jimmy "has made many friends among the Russian sporting fraternity," and the public always made him a betting favorite "even though he'd be riding a goat." Winkfield worked the northeast circuit for Lazareff, from Warsaw to Moscow to St. Petersburg, then back to Moscow and Warsaw. "A notable Russian jockey, [Joseph] Klodziak, an understudy of Winkfield," rode the southern Russian circuit, including Odessa.

Jimmy Winkfield may not have claimed an American national riding championship, as Willie Simms and Soup Perkins had, but he won the Russian national riding championship in 1904, the first year he rode there. He grabbed it from another Yank, the white boy Joe Piggott, who had been leading the list until he was thrown from a horse owned by a cousin of the czar, which wiped out Joe for the season. So it was Winkfield by a wide margin, with eighty-seven wins and twenty-three seconds and thirds. He also pulled off the extraordinary coup of winning all three of Russia's big derbies for Lazareff—a sort of czarist triple crown—namely, the Moscow, Warsaw, and St. Petersburg derbies. Other American riders in Russia included Johnny Hoar, Billy Caywood, and Joe Richards. The Russian commentator visiting the States said that all of them—Winkfield, Piggott, and the others—"have earned salaries in Russia beyond their fondest hopes, considering that their terms in this country were up." But that didn't mean they never wanted to come back.

YANKEE JOCKEYS BACK IN AMERICA

Under that headline, the *Courier-Journal* noted in December, 1904: "This is the time of the year when the American jockey, who has been forced to go to foreign climes on account of his weight, comes sailing for home to remain for the holidays." Among them were Winkfield and another black rider, James Gannon, who had starred at the Harlem track in Chicago several years earlier but now found himself riding and training for "the well known sporting man Joseph Afanazoff, of Warsaw." Winkfield and Gannon were back not only for Christmas but to ride that winter at Hot Springs, Arkansas. Neither had plans to stay in America, though, as they had contracts to return to Russia, where Winkfield continued his storybook career as a rider in Russia, then in France.

VERY FEW African Americans were still in the top ranks at home when Jimmy first left the country. The number of recognizable names of blacks on *Goodwin's* official list of jockeys dropped to fewer than five after 1900. One of the names was Wallace Hicks, who had 80 wins in 1903. Even better was Dale Austin, who had 90 in 1903, 129 in 1904 (making him number seven in the country), and 141 in 1906 (number five). But Austin was also the only prominent black rider on the list in 1905 (out of a total of sixty-six) and in 1906 (out of fifty-one). Then Jimmy Lee came out of nowhere to give Austin a little African American company on the national lists in 1907. If Winkfield was the last of America's great black jockeys, Lee was the last of the near-greats.

Born in Raceland, Louisiana, Lee lit up the Bluegrass his first year, when he was twenty years old. He won the Clipsetta, Latonia Derby, Latonia Oaks, and Kentucky Oaks and then rewrote world racing history on June 5 at Churchill Downs. Until then, only Fred Archer and Monk Overton had won six out of six races in one

Jimmy Lee was the last of the black jockeys to win a major stakes race—the Travers at Saratoga in 1908. Courtesy of Keeneland Association.

day, but nobody had done it when there were only six races on the card. Lee did it that day, capturing every race that the public came to see at Churchill Downs. "It was many a long year before Lee's feat was duplicated," wrote Charles Parmer, "though the *fancy jocks* [jockeys riding for the wealthiest and most fashionable stables at the moment] of the East continually tried to equal the colored boy's mark. Finally, it was duplicated out in Reno, Nevada, on July 15, 1916, when a little [white] chap named Herman Phillips won the full program of six races."

Lee wound up as the country's second-best rider in 1907, with 217 wins, although he was far behind the phenomenal Walter Miller, who for the second year in a row was the only American jockey yet to top 300 (with totals of 364 in 1906 and 340 in 1907). And Jimmy Lee was back the next year with at least six more stakes wins, including the Travers on Dorante, saddled by the black trainer Raleigh Colston. With 114 wins, Lee captured eleventh place on the national list in 1908; he was also the only prominent black rider on it.

No other African American jockey followed Jimmy Lee to glory. He was the last of seven black riders to win the Travers. Winkfield had been the last African American winner in the

Kentucky Derby, Tiny Williams in the American Derby, Simms in the Belmont, Clayton in the Suburban, Pete Clay in the Metropolitan, Hamilton in the Futurity. They all but vanished after the African American Jess Conley finished third in the 1911 Kentucky Derby aboard Colston, named for his trainer.

Why did the black jockeys virtually disappear? "Racialism"—to use the freshly minted word for the omnipresent prejudice of the day—was the underlying reason; even when social and economic factors seemed to explain it, prejudice lay behind them. Of course, the fate of black jockeys had almost been sealed by the Civil War, which ended their two centuries of dominance. As the South and its cavalier fantasies lay in ruins, a small band of black riders enjoyed almost a monopoly in the "West," especially in Kentucky and New Orleans, but they never dominated the entire sport, as they had before the war. They had made spectacular forays into the East, winning five national championships, but during the first decade of the twentieth century, they quickly dropped from sight.

For one thing, it had become almost impossible for an African American boy to become a jockey in the first place. The great black riders had grown up on horse farms, or near them, but by 1910, most African Americans were living in cities, where thoroughbreds were a rare sight—unless you took a train to Coney Island or happened to see them being led into a horse sale at the old Madison Square Garden. So it has been argued that black riders were not pushed out, but that they simply left the farms for urban areas, where the sports were baseball, then football and basketball. But in fact they didn't simply leave the farms. Racial prejudice and violence, lynchings and the terror of the Klan, contributed mightily to that migration, which in turn intensified racial prejudice and violence in the cities. Still, the migration alone was not the only factor—it could not have wiped out virtually all of them.[8]

Writing about Jimmy Lee, historian Parmer, who had known those days, said it was rough riding by white jockeys that drove off the black riders. "Lee's success did not spoil him. He remained a quiet, courteous fellow. But some of his compatriots of color became a trifle cocky in the jockey rooms; especially in the East. The white boys retaliated by ganging up against the black riders on the rails. A black boy would be pocketed, thrust back in a race; or his mount would be bumped out of contention; or a white boy would run alongside, slip a foot under a black boy's stirrup, and toss him out of the saddle. Again, while ostensibly whipping their own horses, those white fellows would slash out and cut the nearest Negro rider. . . . They literally ran the blacks boys off the tracks."[9]

It would have taken much more than on-the-job violence to run them off, however. They had experienced that often enough, all the way back to quarter-racing days, when black boys and white boys battled their way down that gauntlet of parallel paths. The white rider Roscoe Goose, who would win the 1913 Kentucky Derby, agreed that violence in the saddle drove black jockeys away, but he said it was not that the black riders were intimidated. Rather, their employers did not want their jockeys to be at a disadvantage. "People got to thinking that if they had a colored boy up, he'd have the worst of it."[10]

There were two final blows. The first was a literal one, a one-two punch: Jack Johnson's clobbering of the white Tommy Burns for the world boxing title in Sydney, Australia, in 1908, and then his defeat of the white former champion Jim Jeffries at Reno two years later, on the Fourth of July. On the latter night, the news set off a firestorm of racial hatred across the country: "Black Proclaimed Champion, Race Riots Break Out After Fight," "Omaha Negro Killed," "Houston Man Kills Negro," "Outbreaks in New Orleans," "Police Club Rioting Negroes," "Mob Beats Negroes in Macon," "70 Arrested in Baltimore." Four years later, when Frank Moran went down at the hands of the African American fighter, the *Chicago Herald* headlined: "Johnson Is Victor over White Hope," a term that would not have surprised the slave jockeys, who had seen white journalists cast about desperately for such a hope again and again. But Jack Johnson's daring to be great created a certain hell for any black athlete who might dare to do the same. Yet by itself that threat of more prejudice and more violence would not have been enough to wipe out the black jockeys, either. They had been through worse times long ago.

The ultimate blow came in 1908. It was a strike against the entire sport, or what was left of it, after several years of lobbying against racing by the antigambling forces. Fifteen years earlier, New Jersey's ban on the frighteningly democratic pari-mutuel wagering had forced the closure of giant Monmouth Park, only three years old. A few years after that, antigambling forces helped run bookie Gus Walbaum ragged, to the point where he shut down his Saratoga track for a whole season (1896). By 1908, the number of American racetracks had fallen from 314 to 25, with most of the major courses shut down in every state—except in the Big Apple, as racing people were already calling New York, and in two other racing centers, Kentucky and Maryland. Led by Governor Charles Evans Hughes, New York State finally passed a draconian bill that did the trick for the puritans. The legislation made it illegal for anybody to quote odds openly, solicit bets, or record bets in a fixed place. The next three seasons were a disaster for the New York tracks, and they shut down completely in 1911 and 1912.

Closed forever were those bastions of Brooklyn: historic Sheepshead Bay, where Isaac Murphy had piloted Salvator in one of the greatest races of the century; Gravesend, where Willie Simms won his Preakness; and Brighton Beach, where Tony Hamilton outran the *New York Times* and its campaign to get him suspended (Americans who want to soak up some of those memories have only to walk the length of Coney Island). With the New York catastrophe, the great stable owners got out of the sport fast. Milton Young, Haggin, Keene, and the once indestructible Ed Corrigan sold their horses all over the Western world, especially to England, France, Germany, and Argentina. It was only thanks to a few stubborn owners, among them August Belmont II, Joseph Widener, and W. C. Whitney's son Harry, that New York and thus American racing was revived in 1913.

But the great black jockeys never came back. Granted, the closures of so many tracks, the troubles of 1908–10, and the cataclysm of 1911–12, were tremendous blows, but that should not have meant that only white jockeys would survive them. Even the near-great black jockeys never came back. African American riders almost disappeared at top tracks all over the country—except as newly converted steeplechase riders, trainers or assistant trainers, exercise boys, and grooms. There were ultra-rare exceptions to prove the rule, such as the good jockeys Roscoe Simpson and Clarence "Pick" Dishman, and in the 1921 Kentucky Derby Henry King finished tenth aboard Planet. But anyone who would be satisfied with so little might also see progress in the fact that the second-place colt in that Derby was Black Servant, a slight improvement on old David McDaniel's filly, Black Slave.

Jimmy Winkfield later said that big money eased the black jockeys out, that once the sport became a profitable profession, the blacks were increasingly out of the running. An old Tennessean, Nate Cantrell, agreed. Born in 1879, he became an exercise boy, then an assistant trainer. He was about seventeen the year that Isaac Murphy died and Willie Simms won his first Derby. He was interviewed in his nineties, and to this African American, big money meant not only money, but image, agents, negotiations, and matching riders to horses. "In the old days, where if you ran twelve horses, from six to eight of the jockeys were always black," he said. "And it remained that way until more money got in the game. Now then when a lot of money got in the game, the white men then, like they do now and like they've always been, wanted his people to have, not only the money, but also the reputation. And that's when they begin to pick any kind of a boy that would ride with short stirrups [the American crouch] and have a bunch of agents and a bunch of fellas that would canvas around all day and all night to get him on the best horse. And that's how it happened."[11]

LONG AFTERWARD, many people, unaware of the history of the sport, would be offended by black "lawn jockeys." These were hitching posts, which no longer hitched but were simply intended to suggest that the resident had money. The black versions were considered racist, nasty reminders of the plantation past, and indeed they were often offensive caricatures. They were eventually replaced by white-faced statues, which suggested little else than that the resident might have a cement heron or a bathtub Virgin Mary in the garage as well. How could people who were aghast at the earlier black statues know that they reflected not only a slave-ridden past but an age of extraordinary accomplishment and courage by African Americans?

One story is that they date back to George Washington, who commissioned a statue to honor his young black groomsman, Tom Graves. Graves held a lantern for the troops crossing the Delaware, and upon Washington's return was found frozen to death, still holding the reins of some of the troops' horses. Later, when fugitive slaves made their way north on the Underground Railroad to seek freedom in Canada, green strips of cloth attached to a groomsman's hitching post signaled a place of safety; red meant keep going. Ironically, just as the early twentieth century was consigning the real black jockeys to oblivion, the black lawn jockeys were becoming popular, and after World War II, when the real jockeys were totally forgotten, the black-faced statues would grow in popularity, becoming a national fad. Once the new awareness fostered by the civil rights movement exposed them as racist stereotypes of slaves and servants, they were stuffed into the backs of garages to await inquiring antiques dealers from junky little shops down the road.

But what about another reason some whites would give for the disappearance of black jockeys from the nation's racetracks—what about size? Some people, blind to the panorama of America's first sport, would conclude that African Americans were simply too big to be jockeys. Then, after learning that there had been great black jockeys for two centuries, they might decide that, well, they must have *gotten* too big: perhaps after leaving the old horse farms for the cities, they ate more. Entertaining this ludicrous notion for a moment, it is difficult to see how this could have been accomplished so thoroughly—and so quickly—for the black jockeys began disappearing around 1905 and were virtually gone when the sport was revived in 1913, never to return in noticeable numbers.

It is also difficult to follow how their sudden vanishing act could have been brought about by switching from a diet of Southern soul food to a diet of what one can remember about Southern soul food. Or why Dixie breakfasts had created jockeys whereas our modern scraps made running backs. Jimmy Lee, for one, had indeed fought the scale. As Parmer pointed out, Lee gave "most of his attention to reducing, for that *bête noir* of jockeys, overweight, was threatening him." But so did almost all the other jockeys, most famously McLaughlin, Garrison, and those thickening whites who sailed to Europe to extend their careers. Far more whites than blacks were in that exodus of the overloaded.

The silly argument that African Americans tend to be too big to be jockeys is suspiciously modern, advanced long after the fact and based, it turns out, on white fears of the prominent role of African Americans in football and basketball. A television commentator, Jimmy "the Greek" Snyder, offered a famous ad hoc commentary in 1988 to the effect that modern black athletes were big—and hence were having so much success—because their slave ancestors had been "bred" to be big, and in specific to have large thighs. The CBS executives who had hired the Greek to be plainspoken immediately fired him for being plainspoken, although Snyder hardly had been the first person to offer that particular instant "analysis." A *Sports Illustrated* article had suggested it before him, as had other casual thinkers.

In much earlier days, the 1860s, the prominent role of African Americans in racing had led to suspicions that African Americans had been "bred" with quite an opposite goal in mind, to be jockeys, and in the 1890s there were similar fears that they were about to take over America's leading sport. There was also a time in the 1930s when it was thought, or feared, that basketball was such a brainy sport that to be played right it required Jews. Boxers, the fear-stricken concluded through the years, had a huge advantage if they were Irish—no wait, Italian—no wait, African American. But most people missed the operative line in Snyder's remarks, which was not about size at all, but instead about fear. When asked about blacks in coaching and managing, he grumbled that pretty soon they would take over that, too.[12]

In their own time, racial fear stared the black jockeys in the face every day. They were used to it, of course, but at times the provincial white obsession with race—or rather, with any shade of black—could be extremely wearying. Seven paragraphs in the *Thoroughbred Record* in 1924, reminiscing about the black jockeys, would point out that Monk Overton was "as black as ebony," Tommy Britton was "almost as black as Overton," and Willie Simms was "of a lighter hue than was Overton or Britton." Simms was "saddle-colored." Surely not enough credit has been given to the obsessed white writers for their thesaural contributions. The steeplechaser Charles Smoot racked up fifteen years of triumphs and was national champion by 1928. But if, after one of his Saratoga performances, he dared to look up the story in the *Albany Times-Union*, he would find himself identified as "the dusky rider of Pink Star." Granted, this national champion's name would be mentioned—three times even, each time misspelled as "Smooth."

The Saratoga Association, which was about as far north as you could get, would build a recreation center in 1928 for the jockeys and the stable help, with a design feature not usually found in that clime. One wing was for whites, one for blacks, the pool divided by an underwater wall to achieve the same separation. The center was meant to accommodate the sport's many white Southerners, although they doubtless would have preferred not to have their water even swishing back and forth above the wall. It was also an unrecognized symbol of the fact that the rarefied, behind-the-scenes world of racing—the "backstretch," as the entire stable area came to be called—that cocoon that once shielded a few African Americans from the horrors of slavery, now segregated them. Happily, that little swimming pool wall has remained in place to the end of the twentieth century, with any luck to be preserved (unless the Saratoga authorities actually read this) as a reminder of the way America was, but may not be again.

Even that atmosphere of fear and loathing and actual segregation would not have defeated virtually all of the would-be black jockeys. The real problem was that the few who might dare to apply, against the odds, simply could not get jobs—would not be given the opportunity. That would have required not only tolerance on the part of white employers but something far rarer, which was courage, which meant rising above the cowardice of the bottom line. Many companies today limit their hiring of African Americans because they do not want to "hire a lawsuit," which means that they are taking the cowardly, short-range view of that bottom line. Back then, the stable owners and trainers did not want to tackle the real issues, either, but simply wanted to win purses. The white jockey Roscoe Goose's first-hand analysis has the ring of truth. "People got to thinking that if they had a colored boy up, he'd have the worst of it." Instead of forcing the sport to give fair treatment to their African American jockeys, white stable owners simply quit hiring blacks. It was bigotry, in the form of big money and physical threats and outright exclusion, which was as widely practiced as if it were writ, that explained the vanishing of the black jockeys. This was not so unusual, of course, as African Americans already had been excluded from other sports and other areas of American life. Unlike other sports and other fields, however, racing could not have sustained a separate black "league," with black farms, black owners, black tracks, black jockeys. It had to be interracial or not. It chose "not."

IN THE MEANTIME, some of the great black jockeys of earlier days had done very nicely, many of them as trainers. Ed Brown, who as Dick won the fourth Belmont Stakes, made a spectacular transition to independent training. In a career that spanned three decades, he saddled the 1877 Kentucky Derby winner Baden Baden and developed two colts, Ben Brush and Plaudit, that won the Derby after he

Ed Brown was a great jockey in the Civil War years and rider of the
Belmont Stakes winner in 1870. He had an even greater career
as a trainer. Courtesy Keeneland Association.

sold them. Even in the cut-throat New York City area in the 1890s
he ran one of the most respected and successful training stables in
the country. He died at age fifty-eight in 1906.

Billy Walker—who rode in the first Kentucky Derby and won
the third, who was honored for bravery as a child jockey and once
saw the House of Representatives adjourn for a horse race (his)—
enjoyed a wonderful retirement in his beloved Bluegrass. Known as
Billy when he was riding and Will later on, he had invested in real estate and, like Ed Brown, was once described as one of the wealthiest
African Americans in Kentucky. He lived in Louisville and became a
trainer and consultant to John Madden, who produced four Kentucky Derby winners. Walker was a prominent figure in his own right
as well, one of the country's foremost experts on breeding. "He could
trace the lineage of almost any American race horse without references," said the magazine *Turf and Sport Digest*, adding, "Walker's
knowledge of blood lines went even deeper. Not only could he trace
to tap-root every thoroughbred of consequence but . . . he could seg-
regate the entire pack according to . . . their families."[13]

Madden, the country's leading breeder for two decades, would not send his yearlings to the auction block without consulting Walker, and for many Augusts Will himself made the pilgrimage to the Saratoga sales, as an adviser to Madden but also in demand by others at the Springs. "His advice was sought on all sides by prospective purchasers, especially certain richly endowed Eastern financiers," said *Turf and Sport Digest*. "He was well remunerated for this advice, and his Saratoga trips proved well worth his while. At home, in Kentucky, his counsel was in constant demand by horsemen. Consummation of many sales awaited his approval of the individual's bloodlines." Like many great black trainers in the past, reaching back into slavery days, Walker was a revered figure in his profession, with a permanent ticket into inner sanctums that very few whites possessed. "He was privileged to enter any tack [jockeys'] room in the Midwest, regardless of whether men of affluence and high social standing or racing commissioners were present, and invariably was permitted to join in any and all debates which might be in progress."

For fun, he witnessed an incredible fifty-nine straight Kentucky Derbies, four of them from the back of a horse. In his declining years, he liked nothing better than to head out to Churchill from his three-story town house on South First Street. Purely as a hobby, "he became quite an accomplished clocker," said the *Turf and Sport Digest* obituary. "Each morning at Churchill Downs would find him seated among a band of the professional 'split-second' boys." They were paid to record the official times of workouts, on which vast amounts of wagers would later be based. Whenever one of them lost track as a dozen or more horses went by the sixteenth-of-a-mile pole and would yell out, "Who's got the sixteenth?" it was invariably Will who would answer, "I have!" As a reminder of his blessed life, he sported a silver and gold watch attached to a gold horseshoe fob and engraved with a horse and jockey and a name that had meant much to American sports before it was forgotten: "Wm. 'Billy' Walker." He died in 1933, at age seventy-two or seventy-three, survived by his wife, Hannah, and a sister, Delia Allen.

AMAZINGLY, one of the great black jockeys actually kept on riding into the second decade of the twentieth century, winning many of the biggest events of his day and doing far better than the vast majority of American white riders—but not in America. In 1909, when his sport was about to shut down at home, Jimmy Winkfield left stable owner Michael Lazareff and went to Austria and Germany to ride for a Polish prince and a German baron. The Germans saw the American win their Grosser Preis von Baden, worth a hundred thousand marks, and Winkfield was soon a heavy factor in the betting choices. One day, when he was itching to ride one of the baron's fast-looking colts that nobody else thought could run, he asked the baron about it. He told Roy Terrell and *Sports Illustrated*, "I was getting pretty famous over there by then, and the baron said no, if I rode him the people would bet on me and lose their money." Finally, the baron gave in, and Jimmy was stuck on the colt at the start, while everybody else was already fifteen lengths up the track. "Then we get to the stretch, and I give him a cluck or two, and off we go. He run so fast the others never see us comin'. We win by eight lengths."

If living well was the best revenge, Winkfield had plenty of it. In 1913, he went back to Russia to work for another Armenian, Leon Mantacheff. On his salary of twenty-five thousand rubles a year, plus 10 percent of all purses, he treated himself to a valet, a suite at the National Hotel in Moscow, and caviar for breakfast. "I was at the top of the tree." Several other Americans, most of them white, were still riding in Russia, so Jimmy had plenty of friends with whom to compare notes on what was happening back home. What was happening was that the white jockeys were just crawling out of their New York shut-down, and the black jockeys were a thing of the past, so Jimmy was doing very well indeed with Mantacheff in Russia. He told *Sports Illustrated*, "We sure won a lot of races. . . . I won 130 one year riding only three times a week."

Of course, like his mounts, he saw czarist Russia through blinders. "Before the revolution," he said, "that was a good country. And I never had to pay no income tax." He opted not to work for the czar, Nicholas II, although it was not because of Nick's clever racing strategy. In a kingly variation of *noblesse oblige*, the czar would keep only 25 percent of his winnings and give the rest to the owner of the second horse. As a result, of course, His Imperial Highness won an awful lot of races, doubtless many of them with nags that never would have had a chance under a less generous monarch. "He never paid his jockeys nothing, though. Maybe 4,000 rubles, so I never rode for him."

When the Communist Revolution came, Jimmy said, the Russians were "like rabbits in the woods. They didn't know which way to go." The Bolsheviks let the tracks stay open and paid no attention to the people there, even though one of them, Jimmy Winkfield, was a capitalist who had been making the rough equivalent of a hundred thousand dollars a year. "Nobody bothered us so long as we stayed dirty and wore old clothes. . . . But if we ever dressed up, they'd have figured we was aristocrats." The Moscow Jockey Club soon ran out of money, however, so they shipped all the horses south to Odessa on the Black Sea. That resort of the aristocracy was an even more dangerous place, and in April 1919, the revolution's troopers were on the edge of the city. Jimmy would remember telling himself, "This ain't no longer a fit place for a small colored man from Chilesburg, Kentucky, to be."

So he got out, but not by himself. Assuming responsibility for the safety of the racing colony—all the men, women, and children, and its two hundred thoroughbreds—he and a Polish nobleman led them southward first, toward Rumania. It was quite a trip. Villagers fired on them, thinking they were Bolshevik agitators. Others wouldn't give them food, thinking they were gypsies. "Once . . . we came upon this cow. But it was Lent, and no one would eat her. We drive her along for 20, 30 miles, trying to get her to Easter. We finally swapped her for a pig and ate him on Easter Sunday." In Bucharest, the Rumanian capital, they put the women and children on a train to Warsaw.

Then they were off again, but as they took the thoroughbreds past the Transylvanian Alps and across a patch of Hungary and

Czechoslovakia, some of the horses starved to death, some were eaten. When Winkfield and his party got to Warsaw, one thousand miles and two months out of Odessa, they had 150 horses left, but none ever raced again. They were all eaten that winter. Winkficld said he rode a few more times in Warsaw, once before an American VIP, Herbert Hoover, and then he hooked up with Mantacheff again in Paris.

So, by 1920, the world's only great black jockey (the rare survivors at home were not in the "great" category) appeared in the City of Light, the refuge of exiles, rich and poor, from the world over. He met and then married the daughter of a Russian aristocrat, a fellow exile; they had a son, Robert, and a daughter, Lillian. And he was back on top, winning the Prix Eugène Adam. In the celebrated Prix du Président de la République, Winkfield confronted one of the great American white boys, Lucien Lyne, who had ridden with Jimmy back in Kentucky. Lyne was riding the best horse there, Ruban, for King Alfonso of Spain, but Winkfield, on Badahur, beat him. Jimmy rode through the glitter of the Roaring Twenties in Paris, and then he hung up his saddle. "I never made anything like the money I made in Russia, but I saved some, and in 1930, when I was 48, I rode my last race."

By the time the last of the great black jockeys finished his career on the Continent, he had about twenty-six hundred wins in America, Russia, Germany, Austria, France, Italy, and Spain. In his only appearance in England, he finished fourth among twenty-four entries in the St. Leger. After dismounting for good, Winkfield bought a property in a town called Maisons-Laffitte, a dozen miles northwest of Paris, built a stable, and went into training. The Winkfields' was an elegant place, as so many are in France, a stucco home with lush lawns, chestnut trees, and box stalls for nearly thirty horses. Visiting Yanks would drop in on him and hit him up for food money after losing at the races, for which there were plenty of opportunities at one of the half-dozen tracks around the French capital.

Then came another of those nasty interruptions. Just as the Communists had chased him out of Odessa, the Nazis came to

Paris, and he was on the move again. This time Winkfield took his family to America, going to work for the prominent stable owner Pete Bostwick in Aiken, South Carolina. Few at home remembered him or any of the other black jockeys. After all, there weren't many active black jockeys around to remind them. "Today," Charles Parmer wrote of the black jockeys in 1939, "there may be thirteen of them among about 950 licensed jockeys. The steeplechase division has had several in recent years who were daring horsemen; but they had few chances to ride." One of the black steeplechasers was Paul McGinnis, who was national champion in 1936. Winkfield stayed with Bostwick through the war years (Winkfield's son, Robert, left briefly, as a draftee, to help liberate Maisons-Laffitte) and for a time afterward, then he went out on his own, training for several owners. He gave a few rides at Charles Town, West Virginia, to a white apprentice named Bill Hartack, who would tie Eddie Arcaro with a record five Kentucky Derby wins.

There were not many black apprentices for veterans like Winkfield to help. For that matter, there were hardly any black former jockeys left, either. Racing was a sport that had always been, and still is, controlled by money alone, and nobody had much interest in opening up racing to the future. "When I was riding," said Bill Harmatz, a white rider who would mount the first of his five Derby entries in 1955, "there were a couple of black riders [who] tried to make it, and hell, they never got [to] first base. No one would even give 'em a shot."[14]

Winkfield returned to France in 1953 with the intention of selling his Maisons-Laffitte home. A number of French owners, who promised him business, and his wife, who had always wanted to go back, convinced him to stay. It was not an easy decision: daughter Lillian had married a Cincinnati surgeon, Dr. Edmond Casey, and he was a grandfather now. But stay he did, and Robert came over to help him, making it a lot easier. They saddled Francillon, who twice won the Prix de L'Elevage.

In 1960, he was back in America again, for an operation. "I could have had just as good an operation in Paris, but I knew I was going to die, and I wanted to die back in Kentucky." He had the operation but declined to die, instead spending the winter at Lillian's in Cincinnati with his three granddaughters, then deciding—why not?—to cross the Ohio River and take in the 1961 Kentucky Derby.

He had not seen the Derby once in the fifty-eight years since he last appeared in it as "Winkfield, the Great Jockey," to quote the *Courier-Journal* headline. Already alerted to his return by the *Sports Illustrated* piece, which appeared in May that same year, the Turf Writers Association honored him at a banquet in Louisville's richly paneled Brown Hotel, which served its famous Hot Browns (open-face turkey sandwiches), dripping with Mornay sauce. When Jimmy showed up at the Brown to be honored, he was informed that he could not use the front door. Seventy-nine-year-old Jimmy Winkfield, who had won the Derby twice, had to wait outside while his friends made a fuss; eventually, Derby officials ushered him in through the front. Then, having seen his last Derby (won, as he could have told you, by Carry Back, John Sellers up), he went back to France.

BY 1975, there were still no more than ten black thoroughbred riders out of more than a thousand American jockeys. In the few circles where black jockeys were dimly remembered, the foolish latter-day argument had begun about whether African Americans were generally too big to become riders. It kept hitting new lows. Yes, said an official of the Jockey Guild. "The proof of the pudding is they turn out to be basketball players and baseball players and football players." Jockey Bill Harmatz disagreed. "Look at Sammy Davis Jr. He's the size of a jock. I got to think there's just as many small blacks as small whites." So, Harmatz was asked in 1975, did discrimination exist in racing? Yes, he said. "I hate to sound that way, but really I'd have to say it does. Most of the owners would rather have the white riders riding for 'em, I guess."[15]

By then, another ethnic group had become well established. The Latin Americans had launched the biggest invasion of racing (or any American sport) since the English riders came over after the Civil War—led by the brothers Angel and Ismael "Milo" Valenzuela (Milo won the Derby on Tim Tam in 1958) and the Panamanians Manuel Ycaza and Braulio Baeza. One of the turf historians of the 1960s, William H. P. Robertson, said the Latins—from Panama, Puerto Rico, Mexico, South America—were "lighter and, in general, hungrier." Stable owner C. V. "Sonny" Whitney jokingly suggested the language barrier might have helped them win so much: they couldn't understand the orders of the trainers and owners. The Latin Americans were a huge success, often accounting for a third or more of the jockeys in any given major event into the 1980s. Patrick Valenzuela scored the last of their Derby wins, on Sunday Silence, in 1989.[16]

But as the twentieth century ran out, who would be listed as the latest of the great African American jockeys? Sadly, the answer was Jimmy Winkfield, who quit riding in 1930. He died in France in 1974. He was ninety-one.

Great black and white jockeys once competed side by side. This portrait, circa 1891, includes Fred Taral (third from left), Charles Littlefield (center), Willie Simms (fifth from left), and Tony Hamilton (behind Simms). Courtesy of Keeneland Association.

NOTES

1. The estimates on the Native Americans are suggested by Barry Richardson, administrator of the Haliwa-Saponi tribe, based in western Halifax County at Hollister, North Carolina.
2. Thomas Anburey, *Travels Through the Interior Parts of America* (1789; reprint, New York: Arno, 1969), 393. For readability, occasional minor punctuation changes will be made in quotations from older works. Original spellings are retained.
3. Jefferson's assessment of Washington's riding is given by Dumas Malone in *Jefferson and His Time*, vol. 2 (Boston: Little, Brown, 1951), 261. Jefferson on his dilemma may be found in Paul Leicester Ford, ed., *Works of Thomas Jefferson*, vol. 11 (New York: Putnam, 1892–99), 80.
4. Among the white professionals in the South was a Scot who lived near the Charleston racecourse, kept a slave woman, and then sold her. The purchaser placed an ad in the 1754 *South Carolina Gazette*: "RUN AWAY the 7th instant, from Capt. James Mackay, a negro wench called Bess, formerly the property of jockey Mackenzie, who lived at the quarter house." *South Carolina Gazette*, April 1, 1754. The ad ran frequently from April into July.
5. The black-white race was mentioned in Henrico County Records 1677–1692, 64, cited in Alexander Mackay-Smith, *Colonial Quarter Race Horse* (Richmond: Helen Kleberg Groves, 1983), 59–60, 68.
6. Mackay-Smith assesses Curtis, *Colonial*, 81. The comment on Southern trainers was made by John Hervey, *Racing in America*, vol. 1 (New York: Scribner, 1944), 22.
7. Allen Jones Davie, the earliest source on the race, says it occurred "some years previous to the war of the revolution." Based on the fact that imported Janus, who began standing in America in 1757, was the sire of Paoli and the grandsire of the Big Filly, the two horses in the race, a later

authority, Fairfax Harrison, was doubtless right when he guessed the race was in about 1773. See below for full citations for Davie and Harrison.

8. The story of Austin Curtis's big race was first recounted by Allen Jones Davie in "Quarter Racing of the Olden Time," *American Turf Register* (hereafter *ATR*) 3, no. 9 (May 1832), 450–52. Dale Coats, manager of the Duke Homestead State Historical Site and Tobacco Museum, at Durham, North Carolina, reports that a hogshead in the historical literature usually translates to about a thousand pounds, which would have made this stake 100,000 pounds, but Davie's original account specifically calculated it at 147,000.

9. As was typical of the day, Davie did not fully identify the race participants in his published letters. He identified Curtis only as Austin and the other principals by little more than initials ("Col. D—y," "Mr. J," and so on), including himself ("D."). Fairfax Harrison in *Roanoke Stud* (Richmond: Old Dominion, 1930), 71–73, and Mackay-Smith, *Colonial*, 82–84, did fine detective work in filling in the blanks. The Big Filly, which Davie put in lowercase, was the documented "Bynum's Big Filly," bred by Turner Bynum.

10. John Bernard, *Retrospections of America 1797–1811* (New York: Harper, 1887), 155. Rhys Isaac, *The Transformation of Virginia 1740–1790* (Chapel Hill: Univ. of North Carolina Press, 1982), 100. [Anne Ritson], *A Poetical Picture of America* (London, 1809), 79–80, cited in Mackay-Smith, *Colonial*, 56, 68.

11. Davie, "Quarter Racing," 452. Mackay-Smith, *Colonial*, 56–58.

12. The monkey claim is made for Virginia senator John Randolph in Hervey 2, 73. Harrison, *Roanoke Stud*, 15, quotes an early reference to his "uncouth and awkward manner."

13. Marvin L. Michael Kay and Lorin Lee Cary, *Slavery in North Carolina, 1748–1775* (Chapel Hill: Univ. of North Carolina Press, 1995), 32, 37, 40, 43–47.

14. "On Sunday the 7th Instant (July)," *South Carolina Gazette*, July 11–18, 1754.

15. Davie was quoted by Mackay-Smith, *Colonial*, 4. Kay and Cary, 66, 81.

16. Mackay-Smith, *Colonial*, 85.

17. Davie recounts this race in "Remarkable Race in North Carolina Before the Revolution," *ATR* 3, no. 8 (April 1832), 419–20, giving the date as "about 1770." Writing sixty-one years later, he called the Sharrard horse Blue Buck, but this lapse was corrected by Harrison in *Roanoke Stud*, 69–70, 109, and Mackay-Smith, *Colonial*, 85–86, both of whom reprint and, oddly, actually change Davie's text to conform.

18. Philip Vickers Fithian, *Journal and Letters of Philip Vickers Fithian, 1773–1774, A Plantation Tutor of the Old Dominion* (Williamsburg: Colonial Williamsburg, 1943), 245.

19. Davie reports this one in "Sports and Sportsmen of the Olden Time," *ATR* 3, no. 4 (December 1831), 193–94. He guesses the year as "178–," which Harrison and Mackay-Smith understandably treat as another lapse, perhaps a typo, for Davie also says it was "at the time quarter racing was fashionable," which it no longer was in the 1780s. Harrison, *Roanoke Stud*, 70–71, guesses 1772. Mackay-Smith, *Colonial*, 86–87, gives it as 1778, although a caption in his book puts it as 1772. Again Harrison and Mackay-Smith actually alter Davie's text to conform with their dates.

20. "Charles Town, February 9," *South Carolina Gazette*, February 9, 1769, p. 3.

21. "Richard Henderson (?) to Judge John Williams," Williamsburg, November 2, 1778, in Walter Clark, ed., *State Records of North Carolina*, vol. 13 (1896; reprint, Wilmington: Broadfoot, 1993), 491–93.

22. "Flimnap," *ATR* (November 1829), 164. John Irving, *South Carolina Jockey Club* (1857; reprint, Spartanburg, S.C.: Reprint Co., 1975), 43–47. [Fairfax Harrison], *Early American Turf Stock*, vol. 2 (Richmond: Old Dominion, 1935), 188–89.

23. Lieutenant-Colonel [Banastre] Tarleton, *A History of the Campaigns of 1780 and 1781 in the Southern Provinces of North America* (London: Cadell, 1787), 283–333.

24. Ibid., 333.

25. Julian P. Boyd, ed., *Papers of Thomas Jefferson*, vol. 13 (Princeton: Princeton Univ. Press, 1965), 363–64. Ford, 5:39.

26. Jones referred to the "race ground" in his will. See [Jones], Halifax County [North Carolina], Will Book, vol. 3, 355–62.

27. General Assembly Session Records, December 1791–January 1792, North Carolina State Archives.

28. "Extracts from the Diary of Jacob Hiltzheimer, of Philadelphia, 1765–1798" (Philadelphia: Fell, 1893), 13, 23. The Maryland uniform requirements were described in the *Maryland Gazette* of February 11 and October 26, 1768, as copied in a remarkable, although as yet uncataloged, card file of early newspaper gleanings on racing in the John L. O'Connor Collection, National Museum of Racing and Hall of Fame, Saratoga Springs, N.Y.

29. Isaac Weld Jr., *Travels Through the States of North America and the Provinces of Upper and Lower Canada* (London, 1799), 196, quoted by Mackay-Smith, *Colonial*, 274. The ads are mentioned by Jane Carson, *Colonial Virginians at Play* (Williamsburg: Colonial Williamsburg, 1989), 56. The author has not found such ads.

30. One of the more interesting of Washingon's reported experiences on the turf, described here, was not quite as interesting as several historians have supposed. The incident was first reported by Thomas Peter, who married a daughter of Washington's stepson, John Custis. In a letter,

headed "Gen. Washington and Mr. Jefferson" and signed "P.," to *ATR* 1, no. 7, 353, Peter told of seeing Washington's Magnolio lose a race at an Alexandria race meeting. He also told of a colt owned by Thomas Jefferson competing during that meeting, but on a different day, and, or so Peter thought, winning. Peter's date, "about the year 1790," had to have been wrong, since Washington then no longer owned Magnolio (whose name Peter, like many others, misspells as Magnolia). In any event, his letter was misread by one or more later historians, a number of whom turned it into a wonderful but erroneous tale of Jefferson beating Washington at the races. Sources for the other episodes mentioned include the following. An ad, headed "To be run for," in the *Maryland Gazette*, April 23, 1761, p. 2, and May 21, 1761, p. 4, mentioning Washington as a manager. The Robert Sandford episode, Mackay-Smith, *Colonial*, 219, 262. Citations in Carson, 58, 109, 155, 165, and in Harrison, *Belair Stud 1747–1761* (Richmond: Old Dominion, 1929), 92. The references to Altamont are found in Roger Longrigg, *The History of Horse Racing* (New York: Stein and Day, 1972), 210, and to Grey Medley in James Douglas Anderson, *Making the American Thoroughbred, Especially in Tennessee, 1800–1845* (1916; reprint, Nashville: Grainger Williams, 1946), 44–45, 97–98.

31. Hervey 1, 157; Hervey 2, 158; Mackay-Smith, *Colonial*, 208–10.

32. The evolution of Jones's track into a public course was mentioned by Blackwell P. Robinson in *William R. Davie* (Chapel Hill: Univ. of North Carolina Press, 1957), 146. Governor William Davie was Allen Jones Davie's father. William's assessment of Curtis is under his *nom de plume* "Panton" in "The Race Horse Region in America," *ATR* 3, no. 10, 505–7. Jones's Flimnap offspring are mentioned in Harrison, *Early American*, 190.

33. [Jones], Halifax County [North Carolina], Will Book, vol. 3, 355–62.

34. Margaret M. Hoffmann, *Genealogical Abstracts of Wills, Halifax County, North Carolina, 1758–1824* (Weldon, N.C.: Author, 1970), 140. Paul Heinegg, *Free African Americans of North Carolina and Virginia* (Baltimore: Genealogical Publishing, 1995), 215, 376–77.

35. Allen J. Davie, "Marmaduke Johnson's Mare," *ATR* (June 1833), 520. The obituary is in an item headed "Died" in the *Minerva*, Raleigh, N.C., January 5, 1809, p. 3.

CHAPTER 2

1. Balie Peyton, quoted in Anderson, 250. Anderson reprints Peyton's "Reminiscences of the Turf," a series of eight articles published in the now exceedingly rare *Rural Sun*, Nashville, in 1872 and 1873. The Nashville Public Library has the last two, those of May 8 and August 7, 1873, which mention Simon. The series was reviewed and heavily

quoted, though with minor changes, by Albion [pseud.], a racing writer for the *Spirit of the Times* in a series of his own, "Reminiscences of the Turf," on November 24 and December 1, 8, and 15, 1877. This effort was in turn reviewed and heavily quoted both by an anonymous editor in "Early Tennessee Turf History," which ran in two parts in *Wallace's Monthly* 3, no. 12 (January 1878), 1076–83, and 4, no. 1 (February 1878), 32–43, and by Peyton's friend Jo. C. Guild in *Old Times in Tennessee* (Nashville: Tavel, Eastman & Howell, 1878), 244–55. Since comparison shows Anderson was more faithful to Peyton than Albion (and therefore *Wallace's* and Guild), although the latter's changes are minor, the author uses either the extant *Rural Sun* editions or Anderson for quotations.

2. W. Augustus Low and Virgil A. Clift, eds., *Encyclopedia of Black America* (New York: Da Capo, 1981), 14, 15.

3. "Mr. Purry's Account of Carolina," *The Gentleman's Magazine* (London) 2, no. 21 (September 1732), 970.

4. Elizabeth Elliot, *Portrait of a Sport: History of Steeplechasing* (Longman, 1957), 94, quoted in Longrigg, 208.

5. Margaret Hunter Hall, *Aristocratic Journey* (New York: G. P. Putnam, 1931), 211–12, quoted in Randy J. Sparks, "Gentleman's Sport: Horse Racing in Antebellum Charleston," *South Carolina Historical Magazine* 93, no. 1 (January 1992), 23, 24. Sparks is the best modern treatment of the subject.

6. John Irving, *South Carolina Jockey Club* (1857; reprint, Spartanburg, S.C.: Reprint Co., 1975), 11. Sparks, 20, 21.

7. Peyton in Anderson, 249–50.

8. Grosvenor [Thomas Barry], "Memoir of Haney's Maria," *ATR* 6, no. 7 (March 1835), 348–49.

9. Toni Morrison, *Beloved* (New York: New American Library, 1988), 23.

10. Peyton, *Rural Sun*, August 7, 1873, p. 1.

11. Ibid.

12. Peyton in Anderson, 251–52.

13. Robert V. Remini, *Andrew Jackson and the Course of American Empire, 1767–1821* (New York: Harper, 1977), 55–56.

14. John Spencer Bassett, ed., *Correspondence of Andrew Jackson*, vol. 3 (Washington: Carnegie, 1926), 418–19.

15. Harold D. Moser and Sharon Macpherson, eds., *Papers of Andrew Jackson*, vol. 2 (Knoxville: Univ. of Tennessee Press, 1984), 248–49.

16. Moser 2:56–57; 3:141. When he was president, Jackson attacked Dun in a letter about his horse Bolivar: "if his breathing had not been injured, he was one of the first runners ever owned in America. Dunwoody by neglect destroyed him as a runner & ruined my Oscar filly also a runner." Anderson, 273.

17. Thomas Barry, "Memoir of Haney's Maria," *ATR* 6, no. 7 (March 1835), 347, 409. Regarding Peyton and the *Spirit of the Times* commentator, see ch. 2, note 1, above.

18. Albion, *Spirit of the Times*, December 1, 468.

19. Augustus C. Buell, *History of Andrew Jackson*, vol. 1 (1904), 247–51, quoted in Marquis James, *Andrew Jackson, Border Captain* (Gloucester, Mass.: Peter Smith, 1977), 151–52.

20. Peyton in Anderson, 240.

21. Albion, *Spirit of the Times*, December 8, 491.

22. Barry, 348.

23. Andrew Jackson, Edward Ward, James Jackson, "The full blooded running horse Pacolet," *Nashville Whig*, March 23, 1814, p. 4. The white James Jackson, who would have known Simon well, was a direct ancestor of Alex Haley, the African American author of *Roots*.

24. Albion, *Spirit of the Times*, December 1, 468.

25. The author has followed Barry on when this race was held. It should be noted, however, that a Maria–Western Light match was advertised for two years earlier—October 7, 1813, although it may not have come off. The match was either in 1813 or 1815. It would seem certain that they raced only once. Haynie, who was Barry's source, would have remembered if Maria had had two matches with the Ward horse. "A Match Race," *Nashville Whig*, September 28, 1813, p. 2.

26. Barry, 348–49.

27. Unfortunately, Peyton's colorful version was picked up by one historian after another, in recent years by Arthur Ashe via Charles Parmer. Barry's account, of course, was much earlier, was based on Haynie, and was more credible in other ways. Published in the *American Turf Register*, the sport's bible, and doubtless read at the time by President Jackson himself, a huge error like that in Barry's account likely would have been corrected in the *ATR*, which constantly ran emendations. The conjurer, perhaps, "also ran," but not in that race. Writing a few years after Peyton, Albion, of the *Spirit of the Times*, "resolved" the issue with equal imagination, by putting Simon back on Maria and winning in spite of his of the conjurer. For the dubious later versions involving the "conjurer," see Peyton, *Rural Sun*, May 8, 1878, p. 1, and Albion, *Spirit of the Times*, December 1, 468. Guild, 250–51, adds his own doubtful tale, about a race between a horse named Yellow Jacket and Maria, Simon up.

28. The Jackson admirer was Albion, *Spirit of the Times*, December 8, 491.

29. Peyton, *Rural Sun*, August 7, 1873, p. 1, quotes Elliott describing this incident.

30. Foster got a little more than three thousand votes, about 10 percent, in the 1815 election. He ran in 1817 and lost again, though not as badly.

31. Peyton was referring to Major General Sir Edward Pakenham. The *Spirit of the Times* quote is again from Albion, December 8, 491.
32. Guild, 249.
33. "Deaths in Nashville by Cholera," *Knoxville Republican*, June 19, 1833 (from the *National Banner*). Carol Kaplan, of the Nashville Room, Public Library of Nashville, located Simon's death notice while assisting in the research for this work.

CHAPTER 3

1. Stewart's approximate birth date can be calculated from the ages of the horses he rode or trained. For example, he said he was about thirteen when he rode John Stanley at two miles. Foaled in 1818, that colt probably would not have been racing that distance until he was three, or in 1821, which would put Stewart's year of birth at about 1808. He would have been about seventy-six when his memoir was published. Porter put his age then at eighty-four or eighty-five, but she admitted she knew nothing about "the names and dates of races and horses."
2. Annie Porter, ed., "My Life as a Slave," *Harper's New Monthly Magazine* 69 (October 1884), 730–38.
3. As an example of Porter's "dialect," the first quotation ran, in full: "You couldn't ha' lit down on no bigger little yeller rascal dan me when I fust begin to take good notice of myself. Dat I was! A rascal hide an' hyar, sho's you born." The discarding of Porter's often indecipherable misspellings departs from the practice in the rest of this book, which is to retain the original spellings in quotations.
4. Best on Johnson is in Hervey, 2:77–88.
5. *Ibid.*, 82–83.
6. The description of Race Week is based on Samuel Mordecai, *Richmond in the Bye-gone Days* (Richmond: n.p., 1856), quoted in Alexander Mackay-Smith, *Race Horses of America* (Saratoga Springs, N.Y.: National Museum of Racing, 1981), 29.
7. The chestnut occurred to Alexander Mackay-Smith in his reprinting and commentary on the Stewart memoir, "Ante-Bellum Black Trainers and Jockeys," *National Sporting Library News Letter* (December 1979), 1.
8. "Clear the Course," *National Advocate*, May 27, 1823, copied in the O'-Connor Collection, National Museum of Racing.
9. "Match Race," *National Advocate*, May 23, 1823, reprinted in *Notes on the Thoroughbred from Kentucky Newspapers* (Lexington: private printing by Louis Lee Haggin, 1927), 132–33. The *Advocate* was printed in New York.
10. This race was probably the May 26 mile heats won by Prize Fighter, described in the *National Advertiser* that week.
11. Virginia stable operations are described in Harrison, *Roanoke Stud*, 29.

12. "Worthy of Regard," *ATR* 3 (March 1832), 358.

13. An excellent treatment of the Turner revolt is Eric Foner, ed., *Nat Turner* (Englewood Cliffs, N.J.: Prentice-Hall, 1971). The jails are discussed in Frederic Bancroft, *Slave-Trading in the Old South* (Baltimore: Furst, 1931).

14. Johnson's breeding partnerships and Troye's paintings are discussed in Mackay-Smith, *Race Horses*, 9–15.

15. The best treatment of Oaklawn Manor is Lucile Barbour Holmes, *Wrought Iron Gate, Oaklawn Manor 1837* (n.p., n.d.).

16. Susan Eakin and Joseph Logsdon, eds., *Solomon Northup, Twelve Years a Slave* (1853; reprint, Baton Rouge: Louisiana State Univ., 1968).

17. R. L. Allen, "Letter from the South," *American Agriculturalist* (July 1847), 213–14.

18. Holmes, *Wrought Iron Gate*. Mary Porter's strength during the war made her a legend locally, according to a descendant, Thomas Kramer, of Franklin, La., interviewed by the author on May 6, 1998. Historians today are still dealing with the contradiction inherent in the reputation of the Porters and some of the other slaveholders as "kind masters," according to Dr. Glenn Conrad, director, Center for Louisiana Studies, University of Southwest Louisiana, Lafayette, La., in an interview with the author on May 7, 1998.

19. Hervey, 2:88.

CHAPTER 4

1. Ben Perley Poore mentions President Jackson inspecting his horses, in *Perley's Reminiscences* (Tecumseh, Mich., 1866), 190–94. The best discussion of the construction of the White House horse and carriage stables (but not the racing operation) is Herbert Ridgeway Collins, "The White House Stables and Garages," Records of the Columbia Historical Society of Washington, D.C. 1963–1965 (Washington: Columbia Historical Society, 1966), 366–85. See also Collins, *Presidents on Wheels* (Washington: Acropolis, 1971), 47–48, Robert Remini, *Andrew Jackson and the Course of American Democracy, 1833–1845* (New York: Harper, 1981), 402, and Anderson, 243.

2. A. J. Donelson (to Benjamin Cooper?), October ?, 1831, with Jackson's October 21 receipt appended, Papers of Andrew Jackson 1813–1869, eighteen volumes, Library of Congress. All Donelson correspondence cited here is from this unpublished collection.

3. J. M. Selden, Central Course, to Donelson, May 10, 1833. Callender Irvine, Philadelphia, to Donelson, May 15, 1834.

4. Peyton in Anderson, 243–47.

5. "Washington City Spring Meeting," *ATR* 5, no. 10 (June 1834), 534–36.

6. The Washington Jockey Club listed Crowell as the owner of Bolivia when she won the October 14, 1834, sweepstakes, but the *ATR* noted she

was bred by Jackson and actually entered in the race by Donelson. On October 24, in the Maryland Jockey Club program, Donelson was listed as owner, so it is not clear exactly when Crowell assumed possession. He also bought Lady Nashville that fall.

7. That race meeting was reported in the New York *Spirit of the Times*, including April 23, 30, May 7, 14, 21, 28, June 5, 11, and July 6, 1836. See also *ATR* files.

8. Solomon Northup, the free black who had been kidnapped into slavery, remembered the earlier days when he worked at one of Saratoga's grand hotels and met the servants of Southern families. "I found they cherished a secret desire for liberty. Some of them expressed the most ardent anxiety to escape."

9. The later, influential historian John Hervey erroneously assumed Willis was "colored," apparently because he was known by only one name and rode for Johnson, who was famous for his black riders. But Johnson also developed white riders, and John Irving, secretary of the South Carolina Jockey Club, who saw Willis ride, said he was white. Willis did not appear African American in portraits, but looked rather like a Scots-Irish schoolboy. Nor did the extensive contemporary press coverage of Willis ever say he was "colored."

10. The trainers are mentioned in "Notes of the Month," *ATR* 14, no. 1 (January 1843), 105.

11. Troye is the main subject of Mackay-Smith's *Race Horses*.

12. Boston's career is discussed in Hervey 2:213–34, and in both the *Spirit of the Times* and *ATR*.

13. *ATR* pointed out that "Cornelius, a colored lad, was Boston's jockey up to 27th April, 1839," the date of his last ride on the champion. "The South vs. The North," *ATR* 12 (December 1841), 682.

14. Tyrone Power, *Impressions of America*, vol. 1 (Philadelphia: Carey, Lea & Blanchard, 1836), 45, 83–85. The author's copy, badly battered since it escaped Gist Blair's library at what became Blair House in Washington, indicates a heavy reliance on these early foreigners' impressions. For Power's visits to Saratoga Springs, see Edward Hotaling, *They're Off! Horse Racing at Saratoga* (Syracuse: Syracuse Univ. Press, 1995), 17, 23, 68, 164.

15. Even baseball books that acknowledge the role of Hoboken remain woefully inaccurate about the birth of the sport. For long-ignored accounts of how it really happened, see the files of the *New York Herald* for October 21, 22, 24, 25, and November 11, 1845, and other contemporary reportage. See also Hotaling, *They're Off!*, 25.

16. "Boston's Great Race on Long Island," *ATR* 9, no. 7 (July 1838), 313–16.

17. For accounts of Cato and his two great races, and several follow-up mentions, see the files of the *ATR* and *Spirit of the Times* from 1839 through

1843. Porter's definitive account, a milestone in sportswriting, was "Wagner and Grey Eagle Races," *ATR* 11 (March 1840), 116–32. It was reprinted almost verbatim, and with brief commentary, in Henry William Herbert [Frank Forester, pseud.], *Frank Forester's Horse and Horsemanship*, vol. 1 (New York: Woodward, 1871), 253–75.

18. Gay Neale, *Brunswick County, Virginia, 1720–1975* (Brunswick County, VA: Bicentennial Commission, 1975), 127–33.

19. Quoted in Mackay-Smith, *Race Horses*, 115.

20. Herbert, 275.

21. "The Low, Black Schooner," *The Commonwealth*, Frankfort, Kentucky, September 17, 1839, p. 1.

CHAPTER 5

1. Two good sources on early New Orleans racing are Hervey, vol. 2, and Dale A. Somers, *Rise of Sport in New Orleans, 1850–1900* (Baton Rouge: Louisiana State Univ. Press, 1972).

2. Harry Worcester Smith nailed down "Chisel'em's" proper name, Chisholm, in "The Sportsman's Bookshelf," *Thoroughbred Record*, August 8, 1925, pp. 66–68. Smith also uses Abe's family name, Hawkins. Unless otherwise indicated, the race accounts and records for 1843 and 1844 are based on the files of the *American Turf Register*.

3. For details of Kenner's life, see Craig A. Bauer, *A Leader Among Peers, Life and Times of Duncan Farrar Kenner* (Lafayette: Univ. of Southwestern Louisiana Press, 1993).

4. Anderson, 200–207. Later writers have suggested that a rider named Abe (not Abe Hawkins) was on Herald, but Anderson's is the definitive account. Sandy, who was one of Hampton's slaves, was replaced by Tom Mooney after the first heat. See also "The Peyton Stakes," *Kentucky Livestock Record*, June 25, 1881, p. 409. Irving, 90, lists "Chisolm" as riding in South Carolina.

5. Smith, 66–67. Bauer, 93. See also Mackay-Smith, *Race Horses*, on Troye's travels and work. Rosella's comment in her typescript memoir is from the Rosella Kenner Brent Recollections at Louisiana State University Library, Baton Rouge, p. 12.

6. "New Orleans Jockey Club Races," *Spirit of the Times*, April 10, 1847, p. 79, reprinted from the *New Orleans Picayune*.

7. "New Orleans Racing Steeped in History," *Backstretch* (January–March 1976), 14.

8. For more on the "potato chip," see Evelyn Barrett Britten, *Chronicles of Saratoga*, (Brooklyn: n.p., 1959), 1976, and Hotaling, 22, 37, 71, 80, 86–87, and 178.

9. Reprinted in "Orleans Jockey Club," *Spirit of the Times*, May 10, 1851, p. 140.

10. Kent Hollingsworth mentions the "sale" in *Kentucky Thoroughbred* (Lexington: Univ. Press of Kentucky, 1985), 28. Unless otherwise noted, the remaining race accounts and results, from the first Lexington-Lecomte encounter through 1861, are from the files of the contemporary *Spirit of the Times* (which frequently reprinted pieces from the *New Orleans Picayune*). Hervey, vol. 2, and Mackay-Smith provide good background on racing and Troye, respectively.

11. For Harry's leasing of Darley, see Hervey 2:281–83.

12. Hervey, 2:198, mentions Hark. Other black trainers surface in various ancient and near-ancient documents; Stuart and Cornelius, for example, in Irving, 182 and 188; Anthony in the Rosella Kenner Brent Recollections, p. 18; Holcombe and Jack Rosseau, retrospectively, in "Reminiscence of Balie Peyton," *Nashville American*, September 12, 1882; and Jack Richelieu, in Anderson, 254. Cornelius and Hercules are also discussed in Sparks, who quoted Hampton, 27.

13. Quoted in *Spirit of the Times*, April 22, 1854, p. 115.

14. Ten Broeck's patriotic colors are mentioned in "Local Affairs, etc.," *Atlas and Argus*, Albany, N.Y., August 17, 1857, p. 2.

15. Irving, 119, 193.

16. *Ibid.*, 89–90.

17. Bauer, 49–59.

18. "Great Sale of Plantation Negroes," *The Evening Picayune*, New Orleans, February 23, 1859, p. 1.

19. Quoted in Frederic Bancroft, *Slave-Trading in the Old South* (Baltimore: J. H. Furst, 1931), 225–26. Bancroft discusses this slave sale at length.

20. Fanny divorced Butler ten years before the sale. Her diary was published at the height of the Civil War, and afterward Fanny returned to the London stage—all of which guaranteed it a great success. See Fanny Kemble, *Journal of a Residence on a Georgian Plantation in 1838–1839* (London: Longman, Green, 1863), 212. See also Charles E. Wynes's introduction to the reprint (Savannah: Library of Georgia, 1992), vii–xxii.

21. "American Civilization Illustrated," *New York Daily Tribune*, March 9, 1859, p. 5.

22. *Ibid.*

23. Bancroft, 226. Bancroft talked to the witness.

24. "Reminiscence of Balie Peyton," *Nashville American*, September 12, 1882.

25. Bauer, 59–60.

26. A major source for the Civil War military background in this and the following chapter is James M. McPherson, *Battle Cry of Freedom* (New York: Ballantine, 1998).

27. Bauer discusses the alarm and the experiences of the Kenners during the war.

28. Rosella Kenner Brent typescript, p. 22. Hervey, 2:348, tells of the sack of Bullfield.
29. Smith, 66–67.
30. Rosella Kenner spelled Henry's name "Hayman."
31. The only comprehensive records of American race meetings from 1861 through 1869 are in H. G. Crickmore, ed., *Racing Calendars*, vols. 1–3 (New York: W. C. Whitney, 1901).

CHAPTER 6

1. "The Siege of Charleston," *New York Daily Tribune*, August 3, 1863, p. 1.
2. *Ibid.*
3. For a history of Saratoga racing, see Hotaling, *They're Off!* Sewell was later described as an escaped slave, a "contraband," in *Wilkes' Spirit of the Times*, as the newspaper's new proprietor and editor called it, on June 30, 1866, p. 276.
4. In addition to the contemporary *Wilkes' Spirit of the Times*, a major source for the following chapters is the general press of the day, especially the *New York Herald*, *New York Daily Tribune*, and *New York Times*.
5. Joseph Cairns Simpson, "Some Old Time Racing," *Thoroughbred Record*, August 17, 1901, p. 79. The *Thoroughbred Record* is a major source for racing history.
6. For a discussion of the explosion of national sports in the midst of, and just after, the Civil War, see Hotaling, *They're Off!*, 39–75.
7. "The Paterson Races," *Wilkes' Spirit of the Times*, June 18, 1864, p. 244.
8. "Death of Abe, the Jockey," *Turf, Field and Farm*, May 11, 1867, p. 173. This weekly, co-edited by the great turf authority S. D. Bruce, is a major source for post–Civil War racing.
9. Several Travers jokes are found in Hotaling, *They're Off!*
10. Lynn S. Renau discusses Williamson in *Racing Around Kentucky* (Louisville: Lynn S. Renau Antiques Consultant, 1995), 128–29. William Preston Mangum II says Williamson was not sold but loaned to Alexander. Mangum generously shared information from his book, *A Kingdom for a Horse: The Legacy of R. A. Alexander and Woodburn Farms* (Louisville: Harmony House, in press). Mangum also believes the jockey in the Troye picture is John, whom, he says, Richards loaned to Alexander along with Williamson.
11. Smith, 66.
12. The spelling is "Rhynodine" in the records.
13. "From Saratoga," *New York Daily Tribune*, August 11, 1865, p. 1. The *Tribune*, slipping, says "capacity . . . are" and spells it "soubriquet."
14. The 1868 program is reprinted in Hotaling, *They're Off!*, 81.
15. "The Turfman's Referee," Rules and Regulations for the Government of Racing (New York: Brown, 1867), 17.

16. "Death of Abe, the Jockey," *Wilkes' Spirit of the Times*, May 11, 1867, p. 173.
17. Smith, 67.
18. "Death of Abe, the Jockey," *Wilkes' Spirit of the Times*, May 11, 1867, p. 173.
19. For the full list of "U.S.'s," see "Major General U.S. Grant," *Weekly Saratogian*, Saratoga Springs, N.Y., July 23, 1863, p. 1.
20. The *Herald* spelled it "modelled" and "Autiel."
21. "Death of Old Abe," *Turf, Field and Farm*, May 4, 1867, p. 280.
22. The second obituary was "Death of Abe, the Jockey," *Wilkes' Spirit of the Times*, May 11, 1867, p. 173. The St. Louis report resurrecting him was reprinted in *Turf, Field and Farm*, June 1, 1867, p. 339.
23. "Old Abe Dead at Last," *Turf, Field and Farm*, June 8, 1867, p. 361.

CHAPTER 7

1. Crickmore, 3:167.
2. At least Troye expert Mackay-Smith thought it was Joe. Mackay-Smith, *Race Horses*, 329.
3. *Ibid.*
4. Albert is interviewed and discussed by the New York *Commercial Advertiser* correspondent Melville Landon [Eli Perkins, pseud.] in his futuristic book *Saratoga in 1901* (New York: Sheldon, 1872), 12, 13.
5. The news items are from the *New York Times* during the July and August 1871 race meeting at Saratoga.
6. A sample of the "dialect" not used here: "it's gwine on twenty years." Only the spelling has been changed in these quotes. Also, Landon misspelled the track name "Patterson."
7. "The Saratoga Cup," *Spirit of the Times* (no longer *Wilkes' Spirit*), September 14, 1872, p. 65.
8. "Saratoga Races," *New York Herald*, July 15, 1871, p. 5.
9. Henry James's impressions of Saratoga appear in *Portraits of Places* (Boston: Houghton Mifflin, 1883), 324–37.
10. "Cyrus Holloway," *New York Sportsman* 15, no. 15 (April 14, 1883), 260.
11. Many of the details on the early Derbies are from the files of Louisville's *Courier-Journal* and the New York *Commercial Advertiser.*
12. "Derby Day," *Courier-Journal*, May 18, 1875, p. 2.
13. "Derby Day," *Cincinnati Daily Enquirer*, May 22, 1878, p. 4.
14. Brownie Leach told how McGrath didn't get his education in his delightful *Kentucky Derby, Diamond Jubilee* (New York: Dial, 1949), 17.
15. Holloway was misidentified as Halloway in some early records, which may have led to his being confused with the prominent Canadian steeplechase rider of the day, Clement Alloway, although *he* wasn't black, either.
16. "Derby Day," *Courier-Journal*, May 18, 1875, p. 2.

17. The Louisville Cup incident is mentioned in "Louisville Races," *Courier-Journal*, May 28, 1875, p. 4.
18. Renau, *Racing*, 131.
19. Walker is interviewed in "Rider of the Derby Winner in 1877," *Thoroughbred Record*, May 13, 1922.
20. Thomas Froncek, ed., *City of Washington, An Illustrated History* (Avenel, N.J.: Wings Books, 1977), 91.
21. Quoted in Renau, *Racing*, 128–29.

<h3 style="text-align:center">CHAPTER 8</h3>

1. A definitive record of the father has not been located. A Private Isaac Burns, who served in the U.S. Colored Troops, died at Camp Nelson on August 11, 1864. A white, J. J. Burns, died there on August 5, 1863.
2. L. P. Tarlton, "Isaac Murphy," *Thoroughbred Record*, March 21, 1896, p. 136.
3. Walker was interviewed in "Great Jockeys of the Past," *Thoroughbred Record*, November 29, 1924, p. 257.
4. "The Turf," *Courier-Journal*, May 15, 1876, p. 1.
5. Murphy interview in the *Kentucky Leader*, March 20, 1889, p. 3.
6. The interview with Murphy was reported by the pseudonymous racing writer Albion in "Saratoga," *Spirit of the Times*, July 26, 1879, p. 624.
7. The offer to Murphy is mentioned in Tarlton, "Isaac Murphy."
8. The race was June 8, 1885, at the St. Louis Fair Association track.
9. "Great Jockeys of the Past," *Thoroughbred Record*, November 29, 1924.
10. Murphy's ad in the *Kentucky Livestock Record*, March 17, 1883, p. 170.
11. Leach, 34.
12. Leach, 35. Hotaling, *They're Off!*, 127.
13. The spitter was Tommy Luther, quoted by Tom Gilcoyne, historian at the National Museum of Racing Hall of Fame, in a conversation with the author, July 11, 1998.
14. Murphy's failing health is mentioned in *Spirit of the Times*, August 29, 1885, p. 137.
15. California racing at the time is summarized briefly in William H. P. Robertson, *History of Thoroughbred Racing in America* (New York: Bonanza, 1964), 121–23.
16. George Waller, *Saratoga, Saga of an Impious Era* (Englewood Cliffs, N.J.: Prentice-Hall, 1966), 207.
17. Richard L. Cary Jr., "Ike Murphy's Ride," *Daily Leader*, Lexington, Kentucky, February 13, 1896, p. 6.
18. Betty Earle Borries, *Isaac Murphy, Kentucky's Record Jockey* (Berea, Ky.: Kentucke Imprints, 1988), 43, 107, 113. Renau, *Racing*, 135.
19. Quoted in Renau, *Racing*, 135.

20. "Isaac Murphy's Position as a Jockey," *Kentucky Livestock Record*, February 28, 1888, p. 113.

21. Borries, *Isaac Murphy*, 74–75.

22. Interview in the *Kentucky Leader*, March 20, 1889.

23. "The American Turf," *Harper's Weekly*, June 18, 1887, p. 438.

24. In Greek mythology, Erebus was a place of darkness in the underworld, en route to Hades, the abode of the dead. "Colored Jockeys Show the Way," *New York Herald*, September 20, 1889, p. 8.

25. The telegram was reported in "Racing in the West," *Spirit of the Times*, June 7, 1890, p. 1.

26. The *Spirit*'s accounts of the June 25 race are "Salvator! Tenny!" and "Post and Paddock," June 28, 1890, pp. 1019 and 1014–15. A typical Garrison finish is described in "Domino Won the Withers," *New York Times*, June 13, 1894, p. 8.

27. The poem is Ella Wheeler Wilcox, "How Salvator Won," *Spirit of the Times*, July 12, 1890, p. 1082.

28. The cardiac quote is from "Post and Paddock," *Spirit of the Times*, July 12, 1890, p. 1014.

29. "Post and Paddock," *Spirit of the Times*, August 16, 1890, pp. 142–43.

30. The description of those at the clambake is in "Post and Paddock," *Spirit of the Times*, August 30, 1890, pp. 226–27.

31. Pimlico Race Course amended its Media Guide to include Spider as another African American winner of the Preakness (in addition to Willie Simms) after the author discovered descriptions of Spider's Preakness in "Winding Up at Pimlico," *New York Herald*, May 11, 1889, and "Last Day at Pimlico," Baltimore *Sun*, May 11, 1889.

32. "A Monmouth Sensation," *New York Times*, August 27, 1890, p. 3.

33. Vosburgh discussed the August 26 race in "Post and Paddock," *Spirit of the Times*, August 30, 1890, pp. 226–27.

34. Murphy is quoted in Renau, *Racing*, 136. Byrnes in Robertson, 141.

35. The appraisal of Monk's whip is by Henry Brown in "They're Off!" *Abbott's Monthly* 4, no. 8 (February 1932), 7.

36. *Spirit of the Times*, December 1, 1894, p. 670. The play and the Latonia incident are also mentioned in Borries, *Isaac Murphy*, 98–99.

37. The Tupto quote is from "Isaac Murphy's Death," *Thoroughbred Record*, February 15, 1896, p. 79. The subsequent comments are from "Post and Paddock," *Spirit of the Times*, February 15, 1896, p. 135.

38. Philip Von Borries, "Black Rider, Black Ghost," *Kentucky Derby* (Louisville: Churchill Downs, 1987), 158–59, includes the later total of Murphy's record.

39. Leon W. Taylor, "Isaac Murphy, Winner of Fourteen American Derbies," *Abbott's Monthly* 4 (July 1932), p. 46

40. "Post and Paddock," *Spirit of the Times*, February 15, 1896, p. 135. "Local Turf News," *Thoroughbred Record*, March 143, 1896, p. 126.
41. "Lucky Baldwin's Escape," *New York Times*, July 3, 1896, p. 1.

CHAPTER 9

1. "Racing in the West," *Spirit of the Times*, June 7, 1890, p. 1.
2. The rise and fall of the black jockeys is also discussed in Hotaling, *They're Off!*, especially 141–44, 189–92.
3. The statistics on nineteenth-century violence against African Americans and on the migration to the cities are from Charles M. Christian, *Black Saga, The African-American Experience, A Chronology* (Boston: Hougton Mifflin, 1975).
4. The *New York Age* is quoted in Christian, 265.
5. Alden Hatch and Foxhall Keene, *Full Tilt, The Sporting Memoirs of Foxhall Keene* (New York: Derrydalc, 1938), 25.
6. "A Race That Proved a Farce," *New York Times*, June 15, 1894, p. 3.
7. Walter was interviewed in Steve Thomas, "Link to 1895," *Blood-Horse*, April 19, 1986, pp. 2813–14. Perkins is cited in "The Eleventh Suburban," *New York Times*, June 21, 1894, p. 3.
8. "What the Jockeys Say," *Courier-Journal*, May 7, 1895.
9. "Proud Perkins," ibid.
10. Von Borries, 158–59.
11. "Jockeys Retained for Next Year," *Sporting World*, September 1, 1892. "Nubs of News," *Sporting World*, September 2, 1892, p. 1.
12. "A Suburban for Ramapo," *New York Times*, June 22, 1894, p. 3.
13. Von Borries, 158–59.
14. Michael Tanner and Gerry Cranham, *Guiness Book of Great Jockeys of the Flat* (London: Guinness, 1992), 110–11.
15. Leach, 59, details the race. The roses and other Derby traditions are described in the annual Derby media guides, such as the *124th Kentucky Derby* (Louisville: Churchill Downs, 1998), 21.
16. The story of the black jockeys in the Belmont was told in Edward Hotaling, "When Racing Colors Included Black," *New York Times*, June 2, 1996, Sports section, p. 9.
17. "Hamilton May Not Ride," *New York Times*, July 28, 1896, p. 8.
18. Hatch and Keene, 34.
19. "Hamilton All Right," *New York Times*, August 1, 1896, p. 6.

CHAPTER 10

1. Roy Terrell, "Around the World in 80 Years," *Sports Illustrated* (May 8, 1961), 71. In most but not all cases, the spelling is restored to normal, so that where Terrell has Winkfield say "ridin'," here he says "riding," but

no changes are made in the content. Unless otherwise indicated, the Winkfield quotes are from Terrell's remarkable report.

2. "Mr. McDowell's Plan," *Courier-Journal & Times Magazine*, May 4, 1902, sec. 3, p. 2.
3. Leach describes the machine in *Kentucky Derby*, 73.
4. "Starter Holtman Gets Them Off Nicely," *Courier-Journal*, May 3, 1903, p. 3.
5. Tanner and Cranham, 111. Their work is the chief source on the American jockeys in England.
6. The sources for American jockeys on the Continent in 1904, including Winkfield, and their return home that year are two articles, "Yankee Jockeys Back in America" and "Jockey Winkfield Did Well in Russia This Year," in *Courier-Journal*, December 11, 1904, sec. 3, p. 6.
7. Writer Jo Cavallo quoted Winkfield's daughter in an interview on National Public Radio's "All Things Considered," May 4, 1996.
8. The disappearance of the black jockeys is also discussed in Hotaling, 191.
9. Charles Parmer, *For Gold and Glory* (New York: Carrick and Evans, 1939), 150–51.
10. Jim Bolus, "The Black Riders," *Courier-Journal & Times Magazine*, April 27, 1975, p. 19.
11. Winkfield's view is given (though he is not quoted) in Peter T. Chew, *The Kentucky Derby: The First 100 Years* (New York: Houghton-Mifflin, 1974), as reprinted in Chew, "Ike and Wink," *Blood-Horse*. Nate Cantrell is quoted in Bolus, 44.
12. The author conducted the controversial television interview with Snyder.
13. Ben H. "Buck" Weaver, "The Passing of 'Uncle Bill,'" *Turf and Sport Digest* 10, no. 12 (December 1933), 38.
14. Bolus, 19.
15. *Ibid.*
16. Robertson, 555–56.

SELECTED BIBLIOGRAPHY

Albion [pseud.]. "Reminiscences of the Turf." *Spirit of the Times*, November 24–December 15, 1877.

———. "Early Tennessee Turf History." *Wallace's Monthly* 3, no. 4 (January, February 1878).

Allen, R. L. "Letter from the South." *American Agriculturalist* (July 1847), 213–14.

Anburey, Thomas. *Travels Through the Interior Parts of America*. 1789. Reprint, New York: Arno, 1969.

Anderson, James Douglas. *Making the American Thoroughbred, Especially in Tennessee, 1800–1845*. 1916. Reprint, Nashville: Grainger Williams, 1946.

Ashe, Arthur R., Jr. *Hard Road to Glory. History of the African-American Athlete, 1619–1918*. New York: Warner, 1988.

Bancroft, Frederic. *Slave-Trading in the Old South*. Baltimore: J. H. Furst, 1931.

Barry, Thomas [Grosvenor, pseud.]. "Memoir of Haney's Maria." *American Turf Register* 6, no. 7 (March 1835), 347–49.

Bassett, John Spencer, ed. *Correspondence of Andrew Jackson*. 6 vols. Washington: Carnegie, 1926.

Bauer, Craig A. *A Leader Among Peers, Life and Times of Duncan Farrar Kenner*. Lafayette: Univ. of Southwestern Louisiana Press, 1993.

Bernard, John. *Retrospections of America 1797–1811*. New York: Harper, 1887.

Blanchard, Elizabeth Amis Cameron, and Wellman, Manly Wade. *Life and Times of Sir Archie*. Chapel Hill: Univ. of North Carolina Press, 1985.

Bolus, Jim. "The Black Riders." *Courier-Journal & Times Magazine* (April 27, 1975), 18.

Borries, Betty Earle. *Isaac Murphy, Kentucky's Record Jockey*. Berea, Ky.: Kentucke Imprints, 1988.

Bowen, Edward L. *Jockey Club's Illustrated History of Thoroughbred Racing in America*. Boston: Little, Brown, 1994.

Boyd, Julian P, ed. *Papers of Thomas Jefferson.* Vol. 13. Princeton: Princeton Univ. Press, 1965.

Britten, Evelyn Barrett. *Chronicles of Saratoga.* Brooklyn: n.p., 1959.

Brodie, Fawn M. *Thomas Jefferson, An Intimate History.* New York: Norton, 1974.

Brown, Henry. "They're Off!" *Abbott's Monthly* 4, no. 8 (February 1932), 6.

Bruce, S. D. *American Stud Book.* 2 vols. New York: Sanders D. Bruce, 1884.

Carson, Jane. *Colonial Virginians at Play.* Williamsburg: Colonial Williamsburg, 1989.

"Charles Town, February 9." *South Carolina Gazette,* February 9, 1769, p. 3.

Chew, Peter T. *The Kentucky Derby: The First 100 Years.* New York: Houghton-Mifflin, 1974.

Christian, Charles M. *Black Saga, The African-American Experience, A Chronology.* Boston: Houghton Mifflin, 1975.

Clark, Walter, ed. *State Records of North Carolina.* Vol. 13. 1896. Reprint, Wilmington: Broadfoot, 1993.

Clippinger, Don. "Black Jockeys, Derby Glories." *Thoroughbred Record* (May 1990), 59.

Collins, Herbert R[idgeway]. "The White House Stables and Garages." *Records of the Columbia Historical Society of Washington, D.C., 1963–1965.* Washington: Columbia Historical Society, 1966.

———. *Presidents on Wheels.* Washington: Acropolis, 1971.

Crickmore, H. G., ed. *Racing Calendars.* 3 vols. New York: W. C. Whitney, 1901.

Culver, Francis Barnum. *Blooded Horses of Colonial Days, Classic Horse Matches in America Before the Revolution.* Baltimore: Author, 1922.

"Cyrus Holloway." *New York Sportsman* 15, no. 15 (April 14, 1883), 260.

Davie, Allen Jones. "Sports and Sportsmen of the Olden Time." *American Turf Register* 3, no. 4 (December 1831), 193–94.

———. "Remarkable Race in North Carolina Before the Revolution." *American Turf Register* 3, no. 8 (April 1832), 419–20.

———. "Quarter Racing of the Olden Time." *American Turf Register* 3, no. 9 (May 1832), 450.

Eaken, Susan, and Logsdon, Joseph, eds. *Solomon Northup, Twelve Years a Slave.* 1853. Reprint, Baton Rouge: Louisiana State Univ. Press, 1968.

Elliot, Elizabeth. *Portrait of a Sport: History of Steeplechasing.* Longman, 1957.

Fithian, Philip Vickers. *Journal and Letters of Philip Vickers Fithian, 1773–1774, A Plantation Tutor of the Old Dominion.* Williamsburg: Colonial Williamsburg, 1943.

Foner, Eric, ed. *Nat Turner.* Englewood Cliffs, N.J.: Prentice-Hall, 1971.

Ford, Paul Leicester, ed. *Works of Thomas Jefferson.* Vols. 5, 11. New York: Putnam, 1892–99.

Froncek, Thomas, ed. *City of Washington, An Illustrated History.* Avenel, N.J.: Wings Books, 1977.

General Assembly Session Records, December 1791–January 1792. North Carolina State Archives.

Guild, Jo. C. *Old Times in Tennessee*. Nashville: Tavel, Eastman & Howell, 1878.

Hall, Margaret Hunter. *Aristocratic Journey*. New York: G. P. Putnam, 1931.

[Harrison, Fairfax]. *Belair Stud 1747–1761*. Richmond: Old Dominion, 1929.

———. *Roanoke Stud*. Richmond: Old Dominion, 1930.

———. *Early American Turf Stock*. Vol. 2. Richmond: Old Dominion, 1935.

Hatch, Alden, and Keene, Foxhall. *Full Tilt, the Sporting Memoirs of Foxhall Keene*. New York: Derrydale, 1938.

Heinegg, Paul. *Free African Americans of North Carolina and Virginia*. Baltimore: Genealogical Publishing, 1995.

Herbert, William Herbert [Frank Forester, pseud.]. *Frank Forester's Horse and Horsemanship of the United States and British Provinces of North America*. 2 vols. New York: Woodward, 1871.

Hervey, John. *Racing in America 1665–1865*. Vols. 1, 2. New York: Scribner, 1944.

Hildreth, Samuel C., and Crowell, James R. *Spell of the Turf, Story of American Racing*. New York: J. P. Lippincott, 1926.

[Hiltzheimer, Jacob]. *Extracts from the Diary of Jacob Hiltzheimer, of Philadelphia, 1765–1798*. Philadelphia: Fell, 1893.

Hoffmann, Margaret M. *Genealogical Abstracts of Wills, Halifax County, North Carolina, 1758–1824*. Weldon, N.C.: Author, 1970.

Hollingsworth, Kent. *Kentucky Thoroughbred*. Lexington: Univ. Press of Kentucky, 1985.

Holmes, Lucile Barbour. *Wrought Iron Gate, Oaklawn Manor 1837*. [Franklin, La.?]: n.p., n.d.

Hoose, Phillip M. *Necessities, Racial Barriers in American Sports*. New York: Random House, 1989.

Hotaling, Edward. "Exercise in Leaping to Conclusions." *Los Angeles Times*, March 11, 1989, p. 8.

———. "Views of Sport, the Thunder of Hooves, the Ring of Commentary." *New York Times*, August 5, 1990, Sports section, p. 8.

———. *They're Off! Horse Racing at Saratoga*. Syracuse: Syracuse Univ. Press, 1995.

———. "When Racing Colors Included Black." *New York Times*, June 2, 1996, Sports section, p. 9.

Irving, John. *South Carolina Jockey Club*. 1857. Reprint, Spartanburg, S.C.: Reprint Co., 1975.

Isaac, Rhys. *The Transformation of Virginia 1740–1790*. Chapel Hill: Univ. of North Carolina Press, 1982.

"Isaac Murphy." *Kentucky Leader*, March 20, 1889, p. 3.

Jackson, Andrew, et. al. "The Full Blooded Running Horse Pacolet." *Nashville Whig*, March 23, 1814, p. 4.

James, Henry. *Portraits of Places.* Boston: Houghton Mifflin, 1883.

James, Marquis. *Andrew Jackson, Portrait of a President.* Norwalk, Conn.: Easton, 1964.

———. *Andrew Jackson, Border Captain.* Gloucester, Mass.: Peter Smith, 1977.

Johnson, Dr. W. Pegram, III. "Men In Black: Sporting Parsons in the British Tradition." Newsletter. Middleburg, Va.: National Sporting Library, 1998.

[Jones, Willie]. "I Willie Jones. . . ." Halifax County [North Carolina] Will Book. Vol. 3: 355–62.

Kay, Marvin L. Michael, and Cary, Lorin Lee. *Slavery in North Carolina, 1748–1775.* Chapel Hill: Univ. of North Carolina, 1995.

Kemble, Fanny. *Journal of a Residence on a Georgian Plantation in 1838–1839.* London: Longman, Green, 1863. Reprint, Savannah: Library of Georgia, 1992.

Landon, Melville [Eli Perkins, pseud.]. *Saratoga in 1901.* New York: Sheldon, 1872.

Leach, Brownie. *Kentucky Derby, Diamond Jubilee.* New York: Dial, 1949.

Livingston, Bernard. *Their Turf, America's Horsey Set & Its Princely Dynasties.* New York: Arbor House, 1973.

Longrigg, Roger. *The History of Horse Racing.* New York: Stein and Day, 1972.

Low, W. Augustus, and Clift, Virgil A., eds. *Encyclopedia of Black America.* New York: Da Capo, 1981.

Mackay-Smith, Alexander. "Ante-Bellum Black Trainers and Jockeys." *National Sporting Library News Letter* (December 1979), 1.

———. *Race Horses of America.* Saratoga Springs, N.Y.: National Museum of Racing, 1981.

———. *Colonial Quarter Race Horse.* Richmond: Helen Kleberg Groves, 1983.

Malone, Dumas. *Jefferson and His Time.* Vols. 1, 2. Boston: Little, Brown, 1951.

Mangum, William Preston, II. *A Kingdom for a Horse: The Legacy of R. A. Alexander and Woodburn Farms.* Louisville: Harmony House, in press.

McPherson, James M. *Battle Cry of Freedom.* New York: Ballantine, 1998.

Mordecai, Samuel. *Richmond in the Bye-gone Days.* Richmond: n.p., 1856.

Moser, Harold D.; Smith, Sam B.; Owsley, Harriet Chappell; Hoth, David R.; Macpherson, Sharon; and Reinbold, John H., eds. *Papers of Andrew Jackson.* Vols. 1, 2, 3. Knoxville: Univ. of Tennessee Press, 1980, 1984, 1991.

Neale, Gay. *Brunswick County, Virginia, 1720–1975.* Brunswick Co., Va.: Bicentennial Commission, 1975.

"New Orleans Racing Steeped in History." *Backstretch* (January–March, 1976), 14.

O'Connor, John, ed. *Notes on the Thoroughbred from Kentucky Newspapers.* Lexington: Louis Lee Haggin, 1927.

P[eter, Thomas]. "Gen. Washington and Mr. Jefferson." *American Turf Register* 1, no. 7 (March 1830), 353.

Parmer, Charles. *For Gold and Glory.* New York: Carrick and Evans, 1939.

Parton, James. *Presidency of Andrew Jackson.* New York: Harper & Row, 1887.

Peyton, Balie. "Reminiscences of the Turf." *Rural Sun*, Nashville, October 31, 1872–August 7, 1873.

Poore, Ben Perley. *Perley's Reminiscences.* Tecumseh, Mich.: n.p., 1866.

Porter, Annie, ed. "My Life as a Slave." *Harper's New Monthly Magazine* 69 (October 1884), 730–38.

Power, Tyrone. *Impressions of America.* Vol. 1. Philadelphia: Carey, Lea & Blanchard, 1836.

Remini, Robert V. *Andrew Jackson and the Course of American Empire, 1767–1821.* New York: Harper & Row, 1977.

———. *Andrew Jackson and the Course of American Democracy, 1833–1845.* New York: Harper & Row, 1981.

———. *Andrew Jackson and the Course of American Freedom, 1822–1832.* New York: Harper & Row, 1984.

Renau, Lynn S. *Jockeys, Belles and Bluegrass Kings.* Louisville: Herr House Press, 1995.

———. *Racing Around Kentucky.* Louisville: Lynn S. Renau Antiques Consultant, 1995.

[Ritson, Anne]. *A Poetical Picture of America.* London, 1809.

Robertson, William H. P. *History of Thoroughbred Racing in America.* New York: Bonanza, 1964.

Robinson, Blackwell P. *William R. Davie.* Chapel Hill: Univ. of North Carolina Press, 1957.

Smith, Harry Worcester. "The Sportsman's Bookshelf." *Thoroughbred Record*, August 8, 1925, pp. 66–68.

Somers, Dale A. *Rise of Sport in New Orleans, 1850–1900.* Baton Rouge: Louisiana State Univ. Press, 1972.

Sparks, Randy J. "Gentleman's Sport: Horse Racing in Antebellum Charleston." *South Carolina Historical Magazine* 93, no.1 (January 1992), 23.

Stephenson, Wendell Holmes. *Alexander Porter, Whig Planter of Old Louisiana.* New York: Da Capo, 1969.

Stuart, E. R. "Ebony and Roses." *Spur* (May–June 1997), 42.

Tanner, Michael, and Cranham, Gerry. *Guinness Book of Great Jockeys of the Flat.* London: Guinness, 1992.

Tarleton, Lieutenant-Colonel [Banastre]. *A History of the Campaigns of 1780 and 1781 in the Southern Provinces of North America.* London: Cadell, 1787.

Tarlton, L. P. "Isaac Murphy." *Thoroughbred Record*, March 21, 1896, p. 136.

Taylor, Leon W. "Isaac Murphy, Winner of Fourteen American Derbies." *Abbott's Monthly* 4 (July 1932), 8.

Terrell, Roy. "Around the World in 80 Years." *Sports Illustrated* (May 8, 1961), 71.

"The Turfman's Referee." *Rules and Regulations for the Government of Racing.* New York: Brown, 1867.

Von Borries, Philip. "Black Rider, Black Ghost." *Kentucky Derby*. Louisville: Churchill Downs, 1987.

Vosburgh, W. S. *Racing in America 1866–1921*. New York: Jockey Club, 1922.

Waller, George. *Saratoga, Saga of an Impious Era*. Englewood Cliffs, N.J.: Prentice-Hall, 1966.

Weaver, Ben H. "Buck." "The Passing of 'Uncle Bill.'" *Turf and Sport Digest* (December 1933), 38.

Weeks, Lyman Horace, ed. *The American Turf*. New York: Historical Co., 1898.

Weld, Isaac, Jr. *Travels Through the States of North America and the Provinces of Upper and Lower Canada*. London, 1799.

Wheeler, John H. *Reminiscences and Memoirs of North Carolina and Eminent North Carolinians*. Baltimore: Genealogical Publishing Co., 1966.

Wiggins, David Kenneth. *Glory Bound: Black Athletes in a White America*. Syracuse: Syracuse Univ. Press, 1997.

Wilcox, Edna Wheeler. "How Salvator Won." *Spirit of the Times*, July 12, 1890, p. 1082.

SELECTED NEWSPAPERS

American Turf Register (abbreviated *ATR* in notes)
Cincinnati Daily Enquirer
Kentucky Leader
Kentucky Livestock Record
Louisville Commercial
Louisville Courier-Journal
Nashville Rural Sun
New Orleans Daily Picayune
New Orleans Evening Picayune
New York Commercial Advertiser
New York Daily Tribune
New York Herald
New York Sportsman
New York Times
South Carolina Gazette
Spirit of the Times
Thoroughbred Record
Turf, Field and Farm
Virginia Gazette

SELECTED MANUSCRIPTS

Rosella Kenner Brent Recollections. Louisiana State University Library, Baton Rouge.

Fred M. Burlew. "American Colored (Black) Flat Jockeys (1860–1910)." National Museum of Racing and Hall of Fame, Saratoga Springs, N.Y.

Papers of Andrew J. Donelson. Library of Congress, Washington, D.C.

Andrew Jackson Papers. Library of Congress.

Willie Jones Papers. North Carolina Historical Commission, Raleigh.

John L. O'Connor Collection. National Museum of Racing and Hall of Fame, Saratoga Springs, N.Y.

ACKNOWLEDGMENTS

ONE OF THE BEST parts of writing a book is getting to thank everybody.

Greg and Luc contributed a number of edits that saved the day and were especially helpful in guiding me through larger issues raised by the central challenge: how to bring back the great black jockeys—how to convey the victories of these heroes who confronted a crime against humanity.

Henry Louis Gates Jr., chair of Afro-American Studies at Harvard University, was the first to see the value of my proposal. His inspiring response to an essay I wrote on the subject for the *New York Times* and his unwavering encouragement of the book were a godsend.

Tom Gilcoyne, historian at the National Museum of Racing in Saratoga Springs, New York, was my indispensable trainer on sporting matters, as he had been for my last book, *They're Off! Horse Racing at Saratoga*. Phyllis Rogers and Cathy Schenck went far beyond what one could expect even from their matchless repository, the Keeneland Association racing library in Lexington, Kentucky. Director Peter Winants and librarian Laura Rose were in the midst of a move into a new building, yet they still shared the glories of the National Sporting Library in Middleburg, Virginia.

John Hasenberg, whose family has triumphed over a crime against humanity and who has known a hurt similar to ours, came through with the support of a friend and gifted editor. John read portions of the manuscript and offered illuminating suggestions.

From many of the venues where the black jockeys performed came assistance that makes the writer a serious debtor. In Washington, where Jesse rode for the White House racing stable, my gratitude goes to African American studies authority Adrienne Cannon, Travis Westly, and Bruce Martin at the Library of Congress, Dan Lech at the National Agricultural Library, and Richard Allan Baker, historian of the U.S. Senate. In Virginia, home of the great jockey Albert, my creditors include the great modern jockey Ted

Atkinson, Paul Mellon, historian Alexander Mackay-Smith, archivist Edmund Berkeley Jr. at the University of Virginia, and the astonishing Dr. Pegram Johnson, scholar, clergyman, and great-great-great-grandson of Colonel William R. Johnson, "the Napoleon of the Turf," who figures prominently in these pages.

In North Carolina, where Austin Curtis was freed, counsel came from the fountainhead of African American studies, Dr. John Hope Franklin of Duke University, and from Dennis Daniels at the State Archives, historian Thomas E. Baker at the Guilford Courthouse National Military Park, Dale Coats at the Duke Homestead, and Monica Moody at the Halifax State Historic Site. In Tennessee, the unforgettable Simon's precinct, I found such generous lights as the Andrew Jackson authority David Hoth at the University of Tennessee, Chaddra A. Moore at the State Library, and Carol Kaplan at the Public Library of Nashville. I could not bypass the bayous of Louisiana, scene of the great jockey Abe, as well as Dean Faye Phillips at LSU, Dr. Glenn Conrad at the University of Southwestern Louisiana, Michael Diliberto and Myra Lewyn at the Fair Grounds racecourse, and gumbo with Greg at the Mohawk.

In Kentucky—cradle of the champion Ike Murphy—my bluegrass stars have included Ed Bowen, author and pillar of the sport; Jay Ferguson and Candace Perry at the Kentucky Derby Museum; Dr. Anne Butler and archivist Betsy Morelock at Kentucky State; Melissa McIntosh at *Backstretch*, the trainers' magazine; Tony Terry at Churchill Downs; and authors Lynn S. Renau, Phillip Von Borries, and the lamented Jim Bolus. In Amarillo, Texas, J. R. May and the staff at the American Quarter Horse Museum solved a couple of sticky problems. And the American Antiquarian Society in Worcester, Massachusetts, bestowed its awesome privileges. It had the added perk of being just down the pike from Luc in Boston and from Robin Bledsoe's bookshop off Harvard Square, and just up I-395 from that other temple of concentration, Foxwoods.

Back home in Saratoga Springs, New York, where a fugitive hero helped send American sports to a new high, are some of the best things that ever happened to racing, such as Marylou Whitney. At the National Museum of Racing and Hall of Fame: president John von Stade, Linda Toohey, Peter Hammell, Catherine Maguire, Field Horne, and gourmet soup expert Dick Hamilton, not to mention the aforementioned *Maître* and Fran Gilcoyne. And George Stojak, too. Other tipsters at the Spa: Jan and John DeMarco, Heather and Tim Mabee, Alex and John McKee, Gordon Harrower, Monte Trammer, Barbara Lombardo, Elaine and Bill Dunson, and Brenda and Bob Lee.

My jockey cap is doffed to all who sustained Marthe and me in our endeavors, including Stephanie Scott, Jean and Charlie Osgood, Peter Jennings, Senators Charles McC. Mathias Jr. and Malcolm Wallop, Lydie and Iannis Stefanopoulos, Abbot Aidan Shea, Edith and Colonel Carl Bernard, Secretary

Bill Richardson, Monsignor Thomas Duffy, the rest of the Shelter Island Seven (Ed Bradley, Ted and Joe Feurey, Jim Cusick, Phil Cecchini, Pat Mc-Givern), Kathy and Jim Vance, Susan Kidd, Barbara Harrison, Pat Lawson Muse, Wayne Wood, Stephen Lee Grover, Georgia and Carl Day, Norman White, Charlotte Kohrs, Robert Finley, and John Wanzer.

It was the extraordinary Steven Martin, Prima editorial director and Forum publisher, who had the courage to print the long-buried story of these first professional American athletes. Senior editor Jennifer Fox, copy editor Jeff Campbell, and all of the staff at Prima were superb. I also had tremendous help from my editorial assistants, the professional librarian Alex Northrup, author and historian Bryce Suderow, and researcher Rebecca Douglas.

Dear Jenny Bent, literary agent: thank you. Without you, nothing.

Thanks, too, to a couple of racing fans who have been the class of the sport: Elizabeth and Charles A. Hotaling Sr.

INDEX

Boldface entries denote names of horses.